Prehistory of the Eastern Arctic

NEW WORLD ARCHAEOLOGICAL RECORD

Under the Editorship of

James Bennett Griffin

Museum of Anthropology
University of Michigan
Ann Arbor, Michigan

Moreau S. Maxwell, Prehistory of the Eastern Arctic

Linda S. Cordell, Prehistory of the Southwest

Jerald T. Milanich, Ann S. Cordell, Vernon J. Knight, Jr., Timothy A. Kohler, and Brenda J. Sigler-Lavelle, McKeithen Weeden Island: The Culture of Northern Florida, A.D. 200–900

Michael J. Moratto, with contributions by David A. Fredrickson, Christopher Raven, and Claude N. Warren, California Archaeology

Robert E. Bell (Ed.), Prehistory of Oklahoma

James L. Phillips and James A. Brown (Eds.), Archaic Hunters and Gatherers in the American Midwest

Dan F. Morse and Phyllis A. Morse, Archaeology of the Central Mississippi Valley

Lawrence E. Aten, Indians of the Upper Texas Coast

Ronald J. Mason, Great Lakes Archaeology

Dean R. Snow, The Archaeology of New England

Jerald T. Milanich and Charles H. Fairbanks, Florida Archaeology

George C. Frison, Prehistoric Hunters of the High Plains

Prehistory of the Eastern Arctic

MOREAU S. MAXWELL

Department of Anthropology
Michigan State University
East Lansing, Michigan

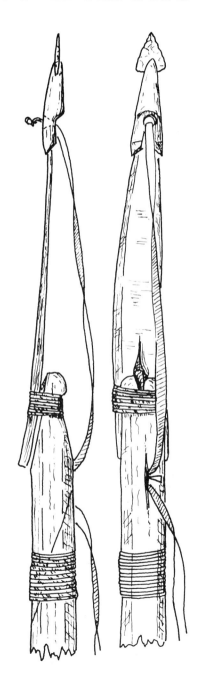

1985

ACADEMIC PRESS, INC.

(Harcourt Brace Jovanovich, Publishers)

Orlando   San Diego   New York   London
Toronto   Montreal   Sydney   Tokyo

ACADEMIC PRESS, INC.
Orlando, Florida 32887

United Kingdom Edition published by
ACADEMIC PRESS INC. (LONDON) LTD.
24–28 Oval Road, London NW1 7DX

LIBRARY OF CONGRESS CATALOGING IN PUBLICATION DATA

Maxwell, Moreau S.
    Prehistory of the eastern Arctic.

    (New World archaeological record)
    Includes index.
    1. Eskimos—Canada, Northern—Antiquities.
2. Eskimos—Greenland—Antiquities.   3. Indians of
North America—Canada, Northern—Antiquities
4. Canada, Northern—Antiquities.   5. Greenland—Anti-
quities.   6. Arctic Regions—Antiquities.   I. Title.
II. Series.
E99.E7M465   1985   971.901'11   84-14488
ISBN 0-12-481270-8 (alk. paper)

47,767

Contents

List of Figures and Tables

FIGURES

TABLES

Preface

A series of dramatic events in 1954 set in motion a major acceleration in the archaeology of the Canadian and Greenlandic Arctic. By the early spring of that year both Eastern and Western nations had stockpiled what were then referred to as "atom bombs." The U.S., with its long-range B-52 bomber, had the ability to deliver such bombs to Russian targets via the short route over the North Pole. A Distant Early Warning Line of radar stations around the Arctic was planned for that future date when the Soviets, too, would have transpolar bomb delivery capability. Surprisingly, however, on May Day the Soviets demonstrated intercontinental bombers, and construction of the DEW Line was begun immediately. By Christmas Eve virtually every type of plane that could carry, or could be modified to carry, a payload arrived in the Canadian Arctic. Bearing tests showed that sea ice 2 m thick could support even the largest Air Force cargo plane, and the logistic scramble was on to build radar stations every 80 km along the 70th Parallel from Cape Dyer on the east coast, across Baffin Island, to the western tip of Cape Lisburne in Alaska.

To most of the early flight crews and construction men the frozen landscape was a frightening place. Previously, it had been familiar only to a few explorers, missionaries, Royal Canadian Mounted Police, Hudson Bay store managers, and, of course, to the 30,000 native Inuit. With hundreds of radar stations requiring thousands of supply flights, expanded native settlements with their own air strips, and, by the 1970s, three or more commercial flights daily to major settlements, the Eastern Arctic rapidly became less forbidding.

In 1957, at the beginning of the International Geophysical Year, Canada had a research team far into the little-known High Arctic on Northern Ellesmere Island, the jumping-off place of early searchers for the North Pole. By the late 1970s and early 1980s exploration for natural resources by helicopter and light plane had made even the High Arctic familiar terrain. Like ants to a picnic, archaeologists rushed to take advantage of flights to such previously inaccessable places as only dreamed of by the archaeological pioneers Mathiassen, Jenness, and Collins. The inevitable result has been a hundredfold expansion of the Eastern Arctic's archaeological literature, most in site reports in the journals. I have been involved from that first winter of the DEW Line to the present and, like many others, have developed a deep love for the Arctic wilderness and also an appreciation of the problems faced by the native people who adapted to its demanding conditions over the past thousands of years. Consequently I feel the time is ripe to tie all this new information together in a synthesis of the region's prehistory. Not the least of my intentions is to provide a target for the lances and harpoons of my colleagues, who will hurl their own interpretations of what happened in the past.

Essentially this book is an attempt to arrange in sequence descriptions of the adaptive technologies, tactics, and strategies devised by the prehistoric Eastern Arctic Eskimo over a nearly 4000-year period. In archaeology such sequencing, to oversimplify the process, is usually done by recognizing significant changes in economic or other cultural activities and correlating them with *supra* and *infra* positions in stratigraphy, major changes in environment, or such chronologies as are afforded by isotopic dating. Separate cultural enclaves can be recognized by discrete differences in artifact styles or ceremonial behaviors, and the movement of people or diffusion of ideas traced from one locality to another.

This interpretive process is less straightforward in the prehistory of the Arctic. Pottery, so useful in more southerly archaeology, with its seemingly infinite variability in shape and design, is very rare in the Eastern Arctic and then only after A.D. 1000. Style changes in artifacts of such hard substances as bone and ivory are more restricted, forcing us to consideration of minute, discrete attributes. Over the millennia there were no major changes in sources of food, or techniques of extracting food from the environment. There are no deeply stratified sites with superimposed layers of cultural activities, and radiocarbon dating is subject to variables not found farther south. While the period of occupation covers several major shifts in climatic conditions, there appear to have been few drastic technological responses to them. Fortunately, the styles of a few artifacts, such as harpoon heads, did change over time, and a rough stratigraphic relationship between sites differentially elevated above sea level provides clues to relative age: Early seacoast settlements now lie high above the sea, for the landmass, relieved of its weight of Pleistocene ice, has steadily risen. In this study I have taken these clues and the interpretations of many other workers in the field to weld an account of the lifeways of the many generations of prehistoric Eskimo.

I hope this account will be of interest to the Inuit, the modern eastern Eskimo, as their own recent concern with their ancient tradition grows. As a summary of research in the region, it will be of value to other scholars, of course, but a wider audience should also find it of interest. There is much to fascinate: Permanently frozen in the soil are such usually perishable items as the wooden tools of some 200 generations of hunting bands, men and women who made their home in this frozen land and their living from animals very difficult to hunt.

This is the story of efficient hunters who maintained their populations with little change over the centuries. The flexibility and high degree of mobility of their band-level organization allowed them to respond to major changes in climate and food availability with little modification of their technology. Above all it is the story of a people living in a balanced state of equilibrium with their ecosystem for four millennia.

Acknowledgments

Many people have assisted in the formulation of this book and the research that underlies it. I thank them all, hold none of them responsible for errors or interpretations that they may not agree with, and apologize to any who may have been inadvertently left from the following list. Foremost are the Inuit of Lake Harbour, the Keemirumiut, and particularly the late Ooloopi Kilikti, to whose memory the book is dedicated. The patient teaching of these friendly people has been invaluable over the 24 years of our association.

Financial help in field research by the National Science Foundation, the National Museums of Canada, and Michigan State University is very gratefully acknowledged. Fieldworkers in this research who have maintained a good humor in the freezing sleet and worked patiently in the cold rain are Robert Christie, William B. Kemp, William Hughes, Bruce Morrison, Moreau S. Maxwell, Jr., H. Allen Maxwell, Peter Kakela, Albert A. Dekin, Thomas Nelson, Douglas Smith, David Munro, Steven Shipman, Robert Arundale, Wendy Arundale, John Maxwell, Geoffry Brower, George Sabo III, David Nugent, Constance Stebbins, Barbara Stebbins, Brian Yorga, Moony Lyta, Pitsula Padluk, Nakasu Qimipik, Natalia Maxwell, Deborah Sabo, Eleanor Maxwell, Douglas Stenton, and Diane Stenton.

The faculty and graduate students of the Department of Anthropology of Michigan State University have been helpful in debating some of my ideas, particularly Charles E. Cleland and William Lovis. Colleagues in Eastern Arctic archaeology and ethnology have freely offered reprints, unpublished material, and illustrations. Their help has been invaluable. They include Charles Arnold, Henry B. Collins, Steven Cox, David Damas, William Fitzhugh, Bryan Gordon, Elmer Harp, James Helmer, John Jacobs, Susan Kaplan, Eigil Knuth, Allen McCartney, Robert McGhee, Fr. Mary-Rousselière OMI, Jørgen Meldgaard, Christopher Nagle, Patrick Plumet, Peter Ramsden, James Savelle, Peter Schledermann, Jane Sproull-Thomson, Patricia Sutherland, William E. Taylor, and Callum Thomson. I particularly appreciate Richard Jordan's careful reading of the manuscript and excellent suggestions for improvement.

Natalia Maxwell was of great help in preparing the illustrations and Margaret Henderson provided valuable editing of some of the early chapters. Last, but by no means least, Jami Yates is warmly thanked for typing the manuscript.

1   Introduction

The Arctic can be raw and damp in summer and I felt chilled to the bone one mid-August day on the south coast of Baffin Island. I was excavating a site where skilled hunters had, 4000 years before, extracted adequate food from this frozen seacoast and developed unique patterns of adaptation. I was well equipped to preserve my twentieth-century comforts in the field. But that day a cold wind blew across the floating ice pans in the Hudson Strait and I was damp and numbed despite four layers of warm clothing.

All day low clouds had covered the sun and moist fog banks had drifted the shoreline. My feet were chilled by contact with the frozen ground, my legs were stiff from squatting, and my back ached from troweling the mud of thawing permafrost. I thought only of crawling into my windproof, rainproof tent, lighting the kerosene stove, and letting its heat soak into my body while I changed to dry clothing and opened my packaged, prepared food. I longed for my goose down sleeping bag, a full stomach, and the warm night-glow of my snug quarters.

Then my scraping trowel struck a flint tool, a tiny burin spall smaller than a paper matchstick. When I tried to lift it from the cold mud my thumb and index finger were too numb to grasp the delicate object. My cold-cramped hand would not serve me, and I stared at the little artifact in frustration.

How had these early hunters done it? For thousands of years human beings had lived here. I, with all the luxuries of my camp, was cold and miserable. Six or seven hours of damp, chilly work had left my hands nearly useless. But prehistoric people had survived here equipped only with a few stone, bone, and ivory tools and great ingenuity. Through summers when the air temperature was in the low 40s (4° C), as it was that day, and through bitterly cold winters, ancient hunters had bested so formidable a competitor as the polar bear to reign as top carnivores in the Arctic. They had eaten well and had provided themselves with clothes and shelter. They had developed impressive technical skill and the varied cultural forms of a social heritage that yet survives in the Arctic.

It was no longer helplessness but awe that I felt as I finally retrieved the tiny engraving tool and gave up my quest for the day. How was it possible for human beings with no resources other than their own skills to accomplish so much in an environment in which the smallest mistake can be fatal? Fascination with this question has driven me north each summer for more than 20 years in search of the impressive record of cultural adaptation preserved within the permafrost.

This fascination with survival and successful adaptation in such a bleak environment began in the winter of 1954. Previously I had had a continuing involvement for several decades in the archaeology of the American Midwest, but little had prepared me for conditions of native life in the Arctic. Through that winter and most of the two succeeding winters I traveled by dogsled over several hundred kilometers of sea ice and snowcovered ground with several teams of Inuit hunters from Frobisher Bay, my most frequent companion being Anakudluk, who has since died. All too often, weather conditions precluded an airdrop of supplies, but the unperturbed Inuit hunted caribou and ringed seal and we seldom were hungry. After a long, hard day's journey they built small snow block igloos, barely large enough for the three of us to sleep, with impressive skill and speed.

In the summer of 1958 the National Museum of Canada provided me the opportunity of making the first archaeological survey of northern Ellesmere Island. For 90 days I backpacked through this beautiful High Arctic wilderness. I developed a sense of where prehistoric hunters would have been most apt to camp, but, more important, I was able to learn much about animal behavior in an area that had been immune to hunting pressures for the preceding 50 years.

By 1960 my graduate students and I had centered our research on the southeast coast of Baffin Island and on the problems of paleoecology and adaptation. Over the succeeding years we have come to know this stretch of Arctic coast and its inhabitants well. Through surveys and excavation we have elucidated the prehistory of the region. But, more important, through the helpful cooperation of the local Inuit we have been able to observe their adaptive behavior through all seasons of the year and to listen to their insightful interpretations of the ancient implements we have recovered.

Primitive hunters and gatherers were always under stress in the environments from which they derived their energy resources, but there have been few conditions in world history that imposed environmental stresses on the hunters and their communities as severe as those of the Eastern Arctic. Yet the archaeological record indicates that predecessors of the Inuit (Eastern Arctic Eskimo), who inhabit the region today, adapted to this intemperate environment sufficiently well to occupy their ecological niche for at least 4000 years. They did so in successful competition with other biologically specialized predators, using tool kits and information resources so efficient that they required little modification over the entire time span.

Archaeological excavations in the Arctic provide a time depth that chronicles the course of this unique cultural adaptation with unusual richness of detail. Through several time periods, permafrost has preserved all the bits and pieces of cultural inventory from scraps of skin boots to wooden knife handles. The cultural history thus recorded yields a picture of the daily life of small communities that is much more complete than the archaeological record normally affords and gives the archaeologist a closer sense of identity with the people who lived there.

The data recovered from this region provides abundant materials for testing hypotheses and propositions focused on the economies of ecology, that is, the way in which energy is cycled through the food chain. Although most primitive groups appear primarily oriented toward hunting, detailed studies show that in many contemporary hunting and gathering societies, wild fruits, nuts, and vegetables, largely gathered by women and children, account for as much or more of the family's energy input as do animal products of the hunt. One of the few exceptions has been the Inuit, who were almost exclusively carnivorous until the nineteenth-century encroachment of industrialized civilization. Arctic people occupied the top rung of the food chain, consuming far larger quantities of meat than do Americans in the twentieth century. The extreme cold of the environment takes a specific energy toll from the human organism in addition to that normally required for maintenance of vital forces. This high fat and protein demand is coupled with other specific stresses that inseparably intertwine ecology and archaeology in the study of Arctic prehistory. However, the primary adaptive mechanism of humans, unlike that of the polar bear, is culture.

The development of an adaptive culture leads us to quite another dimension of ecology. The Arctic is a habitat in which specific knowledge and the pooling and sharing of information is critical. Not only must an Arctic hunter, like any hunting animal, learn all that he can about the habits and movements of his prey, but he must also know and understand the myriad conditions and dangers of sea ice, the many principles and techniques for conserving heat, and the many strategic variables involved in the decision to spend a particular day far inland hunting caribou rather than on the ocean hunting seal. Archaeology provides some strong clues to the ways in which Arctic information was pooled among widely separated communities and transmitted to successive generations.

The rich ethnographic literature of the Inuit of the recent past provides a basis for constructing models that aid interpretation of the data recovered through archaeology. Close similarities between styles of artifacts still used today and those recovered from prehistoric sites allow the archaeologist to make more confident extrapolations into the past than he or she usually feels comfortable in making. But this valuable interpretive tool must be used cautiously. When one looks at the skillfully designed mechanisms and weapons of traditional and modern Inuit, they seem so functionally logical that it is hard to imagine other ways of adapting to the cold climate, seacoast life, and availability of specific sources of food. But the window into time provided by archaeology reveals that there have been a variety of adaptive techniques. Although there are certain fundamental responses that must be made to the environment, the adaptive strategies that have been employed in this region of the world are not all the same through time and space.

To me, the most challenging problem is defining the nature of balanced equilibrium that appears to be the dominant factor in the long course of human occupancy of the Eastern Arctic. In other regions the processes of change seem paramount in cultural prehistories and anthropological models. In contrast, the apparent homeostasis of technologies, ideologies, settlement systems, and lifeways through 4000 years of Eastern Arctic prehistory provides the anthropologist seminal data for the study of balanced equilibrium systems.

The basic conservatism expressed in this equilibrium is simultaneously threaded with subtle changes in the style of artifacts, particularly harpoon heads, thus providing archaeologists with the variants necessary for typological dating. To our untutored eye many of these stylistic changes do not seem functional, that is, more efficient; they seem more the "free play of imagination around a fixed form," as Boas once said of Alaskan needle cases. In itself this is not surprising; the tendency toward innovation is an ubiquitous trait among humans. What is more surprising is that through most periods of Eastern Arctic prehistory a new stylistic variant was seemingly adopted by everyone, so that it appears virtually simultaneously in widely separated locales. Once the variant appeared, others copied it in almost slavish conformity, even though the new style might require more time to make and be apparently less efficient than some previous one.

This leads to two questions. The first deals with the nature of diffusion. Thus far, efforts to identify cultural centers from which changes diffused to the periphery have not proved successful. It is as if everyone in the Eastern Arctic had informational contact with everyone else through the interlocking systems of a multitude of small contiguous bands. The second question is more enigmatic. If the level of conformity was as high as it appears to have been, then who were the innovators and what social or ideological risks may they have run?

All this appears to have taken place within a relatively closed cultural system. In spite of several apparent contacts between prehistoric Eskimo and sub-Arctic Indians, the former borrowed few cultural traits from the latter. All this—the rapid and widespread information exchange among prehistoric Eskimo, their constraints of conformity and apparent reluctance to adopt the techniques of other cultures—suggests strong mechanisms of boundary maintenance that as yet are little understood.

2   The Arctic Setting

INTRODUCTION

To understand and appreciate the complexity and dynamics of prehistoric life in the Arctic, one must look first at the more critical factors of the environment.

The area poleward of 66°30′ north latitude is known as the Arctic Circle. Within its arc the sun's rays so strike the earth that on one day of the year, around June 21, the sun does not set for 24 hours, and on another, around December 21, it does not rise. But the landforms within this circle have variable climates, and thus the Arctic Circle is not a useful limit for the study of Arctic prehistory. The circle includes parts of northern Norway and Finland and much of northern Russian and interior Alaska, but it does not include southern Baffin Island, part of Greenland, both sides of Hudson Strait, and the shores of Hudson Bay as well as the islands at its mouth. Arctic archaeologists are primarily concerned with the prehistoric development of a specific kind of human adaptation in an environment of frozen seacoasts and tree-less tundra. Some of the areas just mentioned that extend south of the Arctic Circle are water-surrounded lands that have been permanently frozen since the fourteenth century, if not before then. They also share other characteristics of the Arctic Circle that include them within the boundaries of Arctic archaeological interest.

Moderating effects of ocean currents create regional diversity in winter temperatures too great to permit definition of the area. A more useful boundary can be derived by linking all those points in the Northern Hemisphere where the mean temperature of the warmest summer months is no more than 10° C (Figure 2.1). This isotherm encompasses more territory than does the Arctic Circle but still excludes parts of the Labrador coast and Newfoundland, where prehistoric people had close cultural linkages with the northern islands of the Eastern Arctic.

Two other common definitions of the Arctic setting also exclude these localities. One of these considers the Arctic to be bounded by the continuous permafrost line, the tundra zone where the ground is permanently frozen, (Figure 2.2). This line very nearly coincides with the 10° C isotherm in the Eastern Arctic, but in Siberia it drops well south of it. The other related definition considers the Arctic to be the area beyond the northern limit of tree growth. These two boundaries tend to coincide because tree roots cannot penetrate the frozen ground, and melt- and rainwater cannot seep down through it. No vegetation of appreciable size can be supported within the area shown in Figure 2.2.

By all of these definitions the Arctic is a distinct ecological zone in which vegetation and animals, including man, have developed distinctive adaptive traits that permit survival under conditions that prevail in no other habitat. Among humans this distinctiveness is seen, particularly in the Eastern Arctic, in the sharp differences between Inuit language, culture, and physical type and those characteristics of the sub-Arctic Indian population of North America. These distinctions appear to have persisted through several thousand years.

It is common practice to divide the North American Arctic into western, central, and eastern regions. Apart from their contemporary importance for administrative and political purposes, these divisions are seldom viewed as having specific boundaries, and they have little relevance for prehistory. Only two major cultural configurations are discernible in the archaeological record, a western and an eastern. The eastern cultures, throughout most of prehistory, extended no farther westward than

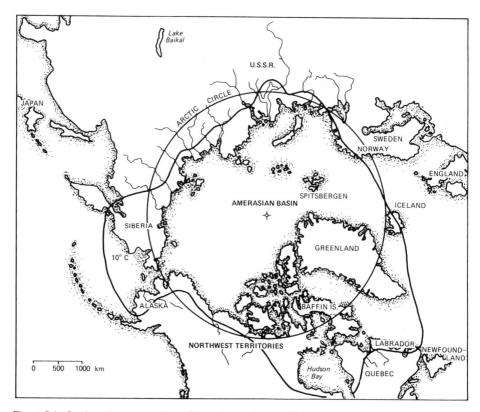

Figure 2.1 Southern boundary of the 10° C isotherm. This line links points where the mean temperature of the warmest summer month is 10° C. North of this line, plants, animals, and humans are Arctic adapted.

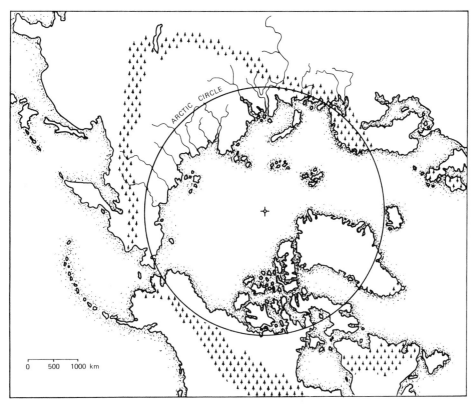

Figure 2.2 The northern tree limit. North of this limit most of the earth's surface is permanently frozen, limiting the root structure of standing trees.

the entrance to Dolphin and Union Strait and the western shores of Victoria and Banks islands. No contested boundary between western and eastern tribes is evidenced, but early sites producing cultural assemblages such as those found to the east on Baffin Island and Melville Peninsula have not been located west of Amundsen Gulf. Both the first and the last migrations into the Eastern Arctic had their inceptions in western Alaska. However, archaeological data does not confirm the concept of a Central Arctic useful in ethnographic analyses. Thus the prehistory of the Eastern Arctic refers to the islands and the mainland littoral from Banks Island east to Newfoundland and the eastern shore of Greenland.

LANDFORMS

The topography of inland regions is only of secondary importance to people oriented toward seacoast living. High mountain ridges impede overland travel; valleys and mountain passes shelter and guide the passage of migrating game animals, but

Figure 2.3 Steep, 600-m-high talus slopes on the shore of Coneybeare Fjord, Ellesmere Island provide few coastal campsites.

human activity is focused on the shorelines. Here the topography of the region has a direct bearing on the breeding behavior and concentrations of sea mammals and is crucial to a hunting people's selection of settlement sites.

The dominant bedrock feature of the Eastern Arctic is the vast Canadian Shield of Precambrian granite, gneisses, and schists. Scoured by Pleistocene glaciers to flat plains in the south, it rises to 2100-m peaks in the north (Figure 2.3). Along the eastern margin of the Canadian Arctic Islands, steep mountains dominate the landscape, dropping abruptly into the sea in all but a few places. A belt of high mountains beginning at 83° north latitude on the northern coast of Ellesmere Island cuts Devon Island in half and continues longitudinally down the eastern third of Baffin Island into the Torngat Mountains of Labrador. Active intermontane glaciers, at elevations above 1200 m, extend southward through this chain.

There are relatively few level spots for human settlement along this rocky coast, but deep narrow fjords provide good ecological conditions for seal, walrus, narwhal, and whale. Prehistoric people took advantage of the topographic diversity of the region to find shelter near these hunting grounds. A rocky coastline in relatively low relief extends southeastward for about 100 km along the western shore of Frobisher Bay on southern Baffin Island. Several good settlement sites are to be found there and the sealing is good. Farther south, sheer cliffs and mountains rise 300 m from the water's edge. Except for a few shallow bays and fjords, it is impossible even to haul a kayak out on the rock-walled shore, but modern Inuit find the best polar bear hunting in these steep mountainous shores and narrow valleys (Figure 2.4). This landform diversity in the Shield area contributed to hunting success in prehistoric time as it does today.

The area also provided stone resources important in the prehistoric cultural inventory. Although flint and chert are scarce, their sources limited to a few sedimentary erosional remnants, there are deposits of graphite, serpentine, and varieties of soapstone that were carved into lamps and cooking vessels and are now

Figure 2.4 Broken Canadian Shield cliffs of the southeastern coast of Baffin Island restrict settlement locations to relatively few coastal sites.

exploited artistically by modern Inuit. Frequent exposures of clear quartz crystals, a wide variety of quartzites, and fine-grained abrasive rocks were the raw materials of tools and weapons for the early hunters.

These hard-rock Archean formations extend westward to the southern tip of Somerset Island, the southeastern corner of Prince of Wales Island, and the eastern half of Boothia Peninsula. West of them, in the southern part of Banks Island, western Victoria Island, and the mainland littoral opposite Victoria Island, Precambrian formations appear as late Proterozoic rocks of the Coppermine Series. These are highly fractured traprocks, dolomites, diabase, gabbro, and basalt. They are interspersed by sedimentary beds of sandstone, limestone, and shale and overlaid by thin sediments (Figure 2.5).

At its western margin just east of Cape Parry on the mainland, the Canadian Shield disappears under the sediments of the Mackenzie Valley geological province. This wide zone of very thick, fossiliferous, limestone beds extends southward, underlying the Great Plains of southern Canada and the United States. Much of the

Figure 2.5 Mechanical, rather than chemical, erosion characterizes the frigid Arctic. Melt water seeps into rock crevices, freezes, expands, and splits off huge slabs.

province was submerged during the Pleistocene and has recently emerged above sea level. A thick mantle of silt and other unconsolidated sediments overlies the limestone, and consequently this area is more severely affected by permafrost action than many other parts of the Arctic.

In addition to the rugged eastern rim of the Canadian Shield, three pronounced arches run north and south and a fourth east and west. The two easternmost ridges, of hard granites and gneisses, follow the northward-trending Melville and Boothia peninsulas. The third, of traprock, extends from the Kent Peninsula into southern Victoria Island. The east–west traprock formation crosses northern Victoria Island from Minto Inlet eastward. These arches envelop three basins of sedimentary rocks: Foxe Basin, with limestone outcrops on Melville Peninsula, Baffin and Southampton islands; Victoria Strait Basin, covering part of the Boothia Peninsula, King William Island, and southeastern Victoria Island; and Wollaston Basin, covering southwestern Victoria Island and part of the coastal mainland across Dolphin and Union Strait.

These weathered limestone regions have low local relief and flat, dry, gravel beach terraces, where many large settlements have been established over time. The gently sloping shores provide easy access from sea to land, both for kayaks in summer and for dogsleds traveling over sea ice in winter. The shallow bottom sediments of Foxe Basin support great quantities of shellfish, on which walrus depend. Deposits of good quality flint, chert, indurated shale, and slate for stone tools are to be found in the limestone outcrops. The Hudson Bay Lowland, a flat and boggy area to the west of the bay that was below sea level at the end of the Pleistocene, is less desirable for human settlement. A layer of unconsolidated marine sediments covers all but the coastal edge, and neither game nor stone resources attract hunters to the flat expanse.

The western fringe of islands in the Canadian Arctic Islands is still little explored, and better known from the air than from the ground. Only one archaeological site has been reported, and it lies on the south coast of Melville, the most southerly island. Melville is one of the Parry Islands, which include Prince Patrick, Bathurst, Mackenzie King, Borden, and Cornwall. A northern group, the Sverdrup Islands, includes Ellef Ringnes, Amund Ringnes, and Axel Heiberg.

The dominant feature of the terrain in these northern and western islands is a strongly folded, disturbed belt, the most conspicuous structural element of which is a major mountain system 2200 km long. Its peaks thrust in two broad arcs from northwestern Greenland to the Beaufort Sea. The westerly arc, a band of folded beds varying in width and local relief, roughly parallels 75° north latitude from southwestern Prince Patrick Island across the middle of Melville Island, most of Bathurst and Cornwallis islands, and the Grinnell Peninsula of Devon Island. The eastern arc tilts north and south through Ellesmere Island, paralleling the Precambrian mountains to the east. It is composed of three nearly parallel belts: one a middle Paleozoic range of limestone, shale, slate, and dolomite, the second a Cretaceous formation of limestone, sandstone, shale, and conglomerate, and the third a range of granite, gneiss, and schist fringing the north shore.

South of the Parry and Ellesmere Island fold belts, two large basins of Paleozoic sediments, the Melville and the Jones-Lancaster basins, extend south to the arches of the Canadian Shield. West and north of the fold belts are the low islands of the Arctic Coastal Plain. These islands of flat-lying Mesozoic sandstones and shales have low coastlines and look, from the air, like recently emerged tidal flats with deltas and braided streams. At the present time the western shores of this coastal plain are locked in pack ice that does not melt in summer. Although the coast has not been adequately explored, it is doubtful whether man ever lived there in the prehistoric period.

Eighty-six percent of Greenland, the world's largest island, is covered by a permanent snowfield more than 1,800,000 km² in area and 3 km deep. The weight of this huge glacier has depressed the earth's crust in the center of the island to more than 350 m below sea level. The coast is fringed with *nunatat,* mountains with peaks that rise above the margin of the glacier and descend to a rocky coast dominated by deep, narrow fjords (Figure 2.6). The island of Greenland rises from the American Continental Shelf, and the Precambrian bedrock is probably part of the Canadian Shield, although mountains of the northeast appear to be extensions of European fold belts.

Local relief of the extreme north coast is relatively low and the land is ice free during the summer. While this coast has not been occupied for several centuries, it appears to have been a desirable camping area in Greenland's prehistory between 4000 and 1000 years ago. The western coast, prehistorically as well as today, is divided by the large Steenstrup Glacier that debouches into Melville Bay from south of the Thule Air Base to Kudlorssuaq. The advance of this glacier is relatively recent, and there are probably a number of prehistoric sites buried forever beneath its ice.

In several places on both Greenland coasts, Mesozoic sediments overlie the Precambrian rocks to south of 70° north atitude. This far south there are hot springs on

Figure 2.6   Nunatat several thousand meters high rise above the Gilman Glacier of northern Ellesmere Island.

the western and eastern coasts. Nearby ancient sites suggest that early hunters enjoyed the soothing warmth of these springs. On most Arctic coasts the land is rising and many prehistoric sites are now above present sea level. In contrast, the weight of inland ice on Greenland is causing the shore to sink, and some sites once on beaches have now been eroded by storm waves.

THE SEA

It is toward the sea that most Eastern Arctic people are oriented, and this apparently has always been so. A low coastal ridge on the south coast of Baffin Island separates a seaward slope from a gently sloping landward side. Many more flat areas suitable for summer tents or sheltered winter houses are to be found on the landward slope. Yet, consistently, from prehistoric camps dated to 2000 B.C. to the past summer's tent site, the seaward side of ridge is preferred and the landward slope ignored. When one's major food source is the sea, a precarious perch overlooking its waters is preferable to the protection and comfort of a land-bound campsite. Constant observation of fish-eating birds, the frequency of seal heads bobbing up in certain tidal rips, and the mass and direction of drifting sea ice store information that is critical to the pool of knowledge to which each sea hunter must have daily access. Even archaeologists who eat dehydrated and freeze-dried foods and have no urgent need for such information tend to select uncomfortably cramped tent sites within view of the changing sea that gives the Arctic life.

The Arctic Ocean is a large, circulating mediterranean fed by Siberian and Russian rivers and by major surface currents flowing north through the Bering Strait (Figure 2.7). The major surface flow is generally clockwise from the Chukchi Sea along the Siberian and European shores. It moves out through the strong Greenland Current paralleling Greenland's eastern coast. The topography creates countercurrents close to shore and diverts some of the flow across the center of the Amerasia Basin toward the vicinity of the North Pole. Here, partially deflected by the submarine Lomonosov Ridge, the current passes southward through the narrow Robeson Channel between Greenland and Ellesmere Island or is trapped in the large, closed gyral of the Beaufort Sea. This Beaufort Sea current, circling clockwise, entraps old pack ice and large fragments of flat glacial ice calved off from the northern shore of Ellesmere Island. These ice islands may circle in the gyral for many years. One, known as T-3, was first discovered in 1950. It has made three complete circuits of the Amerasia Basin at an average speed of 0.11 km/hour, although it has been stalled and virtually motionless for several long periods during this time.

The warm waters of the Gulf Stream flow northward in the Atlantic, passing south of Newfoundland, and eastward toward the north shore of Europe. Near the west coast of Iceland a stream of warm Gulf waters circles back toward the west as the Irminger Current and passes close to the southern tip of Greenland and moves north along the coast as the West Greenland Current.

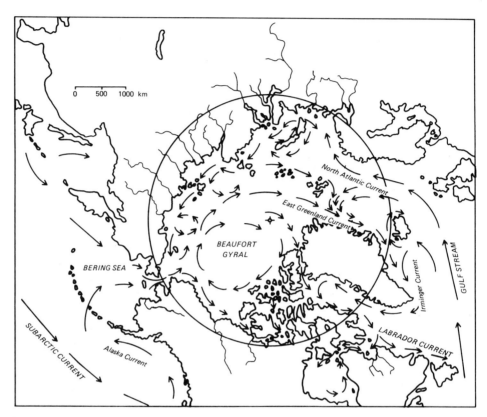

Figure 2.7 Major sea currents and circulation affecting the Arctic environment. The large Amerasian Basin is covered throughout the year with drifting pack ice 3 m or more thick. The greatest discharge of ice and water is along the eastern coast of Greenland.

These waters remain relatively warm as far north as Upernivik and keep a large part of Baffin Bay ice free in winter. At the northern end of the bay the West Greenland Current, now chilled by polar waters, circles west and southward along the east coast of Baffin Island, arriving at the Labrador shore as the cold Labrador Current. Some of this current enters Hudson Strait, flowing westward along Baffin Island to circle Hudson Bay in a counterclockwise direction (Figure 2.8). It passes eastward back into the Atlantic along the northern shore of Quebec. Within the Arctic Archipelago there are only minor currents, mainly following shorelines, but these have a dominant flow from north to south and from west to east. Close to the northern Alaskan shore the current sets west to east, but a short distance offshore this coastal current interfaces with the opposite-flowing Beaufort Sea Gyral. The shearing effect of these opposite currents creates dangerous ice conditions.

Water currents produce situations of critical concern to hunters, both prehistoric and modern Inuit. First, currents directly affect the availability of seal, walrus, and whale because their food content varies with source and temperature. Warmer waters entering the Arctic carry higher quantities of the phyto- and zooplankton, which are at the base of the food chain supporting the sea mammals. But the interface between warmer and colder waters also provides an ecotone, an overlapping of two ecological zones, where food resources are usually richer than within a single current. The diversity of sub-arctic waters (Figure 2.9) places them among the richest in the Northern Hemisphere. The north Alaskan Coast, where warm coastal waters mix with the polar waters of the Beaufort Sea, is such an ecotonal area. So also are the shores of Davis Strait and Baffin Bay between the Canadian Arctic Islands and Greenland. Second, currents and winds have a direct effect on the movement of floating ice. One of the greatest hazards of sea ice hunting is the danger of being far from land on a drifting ice field that the currents have broken from shore. A third factor is that water currents have very direct bearing on the availability of driftwood. People living in temperate regions cannot conceive of the importance of wood to those who live on a treeless tundra. For example, a harpoon tip or spear point can be made of bone, antler, ivory, or stone, but there is no adequate substitute for wood in making the long spear shaft. In prehistoric times large pieces of driftwood must have been a most precious commodity.

Supplies of driftwood are obviously less of a problem where currents flow to the shores from southerly forested regions, such as the coasts of Alaska, the eastern coast of Hudson Bay, and the northern shore of Quebec. Elsewhere, particularly in the center of the Canadian Arctic Islands where most of the flow is out of the Arctic Ocean, driftwood is extremely rare. Since the major drift across the Amerasian Basin is from Siberia toward Ellesmere Island and Greenland, it is not surprising that more driftwood is found on their northern shores than on coasts farther to the south. I once found a section of painted picket fence in small Ella Bay near the

Figure 2.8 Prevailing currents between Greenland and Baffin Island float huge icebergs from glaciers on northwestern Greenland hundreds of kilometers westward through Hudson Strait.

northeastern tip of Ellesmere Island. It could only have come from some Siberian backyard and, locked in ice, traveled slowly across the Arctic Ocean, passing close to the North Pole in its drift.

The range between high and low tides, which occur twice in a 24-hour period, can have multiple effects on seacoast hunting, particularly if these tidal ranges are extreme. The ebb and flow of summer tidal waters exposes sea-floor plankton to more sunlight, causing more rapid growth than is achieved in winter. Strong tidal rips in narrow bays are hazardous to boat travel but are particularly good places for seal hunting. Where the tidal range is extreme and a bay is deep and narrow, the current flowing out of it may be 9 to 16 km/hour as the tide ebbs. Whirlpools in the current test the skill of the most experienced kayak paddler. In winter the fast ice, that is, seawater ice frozen fast to the shore, breaks loose as tides rise and fall. Dangerous open-water tidal cracks, thinly masked with snow, and jumbled masses of hummocky ice form along the shoreline. One must know how to detect and maneuver around these to survive among them.

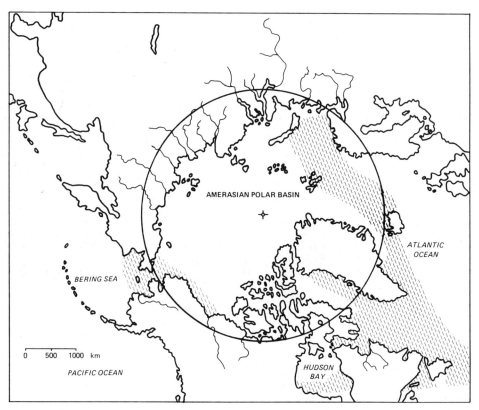

Figure 2.9 The sub-Arctic seas. These waters between the cold Arctic Ocean and warmer Atlantic, indicated by the dashed areas, are very rich in marine life.

Figure 2.10 High (A) and low (B) tides at Pritzler Harbour, southeastern coast of Baffin Island.

In the southeastern quadrant of the Canadian Arctic, near the mouth of Frobisher Bay, tidal ranges, as much as 14 m, are among the highest in the world. North and west, the range decreases to less than 1 m on northern Ellesmere Island and western King William Island. Where the tidal range is over 12 m, as it is on the southeastern coast of Baffin Island, life must be geared to the rhythm of the tides (approximately 12 hours 26 minutes between peaks). Along this rocky coast, boats tied to shore at high tide may rest a kilometer from the sea at low tide. Where the westward set of the ocean current meets strong tidal bores, as at the mouth of Frobisher Bay, even powered schooners must avoid the whirlpools and can leave narrow anchorages only at certain times of the day.

This tidal rhythm is part of the esoteric knowledge of every Inuit child, but not something I have been able to master, much to the amusement of the local inhabitants. The problem is compounded, as every coastal dweller knows, by the fact that the range is constantly varying. In response to different phases of the moon and other features, the range between high and low tides may be much greater in some periods than in others (Figure 2.10).

My first exposure to tidal vagaries came in the summer of 1960 when I excavated several sites on Juet Island with my young son. The peterhead schooner taking us to the island towed a heavy wooden dory that was to serve as emergency transportation if we should need to leave the island. The Inuit crew secured the boat to shore rocks, and left the two of us alone on Juet. Since we had no means of signaling Lake Harbour, I worried about the boat drifting away in a storm. The first night I watched it for hours, pulling it farther and farther upshore as the tidal waters rose. Finally, at about two in the morning, a thin margin of dampness showed that the waters were beginning to recede. I gave a last heroic heave, jamming the heavy boat in the rocks at the peak of the tide, and slept, secure in the knowledge that the boat was safe.

Figure 2.11 Tidal fluctuations in winter create nearly impassable zones of huge ice blocks and saltwater pools between shore and the smooth sea ice. Lake Harbour, Baffin Island.

The next day it became tragically apparent that I had used the floating power of the highest tide of the year. My boat was wedged in a spot that for many months would have a hundred meters of jumbled rocks between it and the water. Essentially it was on the peak of a small mountain, and there it remained, immovable, until the Inuit crew returned a month later and exploded with laughter over our predicament. Thus I added to the many legends of the slightly idiotic, southern-born *kadloona* who are helpless in the north and should be treated affectionately like retarded children (Figure 2.11).

TEMPERATURE AND CLIMATE

Although cold temperatures obviously dominate the Arctic scene, there are many misconceptions about the frigid extremes. The Arctic is not the coldest region in the Northern Hemisphere; nor is it a land of perpetual ice and snow. Moreover, the temperature does not drop in regular rate as one goes northward from the Arctic Circle. It is more the persistence of cold that gives these lands their frigid character. The summers, when temperatures do not often rise above 10° C, are short and the mean temperature of the yearly cycle is −10° C, or lower. This is not to deny the coldness of Arctic winters. Temperatures of −40° C are common, and occasionally −45° C weather prevails. But periods of −50° C or lower are rare. Much colder temperatures have been recorded in the sub-Arctic, where the temperature has dipped as low as −70° C in Verkoyansk and −60° C in the Yukon. Extremes such as these have never been recorded in the Arctic, except at the center of the Greenland ice cap, where no one has yet set up housekeeping.

Statistically there are significant regional differences in ambient temperatures, extreme lows, means, and mean lows. For the most part these are due to the ameliorating effects of ocean waters, which, although relatively low in salinity and covered by 2 m of ice, still radiate 15° of heat when the air temperature is −45° C. Figure 2.12 shows isotherms constructed from mean winter temperatures in the Eastern Arctic. Within these generalized boundaries there are great differences between macro- and microenvironmental conditions. Although a weather map may show the average temperature of a region to be −40° C, the area will include thousands of microlocations where temperatures are much lower or higher. Anyone who while camping in the mountains chooses a protected basin in which to sleep becomes painfully aware of the downward drainage of cold morning air into a valley floor. The Hazen Valley on northern Ellesmere Island is a 68-km-long basin between the United States Range to the north and lower hills to the south. A British meterological team wintering there in 1957 noted the lowest Arctic temperatures yet recorded. An extreme low of −56° C, and a mean low of −46° C prevailed for 3 months that winter. On the other hand, the seacoast barely 48 km away averaged 22° warmer (Jackson 1959).

Ever since the first inhabitants migrated to the Eastern Arctic, people have tended to camp as close as possible to the shore. Since travel was by boat in summer and by

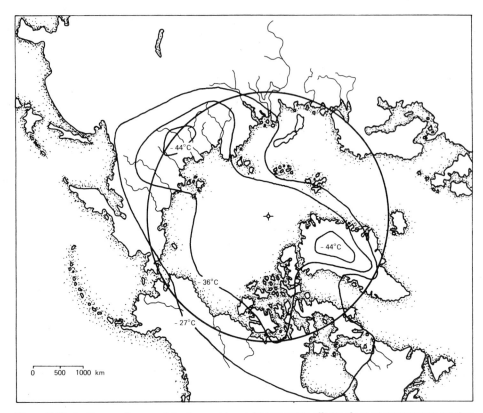

Figure 2.12 Isotherms of mean winter temperatures. The warming effects of ocean currents are particularly apparent in mean winter temperatures.

sled over the sea ice in winter, there was no point in camping farther from the sea than necessary. But also, in winter, the coast is significantly warmer than slopes inland. Given a normal adiabatic rate in which air temperatures decrease with elevation and the fact that seawater radiates heat even under ice, a winter location 12 m above sea level can be as much as 10° colder than a coastal one. Under conditions of extreme cold, degrees of frost must be balanced against the caloric intake of both food and fuel. Gaining extra degrees of heat by locating a camp on the coast simply makes good economic sense. The sensible temperature is of much greater concern to a man hunting on the sea ice than is the actual thermometer reading. Arctic inhabitants were well aware of the windchill factor before it became a daily item in the weather report. A person properly dressed for hunting with only the face exposed is in little danger of frostbite at −20° C in calm air, but with 32 km/hour of wind, the effective temperature drops to −60° C, and exposed flesh can freeze in 30 seconds. Under conditions like these a snow block windbreak can raise the effective temperature 28° or more. Fortunately it is rare to have winds in the Arctic when the temperature is lower than −34° C. When they do occur, the Inuit construct shelters and remain stationary for as long as the storm lasts.

The sensation of winter cold is often less in the Arctic than in regions farther to the south because the air is dry and the dew point very low. In the coldest months of winter, bright middays with temperatures around −28° C make the Arctic a delightful place to be. Summers, even in northern Ellesmere Island, have warm, sunny days when, for a few hours, the temperature may rise to 20° C. The winter snow and ice melt on even the most northerly points of land unless they are covered with glaciers and permanent snow fields. The region at latitudes above 70° north latitude is virtually a desert, with less than 2.5 cm of annual precipitation and generally dry air in both winter and summer. Warmer summer air to the south along Hudson Strait causes higher precipitation and coastal fogs. The moisture-saturated air, frequent rains, and daily temperatures fluctuating between 4° C and 11° C make the sensible cold there more uncomfortable in summer than during the winter months when snow and ice draw the moisture from the air.

Cultural devices such as clothing, shelter, and fuel burning constitute more than 90% of human adaptation to Arctic cold. But physiologists claim at least a slight genetic acclimatization on the part of the Inuit. Their hands and feet are smaller and trunk size and body mass greater than those of peoples living in warmer climates, which conforms to ecological rules that apply to most cold-adapted mammals. Their nasal structure is very narrow, for warming air before it reaches the lungs, which is a trait shared with certain populations in hot, dry climates for opposite reasons. The Inuit also exhibit a physiological response to extremity cooling that circulates blood to and from the surfaces of their hands, allowing them to withstand cold conditions somewhat better than non-Arctic peoples. This latter trait is thought to have a genetic basis in populations long adapted to cold climates. Anthropologists recognize this genetic difference in distinguishing American Indians as being of different racial origins from Eskimos and Aleuts. Furthermore, the Eskimo languages, Inupiat and Yupik, differ from Indian linguistic stocks and in many respects cultural adaptive techniques differ between Indian and Eskimo. It is in the generic use of "Indian" that comparisons are made in the following chapters.

Given some morphological and physiological adaptation of prehistoric Eskimo and modern Inuit, and even with the best of clothing, there is a high energy cost of hunting in extreme cold that probably placed practical limits on the locations that were habitable under prehistoric conditions (Maxwell 1960b). In the fourteenth century A.D. there was apparently a sizable settlement in the vicinity of Lake Hazen on Ellesmere Island, but from the end of that century to the present there have been no inhabitants there. The time of human abandonment coincides with a significant worldwide cooling often referred to as the "Little Ice Age." Large herds of musk-ox and caribou still roamed the basin, and seal and bear inhabited the shore, but this game no longer lured people from the warmer Greenland coastal settlements 160 km away. One explanation for this is that increasing cold in the Hazen Basin tipped the balance for humans between the energy input from meat and fat and the energy cost of hunting and maintaining deep body warmth.

The isothermal map of the Eastern Arctic, with lines connecting points of equal mean January temperatures (Figure 2.13), shows marked regional diversity, mainly

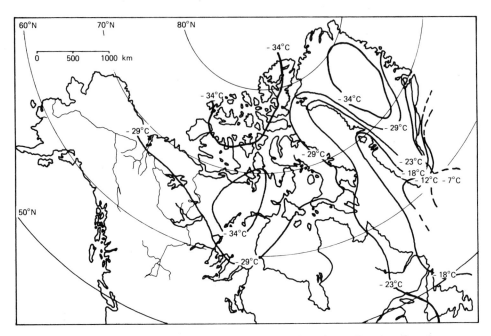

Figure 2.13   Mean January temperatures in the Eastern Arctic show the ameliorating effect of seawater.

caused by ocean currents. Thus northwestern Greenland is much warmer than coasts to the west and south. Paleoclimatological evidence suggests that we can assume similar configurations of warm and cold coasts but that relative temperatures would be significantly higher before the end of the fourteenth century than after. Since settlements before the fourteenth century are found farther north than Inuit settlements since then, it would seem that there were temperature limits to successful prehistoric adaptation. Hypothetically these limits are demarcated by a mean January isotherm of approximately $-34°$ C.

LAND SNOW AND SEA ICE

Annual precipitation is surprisingly low in the Arctic, from about 38 cm a year in the south to 2 cm a year in the far north. Since half or more of this is in the form of summer rain, the annual snowfall is much less than in the sub-Arctic or in the northern Temperate Zone. The dry, cold snow, like desert sand, is kept in motion by winds that pile deep drifts in valleys and on the lee side of ridges. There is seldom more than 30 cm of snow cover on the flat sea ice, and often large expanses are scoured to bare ice by the winds. Where the snow is exposed, it becomes windcompacted to nearly the consistency of styrofoam and strong enough to support a many-ton wheeled aircraft without rutting. This wind-compacted snow can best be cut with a carpenter's saw and is the ideal building material for Eastern Arctic igloos. It is dry, hard, and easy to shape and has thousands of air pockets that make it an excellent insulator. Historic Inuit and earlier people used thin antler and whalebone probes to test the strength and consistency of the snow selected for building, a procedure requiring knowledge and skill accumulated over a lifetime of experience.

Although one speaks of dogsled travel over the sea ice, it is really the thin layer of hard snow on which the runners slide. The sleds can travel over new ice before the snow has fallen and over stretches of wind-scoured ice, but they are easier to control on compacted snow. In summer the snow cover melts long before the thick ice beneath it. Standing at the top of a hill, one can see a traveler in the distance sledding across what appears to be a fjord of open water. Dogs, sled, and man are running on the firm sea ice a few inches beneath the melt water.

Glaciers and permanent snowfields on both Greenland and the eastern margin of the Canadian Arctic Islands are remnants of the last Pleistocene advance. Their margins are a treeless tundra, where the past winter's snow melts in summer and tiny flowers bloom at the very edge of the glaciers. This, like the cold- and warm-water interface of the oceans, provides an ecotone. Relatively speaking, the edge of a snowfield is the best area for late summer and early fall hunting of caribou and musk-ox.

Land snow can be helpful or annoying: an aid or a hindrance to hunting, a source of insulation, a good surface for transportation, or a reason, in a wind-drifting snow blizzard, for a week of immobility and potential hunger. But it is of far less concern to Arctic hunters than sea ice, on which mistakes in judgment or simply bad luck can have lethal consequences.

The adaptive problems associated with sea ice hunting have been the subject of an excellent study by Nelson (1969). The more critical factors involved are essential to an understanding of the Arctic environment. As Nelson points out, the ice-covered sea is much too rich in resources for the Inuit to ignore, but harvesting these requires an impressive body of esoteric knowledge in addition to complex hunting equipment.

> On land he has had to learn intimately the behavior of the game he pursues, but there is little need to pay attention to the ground over which he travels. On the frozen surface of the sea ice that covers the ocean for much of the year, there must be a two-fold adaptation: not only must the behavior of the game pursued from the ice be understood, but it is equally important to know the behavior of the ice itself. (p. 9)

> Sea ice is indeed dangerous, mostly because it is continuously subject to the will of the wind and the forces of current. But were it not so, it would not be nearly as productive for predatory man. Regardless of how and why it has been done, the Eskimos have amassed a large body of knowledge of the sea ice which permits them to move in comparative safety over it during their everyday activities. (p. 10)

At a typical contemporary hunting camp in the Eastern Arctic, where Kemp (1971) made a detailed analysis of the energy input—output balance, 75% of the year's food supply came from hunting on the sea ice. This activity provided more meat than both the interior caribou hunts and the open-water hunting of seal and walrus that occur in summer. Archaeological techniques are not yet sophisticated enough to make this distinction between winter and summer hunting, except when migratory wild fowl are present in the middens. However, we can infer that ancient hunters contended with the same conditions and experienced similar returns on the effort expended in hunting.

Sea ice starts to form at sea, not near the land where the water is relatively warm. If conditions are just right—a low twilight sun, a clear, cloudless sky, cold sea-bottom temperature, and no wind—ice can form in the open sea even when the water temperature and ambient air are both slightly above freezing. The process occurs by radiation to the cold upper atmosphere. The water surface radiates sharp-pointed spicules which, if not disturbed by winds, join to produce brash ice that mutes the chop of surface waters and gives an oily sheen to the water. The building and destroying of ice crystals continues until there is a surface layer, built in part from colder waters beneath. Such ice is grayish at first and unsafe, but thereafter becomes black and is then safe for the knowledgable traveler. Saltwater ice, unlike freshwater ice, is flexible due to its having interlocking crystals. One can only cross new saltwater ice by straddling ones legs, to disperse the weight, and then moving forward by constantly shuffling one's feet. To stop moving is to break through to frigid water. The ability to cross young sea ice, like so many other vital activities, is a competitive skill in conventional Inuit communities. Dogsleds have to be whipped across standing waves of flexible new ice and kept constantly moving. At some point after freeze-up, however, the sea ice is safe to travel.

There is a physical limit to the thickness of Arctic sea ice. In the Eastern Arctic Archipelago this limit is about 2–3 m in a single winter, all of which melts during the summer. Through rafting, one floe riding up over another, the ice thickness can be tripled. These rafted chunks melt more slowly, and, since they are high in the air, the salt content percolates downward, turning the chunk to freshwater, drinkable ice of a bluish color. In the Amerasian Basin the maximum yearly growth is closer to 3–4 m, but even 2 m of ice is strong enough to support an 80-ton aircraft.

After the ice is thick enough to support travel its dangers become greater because they are less obvious. Ice fields many kilometers across are still subject to wind, current, and tide. There is a legend in the Arctic of a community of 30 men, women, and children hunting at the floe edge off the east coast of Greenland. Their ice sheet broke loose and drifted south in the current, melting as it moved into warmer waters. They were finally picked up by a passing ship in the North Atlantic when their ice pan was barely large enough to support them. Many hunting parties have been less fortunate.

Fast ice, frozen to shore, can stretch for kilometers across a bay, but an almost imperceptible wind can break it loose from an open coast. In February of 1956, flying across the Arctic at a north latitude of 70°, I noted that any hunter who had left the Boothia Peninsula the day before for Victoria Island would have been caught on drifting ice in the middle of the passage. The trip is normally a three-day one by dogsled, but east and west shore leads 10 km wide had opened overnight.

The situation is compounded by high tides. In bays where tidal ranges exceed 10 m, rocky knolls become mountains twice a day and are barely awash at high tide. Since ice cannot freeze solidly to their shores, such knolls are surrounded by an ice mush that has the consistency of deep quicksand. Another hazard is the capricious vagary of winter winds. A local breeze can set one ice field many kilometers across in opposition to another, equally large field. When the two come together across a kilometer of open water it is truly a case of the irresistable force meeting the immovable object. Stefansson (1921:145 ff.) describes well the effects of this meeting of giants. Huge blocks are ground off and upended, and pressure ridges 25–35 m high run through the weaker field at speeds of about 4 km/hour. When such an event occurs at night near a sleeping community of snowhouses, everyone must act quickly to pack and move before the settlement is torn apart or destroyed by pressure ice. The long pressure ridges are jumbled masses of ice that last through the winter and obstruct dogsled travel.

Winter hunters setting out from land follow sky signs. Dark areas on low-lying clouds indicate open water, either at the edge of a floe or in the midst of large ice fields, where polynias (open ponds) form. The shores of these ponds are rich with game and hunters follow the circuitous routes of recently frozen leads to reach them. These leads are smooth pathways between ice floes where the fields have broken apart and the open water has refrozen. If there is no interface between ice and open water close enough to reach from the home base, the hunters will concentrate on the breathing holes kept open in the thick ice by seal who must, every few minutes, come up for air.

By April the days are longer, the sun often warm in the −7°C calm air, and the movement of the ice so constant that it becomes a daily factor in the hunting equation. Seal and walrus heave onto the surface between cracks in the ice to sleep in 20-second intervals, alert to slip back into the water if danger threatens. Stalking the basking mammals is emotionally the most satisfying hunting technique to the Inuit, although it is less rewarding than either floe edge or breathing-hole hunting and requires years of acquired skill. There is a special danger to sea ice hunting at this time of the year. Old ice cracks, particularly tidal cracks close to shore, are bridged over with drifted snow. From the surface they look no different from the rest of the snow-covered ice. But they are fragile and quick to give way under a man's weight and drop him into frigid water. Failure to recognize these weak bridges can be fatal.

It is late July before the thick pans of winter ice disappear, even in the most southerly Arctic. By then sea ice is no longer a problem. Long after it becomes impossible to travel on sea ice, one can drive a dogsled some distance along the ice foot, the narrow highway of fast ice between the tidal crack and the shore. Narrow bays and fjords, still ice bound, can be crossed through the snowmelt water if one puts boots on the dog's feet to protect them from sharp ice spicules in melt pools. On the sea it is necessary to thread one's way through floating ice pans by kayak, but if winds and current are right, one can haul out on a small pan, drink freshwater from the melt pools on its surface, and sleep while drifting in the desired direction. This is a time too when seal and walrus climb onto the drifting pans to sleep in the sun and fall prey to stealthy kayak hunters.

The freshwater ice of inland lakes has quite different physical properties. It freezes faster in late fall but is brittle, and thin sheets of it lack the flexibile strength

Figure 2.14 Summer candling ice on Lake Hazen, northeastern Ellesmere Island, is nearly 1 m thick but too weak to support a person's weight.

of saltwater ice. In the dead of winter it may freeze to depths of about 3 m, precluding any ice fishing except at fast-flowing inlets or outlets. In the melting months freshwater ice can *candle* with remarkable speed. In this type of melting, loosely bonded crystals of ice stand vertically to depths of as much as a meter but fall apart at a touch. Whereas 0.5 m of floating sea ice can support a person, 1 m of candled ice can neither support a man's weight nor be penetrated by a boat (Figure 2.14). Summer bands who have crossed firm lake ice to hunt many kilometers inland can return to find that they must walk 80 or more kilometers around a lake that has candled in their absence.

TUNDRA AND PERMAFROST

Summer is a poor time to travel over the inland tundra. In regions of permafrost, melt water cannot sink into the frozen soil and flat areas become morasses of boggy pools. Above the permanently frozen soil there is an "active layer," an 8–15 cm-thick stratum that thaws in summer. This mud supports the tundra flora, various mosses, sedge grass, lichens, and marsh cotton so characteristic of the Arctic ground cover. Willow trees, which have pussy willows late in June and autumn-colored leaves in late August, grow even in the northern part of the Arctic, but they are more like vines and are seldom more than a few centimeters high.

It would be hard to walk very far on summer tundra, even without the numerous pools, bogs, and streams. The moss sod may be as much as 20 cm thick and feels like soft foam rubber underfoot. In low flat areas the sedge grass grows in tough clumps 30–60 cm apart. Walking across this muskeg requires a constantly changing stride in order to step from the surface of one hummock to another. The thick moss sod insulates the frozen earth from the sun's heat and makes archaeology in this region an unusually slow process. One must first peel back the heavy, water-saturated sod and then work down through the cold mud a centimeter at a time as it thaws. In most Arctic locales only 20 cm of midden thaw this way in a single summer. In order to excavate to a depth of 60 cm one must leave the midden exposed and return again and again to retrieve successive layers of the frozen past.

Construction on permafrost generates many headaches for engineers, and pres-

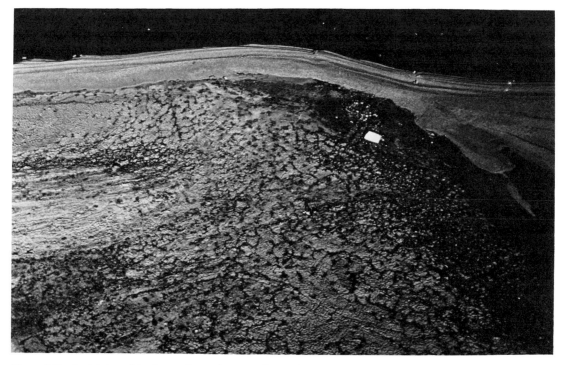

Figure 2.15 Aerial view of tundra muskeg and patterned ground on the shore of Lake Hazen, Ellsemere Island. Frost contraction cracks run inland at right angles to the shore. One of these runs through the excavated Thule house above the rectangular tent (tent is 2 m long).

ents some special problems for archaeologists. One of the many permafrost phenomena is patterned, or polygonal, ground (Figure 2.15). The earth constricts and cracks in the intense cold, and from the air the patterned polygons look like the baked surface of a southwestern mud flat, though Arctic polygons may be 3 m or more across. Melt water flowing into the cracks freezes and expands in ice wedges. As a result, the vertical stratigraphy of many Arctic sites is unreliable, with later materials slumping into cracks and becoming lodged at the level of earlier occupations. To compound the problem, there are slippage surfaces in the permafrost that causes the upper several meters of sloping ground to flow downgrade. This movement obliterates signs of earlier frost cracks and leaves an apparently undisturbed strata of cultural materials that is often, in fact, a mixture of earlier and later artifacts. This solifluction, in extreme cases, will virtually churn the upper layers of permafrost. Through the centuries, the depth of the active layer rises and falls with changing annual temperatures.

SEASONAL HAZARDS OF THE ARCTIC ENVIRONMENT

Cold and the uncertainty of life as a hunter were major problems for prehistoric Arctic dwellers. In this setting animal populations can suddenly disappear without apparent reason, and when this happens, human communities are threatened with starvation. Freezing is an ever-present danger, but drowning is the prime non-disease fatality today and probably was in the past as well. The period during the first formation of ice in the fall, when it is too late to use skin boats but the ice is too thin to support a man's weight, is a time of scarcity for marine hunters. Hunters in search of game must walk on sea ice while it is still dangerous or on newly frozen lead ice. Snow bridges over tidal cracks can break, dropping a person into water that is actually below freezing temperature because of its salinity. With the sudden shock, chilled muscles may not provide enough strength to haul one onto firm ice. Even if one makes it to the surface of the ice, soaked clothes will freeze like a metal straitjacket in a few minutes unless enough of the moisture can be blotted up by rolling in dry snow.

Winter foehns, sudden warm downslope winds caused by the cyclonic passage of air over high mountain ranges, are rare, commoner in the high mountain ranges of Greenland and Alaska than elsewhere in the Arctic, but their effects can be disastrous for herd animals and inland hunters. The downslope winds increase in temperature at the rate of 1° for every 55 m of vertical drop, and within a few hours the ambient temperature can rise from below $-18°$ C to well above the melting point. Deeply drifted snow becomes soft and wet, trapping caribou and musk-ox in inland valleys. If the temperature then falls with equal rapidity the snow bog turns to ice, wiping out the herd.

Under other winter atmospheric conditions a human community or a herd of animals may be blanketed by an ice fog, or ice crystal haze. This makes maneuvering difficult but does not create the problems that a whiteout does. During a whiteout there is snow on the ground and a thin, continuous cloud cover diffuses the sun's light so that the terrain becomes shadowless and there is no discernible horizon. The effect is like being inside a bowl of milk. It is very difficult to walk upright in a whiteout without falling over, but the greatest danger is that of walking off the edge of a cliff without ever seeing the drop-off. A whiteout can last several days, and during one there is no choice but to stay in camp. Even a 10-m walk could be disorienting and possibly fatal.

Snow blindness is a continuing hazard through the winter and parts of fall and spring. When the sky is cloudy, the surface of the sea ice tends to be shadowless and the constant effort required to discern hummocky blocks of ice that can overturn a dogsled and break a leg causes severe eyestrain. Conversely, when there is a bright sun shining on the white snow covering the sea ice, the glare is intolerable without eye protection. With an attack of snow blindness, which also causes nausea and extreme headaches, one has no choice but to sit with bandaged eyes for several days until regaining sight.

Winter nights are long in the Arctic. In the southern part of the range there is approximately 1 month in which there is no appreciable sunlight. This period extends to nearly 3 months north of 75° north latitude. Through all but full-moon nights any hunting during this period must be carried on by dim moonlight and starshine. The long dark period is depressing. For many years it was thought that the Arctic hysteria that occasionally hits northern communities was primarily caused by the depressing effects of the long darkness. Now the condition is attributed more to vitamin or mineral deficiency, but certainly the long dark months are psychologically disturbing.

Summer, spent mainly on the open water, brings a new danger of drowning. Storms with winds of near hurricane force can develop with little warning. Kayaks can easily overturn in such sudden storms or in riptides or when drifting and thawing ice suddenly gives way (Figures 2.16 and 2.17). Otherwise there are comparatively fewer hazards than in winter. Sudden coastal fogs are a frequent problem. They roll in with incredible speed, disorienting anyone at sea in small kayaks without compasses. Another condition, which affects some kayakers more than others, is kayak anxiety. This, like whiteout, is a form of vertigo. Under calm water and light cloud overcast, there is no horizon, and a person sitting close to the water in a small boat experiences a sensation of tipping over when the boat is not. Struggling to correct the imagined condition can overturn the boat in the frigid water. The only solution for kayak anxiety is to sit as motionless as possible and slap the water on both sides of the boat. This enables the tactile senses to compensate for the loss of visual control of equilibrium. There are stories of Inuit men who are so severely affected by this type of anxiety that they have to give up open-water hunting.

Given this difficult environment with all of its hazards, uncertainties, and recurrent seasonal dangers, the natural reaction of temperate-climate dwellers is to wonder why people would stay there rather than move south. There is probably no single factor that can explain this, but certainly the relative abundance of food resources is an important one. For those who have the techniques and knowledge to

Figure 2.16 Summer windstorms on the coast of Hudson Strait may exceed 100 km/hour. This storm picked up our kayak and drove it through the cook tent. John Maxwell and George Sabo, III enjoy coffee in the ruins.

Figure 2.17 Prolonged southeasterly winds in summer drive drifting Hudson Strait pack ice against the Baffin Island coast, precluding any open-water hunting or travel.

utilize these resources, the balance between energy input and output is favorable. The archaeological record of community size and settlement permanence leaves no doubt of this. For several thousand prehistoric years the vicinity of Lake Harbour on the south coast of Baffin Island, for example, was a better place for ancient hunters to live than the much more clement north central part of Michigan.

The key to Arctic abundance, of course, is ecological adaptation. Human adaptation is so specialized in the Arctic that it necessarily has its roots farther south. Before humans could successfully exploit the resources of this frigid zone they would have to have acquired a high degree of preadaptation, learning to live in increasingly colder environments and along coasts that remained frozen for increasingly longer periods of the years. One example of long acculturation is the sophistication in the tailoring of skin clothing in the Arctic. The Paleoeskimos exceeded most sub-Arctic hunters in the ingenuity and efficiency of their clothing. At the same time, effective clothing is so essential in this setting that the necessary knowledge and skills must have been acquired long before living on the Arctic's frozen coasts became a permanent life-style.

PALEOECOLOGY AND PALEOCLIMATOLOGY

The brief geographic description offered in the preceding essentially deals with conditions of modern times. However, in the following text we consider 4000 years of major climatic fluctuations and human responses to them. The variation of these responses is more expected in the Arctic than in other, more temperate, areas of the world.

> In the Arctic, changes in environmental factors have always had a significant impact on human populations. Alternative sources of food, fuel, and raw materials are limited because the ecosystem supplying these needs is a "simple" one and contains relatively few alternative energy paths. Thus Arctic populations must adapt to an ecosystem which is subject to strong control by the physical environment and vulnerable to the effects of environmental change. (Barry *et al.*, 1977:195)

Since 1975, many new data have been added to the study of Eastern Arctic climatic variation. They have come from extensive pollen profiles, evidence of glacial advances and retreats, organic growth records, formation of paleosols, isotopic variations in deep ice borings in Greenland, and to some extent archaeological excavations. The emergent sequence of fluctuation has led archaeologists to attempt correlations between climatic episodes and prehistoric events and to suggest causal relations between the two. These data, both correlations and causal interpretations are best synthesized in Barry *et al.* (1977). There, and subsequently in this volume, they are analyzed in more detail. Here I present only a simplified version (Figure 2.18), which will serve also as an introduction to the major prehistoric sequences.

With virtually all food, most fuel, and many sources of raw materials coming from Arctic animals particularly sensitive to climatic change, it is logical to expect concomitant human response in the form of demographic fluctuation, settlement expan-

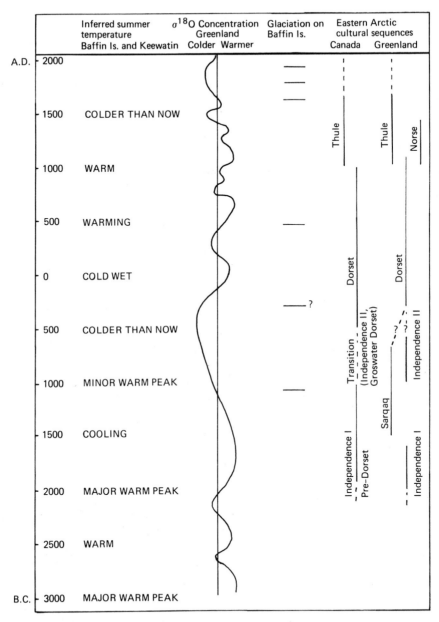

Figure 2.18 The sequence of climatic and cultural events in the Eastern Arctic (adapted from Barry *et al.* 1977).

sion or contraction, and alternative strategies in hunting activities. Relating paleoclimatic change to this human response is a two-step process often leading to confusing and unsatisfactory results for Eastern Arctic archaeologists. The first step is to determine the cooccurrence of the two sets of events, a step fraught with problems. Since the approach to paleoecology is multidisciplinary, determinations of warmer or colder conditions from one discipline may be at variance with that from another. Furthermore, since microenvironmental conditions are critical in this region, extrapolation of data from one region to another may have questionable validity. Fortunately these two problems are smoothing out as more and better data are being recovered.

A more critical problem, discussed in detail throughout the text, is one of determining chronological contemporaneity. Ultimately, virtually all archaeological chronology and many paleoclimatic sequences depend on radiocarbon assessments that in the Eastern Arctic are less than reliable for a variety of reasons.

Having accepted a general cooccurrence of climatic episodes and major aspects of cultural change, as we have here, significant problems emerge in establishing causal relations. The key is in animal ethology—behavior of the land and sea animals on which Arctic people have depended. In simple logic, colder conditions impose more physiological stress on both humans and animals. Foraging and breeding behavior may be constrained, resulting in reduced populations of both. Conversely, warmer conditions should lead to increased populations of both humans and animals. To some extent this logic holds good in the cold and arid High Arctic. But in more southerly latitudes there may be an opposite reaction. Warmer and wetter winters and longer summers may place greater stress on caribou (*Rangifer tarandus*) and ringed seal (*Phoca hispida*), the two prime animals in Paleoeskimo economy. With deeper winter snow and fluctuation between freezing and thawing, caribou foraging areas may become buried or iced over. An unseasonably early spring followed by a freeze may affect the calving, and a prolonged warm period increases the population of warble flies that infest the caribou. On the sea, ringed seal are sensitive to the growth of winter landfast ice through which they maintain breathing holes. Too early and intense a cold period may produce thick ice too quickly for the seal to maintain breathing holes. Even more critical are warmer periods in which the extent of fast ice is reduced and disappears too early in the year. Under such conditions seal populations decline, the size of individuals is decreased, and breeding is attenuated.

Many archaeologists working in the region have found that fitting all this information together produces confusing patterns. The initial expansion into the Eastern Arctic and subsequent increase in settlements took place during climatic conditions warmer than at present. On the other hand, the Dorset culture that follows and is presumably the product of descendants of the earlier inhabitants seems to have developed in response to very cold conditions. It appears to have declined during a subsequent warming trend; yet flourished in climatic conditions warmer than now. No adequate explanation for this apparent enigma has yet been made.

The following synopsis serves as a simplified scenario of those relations between climate and culture that I treat subsequently in more detail. The paleoclimatic data draws heavily from the synthesis of Barry *et al.* (1977).

On eastern Baffin Island, the thermal maximum was reached between 4000 and 3000 B.C., a time of less interisland ice cover and presumably less ice in the Arctic Basin. By 2000 B.C. Paleoeskimo people had entered the Eastern Arctic following a second warm peak c. 2600 B.C. Populations of the Independence I and Pre-Dorset cultures appear to have expanded through the warm-but-cooling trend until c. 1600 B.C. In the following cool period lasting to c. 1300 B.C., Independence I people seem to have disappeared from the High Arctic, and Paleoeskimo penetrated deep into the barren lands west of Hudson Bay.

The period between 1300 and c. 500 B.C. was generally one of cooling but less stable climates, with fluctuating warmer and cooler periods. It is marked by a warm episode around 1000 B.C. during which Keewatin forests reached their most northerly extension and Paleoeskimo people retreated from the Barrens. Three centuries later there was a second brief warm peak. This unstable climatic period between 1300 and 500 B.C. is archaeologically one of the least well-known phases. Relatively few discovered sites have yet been attributed to this period in the lower latitudes between Baffin and Victoria islands. Recovered artifacts from these few suggest some change in economic activity but also a general transition between Pre-Dorset and Dorset. However, in the High Arctic and West Greenland and on the Labrador coast, what appear to be different cultural configurations emerge from a hiatus of 3 or more centuries. In the High Arctic, including northern Greenland, the Independence II culture house types are much like the Independence I structures in addition to exhibiting some new artifact traits. In the general Disko Bay region of West Greenland, the Sarqaq culture has close resemblance to the Pre-Dorset of Arctic Canada yet many traits that are regionally specific, and on the Labrador coast, Groswater Dorset, emerging in this period, overlaps in its early and late phases both Pre-Dorset and Early Dorset. This evidence has led to sporadic and alternative interpretations of the relation between earlier Paleoeskimo (Independence I and Pre-Dorset) and later Paleoeskimo (Dorset) cultures. One camp sees it as a cultural and population continuum; the other attributes perceived differences to separate populations.

The appearance of the cultural configuration universally recognized as Dorset can currently be estimated around 500 B.C. This correlates well with a marked cold peak, colder than present, which may have been reached a century earlier. It marks the onset of permafrost, at least on southern Baffin Island, a retreat of the forest line on Keewatin, and a readvance of the Barnes Ice Cap on eastern Baffin Island. There follows a cooling trend and thriving of Dorset culture. This period of minimal summer temperatures continues to about 100 B.C. Following it there is a short unstable period with probable regional variants and a warming trend punctuated by occasional episodes of cold, wet summers in the four centuries between A.D. 100 and 500. In these four centuries on all but the Labrador and Newfoundland coasts, Dorset sites became markedly scarce. It is now doubtful that this scarcity is a function of limited exploration. Extensive survey along the southeastern Baffin Island coast has produced only two or three small Middle Dorset sites in this formerly extensively settled region. Conversely the number of sites, and presumably populations, increased on Labrador and Newfoundland during this warming trend. Since these latter coasts are normally warmer than most of the Eastern Arctic this expansion is difficult to account for unless it is related to improved hunting conditions for the harp seal (*Phoca groenlandica*), which has always been an important food resource along these coasts.

From A.D. 500 to 1000, Arctic climates continued to warm, with a peak warmth around A.D. 1000. The century before and after this peak saw the major expansion of Norse Vikings into the North Atlantic islands, Iceland, and Greenland and from there to Newfoundland. Crops flourished throughout Scandinavia and winter sea ice was greatly reduced. Surprisingly, this period in which climatic conditions became warmer than they are at present saw a marked florescence of Dorset culture in geographic expansion, settlement size, and tool, religious, and artistic complexity. This climax, currently unexplainable, seems to negate the previous interpretations that correlated Dorset adaptive success with cold, dry winters.

The nature of interaction between Late Dorset people at the end of this period and incoming Thule whale hunters from Alaska is still, as it has been for several decades, a moot question. The two peoples may have interfaced in direct contact or may only have interrelated through cultural diffusion. Alternatively, Dorset culture may have suffered catastrophic decline shortly before the Thule entry. Excavation has yet to resolve these questions.

Shortly after the warm peak of c. A.D. 900–1000, temperatures began cooling until the onset of the Little Ice Age of c. A.D. 1500. Norse farming settlements collapsed from many causes, chief of which was the increasing cold. A presumably greater extent of sea ice inhibited the population of baleen whale, which had been the ethic center of Thule culture, and from the seventeenth century on, Thule culture became fragmented into a number of regionally specific hunting strategies.

3

Pioneers of the Eastern Arctic

Sometime before the end of the third millennium B.C., nomadic bands began pushing eastward from regions of the Bering Strait and the north Alaskan coast into lands that humans had never seen before. Within a few centuries these nomads were roaming the northeastern coast of Greenland and Baffin Island and several hundred kilometers of the Labrador coast.

This migration may well have been the last act of a process that began 70,000 years ago when an expanding world population forced hunters and gatherers to move outward from European centers into unoccupied lands. The expansion into most of North and South America had been completed by 10,000 years ago, but the Eastern Arctic, still at that time covered by glacial ice in the highlands much as it is now, remained unoccupied by human predators. Ice- and snowfields over Foxe Basin and Hudson Bay blocked eastward passage until about 6500 years ago. The withdrawal of the ice did not immediately attract human occupation to the region. Archaeological evidence indicates that no emigration occurred until 4000–4500 years ago but that once started, population of much of the Eastern Arctic took less than 500 years. Why did the occupation start then? Where was the homeland of the emigrants? What was the stimulus for the eastward move? What factors drove people to move so far in only a few centuries?

ORIGIN OF THE MIGRATION

Within North America, there are only three logical points of origin for these early migrations. The emigrants could have split off from prehistoric Indian cultures of the Northeast, from early maritime hunters of the western coast of Alaska, or from inhabitants of some as yet unidentified place between the Eastern Arctic and the western Alaskan Coast.

The suggestion that a tundra and frozen coastal lifeway developed in the east from some prehistoric Northeastern Indian culture and then spread westward fails for lack of evidence. Several authors have noted that certain isolated Arctic stone tool traits are comparable to selected features of Paleoindian artifacts of the Northeast. These, however, never appear in a complex of tools that could be interpreted as a prehistoric progenitor for the earliest Eastern Arctic tool kit. Elmer Harp, William Fitzhugh, and James Tuck have diligently sought evidence of contact between Indians and the earliest prehistoric Arctic hunters on the Labrador and island coasts of Newfoundland, but they concluded that, given the dating of sites and their distribu-

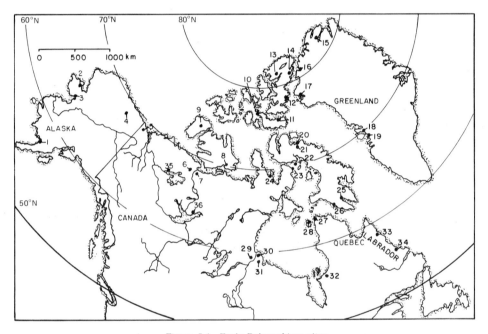

Figure 3.1   Early Paleoeskimo sites.

1. Naknek, Alaska
2. Trail Creek, Alaska
3. Cape Denbigh, Alaska
4. Anaktuvuk, Alaska
5. Engigstciak (Firth River), Yukon Territory
6. Dismal II, District of Mackenzie
7. Bloody Falls, District of Mackenzie
8. Ekulluk sites, Victoria Island
9. Umingmak, Banks Island
10. Port Refuge, Devon Island
11. Cape Sparbo, Devon Island
12. Bache Peninsula, Ellesmere Island
13. Eureka Sound, Ellesmere Island
14. Lonesome Creek, Ellesmere Island
15. Independence Fjord, Greenland
16. Solebakken, Greenland
17. Gammel Nûgdlît, Greenland
18. Sarqaq sites, Greenland

19. Sermermiut, Greenland
20. Pond Inlet, Baffin Island
21. Mittamatalik, Baffin Island
22. Kapuivik, Jens Munk Island
23. Igloolik, Melville Peninsula
24. St. Mary's Hill, Simpson Peninsula
25. Shaymark, Baffin Island
26. Lake Harbour sites, Baffin Island
27. Ivugivik, Quebec
28. Arnapik, Mansel Island
29. Thyazzi, Manitoba
30. Seahorse Gully, Manitoba
31. Twin Lakes, Manitoba
32. Great Whale River, Quebec
33. Saglek, Labrador
34. Thalia Point, Labrador
35. Great Bear Lake
36. Great Slave Lake

tions, there could have been only limited physical contact between the two groups and little or no cultural exchange. Few researchers now question that the earliest Arctic migration moved from west to east, although McGhee (1983) has suggested an early Greenlandic emigration from Siberia via Spitsbergen.

There is somewhat more evidence for the possibility that the earliest migration began either in the interior of Alaska or on its north coast between the Bering Strait and Victoria Island. An interpretation favored earlier by McGhee (1976) proposes two early, but culturally separated, migrations from west to east. The earlier of the two, Independence I, moved across the northern islands of the High Arctic to the northeastern fjords of Greenland (Figure 3.1), whereas a few centuries later, a second migration, Pre-Dorset, traveled the coastal mainland into the more southerly islands. Since the earliest Arctic complex of the Bering Strait is more like Pre-Dorset than like Independence I, McGhee suggested that the origin point for the earliest eastern culture, Independence I, was some place between east and west and that a few centuries later, people spread both eastward and westward.

This interpretation becomes increasingly viable as additional early sites are located that show evidence of Arctic-adapted people. With continued exploration, interior Alaskan complexes may yet show up as progenitors of the frozen coastal culture. Dumond interprets the earliest Arctic Alaskan evidence as demonstrating a subsistence that is "balanced [between] hunting and fishing, with emphasis on caribou and anadromous fish where available" and with only seasonal, during the open-water period, sea mammal hunting (1972:314). His argument that representatives of the complex do not appear in Siberia strengthens the assumption of an interior North American development.

However, the most conclusive evidence to date would place the parental cultural complex far to the west on the northeastern shore of Bering Strait. At the Iyatyet site on Cape Denbigh, Norton Sound, Gidding's work, which began in 1948, identified an ancient stone tool assemblage that he named the Denbigh Flint Complex (Giddings 1964). The uniqueness of this complex as compared to archaeological evidence of more southerly cultures associates these remains with a technology already adapted to tundra and maritime hunting. Spalled burins that have their closest parallels in the Upper Paleolithic of Europe occurred with high frequency, leading Giddings originally to attribute these remains to a general movement of people out of Siberia prior to the Neolithic period.

Although the Denbigh Flint Complex has not proved to be as early as Giddings originally thought, ^{14}C analysis indicates that it is probably as old as 2500 b.c., later research in both coastal and interior Alaska demonstrated that the basic complex, with some temporal and regional variations, could be identified along the Alaskan coast from the base of the peninsula at Naknek around to the Firth River, east of the Canadian–Alaskan border, and inland as far as Anaktuvuk Pass. Stone tools are all that remain in most of these sites, but the similarity of the assemblages recovered from them led Irving (1957) to group them as the Arctic Small Tool tradition. This term and concept has proved useful to archaeologists in both Western and Eastern Arctic. The Denbigh lithics shown in Figure 3.2 are representative.

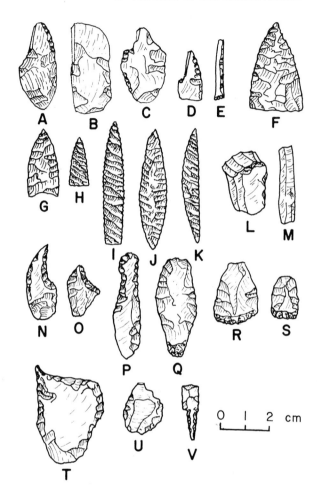

Figure 3.2 Lithic tools of the Denbigh Flint Complex (drawings based on selected illustrations from Giddings 1964).

A–D. spalled burins
E.   burin-spall tool
F–I.   end-hafted projectile tips
J,K.   side blades
L.   microblade core
M.   microblade
N–P.   side scrapers
Q–S.   end scrapers
T.   retouched graver
U.   polished graver
V.   drill.

THE ARCTIC SMALL TOOL TRADITION

Artifacts in this tradition's basic tool kit are, as the name implies, so small that they reflect either a very constrained set of hand motor habits or, as modern Inuit suggest, a population of dwarfs. When I carried the lithic sample from Lake Harbour, Baffin Island, to Denmark for comparison with collections there, I was able to pack nearly 10,000 stone tools in a padded box no bigger than a large suitcase.

The distinctive components of this basic tool kit include a number of artifacts, with or without handles, used to fabricate weapon parts from hard organic substances such as antler, ivory, bone, and wood. Of these, the most distinctive is the spalled burin, not found in most prehistoric Indian sites. The several shapes and sizes shown in Figure 3.2 represent different types, each of which may have been used for some specifically different function. Essentially, the Paleoeskimo used small burins as chisels, for cutting and splitting hard material by successive grooving strokes, or as side scrapers, utilizing the sharp margins of the burin spall scar to shape objects. The burin spall itself was also a fabricating tool. Other toolmaking implements are flaked gravers with tiny, retouched points resembling those of Paleoindian complexes, concave-edged side scrapers that are usually unifacially flaked, and small end scrapers that range in shape from triangular to square but usually have expanded working edges that are broader than their bases. Microblades, tiny parallel-sided flakes 10 mm or less wide and 20–40 mm long, were pressed from variably shaped chert, obsidian, or quartz-crystal cores. These too are tools, not weapons, as are small adzes with polished edges.

The primary hunting implements were presumably harpoons, arrows, and spears of bone, antler, or walrus ivory. A number of carefully flaked, triangular, end-hafted projectile points comparable to other prehistoric artifacts that unquestionably were used as harpoon tips have been recovered (Figure 3.2F and G). The small, thin, narrow, end-hafted flint points with squared bases, or tapering, and bipointed stems (Figure 3.2H and I) are associated elsewhere with bone arrowheads. A wide variety of side-hafted artifacts in this complex appear to have been prepared for setting in the lateral grooves of long bone spear or arrow points. One of the few bits of western

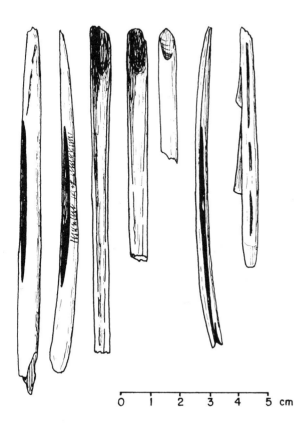

Figure 3.3 Bone points slotted for end or side blades from the Trail Creek caves (drawings based on selected illustrations from Larsen 1968).

0   1   2   3   4   5 cm

Arctic evidence for the function of these side blades comes from the Trail Creek caves (Larsen 1962). The stratigraphy of the caves is less straightforward than one could wish, and most of the recovered artifacts are older than the Denbigh complex. But some of the bone points, side slotted and end grooved, if not of Denbigh time demonstrate how Denbigh side and end blades could have been hafted (Figure 3.3). This basic Arctic Small Tool tradition fabricating and hunting kit can be traced across the Arctic with surprisingly little change in artifact shape from Bering Strait to northeastern Greenland, a straight-line distance of 4300 km. There are, however, some discrete regional and temporal differences between site complexes that are difficult to explain. For example, some sites have produced few or no microblades, eastern assemblages do not have the long, narrow, parallel-flaked side blades of the west, and some sites, such as those of southern Baffin Island and the Denbigh layer at the type site of Iyatyet, include ground and polished stone artifacts that are apparently absent from other early Arctic Small Tool tradition sites.

Despite these site-specific descrepancies, the early phase of the tradition stands out as a unique artifact complex in world prehistory. The essential commonality of the assemblages provides convincing proof of a migration of people rather than merely the diffusion of traits. Whether this tradition originated on the western coast of Alaska, farther west on the frozen coast of Siberia, or among interior caribou hunters in northern Alaska, it is logical to see it as entering the Eastern Arctic from some western location.

PROBLEMS IN DATING EARLY SITES

An understanding of the precise timing of the migration into the Eastern Arctic would clarify the question of origins. The time-related evidence requires more than usual interpretation because of the nature of the ^{14}C samples. The only organic remains in many Arctic sites are caribou antler and bones, cinder-like lumps of charred fat, sea mammal bones, and ivory. These materials differ greatly in both composition and source and thus yield markedly different age assessments. Moreover, the state of the art of carbon dating is such that insufficient study has been made of comparable materials. Corrective factors for the substances involved and the discrepancy between terrestial and sea sources are unknown. Some of the problems involved in converting Arctic radiocarbon years to calendar dates are related to atmospheric changes in ^{14}C–^{12}C ratios, the use of different half-lifes for the variable materials, and assessments of fractionation. Collecting difficulties and alternative statistical procedures further complicate interpretation of the data.

Nine published dates from the Iyatyet (Giddings 1964) and Onion Portage (Anderson 1970) sites range, in their central tendencies, from 2303 to 1801 B.C., with a mean date of 2013 B.C. Dates obtained for the Denbigh Flint Complex in Alaska exceed this range in both directions, the extremes being 3113 B.C. ± 340 years and 1102 B.C. ± 250 years. However, there are statistical reasons for ignoring the earliest date, based on Spaulding's (1958) test of probability that two carbon dates refer to coeval events. Dekin (1975) applied this test to Arctic dates and found only a probability of .05 that the two runs on the Denbigh sample (C-793) dated the same event. One run yielded a date of 2303 B.C., which clusters well with other Denbigh samples, and the other run yielded the 3113 B.C. date. Standing alone, 1000 years earlier, the date cannot be validated statistically for the event recorded in the array of evidence for the Western Arctic Small Tool tradition. Thus the date of 2303 B.C. ± 290 years, or the period from about 2500 to 2000 B.C., is the most acceptable for the earliest formal evidence of this complex in the Western Arctic.

The problem is more acute in the Eastern Arctic because of the dearth of suitable organic materials for dating. Several of the earliest sites contained no organic material other than cinders of charred seal fat or scraps of driftwood. The latter, of course, could have drifted in cold currents for centuries before being deposited in site middens, and the former have proved notably unreliable. The various contentions and interpretations that revolve around the radiocarbon dating are discussed in McGhee and Tuck (1976), Dekin (1975), and Arundale (1981). Currently it would appear that bones, ivory, and charred fat from sea mammals yield calendar dates older than we might expect, while caribou antler, and perhaps caribou bone, yield younger dates than do charred wood samples. A number of methods have been used in attempts to correct for factors that distort the radiocarbon dates. McGhee and Tuck (1976), obviously preferring to accept only charcoal dates from burned indigenous wood (*Salix arcticus*), follow Olsson (1972) in suggesting that 400 years be subtracted from those ages derived from sea sources. Stuckenrath (Dekin 1975) suggests that 200 years or possibly a reduction of 10–20%, might be more appropriate.

Such manipulations have little effect on the relative sequences, but the imprecision involved permits various adjustments that fit the data to personal theories. The issue becomes most critical at the beginning of the Eastern Paleoeskimo time scale for two reasons. First, a literal acceptance of sea mammal dates indicates an eastern occupation at least 500 years earlier than Alaskan dates for the Denbigh Flint Complex. Second, comparative dates are directly related to the questions of whether Independence I and Pre-Dorset are culturally separable elements of the earliest occupation and, if so, which development is the later of the two.

Knuth's (1952, 1954, 1967a,b) careful work on the northern and northeastern coasts of Greenland and his later exploration of northern Ellesmere Island have given us the most reliable dating for the early occupation of the Eastern Arctic. He has a suite of 11 dates for the earliest occupation of northeastern Greenland (Independence I) that range from 1810 B.C. ± 120 years to 1980 B.C. ± 130 (with a mean date of 1884 B.C.). The samples are charred indigenous willow (*Salix*), which should yield accurate results from normal dating techniques. However, a literal comparison of these with the Alaskan dates would have primitive hunters racing across the Arctic toward the east. That interpretation is hardly compatible with anthropological concepts. Better results are obtained when the standard deviations

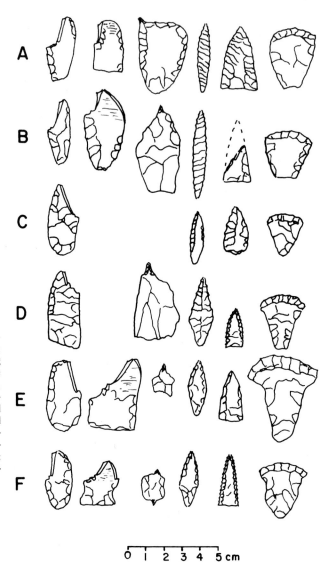

Figure 3.4 Similarity of selected Arctic Small Tool tradition stone artifacts from sites along the Arctic coast (drawn to the same scale): from left to right, unpolished burins, polished burins, retouched gravers, bipointed end blades, triangular end blades, and end scrapers (drawings based on selected illustrations from Giddings 1956, 1964; Harp 1958; MacNeish 1956; Maxwell 1973; Taylor 1968).

A. Denbigh Flint Complex
B. Engigstciak, Firth River
C. Dismal II
D. Thyazzi, North Knife River
E. Arnapik, Mansel Island
F. Shaymark, Frobisher Bay

and sampling errors in the carbon dates of Alaska and those from northeastern Greenland are taken into consideration. This statistical procedure allows for an eastward migration that occurred over about 500 years.

The problem of comparative dating is compounded by sea mammal carbon dates from more southern sites. A charred fat sample from the Pre-Dorset Closure site near Lake Harbour dates 2740 B.C. ± 380 years (GSC 1382). The sample, assumed to be seal fat, is very small, and the date may be too early by 500 years. However, another from the same site yields a date of 2510 B.C. ± 100 years (GAK-1281). Other dates include one of 2435 B.C. ± 155 years (S-589) for a sample of seal bone from Pond Inlet at the northern edge of Baffin Island, a date of 2190 B.C. ± 130 years (GSC-849) on a sample of charred seal fat from the Shaymark site, Frobisher Bay, another from the Closure site, also on charred seal fat, of 2117 B.C. ± 73 years (P-707), and a date of 2008 B.C. ± 168 years (P-107) on walrus ivory from the earliest sites at Igloolik. Subtracting 400 years, or 10% of the carbon age, from several of these dates still leaves the calendar years at the beginning of the second millennium B.C.

The most useful correction is by Arundale (1981), who takes laboratory-derived values for fractionation and sea reservoirs into account (see Chapter 5). Deliberately avoiding the tempting game of manipulating these dates to fit my own pet theories, I simply state that the formal data supports a contention that Paleoeskimo migrants left coastal Arctic Alaska around 2500 B.C., hunted their way eastward, and reached the eastern limits of what was to be their region of later development about half a millennium later. The great similarity in the tool assemblages from sites across the Arctic coast records their passage. This similarity can be seen in Figure 3.4.

FACTORS PROMPTING THE EASTWARD MIGRATION

Anthropologically, the most interesting question about the human expansion into the unexplored east is why it occurred at all. What stimulated a movement into this relatively bleak and hitherto uninhabited region at a time when vast and sparsely inhabited regions stretched southward? Only hypothetical answers can be given, for there is no substantive evidence. Early in my research I had the intriguing idea that when Foxe Basin and Hudson Bay were finally released from their burden of continental ice, and thereby opened to Atlantic fauna, there might have been an ecological explosion of maritime game animals that served as a magnet to primitive hunters. Unfortunately, paleontologists, zoologists, and mammalogists find this doubtful. No such biotic explosion occurred with the withdrawal of continental ice from the Great Lakes. Nevertheless, it is a truism that ecotones tend to be richer than the centers of the interfacing ecological zones, and the juncture of Atlantic and Arctic waters in the extreme Eastern Arctic is such an ecotone. It is feasible to assume that a combination of optimal conditions created an exploitable biomass of sufficient proportions to lure hunters eastward. Anthropologically, however, it is difficult to conjure a picture of a hardy group of pioneers pushing rapidly eastward to discover this rich eastern ecotone. It is unlikely that a small group could have done so and returned to tell Alaskan relatives about its protein wealth.

While the freeing of Arctic Archipelago basins from huge sheets of continental glacial ice may not have triggered an immediate influx of sea animals and humans, it is logical to suggest that climatic change played an important role in attracting early hunters eastward. Paleoclimatic evidence accumulated by Barry *et al.* (1977) indicates many rapid fluctuations in the past 5000 years between periods colder and

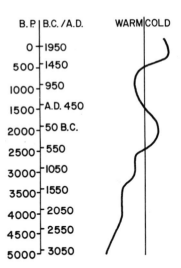

Figure 3.5   Schematic sequence of Eastern Arctic climatic
shifts (adapted from Barry *et al.* 1977).

warmer than at present. A simplified version of this evidence is presented in Figure
3.5. But in the critical period of eastward expansion, both air and water temperatures were warmer than they have been for the four millennia since. Around
3000 B.C., Northern Hemisphere temperatures were phasing out of the heat wave
called the "Thermal Maximum." Hot, dry temperatures that had played a critical
part in the Paleoindian lifeways of the plains and plateaus were waning, but in the
Arctic, seawaters were still warm enough that most of the Arctic Archipelago, and
perhaps even the Arctic Basin, were free of ice during the summer months. The
north coasts of Ellesmere Island and Greenland, now locked throughout the year in
fast ice, were open for hunting and navigation.

Today northeastern Ellesmere and northern Greenland have seashores that are
virtually covered, even in the middle of summer, by drifting ice pans. There are
enough cracks in these floes to provide breathing space for a moderate number of
ring seal, but not enough for the larger bearded seal, nor for the walrus, whale,
narwhal, and beluga. This modern ecological picture of the area does not adequately
reflect the prehistoric one. Knuth's discovery (1952) of a large umiak (a whale
hunting boat made of skin that could hold up to 20 people) on the now-frozen north
coast of Greenland indicates that it has not been many centuries since the coast had
open, navigable waters. This juncture of Arctic Archipelago and Arctic Basin waters
must have been an unusually rich ecotone to draw hunters so far north from their
northwestern Greenland base. Presumably it would have been even richer during
the waning years of the Thermal Maximum.

Much of the same can be said for the coast of Labrador, where Tuck (1976) and
Fitzhugh (1976b) have found traces of the earliest eastern emigrants. At present,
this juncture of Atlantic water and the cold Labrador current, which begins in
northern Baffin Bay, is an area unusually rich in protein resources such as codfish
and harp seal. In the early days of the Paleoeskimo migration, when land and sea

temperatures were warmer than they are now, this ecotone could conceivably have been even richer.

WESTERN POPULATION PRESSURE

The most logical reason for this, or any other migration of people, is population pressure in the homeland. On coastal Alaska we have no direct evidence for such pressure deriving from too many hunters and too many mouths to feed for the available game. In fact, at today's level of archaeological exploration there have been too few sites discovered to suggest this. But warmer waters on the Alaskan coast may have had adverse effects on local sea mammals and contributed to the need for eastward migration. While some of the larger air-breathing sea mammals thrive in areas of more open water, ringed seal require a critical extent of winter landfast ice for breeding and individual growth (McLaren 1958). Declining numbers of this important food source may have made unexplored coasts to the east more attractive.

Field studies conducted since 1970, have increased our knowledge about hunter–gatherer behavior and added complexity to our understanding of the system of hunter–prey relations. The formula is a delicately balanced one and may not always be reflected in the archaeological record.

From the vantage point of modern times it is not easy to reconstruct the factors that culminate in population pressure among hunting peoples. But studies of such modern hunters as the !Kung Bushmen and Australian desert dwellers indicate the fallacy of the Malthusian theory that population will increase to the maximum numbers the environment will support. It becomes increasingly apparent that there are adaptive limits to hunting-band size and both cultural and biological constraints that maintain these limits well below the carrying capacity of the hunting territory. Rather than expanding to the point where energy requirements might strain available per capita food resources, such groups tend to hold their population density to a ratio with the carrying capacity of the land that would permit the environment to support two or more times as many people as it does. One explanation that is offered for this pattern is the ability to survive catastrophe that it confers. There is a wide margin for cyclical failure in the propagation of game herds and plant-food resources or in the efficiency of subsistence activities that can result from fluctuations in the natural environment.

The number of hunting families occupying a given terrain is further reduced, and population pressure concomitantly increased, by what appears to be an additional constraint. Hunting families are apparently reluctant to spend more than limited time and effort in acquiring the necessary food. Since they do not stockpile wealth their work load per nuclear family is less than that of agriculturalists who accumulate a surplus. This energy expenditure, which involves not only the time and effort spent in hunting but also the travel time to and from resource locations, appears to have arbitrary, but restricted, limits of acceptability. Studies of contemporary hunters and gathers indicate that this limit is about 200 workdays per year per nuclear family, whereas the collective load for an agriculturally based nuclear family may be three times that amount. The acceptable limits of this activity have much to do with population pressure but are virtually impossible to measure in prehistoric populations. It is possible that factors in the waning Thermal Maximum upset the delicate balance of population and environment in Alaska without leaving clear prehistoric evidence.

An explanation for the eastward move suggested as early as 1917 by Steensby would have these early hunters following eastwardly migrating musk-ox. An important item of evidence supports this conjecture. Knuth's (1967a,b) excavations in the earliest sites of northeastern Greenland point to 200 or more years of reliance on the musk-ox as the primary source of human energy. But Steensby's hypothesis is suspect for two major reasons. In the first place, the evidence from western Europe, and elsewhere, is that musk-ox distribution was seldom far from glacial margins. Although the paleontological history of the musk-ox during the waning Pleistocene is not as well known as it should be, the animal's eastward migration would be expected to occur earlier than the Arctic Small Tool tradition. It should have preceded that complex by at least 2000 years. Second, and more critically, a number of Arctic explorers, beginning with Stefansson, have been convinced that musk-ox are so easy to hunt and so slow to reproduce that they could not, for long, have been the primary source of energy for any group of hunters (Wilkinson 1972). In fact, except for the expedition of Admiral Peary, who instructed his Inuit hunters to slaughter more than 200 musk-ox on northern Ellesmere Island to support his dash to the Pole, there is only limited and regionally specific evidence for Eskimo reliance on musk-ox as a major energy source (Damas 1969b).

THE RATE OF EXPANSION INTO NEW LANDS

One of the most intriguing questions about the Paleoeskimo emigrants deals with the apparent speed of their eastern expansion. If we accepted the Denbigh date of 2300 B.C. and the eastern Pre-Dorset sea mammal date of 2500 B.C. as absolutes, we would have to see these Arctic Small Tool tradition people as arriving in the east before they occupied the west. Logically we have to allow some time for the migration, and 300–500 years seems to be in the right order of magnitude. In this length of time the initial migration, perhaps splitting into a northern wave toward northeast Greenland and a southern one toward Labrador, would have covered 5500 km of shore. Arithmetically this relation between time and distance is not startling. It would only take a slow, cumulative drift of people, 11 km each year, to accomplish this movement in five centuries. But our models of migration, based on comparative hunting behavior, indicate that such a cumulative drift could only be stimulated and sustained by continuous ecological or social pressure.

Although there are no realistic models for the migration of people into totally unoccupied lands, the traditional eastern Inuit nomadism would seem to furnish a likely way of looking at the movements of early prehistoric Arctic dwellers. In this model hunters tend to stay in those locales they know best, where their consequent ratio of hunting success to expended effort is highest. Inevitably band populations in these locales increase. At the critical point when the relation between population density, environmental carrying capacity, and expended hunting effort reaches unacceptable limits, the band begins to fission. Hunting pressure may be a direct cause of population movement, or it may indirectly cause social tensions and frictions that stimulate fissioning of the band. In response to these pressures, a few families move from the band locale into less well-known terrain. But this expansion into unfamiliar hunting regions takes place in small increments of time and space. The separating family retains some refuge, often kinship ties, in the original home base until it has clearly reached an adaptive level in the new surroundings. Furthermore, such movement may be in any direction, east, west, north, or south, and may not necessarily be lineal as the earliest migration appears to have been.

Archaeological evidence suggests that these eastward migrants were organized into simple, seasonally nomadic, and probably egalitarian bands. Such a social system was characteristic of most Eastern Arctic Inuit until modern times. This is not, however, characteristic of all Eskimo societies. Where natural resources were more concentrated, as for example in parts of Alaska, many settlements reached high levels of population density and were virtually sedentary. Social status within the community was often ranked and some social systems were organized along lineage principles.

It is unfortunate that we have so little information on what happens to the environment of lands hitherto unseen by hunters when humans move into them. In animal ethology there are certainly learned responses to predation, whether by carnivorous animals or humans. Today when most Inuit summer seal hunting is accomplished by motor boat, the naturally curious seal, who will bob their heads above water at unfamiliar sounds, have learned the danger of motor noise. Inuit seal hunters and Michigan deer hunters alike dream of that place, unknown to others, that has never been hunted before. There is probably some substance to this dream. In 1958 I spent 3 summer months, most of the time alone, in northern Ellesmere Island. I was probably the first human to walk through much of the area since Greeley's expedition in 1881, and I was amazed at how relatively fearless the animals were. One morning I awoke to find six young Arctic wolves sitting peacefully around my tent. Another day a wolf jumped on my tent and then for 2 days followed me around like a dog. Fox tried to enter my tent for food, and my efforts to photograph one with a camera that could focus no closer than 1 m, were thwarted because the fox refused to maintain an adequate distance even when I tried kicking it out farther with my foot. Duck, geese, and ptarmigan did not bother to fly when I approached them, musk-ox continued placidly to graze 30 m away from me, and seals played acrobatically in a tide pool about 1 meter from my beachside camp. Had I been a hunter I would have had little trouble getting adequate meat.

Although we may never be able to prove this, the reason for the constant movement eastward may be that hunting on new coasts, excellent at first, began to show dwindling results as animals learned the habits of the new predators and there were always lands never hunted by humans farther to the east.

At the western end of the Eastern Arctic there are few traces of the earliest migration. The carbon dates on such Arctic Small Tool tradition sites as Umingmak on Banks Island and Bloody Falls on the Coppermine River are too recent for the earliest period. The Dismal II site (Harp 1958), 80 km inland and 32 km west of the Coppermine River, is the best candidate for one of the earliest camps although it has not been carbon dated. The recovered stone tools, generally fitting my impression of what an early Arctic Small Tool tradition assemblage should look like, include some of the earliest types, such as expanded-edge-end scrapers and tapered-base arrow tips. But in addition to this and an apparently early but undated site at Mary's Hill on Pelly Bay (Mary-Rousselière 1964), there is so little to mark the passage of pioneers that one wonders if they even paused to cook a stew of seal meat as they passed through. Partly this dearth of sites is due to the vastness of the shoreline and difficulties of exploration. It may also be due to demographic factors: If the food resources were as bountiful as I have implied, one would expect the human re-productive rate to increase and the population to swell during the move east.

The initial group entering the Eastern Arctic from the west may have consisted only of a few bands, perhaps no more than 100 people. Haynes (1966), in trying to account for the rapid spread and apparent demographic expansion of Paleoindians in North America, concluded that an initial crossing of the land bridge of Beringia by only a few bands would, over time, be sufficient. He used the figure of 1.4 persons for the population expansion rate per 28-year generation when people are moving into an environment empty of competitors. Applying this factor to a single Arctic band of 50 persons for 18 generations would result, at the end of 500 years, in a total of 15,000 people. This figure is much higher than any archaeologist's estimate for the earliest Paleoeskimo, even in the most densely settled regions of the east, and an increase of 1.3 persons per generation, or even less, is probably more realistic. Regardless of the factor used, it is apparent that populations in the 500-year move eastward could have been much smaller in the western part of the range, conse-quently producing fewer and smaller campsites and residual middens.

The migrating hunters ultimately pushed around the top of Greenland, down its eastern coast for a short distance, and along the Labrador coast as far as Hopedale. In a symposium of Eastern Arctic archaeologists (Maxwell 1976), the major con-centration of these early people was seen by some archaeologists to be in what was considered a "core area" generally centering on Foxe Basin and the shores and islands of Hudson Strait. From here, populations were thought to have expanded into marginal regions in good times and to have retreated back to the core area when ecological conditions were unfavorable. The availability and apparent reliabili-ty of food resources in the core region made this a reasonable concept. Other regions might have been richer in migrating game animals from time to time, but effective harvesting of them depended on a mini-max economy, one in which minor events affecting animal migration might lead to catastrophic economic collapse and human starvation. Alternatively, resources in the core area were, as they are today, sufficiently diverse, reliable, and capable of sustaining long-term settlement continua.

Currently it is apparent that this core area concept may have been in part an artifact of limited Arctic exploration. Further excavation in the High Arctic and along the northern Labrador coast now make it clear that there were also large populations and long-sustained settlements in these regions as well. It would now appear that wherever food resources were sufficient the early Paleoeskimo settled into their seasonal nomadism and that there was no well-defined center of population and cultural dispersal in the east.

INTERPRETATIONS OF BAND-LEVEL ORGANIZATION

Cultural reconstructions of this pioneering phase of Eastern Arctic Paleoeskimo prehistory rest on little more than the stone tools left behind. While it is true that later sites have remained permanently frozen with preserved remnants of wood, bone, and skin, the early sites in the aftermath of the Thermal Maximum thawed each summer causing most organic material to disintegrate. Some of the sites north of 70° north latitude have yielded a few artifacts of bone, antler, or ivory, but this is a function of the desert dryness found there rather than permanent cold. In southerly, more humid, sites only the dark organic stains of rotted tools and weapons are preserved. Nevertheless, because of the distinct geographic factors that constrain human behavior in the Arctic, I feel safe in extrapolating from prehistory some of the features of more recent band organization. Because of the Arctic's extreme marginality as a human habitat the number of viable cultural alternatives is finite. In this environment, ethnologic analogs seem especially appropriate for interpreting archaeological evidence.

From the beginning there would have to have been a dual economy, maritime and terrestrial, for survival. Unlike in the Western Arctic waters, there are no fur-bearing marine mammals in the Eastern Arctic. Skins of the hair seal are waterproof and adequate for summer wear, but insufficient for below-freezing winter temperatures. For such temperatures, caribou skin is a necessity. Caribou hairs are hollow, and the dead-air spaces within the thousands of these on a pelt provide excellent insulation. On the other hand, while caribou hunting alone might satisfy yearly clothing requirements, caribou, unlike seal and walrus, do not supply enough fat through the year to meet human caloric requirements in this environment; nor, on a treeless coast where driftwood is usually too precious to burn, do they provide combustible fat as do the sea mammals. Southerners are inclined to see the need for fuel in relation to cooking food or warming shelter. In below-freezing Arctic cold there is an even more critical need for heat. Humans can go several days with no food at all or derive sufficient nourishment from slivered shavings of raw, frozen meat. There is no comfort in riding out a −40° C blizzard wrapped only in caribou skins with no available fire, but our insulated body heat will not drop to lethal limits. However, our daily requirement for water is fixed, and in below-freezing temperatures this prime necessity is locked in rock-hard ice. I know from uncomfortable experience that sucking on ice cubes or cuddling up to a bag of ice that might melt to water by morning is no substitute for melting fresh ice over a fire.

Our pioneering population would undoubtedly have been limited in band size to the number of people who hunted together and regularly interacted on a face-to-face basis throughout the year. Comparative figures from ethnographies of contemporary hunter–gatherers provide what seem to be universal limits to the size of such bands. In a world sample of hunter–gatherers (Hayden 1972:211), single-band size ranges from 15 to 50 people. The larger bands are those with plant resources to forage or a necessity for cooperative hunting. Except for seasonal caribou drives most Arctic hunting is an individual rather than cooperative activity, and other than a few berries and leaves in summer, there are no plant foods. Therefore we would expect Arctic bands to be on the low end of this range. There is both modern and archaeological evidence to support a figure of 15–20 persons per band. In 1960 when Inuit of southeastern Baffin Island were still grouped in hunting bands, most consisted of 3–5 families. Those prehistoric sites where clusters of houses suggest synchronous occupation also often consist of 3–5 houses, suggesting bands of 15–20 people.

There are economic reasons why bands of this size are adaptive in the Arctic. If smaller family units were able to sustain themselves within reasonable energy input and output limits, they would probably do so. Within the smaller nuclear or extended family, food resources could be more rigidly managed and would be exhausted less quickly. However, in much of the region, food storage is not possible through the summer months. A social unit with fewer than 4–6 hunters would constantly be oscillating between feast and famine. Hunting failure would mean starvation, and a single walrus would provide an unusable surplus. A system of food sharing within the band, either along lines of dyadic contracts or simple communal distribution, smooths out these oscillations and, in a sense, allows a band to invest its surplus food.

Today and in the recent past the actual size of Inuit hunting bands has varied season by season. A specific family will have at least a temporary band identity. Such a band would comprise the social unit that habitually interacts—small enough to keep resources and work load within manageable limits yet large enough to maximize resource harvesting and food sharing. However, this unit may break into smaller components, sometimes a single extended family, for spring caribou hunting, fishing through holes in frozen lake ice, and open-water sealing. All of these are individual hunting activities in which harvesting success is not affected by increase in numbers. The band may rejoin in late summer for collective char fishing at the fish weirs or for caribou drives when the fall pelts are prime. There are two conditions in which a number of bands may form a virtually structureless aggregate of 100 or more people. One of these is the fall caribou drive, when the size of the herd warrants it.

In this system of hunting, a long double row of *inuksuit* (sing. *inuksuk*, pronounced ee-nook-shook), man-shaped piles of rock, is designed to enclose a stampeded herd

Figure 3.6   *Inuksuit* on hilltop near Lake Harbour, Baffin Island.

(Figure 3.6). Women, children, and oldsters, flapping skins and shouting, jump from behind the *inuksuit* to drive the frightened animals toward concealed hunters or into lakes where kayakers can spear them.

The other situation is when ice conditions, for example, large areas of fast ice, warrant collective hunting at the seal breathing holes. As the sea ice freezes, each seal scratches cone-shaped holes in the thickening ice until, even with a 2-m thickness of ice, it has a hole the size of a silver dollar at the surface. Breathing hole (*aglu*) hunting is an individual affair, each hunter standing motionless with his harpoon ready to plunge through the small hole when a wisp of goose down placed there indicates that the seal is breathing below. However, since each seal has six or more of these breathing spots, the more holes covered by hunters the more chance of collective success. In this activity, women and children often help by frightening the seal from some of its holes to one where the hunter stands poised.

Generally the need for larger bands throughout the world is one of defense. Where there is a necessity for maintaining boundaries of territories that enclose scarce resources or protection is needed from raiding parties seeking to steal women or sacrificial victims, the band must be larger than an ecological optimum. There are occasional ethnographic accounts of conflicts between Inuit bands, wife stealing, and blood feuds, but these appear to have been only sporadic and not along territorial lines. Presumably with low population density there would have been even less friction in earliest Paleoeskimo times and no need for large defense units.

We can make some inferences about the social structuring of these small Paleoeskimo bands from world ethnographies. Yellin and Harpending (1972) have taken issue with the general concept of hunting–gathering bands as fixed social units and suggest, instead, that there are essentially two types of bands, the nucleated and anucleated. In the *nucleated band* there is some permanence, not only of the unit itself but of the members that make up the unit. One is born into a nucleated band, has a lifetime allegiance to it, and is banished from it only as the worst form of punishment. Most of the band's cultural force is directed centripetally and so tends to be endogamous, that is, marriage takes place within the band. Trade and social interaction tend to be intraband rather than interband.

Conversely, the *anucleated band* exists as a social entity, recognized both by temporary members and nonmembers, but its persona is a fluid one. Families come and go at will, leaving one band to join another because of poor hunting in one locale or social tensions within the band. Cultural force in the anucleated band tends to be centrifugal with widening spheres of trade and social interaction. There is a diffusion of material and information rather than the concentration of it within closed units and a freedom of mobility between bands. Although such bands tend to be exogamous, marriage may take place within the band as it sometimes does among the Inuit when a new family moving into the band brings with it an eligible mating partner. The description of a !Kung Bushman band by Yellen and Harpending could apply equally well to an Inuit, and presumably to a Paleoeskimo, anucleated band.

> [The band] is no more than a temporally unstable aggregate of families with links of kinship or friendship [or, in the case of the Inuit, nonkindred formal food sharing partnerships] functioning primarily to smooth the daily variations in exploitative success of its members by food sharing. (1972:247)

The anucleated band results in a higher degree of information sharing over greater geographic space. Therefore, within a large region there will be a greater degree of cultural homogeneity and a more rapid information flow. The widespread stylistic similarity of Paleoeskimo artifacts suggests this fluid patterning of population over the landscape characteristic of anucleated bands.

However, these Arctic bands ought not to be seen as being in a constant state of flux. Ecological adaptation depends both on the relative permanence of the band's location and on the flexibility of its membership. Territorialism is not a feature of Inuit culture, yet there is a relatively specific locale within which a band customarily hunts. Here a significant body of information about animal distribution and behavior, the location of raw materials, and particular dangers is pooled within the band. Under such conditions, patriolocality makes good sense if the band is exogamous. It is the man, raised as a boy hunter in his father's terrain, who must provide game for his new family's subsistence. His remaining, after marriage, in the locale that he knows best provides him with the best chances of hunting success. In exogamous marriages it was not uncommon for the father of the bride to exact 1 or 2 years' bride service during which the groom was expected to hunt for his family of in-laws. This apprenticeship hunting in the locale of another established band widened the groom's knowledge of game behavior and increased chances of his nuclear family's survival.

The flexibility of anucleated bands and the tendency of occasional families to leave for new locales had a two-fold effect in adaptation: It reduced hunting pressures to manageable limits, but it also widened a band's information pool. Kindred ties are important and visiting is a common cultural trait; so as band fissioning took place, visiting kinsmen occasionally hunting in the new locale increased their knowledge of available resources.

Beyond the regulations that governed food sharing, there are few factors for social cohesion that can be inferred for the earliest Paleoeskimo hunters. We have recovered very few artifacts that might reflect a common ideology. However, where all subsistence depends on game animals, without wild plant foods to supplement the diet, it is logical to suppose that a shared system of beliefs existed. Game hunting is an occupation fraught with uncertainties, and success is usually surrounded by a supernatural aura. In a sense, magic becomes as much a part of efficiency as weaponry. A strong belief in proper magic may provide a stalker of caribou or harpooner of seal with the necessary self-confidence that makes the difference between success or failure.

Of the many traditional Inuit magic systems and game treatment taboos, the most commonly held belief distinguishes between land and sea animals. One cannot be eaten with or cooked in the fat of the other. During the hunting of caribou one cannot crack bones or pierce any skin with a needle. Rasmussen (1931) speaks of a Netsilik band forced to remain in melting snowhouses on the cracking sea ice well into the caribou hunting time because the sewing of fall and winter garments was not yet finished. Both Mary-Rouselière (1974), while excavating a 2300-year-old site in northern Baffin Island, and I, while excavating an equally old site in southern Baffin Island (Maxwell 1973), found evidence suggesting this belief goes far back into prehistory. Both Dorset sites, their permafrost middens preserving even tiny fish and bird bones, contained no needles, whereas these are a frequent occurrence in other Dorset sites. Since we had reason to believe that both sites were occupied in the summer, we concluded that these people also did no sewing in caribou hunting season. If it persisted this long, it is not illogical to suppose that this belief, as well as others in traditional Inuit ideology, was held by the earliest Paleoeskimo migrants.

Regardless of what interpretations we make of their nonmaterial culture, there is adequate archaeological evidence that the earliest inhabitants of the Eastern Arctic were successfully adapted to their new environment. The 3000-year span of culture history from 2000 B.C. to A.D. 1000 demonstrates that their way of life was a viable entity that remained unbroken in sequence. Through this continuum the numbers of their sites, and presumably their population, steadily increased until by about A.D. 1000 their geographic range covered most of the shores of Newfoundland, Greenland, and islands and mainland west to Amundsen Gulf. For their material culture, that is, tools and weapons, we have enough information from combined early sites to interpret the technological aspects of their adaptation. In these days of rifle hunting it is still possible to go hungry in the Arctic, and to be able to survive with no more equipment than that of the earliest people seems incredible. Yet the archaeological record suggests only minor changes and modifications to this equipment over the three millennia. Many of these changes seem to reflect only stylistic alterations and not improvements in efficiency. Presumable this basic tool kit, combined with impressive hunting skill, was sufficiently versatile to ensure extraction of the required energy from the hostile environment.

4 The Earliest Paleoeskimo Cultures

INTRODUCTION

Controversy is rife in archaeological interpretation. It is one of its aspects that makes it intriguing to practitioners and bystanders alike. When one is trying to reconstruct from a few bits of stone and ivory a conception of the daily struggle for survival—some feeling for the work and beliefs reflected by these "fossilized bits of behavior"—it is inevitable that different points of view will be expressed. Before describing the various sequential stages of cultural history that follow, a brief account of archaeological discovery may help put some of these controversies in perspective.

European interest in Eskimo life began with Martin Frobisher's limited description of the inhabitants of Baffin Island in 1576 and continued through explorers' accounts but this knowledge was not described in anthropological concepts until Franz Boas did so in 1881. During the intervening three centuries most interpretations of Eskimo origins and development rested on analogy to traditional Inuit behavior, analyses of linguistic change, and simple speculation.

Aside from a few artifacts recovered by Inuit from ancient sites and presented to explorers, Eastern Arctic archaeology began with the activities of George Comer, one of the last of the New Bedford whalers, when he was iced in for the winter of 1900 on Southampton Island. In 1907 Boas described the prehistoric artifacts Comer had recovered and related them to his own knowledge of contemporary Inuit. Fifteen years later, Comer, again while wintering near what is now the Thule air base in northwestern Greenland, excavated in a thick prehistoric midden that is still known as Comer's Midden. On the basis of this material, described by Wissler (1918), of artifacts recovered in Alaska, and of the description of stone tools from Disko Bay, Greenland, by Solberg (1907), the Danish ethnographer, Steensby (1917) divided Eastern Arctic cultural history into "Paleo-Eskimo" and "Neo-Eskimo" stages. He described the former as musk-ox hunters who had followed migrating herds from Alaska into northern Greenland and the latter as bowhead whale hunters of a later period and modern Inuit.

The distinction, although in a somewhat different sense, is used today by Arctic archaeologists, with Paleoeskimo referring to such early cultures as Pre-Dorset, Dorset, Independence I, and Independence II and Neoeskimo referring to Thule, European contact, and modern Inuit.

Systematic archaeology of the Eastern Arctic began with the work of Therkel Mathiassen, archaeologist with the Fifth Thule Expedition of Danish scientists in 1921–1924. Traveling impressive distances under very difficult conditions, these Danish explorers gave us much of the information that is basic to our understanding of the Central and Eastern Arctic. Mathiassen located and excavated prehistoric sites scattered from Bylot Island in the east to King William Island in the west. The data he recovered enabled him to define the Thule culture, which, although not so interpreted at the time, is now seen as ancestral to the modern Inuit. His descriptions of the Thule lifeway and its technological inventory make this one of the best defined prehistoric complexes of North America.

Prior to Mathiassen's first published report (1927), Diamond Jenness of the National Museum of Canada had examined and reported (1925) on a small collection of artifacts sent him by L. T. Burwash from Cape Dorset and Southampton and Coats islands. Jenness perceptively separated the collection of stone, bone, antler, and ivory tools into two components. One fit Mathiassen's definition of Thule culture; the other, composed of flaked stone tools, a peculiar polished stone category of burin-like gravers, and artifacts of organic substances stained a chocolate brown and with gouged rather than drilled holes, he ascribed to a Cape Dorset culture. Cape Dorset, he argued, was not only earlier than Thule but possibly also its progenitor. However, a quarter-century passed before this insightful diagnosis was verified by further archaeological research and chronometric dating techniques.

Meanwhile a long controversy ensued over the place of Cape Dorset artifacts in the prehistoric sequence. Nothing was known at that time to determine either their placement in time or their relation to well-defined Arctic or Indian cultural systems. In many of the Thule houses that Mathiassen had excavated, Dorset objects had been mixed with Thule ones in the middens. Using Jenness' criteria, he correctly identified these in his monograph (1927) but attributed Dorset artifacts to a regional and aberrant variation of the Thule culture, conceding that it might predate well-developed Thule.

Mathiassen reached no firm conclusions on the matter, and Jenness' interpretation remained a viable although unconfirmed hypothesis. The first clear evidence of two separate cultures, Dorset and Thule, was provided by Rowley (1940), who reported on a pure Dorset site, Abverdjar, in the northern end of Foxe Basin. This site, unfortunately still not published in detail, remains one of the best examples of a Late Dorset occupation. Artwork of the inhabitants, living there only for a short time, must rank among the best in the pre-Columbian Northern Hemisphere. Three years later, Leechman (1943) confirmed the distinctness of Dorset culture with the excavation of Dorset sites on northern Labrador.

Any precedence of Dorset over Thule remained unclear, although it was strongly suggested in later work by Holtved (1944) at Comer's Midden in northwest Greenland. His reexamination of this site and later excavation of sites farther north in Ingelfield Land tended to support Jenness' hypothesis but did not provide clear stratigraphic evidence that could clarify the issue.

Henry Collins of the Smithsonian Institution had consistently maintained that Dorset was an early culture, with roots that could ultimately be traced to Alaska. But this speculation was based on logic alone. In 1950 he found the first stratigraphic evidence that Dorset did indeed precede Thule in the Eastern Arctic. That summer, prevented by bad weather from reaching his objective at Cornwallis Island, he was forced to wait at the settlement of Frobisher Bay on southeastern Baffin Island. Never one to sit idly, he decided to excavate the undisturbed portions of a badly mutilated Thule site on the banks of the nearby Sylvia Grinnell River. He found a Thule midden under the thick moss sod and beneath this a 40- to 50-cm layer of ancient and sterile peat, the vegetation ground cover that had formed a sod before the Thule inhabitants had arrived. Beneath this sterile sod on the site he called Crystal II was an earlier uncontaminated layer of Dorset artifacts. Subsequent research has demonstrated that the Dorset occupation was relatively late and the Thule early in that sequence, raising further problems about the relation between the two cultures.

In the years that followed there were disputes about the relative antiquity of Dorset and Thule, but the central problem now shifted to questions of Dorset adaptation to the Arctic environment. Both Thule Eskimo and traditional Inuit made extensive use of the bow drill and bow and arrow. Their tools kits contained complex equipment for open-water seal and walrus hunting; transportation devices included dog-drawn sleds and large umiaks. Their winter houses were constructed with heat-conserving efficiency and entered through tunnels with cold-traps near the living room entrance. There was no evidence for these important elements in any of the excavated Dorset sites. It raised the question of whether Dorset artifacts were truly the remains of an Arctic-adapted culture or those of insufficiently prepared Indians who modified their tool kits to meet tundra conditions as they moved north from boreal forests. Jørgen Meldgaard, who by then had excavated an impressive sequence of sites at Igloolik in the northern Foxe Basin, contended that Dorset had a "smell of the forest" about it (1962). This phrase became the battle cry of adversaries in the debate of whether Dorset was prehistoric Eskimo or prehistoric Indian.

Pertinent new evidence sprang on the scene in 1952. First Giddings (1956) and then Irving (1957) and other researchers began reporting stone tool assemblages from Arctic Alaskan sites that included spalled burins, microblades, and other implements reminiscent of the European Upper Paleolithic. Conceivably these artifacts could be uniquely antecedent to an Arctic-adapted Dorset culture. By this time, Harp (1951) had already demonstrated the improbability of any cultural links between Indians and Dorset people, at least in Newfoundland, although not all scholars were convinced. Larsen and Meldgaard (1958) had found spalled burins at sites in Disko Bay, West Greenland. The associated stone tool complex was termed "Sarqaq" and demonstrated to be earlier than Dorset middens in that region. An assemblage similar to that from Alaska and earlier than Dorset was discovered by

Knuth (1954) in Independence Fjord at the most northeasterly corner of Greenland. Until then, similar discoveries in West Greenland reported by Solberg as early as 1907 had been largely ignored. It appeared that some consensus on the question of Arctic cultural origins was now necessary for a clear understanding of the rapidly accumulating data.

A symposium, appropriately chaired by Diamond Jenness, was convened in 1960 by the Society for American Archaeology to discuss the prehistoric cultural relations between the Arctic and Temporal Zones of North America. Among the seminal papers presented, one of the highlights was Jørgen Meldgaard's (1962) account of a succession of sites on sequentially ascending beach ridges at Igloolik in the northern Foxe Basin. To Meldgaard, the complexes from findspots as high as 62 m above present sea level differed significantly from those at 20 m and lower. The higher, and earlier, he had first called Sarqaq after the complex in Disko Bay, but these later became known as Pre-Dorset. He pointed to such Pre-Dorset traits as bows and arrows, drills and drilled holes, spalled rather than ground-and-polished burins, and possibly domesticated dogs, all missing from the Dorset middens, as demonstrating the presence of an Arctic-adapted people before the appearance of Dorset. In his opinion, Dorset technology was ill suited to northern life and reflected only minimal adjustments from an essentially boreal lifeway. The Dorset culture he believed to be that of an Indian or Indian-influenced population who had migrated from farther south.

Some Arctic archaeologists, particularly those from Canada and the United States, remained skeptical of this two-migration hypothesis of the Paleoeskimo, preferring to interpret the evidence as indicating a cultural continuum between Pre-Dorset and Dorset. More data supportive of this contention began accumulating through the excavations of Collins, Taylor, Harp, and myself. In 1965 Meldgaard returned to Igloolik to excavate in the "transition zone" between 18 and 25 m above present sea level. This work convinced him that although there were major differences between early Pre-Dorset and Late Dorset, the two did indeed form a single cultural continuum.

Meanwhile, carbon dating had indicated a time span from about 2000 B.C. to A.D. 1400 for this continuum. After about the thirteenth century A.D. most of Dorset culture appeared to have been submerged by the efficient technology of Thule immigrants from Alaska. Several authors have seen vestigial elements of Dorset in such relatively modern, though somewhat aberrant, cultures as those of the Sadlermiut, the Angmassalingmiut, and the inhabitants of the Belcher Islands.

Although many points of controversy remain, there is a general consensus among archaeologists that one of the earliest, if not the earliest, eastern Paleoeskimo manifestation of the Arctic Small Tool tradition is the Independence I complex.

INDEPENDENCE I

Eigil Knuth's Danish Pearyland Expeditions began in 1947 and continued for 19 years. Pearyland, at the northeastern corner of Greenland, lying between 81° and

83°40′ north latitude, is 43,200 km² of virtual Arctic desert. Although the largest ice-free region in Greenland, it had been little explored and subjected to no archaeological reconnaissance. Knuth hoped to find evidence of prehistoric people living in this land that had been unoccupied in recent centuries. His first discovery, on the north coast of Greenland, was startling. It was a small campsite with the complete remains of a Thule-type umiak nearby. No Thule settlement was ever found and the hunters must have perished far from home. But the find indicated that, five centuries before, the Arctic seacoast of Greenland, now ice locked and impassable by boat, had been warmer and open for hunting. Before traveling from their wrecked boat the hunters had killed such sea species as the Greenland whale (*Balaena mysticetus*), the narwhal (*Monodon monoceros*), and the bearded seal (*Erignathous barbatus*), all of which no longer live on this northern coast.

Knuth's later finds were more significant in the search for the earliest Eastern Arctic inhabitants. Walking along Independence Fjord and up Jørgen Bronlund Fjord to Midsommer Søernes, he noted small settlements of what he initially interpreted as the summer tent rings of later Eskimo. In more southerly parts of the Arctic such tent rings, often the residue of only an overnight stay, are so unproductive of data as to be hardly worth excavating. But Knuth had little else to focus archaeological attention on as the other scientists on the expedition pursued their special interests. The tent sites were often barely discernible on the wind-swept gravel, with peripheries unmarked, as those of tent sites usually are, by large boulders. Careful scrutiny of the gravel eventually disclosed small flint tools including spalled burins similar to those described the year before by Giddings (1952) in the Denbigh Flint Complex. These tools for grooving and splitting hard substances became the hallmark of the earliest Paleoeskimo and demonstrated a cultural nexus between northern Greenland and the Bering Strait. By 1967 Knuth had collected sufficient data, artifacts and settlement systems, to define the Independence I culture and to have it carbon dated between 1980 and 1780 B.C. An impressive suite of dates between these points are based on analysis of charcoal from locally growing Arctic willow and provide what some would see as the only reliable dates of the earliest eastern Paleoeskimo.

Carbon samples come from 43 settlements, which have a total of 157 dwellings. More than 1700 artifacts were associated with these remains. These settlements were all on old beach sites now 10–21 m above present sea level. Many were on gravel terraces and spits where ancient rivers, now dry, debouched into fjords and are as much as 1 km from the present seacoast. At that elevation there are driftwood logs washed there from Siberian rivers, indicating a more icefree Arctic Basin than is true today.

Knuth has provided meticulously accurate drawings of the dwellings from along the 85-km stretch of Greenland coast he has explored. In a more recent report (1967a) he indicated that house settlements were separated by an average of 14 km, but near Independence Fjord they increased in density. Most of the settlements were small, consisting of 2–6 dwellings and some with only a single structure. An exception was "Pearylandville," on the south shore of Midsummer Lake, with 20 summer and winter residences. Deltaterrassene, at the head of Jørgen Bronlund Fjord, was also unusually large, with 10 dwellings.

The interpretation Knuth and others have made of the Independence lifeway is a bleak one. The distribution of settlements suggest a nomadic existence for most of the year with the 2½ months of winter darkness spent in virtual hibernation. While ring seal, hare, ptarmigan, geese, Arctic char, and other seacoast animals were occasionally hunted, musk-ox appear to have been the main source of food. Unlike caribou, which migrate across the landscape in predictable fashion, musk-ox herds wander in large but restricted ranges. The evidence suggests that these people were unfamiliar with the stone lamp and techniques of heating with sea mammal fat. Their only source of fuel was the scarce driftwood, small dead willow branches, and the barely flammable fat in musk-ox bones. Thus their dependence on easily depleted fuel resources and a wandering food supply forced them to move constantly and made elaborate or substantial dwellings impractical. The small hunting bands of no more than four to six men, women, and children might then, for sociability, have congregated in larger groups of extended families for the dormant period in such locales as Pearylandville.

Population estimates are difficult because, in their wanderings, a single family might use several dwellings in a single year. Many of the campsites have so little refuse they may only have been used for a few nights. In the more intensely occupied northeastern corner of Greenland there may have been as many as 200 people at a given time. A population of 334 people in all of Peary Land would give a population density of 1 person for every 130 km^2, an estimation that is probably close to the right order of magnitude. It is reasonable in light of the region's food resources.

While dispersed inland hunting of musk-ox occupied most of the year, in the spring and early summer larger groups may have congregated for seacoast sealing and in the later summer and fall for lakeside char fishing. This was a critical period in which surplus food had to be stockpiled for the dark winter months. Failure to do this would mean starvation, but sometimes this storage appears to have been more than adequate. In the meat cache in front of one winter house at Kap Holbaek, Knuth found the remains of at least three full-grown musk-ox, two calves, and several hare, fox, and fish. If this single-family dwelling was used for only one winter, as it appeared to have been, it would have meant about 3 kg of meat a day for each person through 3 months of winter darkness.

Dwelling Structures

Structural components of the larger sites consist of three distinct types of dwellings. Common to all three is a centrally located hearth filled with charcoal, bone ash, and rounded cobblestones. These latter, burned and cracked by fire, would have stored heat and released it into the house but were also probably used to heat skin vessels filled with stew. The first and least substantial of these dwelling types has only a thin midden of burned bone, charcoal, and fire-blackened rocks in and around a hearth that is central to a relatively formless area of flat limestone slabs.

Most of these tent locations are isolated, suggesting little more than a single night's camp. But some are concentrated in front of more substantial dwellings in settlements apparently occupied in both winter and summer. That the minimal shelter dwellings were summer camps is suggested by the predominance of Arctic char bones in their middens. However, the use of faunal remains presents difficulties in making seasonality assessments in the Arctic. Fish, bird, and mammal meat taken in the late summer can be cached in the subfreezing weather of fall and winter. Arctic char, though caught in largest numbers during the late summer spawning runs, can also be taken through the winter ice of inland lakes.

The second dwelling type is distinguished by a square fire hearth, actually a box about 40 cm on a side, constructed of thin stone slabs set on edge deep in a gravel surface. Where the house margins, low ridges of gravel or boundaries of small boulders, are discernible, these square fireboxes are centered in ellipses approximately $2\frac{1}{2}$ by 3–4 m. These winter houses have a distinct structural feature well suited for the long period of cold, darkness, and inactivity. Knuth (1954) initially used the term "mid-passage" for these features and the term has stuck in the literature. They are not passages and the term "axial feature" is more appropriate. Such a house is shown in Figures 4.1 and 4.2. The axial feature consists of a double row of rock slabs set on edge and buttressed with small cobbles. This double row is

Figure 4.1   Independence I house with vertical slabs defining the midpassage, or axial feature. Millennia of mechanical erosion have split some of the slabs, which stand about 12 cm above the gravel surface (Polaris Promontory, northwestern Greenland).

compartmented by either a central stone firebox or by two fireboxes, one at each end. Presumably the compartments, with sleeping spaces on either side, served to store thawing meat, fuel, and other family necessities. A relatively rigid framework of driftwood, willow branches, and musk-ox bones lashed together would have supported a musk-ox skin covering, perhaps supplemented on the side walls with snow blocks. Such houses would hardly offer gracious living for the winter. The bleak existence probably resembled that of the Caribou Eskimo, as described by Birket-Smith (1929), who wintered in unheated tents near cached caribou carcasses and in reach of lakes with Arctic char. In contrast the deep pit houses of the Thule inhabitants of 3000 years later, roofed with whale ribs and walrus skins and heated with many stone lamps, seem palatial.

The small elliptical tents heated with open fires of musk-ox bones and dung gathered in the summer and of driftwood and willow sticks would seem to have been unbearably smokey unless door and roof openings were so large that they exposed the inhabitants to the cold. Perhaps the fires were lit infrequently only for occasional cooking and thawing of ice for drinking water. Once the fire had burned down to a few glowing embers, the tent roof might have been nearly closed, with heat coming only from the heated rocks of the "passage" and box hearth. The bitter winter months might have been spent in a virtual somnolent state, the people lying under thick, warm musk-ox skins, their bodies close together, and with food and fuel within easy reach. Trips outside would be required only for collection of ice and snow to melt for drinking water in skin buckets beside the fire, for replenishment of meat supplies from the frozen cache nearby, and for elimination. They undoubtedly dealt with the latter problem as storm-bound Arctic travelers do today, eating and drinking only enough to sustain an inactive body so that the number of body-chilling trips outside can be reduced to a minimum.

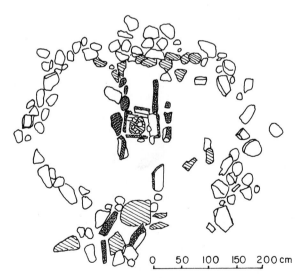

Figure 4.2 Independence I winter dwelling with axial feature. The diagonally hatched rocks are remnants of the floor paving; crosshatched rocks are the vertical slabs that form the axial feature and stone box hearth (after Knuth 1967a).

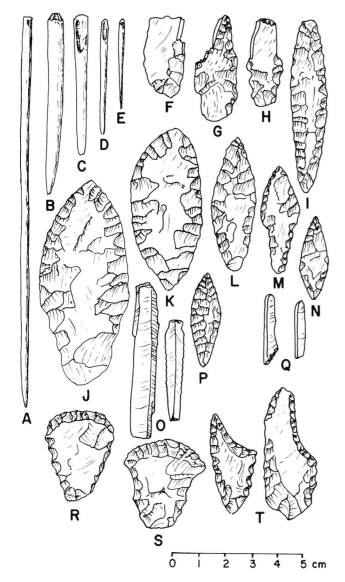

Figure 4.3 Independence I artifacts (drawings based on selected illustrations from Knuth 1967b).

A. bone bodkin or arrow
B. bone flaking punch
C. microblade handle
D. burin-spall tool handle
E. round-eyed needle
F–H. burins
I. side blade
J–N,P. end-hafted knife, lance, and arrow tips
O. microblades
Q. burin spalls
R,S. end scrapers
T. side scrapers

Artifacts

There are few bone artifacts associated with the winter houses of these Eastern Arctic pioneers. The most common are tiny, slender bone needles, which, when complete, have small, round, drilled eyes. Knuth has also recovered round-ended bone flaking punches with scarfed ends for attachment to a handle, small bone shafts with gouged ends that may have been microblade and burin-spall handles, and a long, sharp shaft of bone that might have been the tip of an arrow. Beyond the possible arrow tip there are no nonlithic weapons such as harpoon heads or bone lance tips to suggest hunting equipment.

The stone tool assemblage is more extensive. Typical items are shown in Figure 4.3. Although the relative frequencies of the various tool categories have never been reported, it is clear that most of the major forms of the Denbigh Flint Complex are represented. There are spalled burins, burin-spall tools, long, narrow side blades, triangular end scrapers expanded at the working edge, concave side scrapers, microblades and cores, and large, thin, bifacially flaked ovals (Figure 4.3K) that were probably knives. End-hafted stone weapons (Figure 4.3J, L–N, and P) were all bipointed with tapering stems and must have fitted into sockets of bone foreshafts rather than slotted wooden shafts. Presumably the larger ones were lance tips and the smaller arrow tips.

Initially the similarity of these stone tools to the Denbigh layer at the Iyatyet site

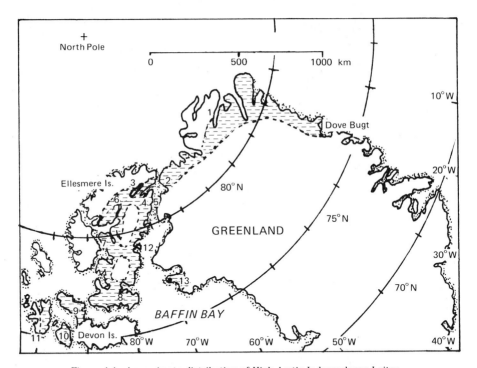

Figure 4.4   Approximate distribution of High Arctic Independence I sites:

1. Independence Fjord
2. Polaris Promontory
3. Lake Hazen
4. Coneybeare Bay
5. Robeson Channel
6. Tanquary Fjord
7. Eureka Sound
8. Grise Fjord
9. Port Refuge
10. Cornwallis Island
11. Bathurst Island
12. Bache Peninsula
13. Gammel Nûgdlît

Figure 4.5   View from the Lonesome Creek site across Coneybeare Bay, northeastern Ellesmere Island. Vertical slab remnants of an Independence house in right foreground.

on Alaska's Norton Sound was striking to archaeologists. But there are discrete yet significant differences. The stone tools of Independence I are larger than those of the Denbigh Flint Complex. In fact some are larger than any others in the Arctic Small Tool tradition. None of them are ground and polished, whereas some of the burins and gravers in Denbigh are. The weapon tips of Independence I do not have squared bases, as many of the Denbigh ones do, and the tapered stem or bipointed shape is so entrenched in Independence I that it appears on tools of practically all categories. Often these tapering proximal ends on arrow tips, burins, knives, and side and end scrapers have small, multiple side notching for binding, a trait absent in the Denbigh Flint Complex.

Knuth has traced the Independence I culture for 900 km south along Greenland's east coast (Figure 4.4). To the west there are sites on Polaris Promontory and across the Robeson Channel to a single box-hearthed house on Ellesmere Island's Coneybeare Bay (Figure 4.5). In 1980 and 1981 Sutherland located additional sites in the valleys west of Lake Hazen that link to sites on the northwest coast of Ellesmere Island along Tanquary Fjord and Eureka South found earlier by Knuth. Charcoal dates from these most westerly sites range from 1980 to 1910 B.C., indicating relative contemporaneity with the settlements on Independence Fjord.

INDEPENDENCE I AND PRE-DORSET

While Eigil Knuth was exploring the northeast corner of Greenland, another Dane, Jørgen Meldgaard began a series of excavations on raised gravel beaches of the northern tip of Melville Peninsula near the head of Foxe Basin. The earliest culture manifestation here, originally called Sarqaq, came to be called Pre-Dorset, was carbon dated on a sea mammal material to an age as early as Independence I, and, like Independence I was comparable in its lithic artifacts to the Denbigh Flint Complex. As Pre-Dorset became better known through excavation of scattered sites throughout the more southern Eastern Arctic many archaeologists considered Independence I to be simply a regional variant, a specific High Arctic adaptation, of the more widespread Pre-Dorset culture. Given the impressive distances involved in the eastern spread of early Paleoeskimo and the Arctic Small Tool tradition such regional diversity of a single basic culture seemed reasonable. Early migrant bands from Alaska might have fanned out as they moved and their numbers increased. The ultimate geographic distribution might have become nearly a right triangle, with some bands moving along the southern base while others traveled north along the hypotenuse. At the eastern limit of the range, people on the south coast of Baffin Island and north coast of Labrador would have been nearly as many air kilometers away from bands at Independence Fjord as the latter were from the western cape of Alaska. Given this geographic dispersion and regional ecological differences, the development of specifically adaptive technologies was to be expected. Discrete differences between the two cultural complexes, such as bipointed end blades in the north and square-based triangular ones in the south, occasional polishing on burins and end blades and rare side-notched straight-based knives in the south and the absence of polished stone tools, frequency of side-notching, and larger tools in the north, could all be attributed to this.

In the 1970s McGhee (1976, 1979) offered a convincing alternate view of these two as separate and distinct cultural complexes. Basing his interpretation on evidence from his excavations in 1972 and subsequent years at Port Refuge on the northwestern tip of Devon Island, he concluded that Independence I was the initial migration into the Eastern Arctic perhaps from some western center other than the Denbigh Flint Complex homeland. Pre-Dorset people coming from the Bering Strait, he felt, did not enter the region until at least 300 years later.

The Port Refuge Sites

Between 1972 and 1977 McGhee located more than 100 camps and dwelling sites along 20 km of coastline near the small Port Refuge Bay on Devon Island's Grinnell Peninsula. The shoreline at this south-central spot in the High Arctic is locked in ice through most of the year. But contrasting currents near Port Refuge keep a large lake, or polynia, of open water in the sea ice even through the coldest months. The polynia, discovered in 1851 and known since as Penny's North Water has probably remained open intermittently since the earliest Paleoeskimo pioneers sighted it. It is a natural magnet for air-breathing seal, walrus, and whale, which may well have been the attraction that led the first people to camp here.

McGhee has separated the sites into three major components and several minor ones. Two, the Upper Beaches and Cold components, he considers to belong to the Independence I culture; the third, the Gull Cliff component, more nearly relates to the Pre-Dorset culture of farther south in Foxe Basin.

The Upper Beaches and Cold sites are raised, barren beaches of limestone gravel 22–24 m above present sea level. In this High Arctic aridity the only plants on the sterile limestone are small clumps of moss and saxifrage that feed on nutrients left from the refuse of human hunters 4000 years before. Aside from the patches of vegetation, the only signs of structural features are concentrations of small cobbles, box-like hearths of larger limestone slabs, and occasional traces of axial features. In some, a shallow depression has been scooped out on both sides of the features to form a low ridge of gravel outlining a rectangular-to-elliptical tent margin. Elsewhere at other times and places in the prehistoric Eastern Arctic, tent sites are reused in subsequent years as families return to the same campsite, or useful boulders and flat rock slabs are shuffled about in making new tent platforms. This is not the case for the Independence I features at Port Refuge where a dwelling once abandoned was left intact. Furthermore, settlements of 5–20 houses were arranged in linear fashion along a beach and so isolated that they were 20 m or more apart. It is as if, as McGhee has suggested (1978), these early hunters feared human ghosts that might linger in the vicinity of older houses. On the basis of midden density, complexity of feature construction, and artifact concentration, McGhee groups the structures into work stations, short-term campsites, and dwellings, none of which were occupied for more than a few months at most. Structures identified as winter dwellings were shallow, oval depressions 2 m wide by, at most, 4 m long with stone box hearths and traces of parallel-rowed axial features. Work space within these dwellings appears to have been uniformly segregated. If one were to stand at the rear of houses facing downslope toward the seacoast, one would find more artifacts associated with weaponry on the right-hand side and more of those associated with sewing and food preparation such as burin spalls, microblades, and needles on the left of the axial feature. Although the large number of recovered burin spalls tends to swamp this distribution, it at least suggests division within the house of male and female activities (Figure 4.6).

Artifacts

Five hundred and ninety lithic artifacts and 56 of bone, antler, and ivory were recovered from the Cold and Upper Beaches components. The stone artifacts fill all the categories of the Arctic Small Tool tradition: microblades and cores, spalled burins and burin spalls, various sized bifaces interpreted as knives, harpoon, lance, and arrow end blades, end and side scrapers, gravers, crude adzes, drills, and retouched flakes. Although falling generally into assemblages of the tradition, many of the artifacts display discrete attributes more like those of Independence Fjord

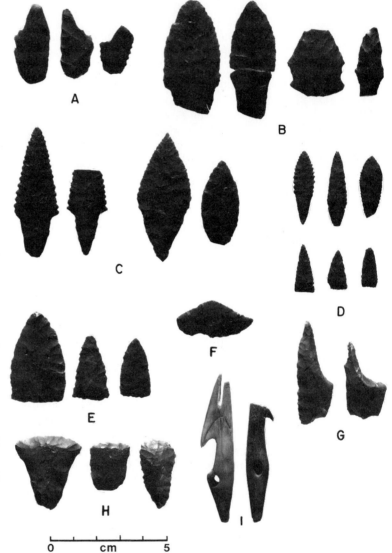

Figure 4.6 Independence I artifacts from Port Refuge, Devon Island (selected from National Museums of Canada photographs, courtesy of Robert McGhee).

A. burins
B. stemmed and side-notched end blades (knives?)
C. tapering-stemmed and unstemmed end blades (lance tips?)
D. tapering-stemmed and straight-based end blades (arrow tips?)
E. straight-based end blades (harpoon tips?)
F. side blade
G. side scrapers
H. end scrapers
I. harpoon heads

than Pre-Dorset manifestations to the south (Figure 4.7). More of the lance, arrow, and harpoon end blades are bipointed, often with fine serrations along lateral edges and small, but distinct, shoulders between point and stem. Except for the edge of adzes, none of the stone tools, burins or end blades, display any trace of grinding and polishing. There are subtle differences between these materials and those of Peary Land. In the latter region, square-based, triangular arrow and harpoon tips have not yet been found as they have in the Independence I components of Port Refuge. Many of the stone tools in Greenland are larger than those of the Cold and

Upper Beaches components. But it should not be surprising that such discrete differences exist since the two regions are more than 800 km apart.

Evidence from the box hearths, midpassages, and lithic artifacts tends to be convincing, but the strongest indication that Independence I was a cultural complex separate from Pre-Dorset comes from the bone, antler, and ivory artifacts.

Most artifacts of organic substance are unidentified scraps of cut antler, bone, and ivory or multibarbed fragments that might be from fish or bird spears. Thirty slender slivers of bone were needles, like those from Independence Fjord, with blunt ends and tiny drilled eyes. The most surprising objects were two ivory harpoon heads from the Upper Beaches component. These were unlike any others from the Eastern Arctic's prehistory. The ends were slotted for a stone end blade parallel to a

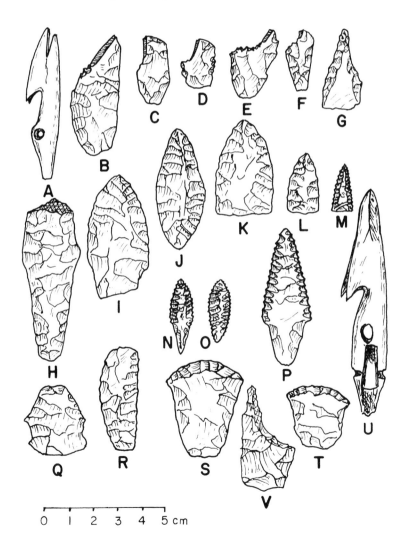

Figure 4.7 Independence I artifacts from Port Refuge, Devon Island (drawings based on selected illustrations from McGhee (1979).

A. barbed, nontoggling harpoon head
B–F. spalled burins
G. drill
H–Q. varieties of end blades
R. side blade
S,T. end scrapers
U. open-socket, double-barbed harpoon head
V. side scraper

round drilled line hole (Figure 4.7A). Two holding barbs were cut into one side, and the proximal end was a rounded peg that would have fit into a round socket on the end of the harpoon shaft. It is particularly this proximal end that is distinctive. All other prehistoric Eastern Arctic harpoon heads heretofore found had been a "female" type, with open or closed sockets into which a foreshaft would fit. Furthermore, most of these would toggle, that is, rotate in the prey's body perpendicular to the pull of the harpoon line, whereas the Port Refuge ones would not. Since the shape and style of harpoon heads in the Arctic varies through time as regularly as those of pottery vessels farther south in Indian country, these two heads clearly did not fit in any Pre-Dorset assemblage. The only similar one yet recovered comes from the West Greenland site of Itivnera more than 1900 km away and occupied possibly 1000 years later (Figure 5.14J).

Although there appears to be little distinction between house features and stone artifacts from the Upper Beaches and Cold components, two antler harpoon heads from the Cold site differ significantly from the ivory ones of Upper Beaches. The one complete one from the Cold component is self-bladed rather than stone tipped, but like those from Upper Beaches has bifurcate spurs on one lateral edge above the line hole (Figure 4.7U). Unlike them, it has an open "female" socket and ends in a single, proximal spur. It thus seems to combine attributes of both Independence I and Pre-Dorset, suggesting that Cold site hunters occupied the bay somewhat later than those of Upper Beaches.

Of itself, the discovery of an Independence I occupation in these latitudes would not have been surprising. But immediately seaward of the Upper Beaches component, and at a sea level elevation 2–3 m lower, McGhee located the Gull Cliff component, which clearly appears to have been Pre-Dorset and not Independence I.

The Gull Cliff Component

On equally barren gravel beaches 2–3 m lower than the Independence I, McGhee located a different series of sites. These were seemingly unpatterned concentrations of cobbles, tools, and animal bones, representing all that was left of short-term camps. Unlike features of the Cold and Upper Beaches components, these Gull Cliff dwellings had no vertical slab fireboxes or traces of midpassages. Furthermore, they were clustered in groups of 2–5 tent sites in contrast to the sites on higher beaches where the settlement pattern was one of isolated dwellings paralleling the coastline.

Stone tools of Gull Cliff differ only slightly from those attributed to the Independence I occupation. They fall into the same familiar categories, but individual tools demonstrate subtle though distinctive differences (Figure 4.8). Burins and side and end scrapers tend to be smaller and thicker and flaked with less skillful control. Two of the spalled burins were polished at their distal ends (McGhee 1976:18). Bifaces hafted to the ends of knife handles, arrows, and lances are not bipointed but rather end in straight, parallel-sided or slightly side-notched stems. The most convincing difference is in the shape of Gull Cliff harpoon heads. The most complete of two

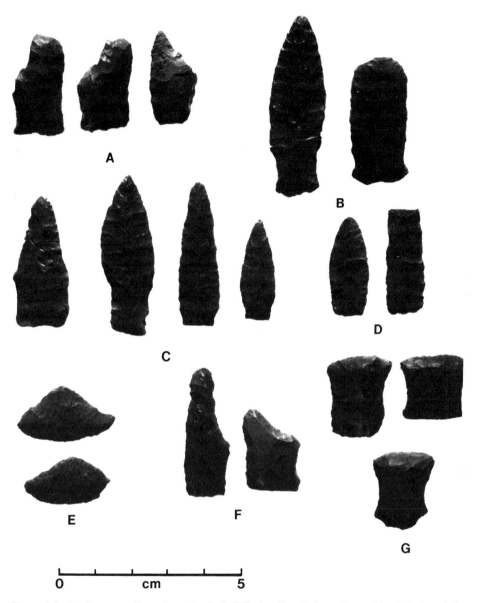

Figure 4.8 Pre-Dorset artifacts from the Gull Cliff site, Port Refuge, Devon Island: (selected from National Museums of Canada photographs, courtesy of Robert McGhee).

A. burins   E. side blades
B. side-notched end blades   F. side scrapers
C. stemmed end blades   G. end scrapers
D. unstemmed end blades

recovered is self-bladed, has a single lateral barb, an open foreshaft socket, and two sharp, proximal spurs. It is clearly meant to toggle in the body of a struck seal. The resemblance of this head to the earliest ones found by Meldgaard (1962) in Pre-Dorset sites at the northern end of Foxe Basin is striking.

There is little difference in the variety of animals the Upper Beaches and Gull Cliff people hunted. Ninety percent of the animal bones recovered from both sets of sites are of ring seal (in contrast to sites in northeastern Greenland where the dominant prey was musk-ox). Supplementing this food source were very few caribou and several duck, hare, and fox. In fact there are more smaller mammals and birds than normally represented in early Arctic sites.

Available carbon dates from driftwood and seal bone do little more than indicate that Gull Cliff was the youngest of the components and suggest contemporaneity of the others with those of Peary Land. They tend to support the contention that the two occupations at Port Refuge were separated by at least three centuries. Does this mean that there were two migrations into the Eastern Arctic and that Pre-Dorset people were "neither the ancestors nor the descendants" of those who lived at Cold and Upper Beaches (McGhee 1979:87)? Or does it simply mean that a single initial migration split into northern and southern waves and that Gull Cliff represents a penetration into the High Arctic of Pre-Dorset people who had settled more southerly coasts at least three centuries before?

If there was, indeed, an earlier migration preceding the one giving rise to Pre-Dorset, its traces in the south may have been masked by later occupations and the thicker vegetation mantle. Dispersed Independence I linear settlements would be more visible on barren High Arctic gravel beaches than in the southern Arctic where most early sites are covered by sod. On the south coast of Baffin Island, for example, the moss sod is 10–12 cm thick, and suitable tent locations are rare enough that they might have been used through several centuries. Under such circumstances, finding a single Independence dwelling in the midst of Pre-Dorset middens would be fortuitous. But there are some clues suggesting they might be there. The Arnapik site (Taylor 1968) on Mansel Island is a sparsely vegetated gravel beach 300 m long with 120 findspots. Although most of the stone artifacts (there were none of organic substances) and structural features fit well into an early Pre-Dorset category, a few of the findspots had barely discernible traces of slab fireboxes and midpassages (Taylor 1968:13). Independence-like bipointed end blades and expanded-edged end scrapers, though rare, appeared in the site's assemblage.

The early Pre-Dorset Shaymark site at Frobisher Bay on southern Baffin Island (Maxwell 1973) had been badly disturbed when we first located it. We could only surface collect this ancient gravel beach 15 m above present sea level. But two clusters of rocks and chert flakes slightly higher than the rest of the beach, produced two expanded-edged end scrapers, four tapering-stemmed burins, a flaked and polished adz and a thin, triangular harpoon end blade, all surprisingly like those of Independence I. Twelve km southeast of that site, in Burton Bay, Jacobs (1981) located a midpassage structure of small boulders on an ancient raised beach.

Unfortunately the careful residents of this dwelling had left behind no artifacts, not even a flake of chert.

These scattered clues suggest three alternative interpretations: (1) that an early occupation of spaced-apart dwellings was obscured by settlements three centuries later, (2) that any early Arctic Small Tool site in the Eastern Arctic might contain variants of tools and structures that for some reason tended to concentrate differentially in different locales, or (3) that a parental culture such as Independence I gradually evolved in the south to what we call Pre-Dorset but retained its original form in the High Arctic.

A fourth possibility is suggested by the increased exploration and excavation along the northern Labrador coast. Here, in the earliest sites, houses with axial features are associated with tapering-stemmed or bipointed end blades with serrated edges and burins without facial grinding or polishing, all attributed to Independence I influence (Cox 1978; Fitzhugh 1980; Tuck 1975, 1976). This might indicate that in at least part of the time span of early Paleoeskimo, separate cultural traditions were developing—Pre-Dorset in the core area of Foxe Basin and Hudson Strait and Independence I in the High Arctic, northern Labrador, and possibly the Disko Bay region of Greenland. Test of such a proposition could be made along the eastern coast of Baffin Island where cultural linkage between Labrador and the High Arctic might be found. Unfortunately most of this coast has been submerged by the weight of active glaciers, leaving no trace of early sites.

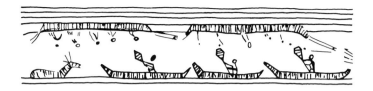

5

Pre-Dorset

Much of the controversy about Independence I and Pre-Dorset could be resolved by adequate carbon dates. But, as discussed in Chapters 3 and 4, there are several problems in the dating technique specific to the Arctic. The more critical of these relates to the sea and most of the faunal artifacts recovered are from sea animals. Here, in comparison to land reservoirs, there are differences in the proportions of ^{12}C, ^{13}C, and ^{14}C (*fractionation*) and in the isotopic content of the sea reservoir itself. Unfortunately there are many early sites from which the only recoverable organic materials are cinders of charred fat, presumably of seal. In the 1970s an attempt was made (McGhee and Tuck 1976) to rectify the situation by accepting as valid only those dates derived from indigenous Arctic willow or locally growing trees. This conservative approach had two major effects. It eliminated from consideration a majority of the previously dated Pre-Dorset sites and supported the hypothesis that Independence I was earlier than Pre-Dorset and separated from it by about three centuries.

In a later treatment of the subject, Arundale (1981) has corrected the dates of various organic materials by incorporating laboratory-derived fractionation and sea reservoir factors (Table 5.1). The table she thus assembles utilizes all available dates and demonstrates remarkably few inconsistencies. Most important, it indicates contemporaneity between High Arctic Independence I and Low Arctic Pre-Dorset, with, if anything, a two-century precedence of Pre-Dorset. (I use these, indicated as *corrected dates*, from this point on.)

If we add to this the sort of flexible treatment of carbon dates for which Arundale argues, we would conclude that the earliest occupation of the Eastern Arctic begins about 2000 B.C., with contemporaneous settlements of people adapted in slightly different ways to both High and Low Arctic. The High Arctic adaptation appears to terminate around 1700–1600 B.C., perhaps as increasing cold led to starvation and dwindling populations. In the more southern Arctic, Pre-Dorset as a recognizable cultural complex continues to a period between about 900 and 600 B.C. Discrepancies in its terminal dating are due largely to individual interpretation and regional variation, as is discussed later in more detail. In some locales there is a gradual

Table 5.1
RADIOCARBON DATES FOR INDEPENDENCE I AND PRE-DORSET SITES[a]

Site	Culture	Lab no.	Material	Uncorrected age (radiocarbon years)	Corrected ages (radiocarbon years)[b]	Date (B.C.)
Closure KdDq-11-8	Pre-Dorset	GSC-1382	Charred fat	4690 ± 80	4225 ± 383	2275
Mittimatalik	Pre-Dorset	S-589	Seal (?) bone	4385 ± 155	4100 ± 167	2150
Closure KdDq-11-6	Pre-Dorset	Gak-1281	Charred fat	4460 ± 100	3995 ± 112	2045
Kettle Lake S.	Independence I	K-1260	Willow charcoal	3930 ± 130	—	1980
Gammel Nûgdlît I	Independence I	K-1628	Whalebone	4500 ± 110	3895 ± 125	1945
Portfjaeld	Independence I	K-928	Willow charcoal	3890 ± 120	—	1940
Portfjaeld	Independence I	K-929	Willow charcoal	3860 ± 120	—	1910
Pearylandville	Independence I	K-939	Willow charcoal	3840 ± 120	—	1890
Q. Rose Is.	Pre-Dorset	I-5250	Charcoal	3830 ± 115	—	1880
Dog Bight L-5	Pre-Dorset	SI-2521	Charcoal	3810 ± 75	—	1860
Kaleruserk (52-m terrace)	Pre-Dorset	P-505	Antler	3700 ± 300	3810 ± 302	1860
Kettle Lakes	Independence I	K-1261	Willow charcoal	3810 ± 130	—	1860
Verdanaes	Independence I	K-1062	Willow charcoal	3800 ± 120	—	1850
Portfjaeld	Independence I	K-930	Willow charcoal	3790 ± 120	—	1840
Kaleruserk (52-m terrace)	Pre-Dorset	P-207	Ivory	3958 ± 168	3783 ± 179	1833

Site	Culture	Lab No.	Material	Age ± error	Corrected age	Year
Vanfaldnaes	Independence 1	K-932	Willow charcoal	3780 ± 120	—	1830
Vendanaes	Independence 1	K-1061	Willow charcoal	3760 ± 130	—	1810
Kettle Lake N.	Independence 1	K-1262	Willow charcoal	3760 ± 130	—	1810
Kaleruserk	Pre-Dorset	P-209	Ivory	3906 ± 133	3731 ± 148	1781
Shaymark	Pre-Dorset	GSC-849	Charred fat	4140 ± 130	3675 ± 144	1725
Kaleruserk (52-m terrace)	Pre-Dorset	P-208	Antler	3560 ± 123	3670 ± 128	1720
Thalia Pt. 2	Pre-Dorset	GSC-1264	Charcoal	3660 ± 140	—	1710
Gammel St. V	Independence 1	K-1196	Willow charcoal	3620 ± 100	—	1670
Closure KdDq-11	Pre-Dorset	P-707	Charred fat	4067 ± 73	3602 ± 95	1652
Okak 6	Pre-Dorset	SI-2507	Charcoal	3475 ± 75	—	1525
Sarqaq	Pre-Dorset	K-807	Peat	3360 ± 120	—	1410
Annawak	Pre-Dorset	P-708	Charred fat	3814 ± 69	3349 ± 92	1399
Sarqaq	Pre-Dorset	K-146	Wood	3340 ± 140	—	1390
Bloody Falls	Pre-Dorset	S-463	Charcoal	3300 ± 90	—	1350
Wellington Bay	Pre-Dorset	I-2057	Charcoal	3180 ± 120	—	1230
KjNb	Pre-Dorset	I-5978	Charcoal	3160 ± 95	—	1210
Itivnera	Pre-Dorset	K-1193	Willow charcoal	3140 ± 120	—	1190
Loon	Pre-Dorset	P-710	Charred fat	3577 ± 69	3112 ± 92	1162
Kapuivik (44-m terrace)	Pre-Dorset	P-210	Antler	2898 ± 136	3008 ± 140	1058
KdDq-13	Pre-Dorset	M-1531	Charred fat	3480 ± 200	3015 ± 209	1065

[a]Data is from Arundale 1981 with additions by Maxwell.

[b]Ages have been corrected by incorporating laboratory-derived fractionation and sea reservoir factors except for wood and charcoal samples.

blending of Pre-Dorset into Dorset and in others the change is more pronounced. In some regions, perhaps marginal to centers of greater concentration, there may have been distinctive transitional modifications. In others, an early withdrawal of Pre-Dorset people and later return of developed Dorset leaves an occupational hiatus.

The earliest dated sites, based on Arundale's corrections, are at Mittamatalik (Pond Inlet) on the north coast of Baffin Island and the Closure site near Lake Harbour on the south coast of Baffin Island, both dated about 2000 B.C. Sites dated between one and one-half and three centuries later are at Kaleruserk near Igloolik on Foxe Basin, the Shaymark site near Frobisher Bay on south Baffin Island, and Site Q on Rose Island, the Dog Bight site, and the Thalia Point site all on the north-to-central Labrador coast. There are other, as yet undated, sites that appear to be equally early on the basis of their stone tools. These include sites on strand lines of Jens Munk Island higher than the nearby dated levels at Kaleruserk (Meldgaard 1962), Arnapik on Mansel Island (Taylor 1968), and the Meeus, Pita, and Mungiok sites near Ivugivik on the northeastern corner of Hudson Bay (Taylor 1962). One would expect equally early sites on the eastern coast of Baffin Island, but several searchers have failed to find any. This may partially be due to coastal subsidence, particularly along the southern part where the weight of still-active glaciers is depressing the land.

The distribution of these early sites suggests a major area for developmental Pre-Dorset culture that would include the north coast of Baffin Island, the west coast of the Foxe Basin, islands in the mouth of Hudson Bay and its northeastern corner, the south coast of Baffin Island, and the north coast of Labrador.

A small site that typologically appears early is St. Mary's Hill on Pelly Bay, but no other early Arctic Small Tool sites have been reported from here to the Alaskan–Canadian border 1770 km to the west. Near this border, at the Engigstciack site on the Firth River, there is a Denbigh Flint Complex layer, but this, with a corrected date of 1368 B.C., is much too late to be ancestral to Pre-Dorset. This absence of early sites cannot be wholly a function of the yet unexplored tundra vastness. For example, Harp (1958) has carefully and unsuccessfully explored the south coast of Coronation Gulf. Future work is unlikely to turn up more than the scattered, thin camps of small bands wending steadily eastward, staying in one location only long enough to leave mere traces of middens. One site, lying between the Canadian border and Pelly Bay, appears to be just such an early Arctic Small Tool tradition locus. This is the Dismal II site (Harp 1958), found 80 km inland and 32 km west of the Coppermine River. Although the recovered artifacts are relatively undistinctive representatives of the Arctic Small Tool tradition, a few discrete traits such as expanded-edge end scrapers and tapered-stemmed points give a general impression of antiquity.

The concentration of sequential sites farther east points to a decline in nomadism. This decline led to a system of centrally based wandering with seasonal energy source exploitation in different locales and periodic returns to winter settlements. The primary reasons for this development in the eastern core are ecological. Although there may be regional variations in emphasis, the Canadian Pre-Dorset culture seems based essentially on exploitation of both terrestrial and sea mammals. In fact some have seen the minor difference between the Alaskan and Canadian aspects of the Arctic Small Tool tradition to be attributable to greater emphasis on sea mammal hunting in Pre-Dorset and on land mammal hunting and fishing in the Denbigh culture (Dumond 1977). There is marked variability, however, in the food resources within the total range occupied by Pre-Dorset people. Some loci, mainly the eastern coasts, provide access to migrating harp seal and their whelping beds; others are on the major caribou spring and summer migration routes from below the timberline to the tundra coasts. Some coasts are periodically visited by migrating herds of walrus, beluga, and narwhal, and others are within the restricted wandering zones of musk-ox. In some regions hunters can rely only on such local residents as ring and harbor seals, caribou, and, in season, anadromous fish.

A large body of biological, oceanographic, and paleoclimatological data is available for the Eastern Arctic. All this evidence points to a particular region in which no one food animal is uniquely numerous but in which the number of available species and individuals within each species is sufficiently great to assure a constantly favorable amount of food energy for the amount of work it takes to extract it from the environment. This diversity appears to be effective within a wide range of environmental conditions and animal behavior. These conditions, offering persisting quantities of food to be acquired by reasonable amounts of labor, appear to be best met in the Baffin Island, Hudson Strait, Foxe Basin, and northern Labrador regions, which collectively have been called the "core area" (Maxwell 1976a; Figure 5.1).

Figure 5.1 The region (shaded) referred to in the text as the core area of Pre-Dorset and Dorset development.

Within the core are the best indications yet published of long, persistent occupation from an early Pre-Dorset period to the modern resident Inuit. Through time and varying periods of clement and inclement ecological conditions, the influence of this core area appears to have expanded and contracted. This situation often may have had disastrous results as populations moved into marginal areas under favorable ecological conditions and then later starved as climatological factors altered.

Within the core area, caribou migrated northward from the mainland along the Melville Peninsula and across sea ice to Bylot Island, while substantial resident herds on Baffin Island moved seasonally from their winter foraging in interior, wind-swept valleys to the seacoasts and to islands in Nettling Lake in the summer. Musk-ox were available on the Melville Peninsula and perhaps prehistorically on at least the northwestern tip of Baffin Island (Mary-Rousselière 1974). Narwhal and beluga could have been hunted in the straits and on outer seacoasts, and some of the harp seal would have passed the shores of Hudson Strait and Lancaster Sound in their annual northward migration as the major part of the herd moved along the Labrador Coast toward the High Arctic. Five additional species of seal, several species of fish, and caribou in the nearby interior provided abundant food resources on this coast. Most important, this core region was unlike the western part of the Pre-Dorset range in that walrus and large bearded seal were common. These potential food resources were supplemented by a high population of the more widespread and dependable ring and harbor seal, by frequent flocks of migrating duck and geese and by wolves, fox, hare, and, occasionally, polar bear.

Empirical proof that the reliably recurring resources of the core area led to a more settled existence comes from the sites themselves. Both carbon dates and typological analyses demonstrate relatively continuous occupation, often on the same descending beaches or within the same bays, from the earliest Pre-Dorset to modern settlements. Button Point, on the south coast of Bylot Island, although so churned by frost action that stratigraphic analysis is impossible, has produced artifacts typologically ascribed to earliest Pre-Dorset (Mathiassen 1927:Plate 61-17) and to latest Thule. The nearby Mittamatalik site near Pond Inlet and other sites on northern Baffin demonstrate a similar range (Mary-Rousselière 1976). At Igloolik and on nearby islands, where settlements shifted downward on descending gravel beaches as sea level declined from 62 to 4 m above its present level, occupation was continuous. This was also the case around North Bay near Lake Harbour on southern Baffin, where occupation appears to have been relatively unbroken from 2000 B.C. to the present.

Furthermore, within this core area and throughout both Pre-Dorset and Dorset periods, there appears to have been a regularity of interaction among these geographically distant groups. This is marked by exchange of technological information to the degree that minor discrete style differences on artifacts appear to emerge almost simultaneously throughout the core area (Figure 5.2). In the Late Dorset period, artistic carvings demonstrate a similar commonality in ideological magic and religion.

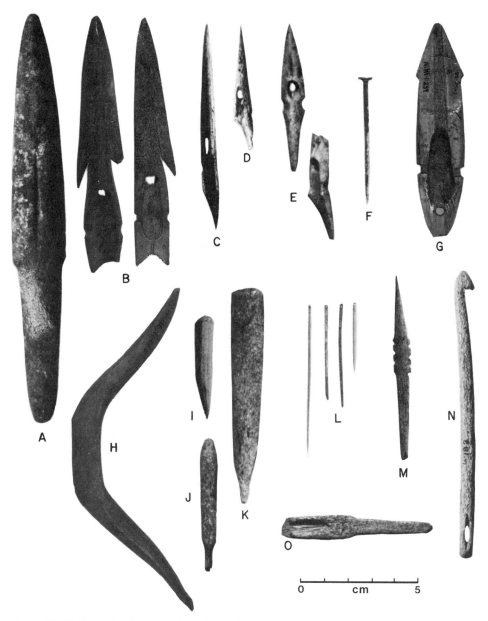

Figure 5.2 Nonlithic Pre-Dorset artifacts from different localities—A, B, E, G, H, J–L, Igloolik region, Melville Peninsula; C, I, M, Buchanan site, Victoria Island; F, Menez site, Victoria Island; D, N, Umingmak site, Banks Island.

A,G.   lance heads
B–E.   harpoon heads
F.   wound pin(?)
H.   bow brace
I–K.   flint-knapping punches

L.   needles
M.   fish spear
N.   sling handle
O.   antler scoop

CATEGORIES OF PRE-DORSET ACTIVITY

Unfortunately, paleoclimatic conditions have restricted the preservation of Pre-Dorset remains of antler, bone, and ivory to only a few sites; nor are any available from the Denbigh Flint Complex for comparison.

At least the early phase of Pre-Dorset development took place during the warmer-than-present but cooling climate following the postglacial climatic optimum. Warmer climates subjected organic remains to the same alternate freezing–thawing cycles and destructive effects of moisture that have decayed such materials elsewhere in the world. At Lake Harbour, and presumably throughout the more southern Eastern Arctic, permafrost, which locks cultural residue in frozen ground until exposed by archaeologists, does not begin until some time between 700 and 500 B.C. With very few exceptions there are no earlier sites this far south that have produced artifacts of organic materials. North of 68° north latitude, the climate was drier and perhaps colder, so that several sites have yielded nonlithic tools. Most of our information about Pre-Dorset bone, antler, and ivory artifacts and their stylistic changes through time have come from the various sites in the Fury and Hecla Strait region near Igloolik (Meldgaard 1960a,b, 1962). Unfortunately, Meldgaard has only published syntheses and preliminary reports. But to many of us, he has been generous in personal communications and we have had access to his collections in both the National Museum of Man in Canada and the National Museum of Denmark. In interpreting a general picture of the lifeway in Pre-Dorset times, I will combine this information with the scanty evidence from other sites without particular concern with regional and temporal variations.

Sea Mammal Hunting

Pre-rifle hunting practices of the modern Inuit illuminate our understanding of prehistoric artifacts associated with sea mammal hunting in this region. We have no published faunal lists from any of the Pre-Dorset sites except Gull Cliffs at Port Refuge, but remains of ringed seal (*Phoca hispida*), bearded seal (*Erignathous barbatus*), and walrus (*Odobenus rosemarus*) have been reported from a number of sites. A beluga vertebral disk was found at Arnapik, and a piece of narwhal ivory at Port Refuge. These remains, the presence of harpoon heads, and the prevalence of coastal sites all imply that Pre-Dorset hunters were hunting the same prey that their descendants do. The larger whales and, at least in the core area, the harp seal (*Phoca groenlandica*) may be exceptions to this. Migrating harp seal, the most agile and acrobatic of the seals, are the most difficult to hunt. They arrive at Grise Fjord on southern Ellesmere Island in late spring, but the Inuit there make no attempt to hunt them until late summer when they become more quiescent just before returning to birthing locations off Newfoundland. However, the locations of Pre-Dorset sites along the northern Labrador coast suggest that harp seal may have been an important food source there during quiescent and breeding periods.

Hunting at winter breathing holes in landfast ice is one of the more reliable and productive ways of taking seal. As described in Chapter 3, if the sea ice has not frozen too rapidly or too thick, each seal makes and keeps open a group of cone-shaped breathing holes that are barely discernible on snow-covered ice surfaces. Some ethnographers have maintained that for successful breathing hole hunting one needs dogs able to sniff out the holes. But I have found that dogs are not essential; in fact when working with dogs, I have spotted breathing holes that they have missed, and if early hunters had not had dogs they still could have hunted this way. Other aspects of the hunt, once a breathing hole has been spotted, are familiar to all who have read accounts of Inuit life. There is a long, cold, motionless wait for that instant when a fluttering strand of goose down placed in the top of the hole indicates a breathing seal. The sudden accurate thrust with cold-numbed arms and the rush to widen the ice hole with a bear bone or ivory chisel on the butt end of the harpoon have been described by many writers. The heavy animal must then be hoisted out before it drags hunting gear, or even hunter, back into the water.

This style of hunting is most productive when there are enough hunters to watch most of the breathing holes within a 1-km radius since a seal may use many such holes in the course of a day. The Thule people developed a number of special devices, still retained by more recent Inuit, to augment the basic breathing hole hunting gear. A curved antler rod helped them determine the shapes of breathing hole cones. The seal breathes with its back to its underwater ice den and if the hole is asymmetrical the hunter may thrust accurately yet still miss the seal. Thule hunters had small stools of driftwood on which to wait and pads of bear skin to warm their feet and to muffle sound. This was crucial because the seal has acute hearing. Special supports secured in the snow held the harpoon ready, and intricate devices kept the wisp of down in the breathing hole. There were scoops to ladle ice chips from the hole and seal claw scratchers to attract the curious seal. On the breathing hole hunting harpoon, a thrusting rather than thrown weapon, the line from the harpoon head was wrapped loosely around the shaft so as not to fall loose as it does on a thrown harpoon.

The thrusting harpoon could be used at the ice floe edge where the fast ice meets open water and bearded seal and juvenile ring seal tend to congregate. It was also useful on shore where walrus may haul out and on the sea ice when basking seal are stalked. But open-water summer hunting from boats required a lighter, thrown harpoon. In summer when the saline seawater is flooded with fresh melt water its density is lowered. Sea mammals then have lost some of their fat, and killed seal are apt to sink. Retrieval becomes as important as wounding an animal. Nearly 1000 years ago, Thule hunters had developed a special kit for this open-water harpooning (see Figure 8.13, p. 269). It included a light harpoon for throwing or for projecting with a hand-held throwing board. It was a jointed arrangement of harpoon foreshaft, socket, and toggling head that released from the harpoon when the head penetrated the seal's body. The line from the head fastened to a small perforated piece of ivory that slipped over a peg on the harpoon shaft and held the line tight until moment of impact. The opposite end of this line was fastened to inflated seal stomach floats that could pull a weakening, injured seal to the surface as it attempted to dive. An elaborate suite of mouthpieces and ivory toggles were used to inflate the floats and tie them to the harpoon line. On the kayak there were round platforms to hold the coiled line and carved ivory pieces to support the harpoon in readiness. ,

These distinctive harpoon sets can easily be distinguished as summer and winter kits, and many of their component parts should appear as archaeological specimens if they once existed in the cultural inventory. Unfortunately we have recovered only the heads of harpoons from Pre-Dorset sites and cannot tell whether they were used for both open-water and sea ice hunting. Tentatively, in the absence of any float gear and sites located near regions of fast ice, I conclude that little if any hunting was attempted from boats on the open water. Pre-Dorset hunters may even have been restricted to hunting seal and walrus at the floe edge or on land where they hauled out.

Archaeologists have recovered the earliest types of these Pre-Dorset harpoon heads from sites at Igloolik, Pond Inlet, and Mittimatalik (Figures 5.2B and 5.3 first two at upper left). These toggling heads have drilled line holes and open sockets into which flattened foreshafts would fit. Binding passed through side notches over these foreshafts holding them in tightly against the socket yet loose enough that the foreshaft could slip free once the animal's body was penetrated. A strong single barb or two symmetrical barbs were cut into the sides and on the proximal ends were two symmetrical spurs. A harpoon head reported by Mathiassen (1927:Plate 1, p. 208) from Igaqdjuag had a stone side blade in place of a single barb. "Blood grooves" running from the line hole toward the point or from the barbs are salient features of these implements.

Harpoon heads of this type date to at least as early as 1960 B.C., based on corrected carbon dates at Igloolik, and, if a corrected date from Port Refuge can be trusted, to as late as 1375 B.C. There is as yet no indication whether there may be temporal difference between single- and double-barbed forms. Meldgaard (1977) considers this type to begin a "Type line A" (Figure 5.3), which loses its side barbs around 1500 B.C. and continues with discrete stylistic transitions into developed and Late Dorset.

There is an apparently equally early type, found in the same sites and on the same elevations at Igloolik, which is barbless and self-bladed and ends in a long, narrow, medial spur (Figure 5.2E). Like the preceding type, it has an open socket and a drilled line hole. The second of two recovered at Gull Cliff, Port Refuge, though broken would appear to be of this type. Its temporal range (corrected dates) seems to extend from 1490 B.C. at the Umingmak site (Figure 5.2D) to 960 B.C. at the Buchanan site on Victoria Island (Taylor 1967), to terminal Pre-Dorset in 665 B.C. at the Seashore Gully site near Churchill (Nash 1969). Through time, this type becomes sharper and more slender and its proximal spur becomes relatively shorter. Interestingly, both the Umigmak and Buchanan sites are inland, the former associated only with musk-ox bones and the latter with caribou. Here harpoons may have been used in hunting these animals, particularly caribou after they had been driven into open lakes.

The few harpoon heads recovered from Pre-Dorset sites have all been self-bladed. But many others must have been slotted for end blades. Most Pre-Dorset compo-

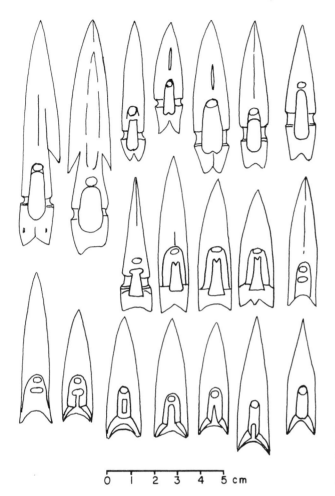

Figure 5.3 Development of Type line A harpoon heads from earliest Pre-Dorset through developed Dorset (based on sketches by Meldgaard, personal communication, 1977).

nents, including those where there has been no organic preservation, have a number of straight-based, triangular, bifacially flaked blades too large for arrow tips that must have fitted on antler or ivory harpoon heads. Many of these are delicately serrated on lateral edges and a few, late in the sequence, have angular, indented bases (Figure 5.4FF).

Harpoons must have been thrust or thrown by hand since no throwing boards or other projecting devices have been found. A possible, but doubtful, exception to this must be noted. Both Igloolik and Umingmak sites have produced curious slender antler and ivory artifacts that resemble large crochet hooks (Figure 5.2N). These fragile-appearing artifacts may have been used as dart slings. If so, they could only have been used with the lightest of harpoons or darts. A small loop would have been tied on the dart shaft and whipped forward by the hooked rod held in the hand. No other functional attribute has been suggested for these artifacts.

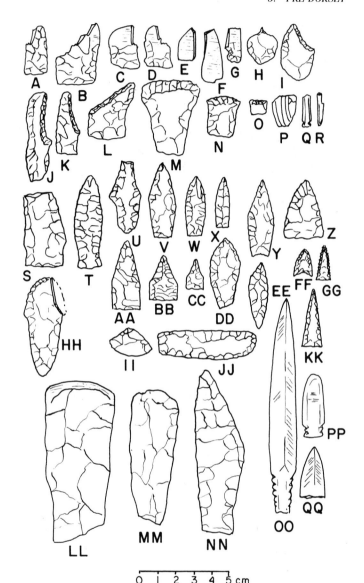

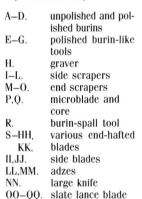

Figure 5.4 Characteristic Pre-Dorset lithic artifacts from several sites—A, K, N, T, X, AA, II, Port Refuge; B, C. J. L, M, S, V, DD, JJ, Arnapik; D, I, U, HH, KK, LL, Shaymark; E, Annawak, Lake Harbour; F, H, BB, CC, EE, FF, MM, QQ, Closure, Lake Harbour; G, O–R, W, GG, PP, Loon, Lake Harbour; Y, OO, Bloody Falls, Coppermine River; NN, Buchanan, Victoria Island (drawings based on selected illustrations from McGhee 1976, 1979; Maxwell 1973; Taylor 1967, 1968).

A–D.	unpolished and polished burins
E–G.	polished burin-like tools
H.	graver
I–L.	side scrapers
M–O.	end scrapers
P,Q.	microblade and core
R.	burin-spall tool
S–HH, KK.	various end-hafted blades
II,JJ.	side blades
LL,MM.	adzes
NN.	large knife
OO–QQ.	slate lance blade and knives

Terrestrial Hunting

Bones of musk-ox, caribou, polar bear, hare, fox, and birds in some Pre-Dorset middens attest to active inland hunting. For taking this game they used both bows and arrows and lances. Antler bow brace and handle segments (Figure 5.2H) indicate that the bows were small and sharply recurved. They were probably complicated constructions of jointed driftwood fragments and steamed and straightened antler and musk-ox horn. This composite was bound tightly with sinew and backed with braided sinew strands. It was probably only lethal within 20 m or less. Arrows had long, slender bone or antler foreshafts, ending in blunt ends or gouged beds for bipointed stone tips. Others, of driftwood or antler, were slotted at the end for square-based triangular points. The straight-based flint arrow tips are usually very small and thin. Many have minutely serrated edges and some were polished on dorsal and ventral faces before final retouch.

In the Western Arctic Denbigh complex there are long, narrow side blades that presumably were hafted in lateral grooves on bone points. These do not appear in Pre-Dorset. The only stone side blades recovered are too heavy for such purpose and were probably fitted to lances and knives.

Characteristic Pre-Dorset lance heads, of antler, are long and open socketed. They are perforated for a line hole near the base with a groove running from this hole to the base (Figure 5.2G). Flat, tapered foreshafts would have fit in these sockets and been held by binding. The line hole near the base suggests that heads were designed to slip from foreshafts and hang loosely attached to lance shafts. This detachable, but nontoggling head makes sense when we consider that spear shafts, made of small pieces of precious driftwood lashed together, were the most valuable part of the weapon. The thrashing of wounded animals would be less likely to shatter them if the head slipped free. Lance heads were either shaped to a sharp, bladed point or slotted for large, triangular stone blades (Taylor 1963b). A number of sites such as Kaleruserk (Igloolik), Sarqaq (West Greenland), and some of those in northern Labrador have produced relatively large, tapering-stemmed points with pronounced shoulders and often serrated lateral edges (see Figure 5.13E). Presumably these also were tips for lances but would fit none of those yet found.

The recovered lance heads have had half-moon-shaped stone side blades set in slots just above the socket or low lateral ridges in lieu of side blades. Stylistic attributes of these lances change little through the span of Pre-Dorset to Late Dorset.

There is some evidence that large domesticated dogs of the Greenlandic variety may have helped the spear hunters, particularly in bringing polar bear to bay. Meldgaard (1962) has reported a few dog bones scattered throughout the Pre-Dorset sequence at Igloolik, although the morphological data on these animals has not been published.

In the much later Thule period, barbed side prongs for bird spears are common (see Figure 8.16, p. 275). There is little evidence for such specialized equipment in Pre-Dorset, although a barbed point from the Umingmak site closely resembles these side prongs. Other unilaterally barbed points from Gull Cliff may also have tipped darts for hunting birds or spearing fish.

Fish, particularly when dried for the lean autumn months before freeze-up, would have played an important role in the diet. Many of the sites lie near what are now favored spots for char fishing. The stone weirs and fish traps in nearby streams are centuries old but still used today. Conceivably they could have been built initially by Pre-Dorset people. They are designed for the anadromous Arctic char, which in late spring leave for the sea from inland lakes in near-starving condition. By early August they return upriver, fat and ready to spawn.

Several artifacts have been identified as Pre-Dorset fishing gear. There are small bipointed bone gorges and unilaterally barbed points, both of which are interpreted as fish spears. These, and small antler barbs, may have been lashed to the ends of fishing leisters. The leister, a particularly efficient weapon for fishing at weirs, is still used today. It is basically a trident on a long shaft with a sharp point in the middle (Figure 5.2M) and springy, barbed sidepieces. When the center spike pierces a fish, the sidepieces surround and hold it and can then be sprung apart to drop it on the shore. Some barbed fish spears with line holes were apparently used as small harpoons. One of these comes from a mixed site at Peale Point near Frobisher Bay (Maxwell 1980). Here a late Thule house pit had cut through an earlier Pre-Dorset midden thought, on the basis of burins weathered out of sod blocks in the house, to be coeval with the nearby Shaymark site (corrected date of 1750 B.C.). At the bottom of the house fill, protected by 50 cm of permafrost, was a bilaterally barbed fish harpoon head identical to others of the Dorset period. Since no other Dorset remains were found in this house 15 m above present sea level, I conclude that it belongs to the Pre-Dorset period.

Domestic Activities

Most of the stone tools were used in domestic activities. The most ubiquitous are microblades, 10 mm or less in width, pressed from randomly shaped cores. These slivers of stone are incredibly sharp, in fact, sharper than the finest Sheffield steel, due to the conical nature of fracturing hard material. While it is not difficult to observe their edges with the naked eye, under magnification they seem to verge outward into infinity. They are potentially so useful, one wonders why their use ended with the demise of Paleoeskimo culture. Frequency percentages in site complexes indicate that they increase proportionately to other stone tools through the Pre-Dorset sequence, but they are present from the beginning as they are in the Western Arctic Small Tool tradition ancestral sites. These tiny tools were probably as multifunctional as our pocket knives, but they would have been particularly effective in cutting skin patterns for clothing and in butchering. Many are side notched near the proximal end for binding into a pencil-thin wooden handle.

In many sites there is a relative difference in raw materials used for microblades. The earliest microblades are of flint or local chert, but in time the frequency of those made from quartz increases. Chert microblades are often retouched along lateral edges for use, which makes them less friable and tougher. I suspect that the two types may have been used for different purposes. the chert retouched ones for woodworking and cutting through tough skins and joints and the quartz ones for sharper and more-delicate cutting. There have been a number of attempts to delimit the intrasite distribution of these ubiquitous artifacts. Where successful, these distributions have a positive correlation with needles and therefore indicate more frequent use by women than by men.

Small bone and ivory needles, round in cross section with one blunt end, have improbably small, drilled eyes. They attest to cut patterns and tailored costumes unlike those of Indians of the boreal forest. Bone awls are very rare, surprising in light of the delicacy of the needles. However, these sites produce quantities of the extremely small spalls pressed from burins. Many of these have been retouched at one end to sharp points presumably for pricking holes in leather for the fragile needles.

Whereas Independence home hearths are well defined, there is no such clear evidence of heating and cooking in Pre-Dorset sites. Clusters of small, blackened rocks inside what we have interpreted as Pre-Dorset dwellings indicate that most fires were made of lumps of flammable seal fat laid on flat stones. At some sites, Arnapik for example, heat-cracked igneous cobbles, carried in from some distance, suggest that meat that was not eaten raw may have been boiled by dropping heated rocks into skin vessels. In the Sarqaq variant of Pre-Dorset on West Greenland there are small, well-made, round steatite bowls (see Figure 5.14K). These are presumably oil lamps with wicks held up by small soapstone cones. Fragments of such small, round, soapstone lamps are also found, but rarely, in Canadian Pre-Dorset sites. Their infrequency suggests that they were carefully curated.

In the domestic activity category there is a wide variety of flint cutting implements and tools designed for working hard substances such as bone, antler, ivory, and soapstone. The most characteristic of these ivory-working tools is the spalled burin, constituting 20% or more of the total stone tool assemblage in most Pre-Dorset sites. This artifact is made by striking a wide, thin flake roughly 25–30 mm long and 15–20 mm wide from a pebble core. Since many burins, particularly the earlier ones, are only flaked on the face opposite the core surface, some of the preforming may have been done on the core itself. Many, but not all, of the flakes are then shaped like a mitten, with the edge along the "forefinger" next to the "thumb" bifacially retouched to provide guidance to the subsequent burin spall. In retrofitting recovered burin spalls to the burin from which they were pressed, I have found that the next step was to make a small notch at the distal spalling corner to serve as a striking platform. A spall could then be pressed off this corner by using a bone punch, although I have found it easier to simply hold the burin preform between my thumb and finger and, pressing down hard on the piece of antler, flip off the burin spall. The first of these spalls will be triangular in cross section since it comes from a bifacially flaked edge. Subsequent ones pressed off in sharpening the tool will be rectangular in cross section and leave small hinge fractures on the burin.

There are many varieties of these Pre-Dorset burins. Some are basally thinned and side notched for hafting; others are so thick they could only have been held between thumb and finger. At the distal end, some are beaked, some have vertical spall scars, and some flare backwards. Some are right-handed and others left-handed. On the southeastern coast of Baffin Island where several thousand burins have been recovered, there are certain variations of the distal, or working, edge. These include forms on which (1) the distal end is also spalled ("shaved" in some terminologies), (2) the distal end is unifacially retouched, (3) the distal end is bifacially retouched, and (4) the distal end is ground and polished on both faces to a very thin but rounded distal edge (Figure 5.5). The shaved burin may also be ground and polished but only on the face opposite to the core from which it was struck.

Most of us have tried to classify these burins so that they would indicate temporal changes. I have rejected my own attempt (Maxwell 1973a), finding that all four types persist through not only Pre-Dorset but Dorset as well. I now think that because each of the four variations produces a different-shaped groove, they may have been used for discretely different functions. McGhee (1980) has interjected a proposition that dampens hopes of using these tools as time markers. At Port Refuge, where he is able to consider stone assemblages house by house, he finds, for example, such similarity between burins and side scrapers in one house and disparity between comparable tools in other houses that he can attribute differences to individual skill and whim. The difference between assemblages in separate, presumably contemporaneous houses, is comparable to what I previously (1973a) would have considered time-linked types.

There are, however, some changes through time. Later burins are polished on one or both faces a greater percentage of the time. They tend to be more often bifacially flaked and side notched. But this difference is apparent only in terms of proportionate frequency. The primary purpose of the burin is logically as a grooving and splitting tool. However, after examining several thousand under the microscope, I

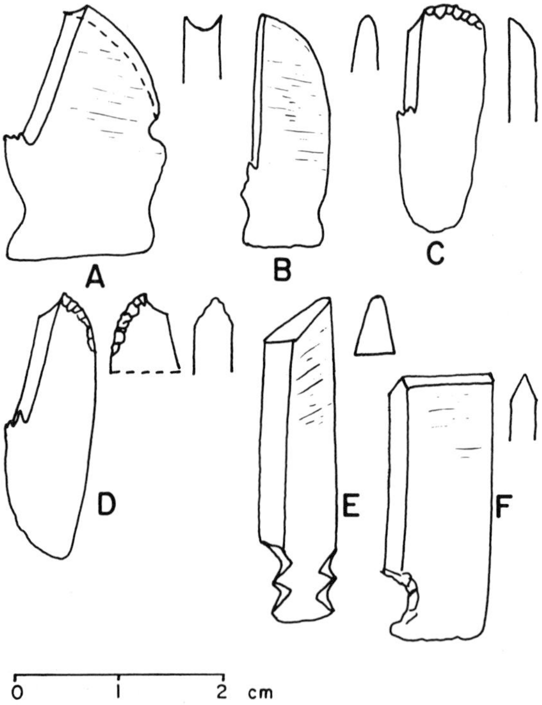

Figure 5.5 Characteristic shapes of Eastern Arctic burins and their cutting surfaces.

A. polished form with spalled (shaved) distal edge
B. polished form with polished distal edge
C. unpolished form with unifacially retouched distal edge
D. unpolished form with bifacially retouched distal edge
E. polished burin-like tool with angular distal end (Igloolik Angular-tipped type)
F. polished burin-like tool with squared distal end (Dorset Burin-like type)

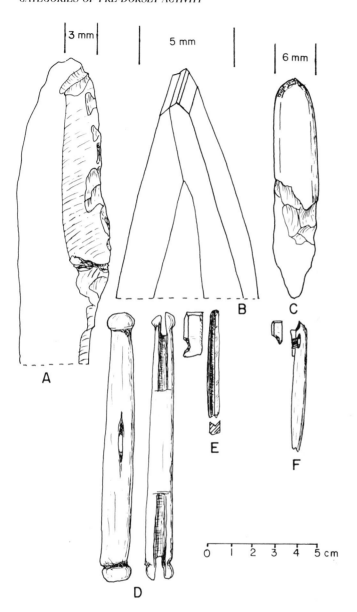

Figure 5.6 Burin and burin-like tools.

A. enlarged burin-spall face (actual size 3 mm) with flakes pressed off through use as scraper

B. enlarged corner tip of square-ended burin-like tool showing polished facets (actual size 5 mm)

C. crushed working corner of well-used, square-ended burin-like tool

D. wooden handle for Early Dorset burin-like tool

E. grooved ivory support piece that fits into lateral groove in wooden, burin-like tool handle

F. Late Dorset side-hafted burin-like tool (Tiriak type)

find more evidence of wear on margins of the spall scar than on the distal corner (Figure 5.6). The face of this scar is like a hollow-ground steel skate blade and extremely sharp. In carving an ivory harpoon head experimentally, I found this edge very effective in shaping the distal end whether I pulled the burin toward me or pushed it away (Figure 5.7).

Another tool used for grooving hard materials in Pre-Dorset times has had a

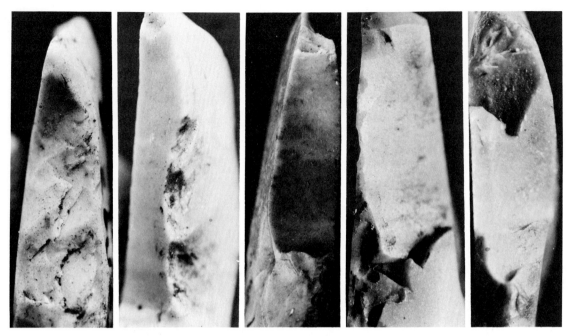

Figure 5.7 Macrophotographs of burin use wear (not all to same scale—average width of burin-spall scar is 3 mm). Tip wear is from use as a grooving tool, and side wear is from pushing or pulling as a side scraper.

controversial history. This is the so-called "burin-like tool," which becomes much more common in the Dorset period. On these artifacts the face, which would normally be a burin-spall scar, and the working corner are formed by grinding and polishing. There are two distinctive variants of this graver. The first, and perhaps the older of the two, has an angular tip at the distal end (Figure 5.5E). The second has a squared distal end and a sharpened working corner (Figure 5.5F). Both coexist in some Dorset assemblages but are always made of different materials— the angular-tipped one of nephrite (which never appears in Pre-Dorset sites) and the square-ended one of chalcedony or flint. This suggests that they were used for different purposes. However, in Labrador Dorset both forms are often made of the same nephrite material.

Early reports from the Igloolik excavations indicated that the spalled burin was restricted to the Pre-Dorset sequence and the burin-like tool to the Dorset. This has led some investigators to attribute the presence of polished gravers in Pre-Dorset sites to mixture and contamination. However, they have now appeared in so many Pre-Dorset assemblages, though always rare, that they must be considered part of the early tool kit. Similar polished gravers constitute a minor element of the Denbigh Flint Complex at Iyatyet, and the angular-tipped variant has been reported from the Meeus site (Ivugivik), Closure and Annawalk sites at Lake Harbour, the Umingmak site on Banks Island, and Saglek Bay and Okak sites on northern Labrador. Corrected and rounded dates for these sites ranges from 2000 to 1500 B.C. The earliest reported appearance of the square-ended form comes from the small square on the Closure site that produced a corrected carbon date of 1650 B.C. By 1150 B.C. at the nearby Loon site, they had become slightly more numerous.

A wide variety of bifacially flaked blades have been interpreted as knives. Shapes include ovals, straight-based forms, and a few with straight, parallel-sided stems. Some appear to have been deliberately asymmetrical. A few have shallow side notches, but deep and distinctive side notches do not appear until late Pre-Dorset. Slate, formed by grinding, was very rarely used for knives. Three fragments from later Pre-Dorset sites and one from the early Closure site, all near Lake Harbour, and one complete artifact from Bloody Falls (McGhee 1970a) at the western end of the range are the only ones reported.

Side and end scrapers are relatively common at these sites. Working edges on the former are steeply and unifacially beveled and range from a straight transverse edge to one that is deeply concaved. The latter vary in size but the majority are of thumbnail size or smaller. A few, particularly some in the Greenlandic Sarqaq variant, are large enough to use in dressing skins but most are not. Their size and indications of use wear suggest that most, like the side scrapers, were used in shaping hard substances such as ivory harpoon heads.

To complete the tool kit, there are crudely flaked adzes with polished bits, flaking punches of seal or walrus penis bone, fine-grained abrading stones, and random-shaped flakes retouched for a variety of functions including tiny points for graving, drilling, or reaming.

Art and Ideology

From its beginning, Dorset has a rich art, much of it reflecting magic and religious ideas. There are only faint traces of this art's origin in Pre-Dorset, perhaps because so few sites have preserved organic remains. A fragment of polished bone from Port Refuge was engraved with crude cross-hatching, and there are scratched geometric designs on a needle case and a caribou scapula from Igloolik (Figure 5.8A). There is

Figure 5.8 Pre-Dorset artistic pieces from the Igloolik vicinity: engraved caribou scapula and deliberately cut ivory maskettes (from photographs by Elmer Harp, Jr.).

at least one small, crudely carved, ivory seal from Igloolik as well. A badly eroded antler maskette from Kugaruk on Pelly Bay (Mary-Rousselière 1964:Plate 1, no. 15) appears to be a precursor to the many human maskettes of Early Dorset. So also are two fragments of ivory maskettes from terminal Pre-Dorset at Igloolik (Figure 5.8B). The shape of these fragments is particularly interesting. Many Dorset masks and maskettes are incised with an X across forehead and cheek intersecting at the bridge of the nose. There is apparently deep ideological significance to this X since the central forehead on human figurines is often excised, leaving a horned appearance. The Igloolik fragments are so cut at the top and broken at the bottom that only half of the X remains.

Shelters, Dwellings, and Settlements

The picture of Pre-Dorset shelters is a confusing one. Many of the sites such as Gull Cliff and Arnapik have only localized clusters of small rocks and artifacts and

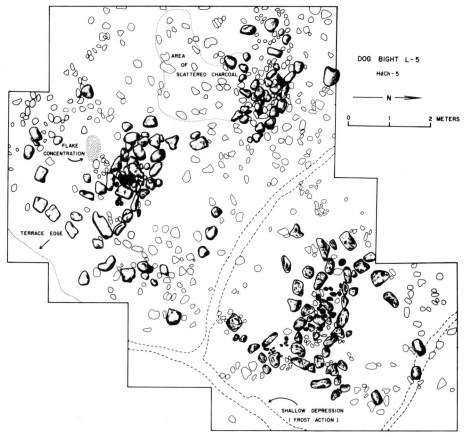

Figure 5.9 Plan of early Pre-Dorset houses with axial features, Dog Bight L-5 site, Labrador (after Cox 1978).

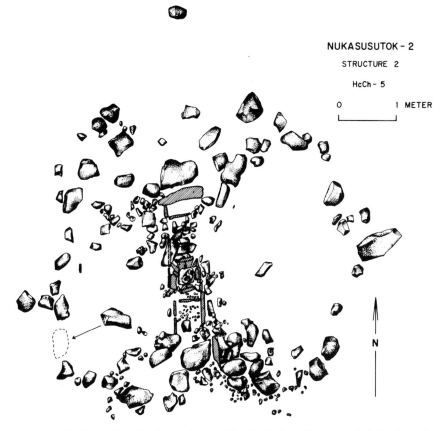

NUKASUSUTOK - 2

STRUCTURE 2

HcCh - 5

0   1 METER

N

Figure 5.10 Plan of late Pre-Dorset house with axial feature, Nukasusutok 2 site, Labrador (after Cox 1978).

stone débitage concentrations. The Closure site at Lake Harbour, occupied for four centuries between 2000 and 1600 B.C. according to corrected carbon dates, is also like this. In a statistical analysis, Dekin (1976) concludes that these clusters are the residue of elliptical tents 2 m long by 1.5 m wide. Skirts of the tent were turned inside, with small boulders holding them down against the wind. Inside the tent enclosure, but not in a defined hearth, charred flat rocks indicate that cooking and heating was accomplishd by burning lumps of seal fat on them.

Midpassages and box hearths may also be present in Pre-Dorset houses, challenging their exclusivity in the Independence I culture. Some of the Greenlandic Sarqaq houses have central box hearths as do the Pre-Dorset houses at Igloolik (Meldgaard 1962). Peculiar paved areas at the Seahorse Gully site near Churchill resemble midpassages (Nash 1972). In extensive survey of the southeast coast of Baffin Island, no midpassages have been located, with the possible exception of the one at Burton Bay, which cannot be dated. On the other hand, house sites on the northern coast of Labrador have midpassages of small boulders or of vertically placed stone slabs with central hearths (Figures 5.9 and 5.10; Cox 1978). Does this indicate a nexus with High Arctic Independence I, or are these winter dwellings and others summer tent sites? The long continuation of the midpassage trait through later Dorset until the fifteenth century A.D. would incline me to the latter explanation (Maxwell 1981).

Along the south coast of Baffin Island, settlements of this period are more often on exposed outer coasts than on deep sheltered bays. The pattern of settlement appears to be one in which 30 or more people congregated in one season of the year and then dispersed to camps of 1 or 2 families for the rest. Every likely campsite at elevations between 10 and 15 m above present sea level along the 420 km of coastline over which I have walked or along which I have kayaked has been searched. At several campsites only a small cluster of flakes and a very few artifacts were recovered. Only the Closure site, occupied intensively for a long time, has evidence of more than small, short-term camps. Later, around 1150 B.C., these annual gatherings appear to have moved a kilometer eastward to the Loon site at the head of Tanfield Valley. Since both Loon and Closure are far from fishing rivers or caribou crossings, we would logically expect these aggregates to assemble in winter for cooperative breathing-hole hunting on the nearby fast ice. If so, the Closure findspots may be the remains of winter snowhouses and not summer tents.

PRE-DORSET REGIONAL VARIATIONS

In the early 1980s the state of the art of Arctic archaeology is still hardly sufficient for definitive statements about regional enclaves of Pre-Dorset culture. Problems with carbon dates and precise chronometry throw analyses into the often subjective realm of typology. The vast area has been little explored. The sites are small, often the residue of transient camps, and in limited tool assemblages, sampling may not recover some critical items more carefully curated than others. Burins and burin spalls are numerous. But if I, with laughable ability in knapping, can make a burin in under 5 minutes, skilled flakers could turn out one almost faster than they could search for a lost one in the underlying gravel. Bifacial end blades would have taken longer to make, and a soapstone lamp longer yet. The odds of recovering a lamp, or even a fragment thereof, in an assemblage of 40 stone artifacts are very slim. Few sites have preserved the harpoon heads and other antler and ivory weapons that reflect stylistic change better than stone tools. Attempts to seriate minor style fluctuations in the latter have come to grief, and variations, as evidenced at Port Refuge, may be as much the result of idiosyncratic behavior as culturally relevant development. Nevertheless, one would expect some local variation given the geographic space involved.

The western end of the range appears to have had sizable populations only after the latter part of the fourteenth century B.C. On the basis of typology, these inhabitants of Banks and Victoria islands returned to the west from the core area only in the latter half of Pre-Dorset development. Carbon dates from the Umingmak and

Shoran sites on Banks Island were based on mixed sea and land materials and are not subject to correction. But charcoal dates from Menez, Buchanan, and Wellington Bay on Victoria Island and Bloody Falls on the mainland suggest that this move westward did not take place before 1400 B.C. and that populations remained here at least until the middle of the 900s B.C.

The nonlithic artifacts from the Umingmak and Shoran sites on Banks Island and Menez, Buchanan, and Wellington Bay do not differ from those of a comparable age at Igloolik (Figure 5.11). Antler harpoon heads are long, very slender, and sharp with a single, medial dorsal spur, needles are blunt ended with tiny drilled holes, and many of the spalled burins are polished. These and other traits clearly indicate a core area homeland for this western complex. But there are distinctive traits that set it apart from other sites of the period. Microblades are rare to absent while relatively large tools of quartzite are common, triangular end blades are often concave based, and there are a few fragments of worked copper. A particularly distinctive tool is a small, bifacially edged, quartzite knife that is not unlike the larger and more modern *ulu*, or woman's knife (Figure 5.11). Whereas the eastern economy is based primarily on seacoast hunting, the emphasis in the west is much more interior oriented. Both Umingmak and Shoran sites have hundreds of musk-ox bones, and the Victoria Island sites are inland along the Ekaluk River near caribou

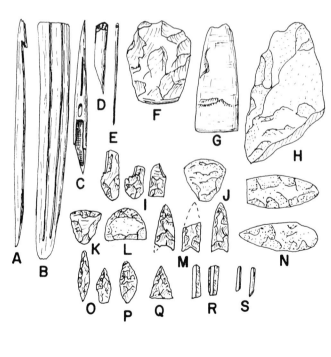

Figure 5.11 Sample of Pre-Dorset artifacts from Banks and Victoria islands—A–E, G, L, M, Buchanan site, Victoria Island; F, I, J, K, N, R, Umingmak site, Banks Island; H, O, P, Q, S, Menez site, Victoria Island (drawings based on selected illustrations from Taylor 1964, 1967, 1972).

A. sling handle(?)
B. ivory knife
C. harpoon head
D. flaking punch
E. needle
F. adze
G. slate rubbing tool
H. quartzite chopper
I. unpolished and polished burins
J. quartzite *ulu*-like knife
K,L. end scrapers
M. end blades
N. quartzite knives
O. end blades
P. side blade
Q. triangular harpoon end blade
R. microblades
S. burin-spall tools.

0 1 2 3 4 5 cm

drive *inuksuit*. Both animals were apparently hunted with harpoons. The Bloody Falls assemblage, with no preserved nonlithic artifacts, differs from the others, and from the rest of the Arctic Small Tool tradition, in its long, polished slate lance head (Figure 5.400). Otherwise its stone tools are more like those of the core area.

This western region of Coronation and Amundsen gulfs seems to have been a dispersal center for Pre-Dorset bands that followed migrating caribou deep into the interior. Remains of small hunting bands, collectively called the Canadian Tundra–Taiga tradition, extend south of present tree line in the District of Mackenzie. These Paleoeskimo, whose stone artifacts most closely resemble those of Wellington Bay, were specifically adapted to inland caribou hunting and fishing, returning to the coast for sealing only occasionally. Evidence suggest that they may have followed the Mackenzie caribou herd in its seasonal migration, penetrating ever deeper southward, until by 900 B.C. they may have been as far south as Lake Athabasca (Noble 1971; Wright 1972). The thinly middened campsites contain small, triangular end blades with concave bases like those of Banks and Victoria islands, small polished burins, rare microblades, and copper fragments. The distinctive bifacially edged, quartzite *ulu* appears in these sites as well as such traits as split-pebble Chi-tho scrapers, hafted drills, side-notched end blades, and large roasting pits typical of Indian sites. Since some of these sites are surely mixed, these latter traits may not relate to Pre-Dorset occupations.

Paleoeskimo sites with artifacts similar to Pre-Dorset continue through interior sites near Dubawnt, Aberdeen, and Baker lakes (Gordon 1975, 1976), and down to the coast of Churchill. If stone tool typology is an accurate measure, these sites are the residue of Pre-Dorset people who were more oriented to the interior and only distantly related to Pre-Dorset hunters farther to the west. In all probability they were living in symbiotic relation with the Keewatin caribou herd, which follows a more northeasterly migratory path than the Mackenzie one (Gordon 1975).

The period of this inland movement, between 1200 and 900 B.C., coincides with a time of increasing cold. Previously, around 1700 B.C., warmer weather had encouraged tree growth to about 280 km north of its present limit (Nichols 1967). But by 1500 B.C. the tree line retreated southward, as did Indian hunters of the boreal forest. Trees killed by frost led to massive forest fires along the front, perhaps extending the tundra barrens to south of their present margin. Paleoeskimo occupation of these barrens appears to have advanced and retreated as Indian groups abandoned and recovered hunting territories. According to Gordon (1976) the terminal carbon date of 835 B.C. for Pre-Dorset at the Migod site marks "the end of their occupation when the hunters may have retreated north and east to the Coast" (p. 264).

The Seashore Gully site at the southeastern terminus near Churchill, a terminal Pre-Dorset site according to a corrected carbon date of 950 B.C., has produced strange stone artifacts yet unfound in other Pre-Dorset sites (Figure 5.12). Here, along with such expected traits as polished and unpolished spalled burins, polished burin-like tools, burin spalls, side-notched knives, and an oval steatite vessel, there is a peculiar complex of large stone artifacts. These included mattocks, adzes,

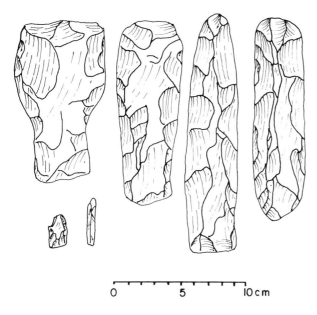

Figure 5.12 Large, flaked stone tools from the Seahorse Gully site compared to a typical Pre-Dorset burin and microblade of the same scale (artifact on top right 15 cm long (drawings based on selected illustrations from Nash 1969).

gouges, picks, planes, and knives that have no parallel elsewhere in Paleoeskimo sites (Nash 1969, 1972). Of these sites only the Seahorse Gully locale, more sea-coast-oriented than the others, continues into the Early Dorset phase.

Interpreting the Paleoeskimo occupation of the northern Labrador coast has varied with increasing exploration. Initial impressions were that this was a marginal area, occupied only in times of sea animal surplus. Later investigations by the Torngat Project (Fitzhugh 1980; Jordan 1978) have discovered a number of sites, suggesting that this coast may have had a long-term, intensive occupation. Current evidence restricts a Pre-Dorset occupation to the northern one-third of the Labrador coast—from Hopedale Region north to Cape Chidley—with concentrations around Saglek Bay to Okak (Cox 1978; Fitzhugh 1976b, 1980; Jordan 1978; Tuck 1975, 1976). Initial occupation around 1880 B.C., based on charcoal carbon dates, is nearly as early as that of Independence Fjord and the Foxe Basin and southern Baffin Island regions. There appears to have been continuous occupation, with its greatest intensity around 1500 B.C., and then dwindling populations to around 1350 B.C. Between then and the middle of the eighth century B.C. there may only have been intermittent settlement or even abandonment of this coast. This abandonment may be partially due to encroaching Indians. The degree to which we should view Labrador Pre-Dorset as a regional variant, differing significantly from such sites as those on northern and southern Baffin Island, those near Igloolik, and those on Mansel Island, depends largely on individual interpretation. No organic material was preserved, but combined stone tools from all of the early Labrador sites include the typical Arctic Small Tool tradition categories frequently discussed in this volume. Both Cox (1978) and Tuck (1975, 1976) see a closer resemblance of some of these traits to those of Independence I and Sarqaq of West Greenland than to core area

Pre-Dorset. Their interpretation centers on end blades, presumably for arrow and harpoon tips, and the early appearance of axial feature houses. The most common small end blade of Labrador Pre-Dorset is a square-based, narrow, thin triangle often with fine serrations on lateral edges. This also is the predominant form in the core area and constitutes 60% of the small end blade sample at Port Refuge (McGhee 1979). Several of the small end blades from Labrador, and from Independence I, are bipointed with tapering stems, but so, also, are a few from most core area sites. The best evidence for a Greenlandic relation is an end blade form with serrated edges, a tapering stem, and a sharp, distinctive shoulder. These have been reported from Greenland and Port Refuge (see Figure 4.7P), but they also appear in the Kaleruserk site at Igloolik and the Closure site on south Baffin Island. Given the distances involved from Okak to Port Refuge and Greenland on the one hand, and from Okak to Baffin Island on the other, a southern connection would seem more logical. I have no difficulty in relating Labrador Pre-Dorset to the core area, particularly since its assemblages include polished, angular-tipped burin-like tools, which certainly do not appear in Independence I (Figure 5.13). However, the fact that axial feature houses have yet to be reported from the core area but persist through the Labrador Pre-Dorset span, as they do in the High Arctic and Greenland, cannot be ignored.

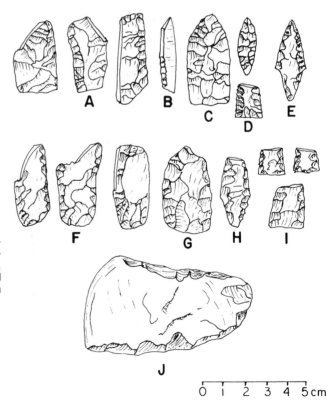

Figure 5.13 Early Paleoeskimo artifacts from coastal Labrador; A–E, Saglek; F–J, Thalia Point (drawings based on selected illustrations from Tuck 1976; Fitzhugh 1976b).

A.   burins
B.   polished angular-tipped burin-like tool
C–E. end blades
F.   burins
G–I. end blades
J.   adze

To date, the only published Pre-Dorset sites in the High Arctic- north of the Parry Channel, are Gull Cliff at Port Refuge (McGhee 1979) and Cape Sparbo on the northern coast of Devon Island (Lowther 1962). Cultural traits here do not differ significantly from those farther south and seem to reflect only occasional penetrations by people more at home in the core area. On the other hand, Schledermann (1978b), working in an uniquely rich ecological zone around the Bache Peninsula of eastern Ellesmere Island, interprets his evidence as reflecting a long continuity of early Paleoeskimo. He suggests that this includes a local transition from Pre-Dorset to Dorset, which would imply a distinctive High Arctic variant and support the belief of some researchers that some of Dorset's traits had their genesis far to the north.

Sarqaq, known mainly from sites on Disko Bay and near Godthaab, Greenland, was the first early Paleoeskimo variant discovered in the Eastern Arctic and in some ways remains the most distinctive. It is probably part of a general Pre-Dorset sphere, but retention of the term Sarqaq serves to underline its unique nature. Published reports are unfortunately scanty, but in those available there is an impression of stylistic homogeneity within the complex. Certain basic tools demonstrate a higher degree of standardization than is customary in other Pre-Dorset assemblages, Some traits, common here, have not been reported from other Pre-Dorset sites. Sarqaq settlements may have tended to be more sedentary, with greater contact and information exchange among larger groups of inhabitants.

Palynological studies (Fredskild 1973) indicate some differences between the climatic succession we have discussed before and the conditions under which Sarqaq developed. Available carbon dates suggest an approximate period for Sarqaq development of 1500–500 B.C. Optimal conditions in the Sarqaq region began by 2500 B.C. with the immigration of birch trees and reached a peak, warmer and drier than today, at about 1650 B.C. By 750 B.C. the climate had again become colder and more humid.

The Sarqaq complex is best known from early sites around Disko Bay (Larsen and Meldgaard 1958) and the later site of Itivnera east of Godthaab. The early site at Sermermiut at the entrance of Jacobshavn was initially improperly carbon dated to 810 B.C. Revised dates (Fredskild 1973) indicate a sterile humus (Sermermiut B Layer 2) beneath the Sarqaq layer dated 1560 ± 120 B.C. and the Sarqaq zone Layer 3 dated 1410 ± 120 B.C. The apparent beginning of the complex, then, was in a warm, dry, but beginning-to-cool climate.

Structural remains on the early Sarqaq sites around Disko Bay suggest possible affinities with the Independence complex of the High Arctic. Box hearths, boulder pavements, and rock alignments resembling midpassages have all been reported. But published information on the sites is yet too scanty to permit further interpretations of diffusion.

Much of the uniqueness of Sarqaq lithic assemblages (no early Sarqaq nonlithic artifacts and only a few from Itivnera have been reported) can be attributed to the high percentage of grinding and polishing on several classes of artifacts (Figure 5.14). The dominant raw material, *angmaq,* is a grainy silicified slate, a material that is perhaps best prepared by grinding. The lithic inventory includes arrow tips of

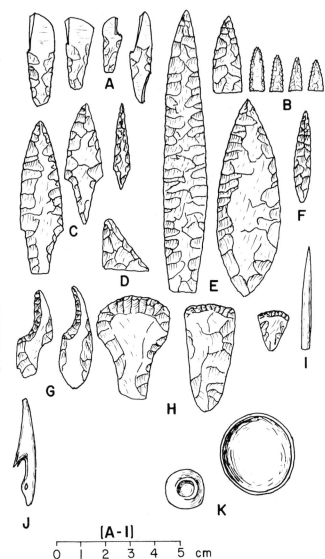

Figure 5.14 Sarqaq complex artifacts (drawings based on selected illustrations from Larsen and Meldgaard 1958; Meldgaard 1961; Rosing 1962). J and K are not in same scale as A–I.

A.   polished burins
B,C,E,F. end blades
D.   side blade
G.   side scrapers
H.   end scrapers
I.   polished stone drill
J.   nontoggling harpoon head with bifurcate barbs
K.   small, round stone lamp with cone-shaped wick holder with depression in the top

triangular, stemmed, and bipointed forms with lateral edges that are usually finely serrated and faces that range from unground to completely ground, polished, and keeled. Most spalled burins are bifacially ground and polished on distal faces, taper to narrowed proximal ends, and have angled working surfaces. Burin spalls, partially ground adz blades, relatively large, stemmed end blades (for lances?), concave side scrapers, and triangular end scrapers combine with the arrow tips and burins to dominate the inventory. The relatively low frequency of microblades (of jasper and flint) was originally thought to be the result of site contamination by Dorset occupants. Microblades are now recognized as an integral part of the Sarqaq complex.

The late Sarqaq Itivnera site is one of the most extensively excavated loci. It lies nearly 150 km inland from the coast of Godthaab on the shore of Kapisigdlit Kangerdluat Fjord and on a natural caribou route. Ninety percent of the recovered faunal bones from the site were caribou (Møhl 1972).

Four carbon dates appear to bracket the Sarqaq occupation at Itivnera. Sterile humus below the cultural layer dates to 1250 B.C.: 3200 ± 120 radiocarbon years (K-1192), Sarqaq Layer 3 to 1190 B.C.: 3140 ± 120 radiocarbon years (K-1193), a Sarqaq floor to 1010 B.C.: 2960 ± 100 radiocarbon years (K-588), and sterile peat above the cultural layer to 340 B.C.: 2290 ± 100 radiocarbon years (K-1194).

The structural remains are of shallow pit houses about 8 m in diameter with a central stone box hearth but apparently lacking the midpassage stone alignments of earlier Sarqaq, although complete diagrams have not yet been published. Unlike the coastal sites, a few nonlithic artifacts were recovered from the site. There is at least one nontoggling, bifurcate barbed, "male" harpoon head similar to one from Upper Beaches at Port Refuge (Figure 5.14J). The rest are less distinctive: walrus bone stone flakers, double-pointed fish gorges, an ivory hammer, a caribou leg bone scraper handle, and a burin-spall awl handle (Meldgaard 1961).

Attributes of the lithic artifacts differ somewhat from those of the coast (Figure 5.15). More of the tools are made of a white quartzite, most arrow and lance tips have tapered stems (whereas more of the arrow tips on the coast are triangular and square based), and many of the Itivnera end scrapers are larger. The site produced a somewhat greater frequency of microblades and polished saws as well as a polished drill or bodkin (Figure 5.14I). There were also perfectly round soapstone lamps ranging in diameter from 16 cm to less than 2 cm with small stone cones to hold wicks of marsh cotton (Figure 5.14K, 5.15G). Fire-cracked rock in Sarqaq sites, however, indicate that cooking was done in skin vessels with heated rocks rather than in stone vessels.

The beginning of Sarqaq at about 1500 B.C. nearly coincides with the disappearance of Independence I from the High Arctic, and the presence of axial feature structures in early Sarqaq has led many to conclude that they are the southern descendants of the early pioneers driven from the north by increasing cold. However, many lithic traits not present in Independence I assemblages but common in those of Canadian Pre-Dorset suggest an origin to the west of Baffin Bay. From its beginning Sarqaq appears to have been a cultural enclave developing its distinctive technology over a millennium of isolation. The initial interpretation of the culture (Larsen and Meldgaard 1958) was that it collapsed and was followed by a later immigration of Dorset people. Taylor (1968), on the other hand, presented a convincing seriation for the development of Sarqaq into Dorset as presumably the rest of Pre-Dorset does. Unfortunately, although natural resources along this coast are rich and must have supported extensive settlements of Paleoeskimo, reports of

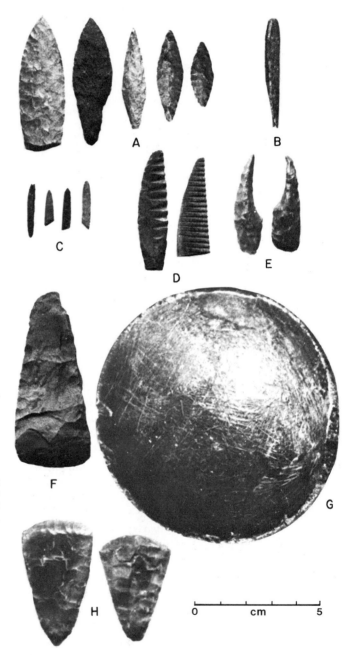

Figure 5.15 Artifacts from the Itivnera site, southwestern Greenland (from photographs by Elmer Harp, Jr.).

A. stemless and tapered-stemmed end blades
B. bone flaking punch
C. burin spalls
D. stone saws(?)
E. side scrapers
F. adz
G. steatite bowl
H. end scrapers

excavated sites are meager. To date, the earliest Dorset remains published would appear to belong typologically to a period around the beginning of the Christian era—several centuries after the most recent reported Sarqaq site.

PRE-DORSET CHANGE AND TERMINATION

Few archaeologists working in the Eastern Arctic would quarrel today with the statement that Pre-Dorset culture merges into Dorset without additional influences external to the continuum; nor would they quarrel with the statement that there are recognizable differences between the site contents of early Pre-Dorset settlements and those of developed Dorset. There is, however, dispute over the nature of transition from Pre-Dorset to Dorset, over the existence or nonexistence of guide fossils (artifacts that signify a specific time period), and over the distinctiveness of early, middle, or late Pre-Dorset assemblages. Many factors contribute to these disputes. With regard to the transition from Pre-Dorset to Dorset, climatic change is a major reason for apparent differences between the two. Pre-Dorset times were relatively warm, and, as stated before, there are very few artifacts of organic substances from Pre-Dorset sites south of the Arctic Circle. In contrast, the onset of permafrost coincides with what is generally recognized as the beginning of the Dorset period. Consequently, wood, sinew, and feathers, along with ivory harpoon heads, are preserved in early Dorset sites. In these more southerly locales, comparisons between the two phases of the continuum can only be made on the less distinctive stylistic variations of stone tools.

A certain amount of the confusion comes from subjective comparisons of artifacts in a specific class with those from another region. To one observer the two sets may look alike, whereas to another they may look significantly different. Difference of opinion rests partially on the fact that there are still few Pre-Dorset sites excavated and reported in full, their assemblages are often scanty, and in some locales sites within the continuum that are closest in time may still be separated by several centuries. Through these centuries, in other regions, slow stylistic shifts may camouflage what elsewhere appears to be the dramatic appearance of a new form. Ultimately many of these problems will be resolved with greater objectivity of analysis supported by statistical treatment. Until then the best indications of change within the Pre-Dorset period come from Igloolik, where the full continuum is expressed on successively descending beach ridges, and from the southeast coast of Baffin Island centered on Lake Harbour. The former has preserved artifacts of organic substances; the latter has not. However, the Igloolik material has not been published in full, and quantified information is not available. The following statements of lithic change come from the Lake Harbour sequence of 12 sites, all of which except one are dated by ^{14}C analysis (Table 5.2).

The early Pre-Dorset is represented by two sites, Annawak and Shaymark, and four components of the Closure site, KdDq-11, KdDq-11-6, KdDq-11-8, and KdDq-11-10. These range in corrected dates from 2275 to 1399 B.C. and collectively

Table 5.2
FREQUENCY PERCENTAGES OF LAKE HARBOUR PRE-DORSET AND EARLY DORSET LITHIC ARTIFACTS[a]

Artifact	Early Pre-Dorset (2275–1399 B.C.)		Middle Pre-Dorset (1162–975 B.C.)		Late Pre-Dorset (628–600 B.C.)[b]		Early Dorset (475–410 B.C.)	
	(n = 1534)	(n = 495)	(n = 513)	(n = 243)	(n = 1170)	(n = 383)	(n = 6805)	(n = 3832)
Spalled burins	20.00	64.00	21	43	6	20	1.00	2
Burin spalls	48.00	—	22	—	18	—	0.01	—
Microblades	20.00	—	31	—	50	—	44.00	—
Ground and polished burin-like tools	0.04	1.00	1	2	2	7	5.00	9
Slate knives	0.03	1.00	4	9	5	17	16.00	28
Triangular and double-tapered end blades	7.00	21.00	10	21	5	15	17.00	30
Side and end scrapers	4.00	11.00	9	20	7	20	8.00	14
Soapstone vessel fragments	0.01	0.02	0	0	3	10	7.00	12
Side-notched end blades	0.04	1.00	2	5	4	11	3.00	6

[a]The first column of percentages for each period includes burin spalls and microblades; the second column does not.
[b]This is an estimated range.

have a total of 2070 stone artifacts. Middle Pre-Dorset is represented by three sites, Loon, KdDq-13, and KdDq-23, ranging from 1162 to 975 B.C. and collectively totaling 627 stone artifacts. Late Pre-Dorset is represented by two sites, Killulugak and Avinga, ranging from 628 to an estimated 600 B.C. and collectively having a total of 1309 stone artifacts. Early Dorset is represented by one site, Tanfield/Morrison, ranging from 475 to 410 B.C. and having a total of 7222 stone artifacts.

In comparing the lithic assemblages of these sites, there are no specific changes that allow us to make cultural distinctions between early, middle, and late aspects of Pre-Dorset. Through the 1400-year period from approximately 2000 to approximately 600 B.C., there are certain shifting levels of popularity in artifact classes as reflected in their frequency percentages, but few of these percentages reflect straight-line increases or decreases. In all these sites, microblades and burin spalls constitute the most ubiquitous classes, and together they account for 60–80% of the stone tools from most sites. Consequently they tend to swamp the significance of other tool classes (Table 5.2). Burin spalls, and particularly burin-spall tools in which the proximal end has been modified by flaking or spalling, are among the very few artifacts that could be considered guide fossils for Pre-Dorset. In developed Dorset sites, even where spalled burins may constitute 7% of the total stone tools, spalls are absent or extremely rare. Microblades increase in relative popularity, with quartz-crystal ones increasing relative to chert ones. Spalled burins tend to decrease in relative frequency and demonstrate a general tendency over time toward bifacial modification and deliberate polishing. These two shifts appear to have greater regularity in some early Pre-Dorset sites elsewhere, but in southern Baffin Island some sites from which recovered burins show no polish, or only a trace, are later than sites in which polished burins have a higher frequency.

According to reports from Igloolik, the spalled burin does not continue in use after the beginning of Dorset, when the polished burin-like tool first appears, and therefore becomes a guide fossil for beginning Dorset. Elsewhere, in a number of locales where sizable stone assemblages have been recovered, the ground-and-polished burin-like tool appears as a trace in the earliest Pre-Dorset sites. In the Lake Harbour sequence the angular-tipped burin-like tool is present in the earliest part of the Closure site (3 of 1427 stone tools) and in the Annawak site (1 of 177 stone tools). The square-ended burin-like tool is apparently later, appearing as a trace in the later part of the Closure site (1 of 1427 stone tools at a corrected date of 1665 B.C.). It increases to 1% of the assemblage at the Loon site (5 of 501 stone tools at a corrected date of 1162 B.C.). Slate as a material for tools has a parallel development. Flaked and partially ground slate adzes appear in a number of early sites, to be replaced in later Pre-Dorset and Early Dorset by harder materials such as quartzite and nephrite. But slate knives, either flaked or ground and polished, increase only slightly from traces in earliest Pre-Dorset to a sudden profusion at the beginning of Dorset. Side-notched chert knives are also rare early but become more common in late Pre-Dorset. Soapstone lamps, oval in Pre-Dorset and rectangular in Early Dorset, are extremely rare until near the end of Pre-Dorset when they become common.

The tip fluting of harpoon end blades, more common in other sites than at Lake Harbour where the available raw material is of poor quality, first appears in the Killulugak sites at a corrected date of 628 B.C. This site also provides the first appearance of nephrite, which becomes the preferred material for angular-tipped burin-like tools. Throughout the southern Baffin Island Pre-Dorset there is a gradual increase in the variety of stone materials used, a decrease in the use of retouched flakes, and a decrease in the ratio of waste flakes to finished artifacts. Many of these developmental changes are discussed in greater detail in Maxwell (1976).

Changes in artifacts made of organic substances (Maxwell 1976) are best illustrated from the publications and informal communications about the sequence at Igloolik. Here the change from Pre-Dorset to Dorset in the sites ranging from 20 to 24 m above present sea level (a period from about 800 to about 450 B.C.) appears to be more dramatic than at Lake Harbour. Harpoon heads go through a rapid sequence of stylistic variants, from an open socket, to a partially closed, flanged, T-shaped socket, to a closed socket with one or two holes on the dorsal surface, to a closed socket with a narrow triangular slice on the dorsal surface (Figure 5.3).

Certain artifacts such as ice creepers, sled shoes, toy sled models, and snow knives make a sudden appearance at what is considered the beginning of the Dorset period at Igloolik and also on the southeastern coast of Baffin Island. This plus a sudden proliferation of slate knives, useful for separating sealskin from blubber and blubber from meat but too soft for other functions, and the disappearance of bows and arrows for caribou hunting suggests a significant shift in emphasis toward more sea ice hunting in the Dorset period.

The causative effect of climate on Pre-Dorset and Dorset cultural change has yet to be determined, yet there is adequate indication of the concurrence of successive warm and cold periods and significant events in the continuum. The best, and most detailed, evidence is in Barry *et al.* (1977). Abstracting their data yields the following sequence: In the Eastern Arctic the Thermal Maximum ended at about 3000 B.C., a millennium before human occupation. There followed a general cooling, but by 1850 B.C., after the entrance of Arctic Small Tool tradition people, summer temperatures may have been as much as 3° C (5.5° F) warmer than they are at present—little colder than the middle western United States today. This period of progressive cooling with a few intermittent warming trends presumably lasted until about 1400 B.C. During this time, Independence I people abandoned the High Arctic, at about 1600 B.C. In Labrador, carbon dates and site densities indicate an apparent population reduction between 1550 and 1150 B.C. (Cox 1978). This may also be related to the cooling period or, conversely, to a northern penetration of Indians at this time (1978:103). It is during this prolonged cooling trend that Pre-Dorset people of the Canadian Tundra–Taiga complex penetrated southward to even colder winters in the Keewatin Barrens through terrain formerly hunted by Indians. By 1200 B.C. glaciers were advancing on southeastern Baffin Island. The cooling trend was broken by a brief warming period between about 1200 and 800 B.C. immediately followed by a marked cooling period during which, by 600–500 B.C., the temperatures were colder than they are today.

This date of 600–500 B.C. correlates nicely with a number of sites, locked in permafrost until their excavation, that have generally been accepted as early, or beginning Dorset. Most of these sites have produced the peculiar harpoon head called "Tyara Sliced" by Taylor (1968; see Figure 7.1B, p. 168), which seems to be a convenient time marker for beginning Dorset. Seven corrected dates for only those levels in the following sites in which Tyara Sliced harpoon heads have been recovered are 564 B.C. (Alarnerk), 505 B.C. (Agliruuijaq), 490 B.C. (Arnakadlak), 435 B.C. (Tyara), 420 B.C. (Nunguvik House 46), 410 B.C. (date derived from willow twigs; Tanfield), 397 B.C. (T-1), and 395 B.C. (Tyara). Three carbon dates from Labrador Early Dorset (Table 7.1), which has not produced preserved harpoon heads, range from 535 to 450 B.C. (A date of 895 B.C. is certainly too early.)

THE PRE-DORSET–DORSET TRANSITION

Some of the difficulty in determining a meaningful distinction between Pre-Dorset and Dorset cultures can be seen in an examination of assemblages from the Killilugak and Avinga sites on the southeastern coast of Baffin Island, the complex of Groswater Dorset sites on the Labrador Coast, and the Independence II complex from the High Arctic (Table 5.3).

The Killilugak Site

This site located on the small Okialivialuk Peninsula near Lake Harbour differs significantly from others in the Pre-Dorset-to-Dorset continuum on Baffin Island's south coast (Maxwell 1973a). A date of 3043 ± 63 radiocarbon years (P-699; corrected by Arundale [1981] to 628 ± 88 B.C.) derived from charred seal fat occurs in what may be considered a transitional period. Unlike other sites in the Lake Harbour region the small, flat surface between rock outcrops 10 m above sea level has a very thin cultural midden overlying bedrock; there are no rocks, depressions, or sod buildups to suggest dwelling shelters. The 503 artifacts and flake residue recovered from the site appeared to be randomly distributed without tendency to cluster (Figure 5.16). Microblades, more of chert than of quartz crystal, constituted 69% of the total stone tool assemblage. This fact plus the significant number of side blades (presumably for lances), side-notched chert knives, and bifacially flaked fragments has led me to the inference that this was an open-air station for processing caribou meat and skins. The location of the peninsula is such that caribou might well have been killed nearby as they migrated in late summer from the interior to the coast.

The significance of the site is less in its function than in some of the discrete attributes of its artifacts, which are in part characteristic of Pre-Dorset and in part Dorset. The spalled burins are more characteristic of Pre-Dorset in their relative frequency but they are also discretely unique. The 347 microblades and 31 burin spalls swamp the relative frequencies of other artifact categories. When they are removed from the total assemblage, burins constitute 18% of the remaining 125

Table 5.3

RADIOCARBON DATES FOR INDEPENDENCE II, TRANSITIONAL PRE-DORSET, AND GROSWATER DORSET SITES[a]

Site	Culture	Lab no.	Material	Uncorrected age (radio-carbon years)	Corrected ages (radio-carbon years)[b]	Corrected date (B.C.)
Engnaes	Independence II	K-1544	Willow charcoal	3080 ± 100	—	1130
Buchanan	Pre-Dorset	I-2054	Charcoal	2990 ± 125	—	1040
Itivnera	Pre-Dorset	K-588	Juniper	2960 ± 110	—	1010
Buchanan	Pre-Dorset	I-2053	Charcoal	2910 ± 105	—	960
Menez	Pre-Dorset	I-2058	Charcoal	2880 ± 105	—	930
Nukasusutok 2	Pre-Dorset	SI-2988	Charred fat	3315 ± 85	2830 ± 100	880
Sarqaq	Pre-Dorset	K-518	Birch	2760 ± 100	—	810
Vanfaldnaes	Independence II	K-934	Driftwood	2740 ± 100	—	790
Buxhall	Groswater Dorset	SI-930	Charcoal	2720 ± 125	—	770
Tikoralak 2	Groswater Dorset	GSC-1179	Charcoal	2690 ± 140	—	740
St. Johns Is.	Groswater Dorset	SI-2990	Charcoal	2645 ± 65	—	695
Seahorse Gully	Pre-Dorset	S-521	Seal bone	2900 ± 100	2615 ± 117	665
Engnaes	Independence II	K-1522	Willow charcoal	2610 ± 100	—	660
Killilugak	Pre-Dorset	P-699	Charred fat	3043 ± 63	2578 ± 88	628
Thalia Pt. 2	Groswater Dorset	GSC-1381	Charcoal	2540 ± 160	—	590
E. Pompey Is.	Groswater Dorset	GSC-1367	Charcoal	2520 ± 160	—	570
Hellebaek	Independence II	K-1059	Willow charcoal	2510 ± 110	—	560
Kapuivik (24-m terrace)	Pre-Dorset	P-211	Antler	2354 ± 135	2464 ± 159	514
Tikoralak 5	Groswater Dorset	GSC-1314	Charcoal	2400 ± 160	—	450
Tikoralak 3	Groswater Dorset	GSC-1217	Charcoal	2340 ± 140	—	390
Buxhall	Groswater Dorset	SI-931	Charcoal	2255 ± 55	—	305
Red Rock Pt.	Groswater Dorset	SI-875	Charcoal	2200 ± 120	—	250

[a]Data is from Arundale 1981 with additions by Maxwell.
[b]Ages have been corrected by incorporating laboratory-derived fractionation and sea reservoir factors except for wood and charcoal samples.

Figure 5.16 Artifacts from the Killilugak site, Lake Harbour vicinity, southeastern Baffin Island.

A. burins with spalled and then polished working surfaces
B. polished burin spalls
C. triangular end blades
D. side blades
E. triangular lance tip
F. two side-notched end blades
G. five corner- and side-notched end blade base fragments
H. slate knife and two slate knife base fragments
I. microblades
J. slate angular tipped burin-like tool, base of nephrite burin-like tool, top-small angular tipped burin-like tool of nephrite and bottom-burin-like tool of quartz crystal
K. transverse edged scraper with ground and polished working edge
L. side scraper
M. end scrapers
N. biface fragment
O. slate rubbing tool

artifacts. Three of these burins are on random flakes and three are on bifacially flaked fragments. The rest constitute a unique type that does not appear earlier and remains in the continuum as a scarce element for only a century or two. The burin is small, more or less rectangular, bifacially polished on both distal faces, and bilaterally side notched. The working face was formed by removing a short burin spall. The scar left was then ground and polished but not so completely that concavity of the burin scar or the bulb of percussion were obliterated. The tool differs both from Pre-Dorset burins, on which the working face (or spall scar) was never polished, and from Dorset burin-like tools, on which the working surface though ground and polished was first formed by very steep flaking retouch. The greatest significance of this type is that a virtually identical artifact appears in, and is restricted to, the contemporaneous Groswater Dorset of Labrador (discussed in the following section). It also appears on the 24-m terrace of Igloolik at Kapuivik, which should date to around 700 B.C. Of the burin spalls recovered from the Killilugak site, 74% had been pressed from burins of this type and were modified for use as tools. Other traits more characteristic of Pre-Dorset are a higher ratio of trimming flakes to finished artifacts and a higher frequency of retouched flakes, including one pointed graver of Pre-Dorset type (15%, $n = 125$).

Traits more characteristic of Dorset are the introduction of nephrite for angular-tipped burin-like tools, an angular-tipped, crescentic burin-like tool of slate, a square-ended burin-like tool of quartz, triangular end blades (2 with tip fluting), and slate knives with sawed side notches. Fifteen of the stone artifacts recovered from the site were side-notched and corner-notched chert end blades. An additional 19 tip and median biface fragments are probably residue of such artifacts. Part of this relative frequency of 27% ($n = 125$) may be related to site function, but an increase in side notching is also a Dorset characteristic. The unfortunate absence of nonlithic tools led me initially (Maxwell 1973) to consider the site as being terminal Pre-Dorset, but it might equally be considered to lie at the beginning of the Dorset phase.

Traits from the 24-m terrace at Kapuivik, in addition to burins like those of Killilugak, are side-notched end blades, burin spalls and burin-spall tools, the first appearance of nephrite, a large needle or bodkin with a long, oval hole, a cut maskette similar to Dorset ones, and harpoon heads with open or flanged sockets· that appear to be antecedent to the Dorset Tyara Sliced harpoon heads. At approximately the same time, or perhaps somewhat later, an unusually large harpoon head (12 cm long and 4 cm wide) with a tranverse line hole and sliced socket appeared at Igloolik, the only place it has yet been found (Figure 5.17). This large head might have been needed in hunting beluga, which have soft skin that tears easily, and might indicate the beginning of a new resource exploitation. Later in Early Dorset the form becomes smaller and marks the beginning of a series of harpoon heads with tranverse line holes that continues until the end of the Dorset period.

On the coast of Labrador north of Nain increasing exploration has suggested a continuum of occupation from early Pre-Dorset to Early Dorset, if not of cultural complexes and culture bearers. Cox (1978) has divided this continuum into a number of segments: early Pre-Dorset from 1850 to 1550 B.C., late Pre-Dorset from 1550 to 1250 B.C., transitional or terminal Pre-Dorset from 1250 to 850 B.C., Groswater Dorset from 850 to 250 B.C., and Early Dorset from 550 to 50 B.C.

Early Pre-Dorset, reliably carbon dated between 1880 and 1525 B.C., appears to have been concentrated in the larger bay–fjord complexes of Saglek, Hebron, Okak, and Nain. The diagnostic traits and possible relations to Independence I have been discussed in the preceding. In late Pre-Dorset there was an addition of relatively large concave-based triangular end blades, parallel-stemmed end blades, and ground or notched burins. Edge serration of end blades dropped from the inventory.

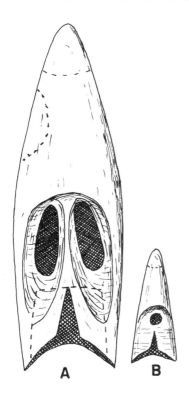

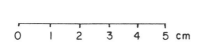

Figure 5.17 Early Dorset harpoon heads: (A) large head perhaps used for beluga hunting compared to (B) a typical Early Dorset harpoon head in the same scale. Some heads of this form have unilateral or bilateral side blade slots.

The most recent of the late Pre-Dorset sites, termed "terminal Pre-Dorset" by Cox (1978), is Nukasusutok 2 near Nain with a corrected carbon date of 880 B.C. (see Table 5.3). It is followed by Groswater Dorset, carbon dated from 770 to 250 B.C. In its most recent phases it overlaps, but is seen as different from, Early Dorset. Opinions differ over the issue of whether it developed out of an indigenous late Pre-Dorset or represents a new and distinct cultural complex entering the northern coast (Cox 1978; Fitzhugh 1972, 1976b, 1980; Jordan 1980; Tuck 1975, 1976).

Groswater Dorset

This complex in the transitional period has more reliable carbon dates based on the charcoal of indigenous trees. Their range overlaps Early Dorset, emphasizing the contention by Cox (1978), Fitzhugh (1972, 1976, 1980), and Jordan (1978) that there is a cultural difference between Groswater Dorset on the central Labrador coast and Early Dorset as it is manifested on the northern coast. Seven dates based on indigenous wood have been published for Groswater Dorset (Table 5.3). The earliest, 770 B.C.: 2720 ± 125 radiocarbon years (SI 930), at the Buxhall site, Fitzhugh considers too early because another carbon sample from a nearby hearth in the same site is dated 305 B.C.: 2255 ± 305 radiocarbon years (SI 931). I would be inclined to accept the earlier rather than the later date. Other dates range from 740 B.C. at Tikoralak 2 to 250 B.C. at Red Rock Point. Early Dorset theoretically has a carbon date of 895 B.C. at the Labrador site of Iluvektalik (Cox 1978), but this is earlier than anyone would currently consider the beginning of Dorset and most of the Early Dorset Labrador dates cluster around 500 B.C.

According to Fitzhugh there is a distinctive difference between late Groswater Dorset assemblages and contemporary Early Dorset ones (Figure 5.18). Groswater Dorset, with its greatest concentration around Hamilton Inlet, is characterized by

Figure 5.18 Groswater Dorset artifacts from the coastal Labrador sites of Tikoralak, Buxhall, and Postville (from Smithsonian Institution photographs, courtesy of William Fitzhugh).

A. burin with polished working surface
B. burin with polished face and working surface
C. box-based end blades
D. corner- and side-notched end blades

E. side blade
F. square-based end blade
G. microblade
H. whetstone
I. end scrapers

the type of spalled, then ground-and-polished burin described previously (called "spalled burin-like tools" by Fitzhugh). There are also burin-spall tools, a wide variety of side- and corner-notched end blades (including a distinctive box-based type), flared end scrapers, round and oval side blades, a high frequency of microblades, and a few fragments of oval soapstone lamps. At the Thalia Point 1 site (590 B.C.), nephrite appears for the first time, including a polished, side-notched nephrite knife and a fragment of the true square-ended, polished burin-like tool. At the Tikoralak 2 site a crescentic, polished, angular-tipped burin-like tool remarkably like the one from Killilugak was recovered (also see Cox 1978: Figure 2aa). In contrast to Early Dorset assemblages, there are few triangular end blades, and those recovered have none of the tip fluting characteristic of Labrador Dorset. None of the Groswater side-notched knives are multiple notched as in Early Dorset, and there are very rare fragments of slate knives. Other traits appearing in Early Dorset but not in Groswater Dorset are soapstone cooking pots, tabular burin-like tools of nephrite, and semi-subterranean dwellings.

In summary, I would see Groswater Dorset as uniquely similar to both Killulugak and the 24-m site at Kapuivik. On the other hand, several of the Labrador archaeologists consider cultural ties to be closer to Independence II, a supposition based in part on the presence in both of paved axial house features and box hearths. The linkage of discrete attributes among these widely dispersed sites implies shared information. But whether this can be attributed to diffusion of styles, migration of people, or commonality of economic activities cannot be answered at this time. Recognition of the distinctiveness of this variant is summarized in Fitzhugh's statement (1980:598) that Groswater Dorset is "an evolved Pre-Dorset form influenced by Dorset traits developing elsewhere but not ancestral to later Dorset development in Labrador."

Independence II

As we have discussed earlier, the Independence I people appear to have abandoned northern Greenland by about 1600 B.C. Their departure, or extinction, coincides with a prolonged cooling trend that probably bears a causal relation to the disappearance. Approximately 600–1000 years later the same region was reoccupied by people of what Knuth (1967a,b, 1968) has termed the "Independence II" culture. Initially Knuth located 8 settlements consisting of a total of 31 dwellings on Independence Fjord of northeastern Greenland and on Polaris Promontory of northwestern Greenland. Later he found two sites on northern Ellesmere Island, one on each of the eastern and western coasts. More recently, McGhee (1981b) and Sutherland (1981) have identified Independence II sites at Port Refuge on Devon Island and in the interior of northern Ellesmere Island, respectively.

Carbon dates currently available could be used to defend either of two competing interpretations. As is discussed in the following, many of the traits of Independence II are similar, if not identical, to those of the core area in a time of transition that should fall between 800 and 500 B.C. There are three carbon dates from the Engaes site (on indigenous Arctic willow): 1130 B.C. (K-1544), 1110 B.C. (K-1544), and 660

B.C. (K-1522). Two of these appear to be too early, but they would tend to support one hypothesis on the development of Dorset culture, that is, that certain traits first developed in the High Arctic and spread southward to the core area. A third willow date, from the Hellebaek site, is 560 B.C. (K-1059), and two dates on musk-ox bones from two other sites are both 420 B.C. (K-3360, K-3361); Knuth 1981). These latter three dates, according to some interpretations, would seem a century or two too recent. Alternatively they would support a second hypothesis that the transition into Dorset was a core area phenomenon that took a century to diffuse northward into the High Arctic where transitional traits persisted.

Other than site location, settlement type, and dwelling architecture there is little to link Independence II with Independence I. There is no discernible similarity between the lithic and nonlithic artifacts of the two periods other than the fact that both are part of a general, long-lived Paleoeskimo tradition. The similarity in sites, however, is striking and must indicate some nexus even though separated by 800–1000 years. In the Port Refuge–Porden Point vicinities of northwestern Devon Island, McGhee located 12 sites with a total of 50 dwellings (1981b). Here Independence II structures were on the same beaches as, although 6 m closer to sea level than, the earlier Pre-Dorset and still earlier Independence I dwellings. Like the Independence I components, but unlike the Pre-Dorset ones, the Independence II settlement type was one of linear, widely dispersed dwellings. Structures are of the familiar midpassage type, with parallel slabs of stone set vertically along the short axis of the house interior like Independence II houses from Greenland. The isolated stone box hearths of Independence I have now disappeared and are incorporated as one or two compartments within the midpassage. Usually, but not always, the midpassage runs at right angles to seacoasts, open ponds, or rivers. At the backs of some houses, presuming that the front faces the water, wings of stone slabs angle outward to provide additional storage areas against the back wall (Figure 5.19).

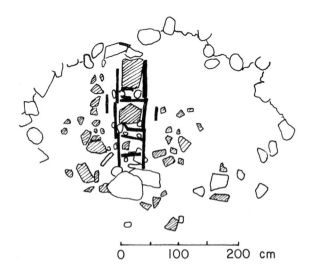

Figure 5.19 Independence II structure from Greenland: Hatched rocks are horizontal floor remnants and blacked-in rocks are the vertical parts of the midpassage (drawing based on illustration from Knuth 1967b).

0   100   200 cm

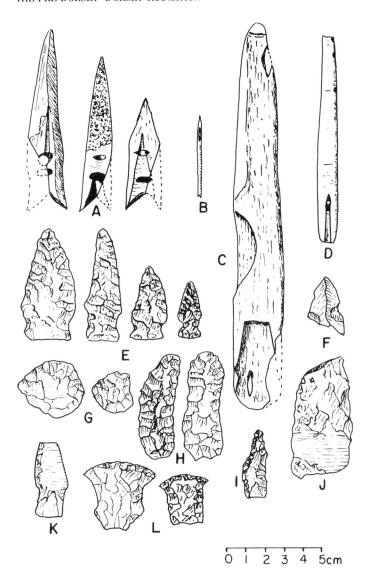

Figure 5.20 Independence II artifacts from Port Refuge, Devon Island (drawings based on selected illustrations from McGhee 1981b).

A. harpoon heads
B. needle
C. lance head with side blade slot
D. harpoon foreshaft
E. side- and corner-notched end blades
F. tip-fluted biface
G. side blades
H. bifaces
I. side scraper
J. polished adz
K. burin-like tool
L. end scrapers

Independence II artifacts bear closer typological relation to terminal Pre-Dorset, developing Dorset, or Early Dorset of the core area than to any preceding material yet reported from the High Arctic (Figures 5.20 and 5.21). Neither spalled burins nor spalled-and-polished ones of the Killilugak and Groswater Dorset type have been located, but there are 2 squared-ended burin-like tools and a third fragment, all perhaps unfinished, from the Port Refuge vicinity. Among the most characteristic lithic tools are a variety of side-notched end blades. When the 122 microblades are removed from the total Port Refuge lithic assemblage (*n* = 208), these notched

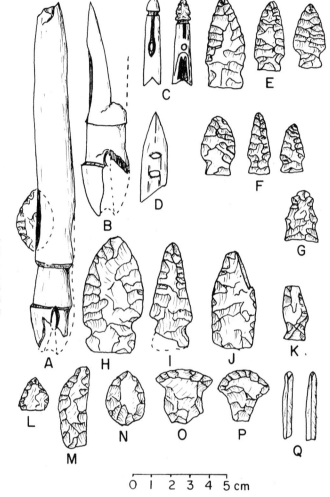

Figure 5.21 Artifacts attributed to the Independence II complex—A–C, H–J, L, Q, northeastern Greenland; D–G, K, M–P, Port Refuge (drawings based on selected illustrations from Knuth 1967b; McGhee 1976).

A,B. cloven-hoofed, side-bladed lance heads
C.   flanged-socket harpoon head with end blade
D.   pierced-socket harpoon head
E–I.   side-notched end blades
J.   burinated end blade
K.   unfinished burin-like tool
L–N. side blades
O,P.   end scrapers
Q.   microblades

blades, some perhaps knives but other undoubtedly tips for lances and slotted harpoon heads, constitute 33% of the remainder ($n = 86$). Presumably much the same relation is true of the Greenlandic assemblages, where the artifacts are somewhat larger, perhaps because of better sources of raw material. This emphasis on notched points tends to link Independence II with Killilugak and Groswater Dorset, but to set the three apart from both earlier Pre-Dorset and the earliest Dorset. For example, at the Loon site, with a corrected date of 1162 B.C., side- and corner-notched end blades constitute only 3% when microblades and burin spalls are removed from consideration ($n = 284$). This frequency increases only slightly in subsequent Pre-Dorset sites. It jumps to 27% at the Killilugak site ($n = 125$), but drops to 6% in the developed Early Dorset Tanfield/Morrisson site ($n = 3832$), which should date generally to a 500–400 B.C. period.

Oval or disk-shaped side blades are common to the three transitional components, but there are also distinctive trait variations. Triangular, straight-based end blades, common in earlier Paleoeskimo and later in Dorset in both the High and Low Arctic, are missing from Independence II. They appear to be rare or absent in Groswater Dorset (end blades in Fitzhugh 1976:Figure 4e, m and Cox 1978:Figure 4t although not so labeled appear to be of this type) but present in Killilugak. Tip fluting of end blades is present at Port Refuge (one specimen) and at Killilugak (two of six artifacts) but absent in Groswater Dorset. Both Independence II and Groswater Dorset have flaring end scrapers and fragments of round-to-oval soapstone vessels, but Killilugak has neither trait.

Antler, bone, and ivory artifacts in Independence II most closely resemble those from Igloolik at Kapuivik on the 24-m terrace and Alarnerk on the 23-m terrace. Both Greenlandic and Port Refuge sites have produced side-bladed lance heads and needles that are sharpened at both ends and have elongate eyes. A harpoon head from Greenland (see Figure 5.21C) is slotted for a notched end blade and has a flanged, partially open socket similar to Meldgaard's (1977) Type A-11. The three harpoon heads from Port Refuge are of Type A-12 (McGhee 1981b:22), with sockets that are essentially closed but have holes pierced through the dorsal surface.

Summarizing the Transition

Available carbon dates suggest that some form of cultural change was taking place in the Eastern Arctic between 800 or 700 and 500 B.C. We have discussed in the preceding the empirical data for this change, but there is also an impressionistic dimension that should not be ignored. The researchers who have worked in sites of this period all have expressed varying impressions of the difference between these sites and both of what preceded and of what followed this period. Meldgaard (personal communication, 1977) once used the term "stressed" for the populations living on the beaches between 24 and 22 m above present sea level at Igloolik. He admits the subjective nature of this term but considers it apt in reference to what appears to be a rapid sequence of styles and experimentation. McGhee (1981b:38) postulates a population decline of Arctic Small Tool tradition people in both Alaska and the Eastern Arctic between about 1000 B.C. and a population expansion of Early Dorset. Fitzhugh (1976a) suggests it was a time of population response to dwindling caribou herds in Quebec. Elsewhere (Maxwell 1980) I have been inclined to think of the transition as an interregnum between two lifeways that were both in states of relative equilibrium.

My 400-km survey of the seacoast on southeastern Baffin Island tends to support both a decline in population and a decrease in relative sedentism in this period. In contrast to the many Dorset and Pre-Dorset sites our field crew has located, only the short-term Killilugak site near Lake Harbour and a small artifact and débitage cluster at Markham Bay, apparently a caribou lookout station, can be attributed to this period. While there is a greater cluster of Independence II sites on northwestern Devon Island and in northeastern Greenland and a concentration of Groswater Dorset around Hamilton Inlet, both McGhee (1981) and Fitzhugh (1980) see these as transitory camps.

Neither paleoecological evidence nor understanding of animal response to climatic change are sufficiently precise to define the type of change taking place. As stated before (see Barry *et al.* 1977), a general cooling period in the Eastern Arctic after the Thermal Maximum culminated in extremely cold winters around 600 B.C. However, this trend was briefly broken by a warm spell between about 1200 and 800 B.C. The latter century of this relatively warm episode coincides with the reentry of people into the northern Arctic, an occupation that was presumably abandoned in the increasing cold of the fifteenth and sixteenth centuries B.C. On the other hand, the cultural transition we are examining may be a response to the long-term progression of colder winters.

The effects of warmer or colder seasons on the marine and terrestrial animals so critical to this hunting culture should provide significant clues to this problem. Unfortunately, the ecological response of seal and caribou can be modeled four different ways. For example, warmer winters may place less stress on caribou calves, leading to herd increase, but, conversely, they may result in more snow cover, less available forage, and herd reduction. Spring icing, particularly in the sub-Arctic and under foehn conditions in Greenland, is especially critical for caribou as are ice thickness and extent for seal (these factors and their effects are discussed in detail in Arundale 1976, Dekin 1975, and Fitzhugh 1976a). The strongest suggestion that this brief warming episode reduced caribou populations comes from the barrens of Keewatin where this was a period of fires and forest-edge fluctuations that certainly must have affected caribou behavior and mortality.

It may not be necessary to decide whether seal and caribou waxed or waned in response to cold or warmth but simply to state that it was a time of instability for both animals and climate. For humans, the old traditional hunting techniques and magic might no longer result in adequate levels of success. A rebalancing of the disturbed equilibrium required some specific response undoubtedly compounded of both technology and ideology.

The nature of this response, to return to Meldgaard's (1977) impression, was one of experimentation. Both Pre-Dorset and Dorset economies were dualistic, depending in the main on both caribou and seal. However, there is a general impression that caribou hunting may have been more important in Pre-Dorset and that sealing had preeminence in Dorset. In the transition period the bow and arrow, useful in stalk hunting, disappears. None of the end blades yet recovered from Independence II sites or from other sites dating to this period, are light enough to have tipped arrows propelled by weak driftwood bows. Alternatively, such arrow tips are frequent in earlier Pre-Dorset sites. A possible explanation for the disappearance of this useful weapon, and its total absence throughout Dorset, is a change in the manner of caribou hunting. Instead of stalking within bow and arrow range, it now became feasible to drive the animals into open lakes where they could be speared with lances tipped with notched stone points. In time, as caribou herds dwindled and migratory patterns changed, this strategy, coupled with a less than adequate technology for extensive sea mammal hunting, became insufficient. The ultimate response was the development or improvement of sea ice hunting techniques as increasing cold extended the range and duration of winter ice. This new economy, geared to climates colder than ever before, enabled the return to a new dynamic equilibrium that we refer to as Dorset.

In this summary it remains only to define Dorset in terms of a trait list that will serve to distinguish it from what has gone before. Whether this collection of traits has its inception somewhere within the core area or whether it represents a coalescence of experiments in several different regions cannot be determined now. Regardless of where it first developed, the following characteristic elements serve to define its first appearance, nearly simultaneously, in widely dispersed locales: (1) rectangular semisubterranean dwellings, (2) a marked increase in triangular projectile points (predominantly for sealing), often with fluting at the distal tips, (3) an extensive ground-slate industry, including knives that are multiply notched, (4) multiple-notched chert end blades, (5) rectangular soapstone vessels, (6) an increase in two distinct forms of burin-like tools, (7) an increase in the use of nephrite, quartz crystal, and other scarce stone resources, (8) the appearance of two distinctive harpoon head types, Tyara Sliced and Dorset Parallel Sliced, (9) broad sled shoes and sled models, (10) ice creepers, (11) snow knives, (12) a rich, presumably magic-related art, and (13) the complete disappearance of such useful artifacts as the drill and bow and arrow.

While many early Dorset sites may lack some of these traits, significant parts of the assemblage are distinctive in Eastern Arctic prehistory. In some locales, such as northern and southern Baffin Island and the mouth of Hudson Bay, these traits are combined with others, particularly fabricating tools, retained from the earlier Pre-Dorset technology. This is particularly clear in the case of the Avinga site, which can only be interpreted as an Early Dorset occupation that was settled in the cooling period immediately before the onset of permafrost.

The Avinga Site

The site, in Tanfield Valley 26 km southeast of Lake Harbour, lies at an elevation of 8.5–9 m above present high tide. In 1962 it was briefly tested; then in 1963 it was sectioned with a test trench 3 by $4\frac{1}{2}$ m. At that time, it was thought to lie typologically between the Pre-Dorset Loon site at 15 m above sea level and the Early Dorset Tanfield site at 7 m above sea level (Maxwell 1973a). In 1976 our field crew returned to the site and excavated three additional $1\frac{1}{2}$- by $1\frac{1}{2}$-m squares. In the original set of excavations, I had interpreted the occupation as having shortly preceded the onset of permafrost. The later excavations added additional information to confirm this. Three Early, and Early-to-Middle Dorset sites (Tanfield/Morrisson, Kemp, and Kakela) lie within 30–150 m of Avinga within the same valley. Kemp, in

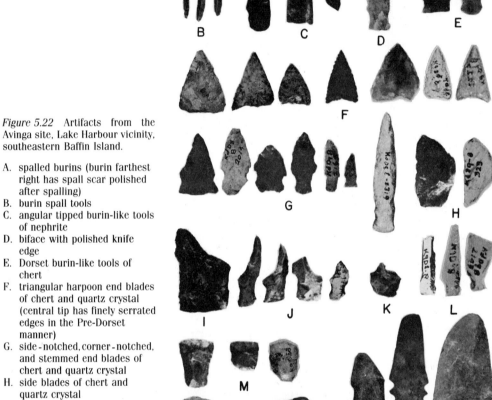

Figure 5.22 Artifacts from the Avinga site, Lake Harbour vicinity, southeastern Baffin Island.

A. spalled burins (burin farthest right has spall scar polished after spalling)
B. burin spall tools
C. angular tipped burin-like tools of nephrite
D. biface with polished knife edge
E. Dorset burin-like tools of chert
F. triangular harpoon end blades of chert and quartz crystal (central tip has finely serrated edges in the Pre-Dorset manner)
G. side-notched, corner-notched, and stemmed end blades of chert and quartz crystal
H. side blades of chert and quartz crystal
I. transverse-edged scraper
J. concave side scrapers of chert and quartz crystal
K. retouched flake with graver tip
L. quartz crystal microblades
M. end scrapers of chert and quartz crystal
N. slate knives
O. abrading stone

particular, within 0.5 m of the same elevation is subject to the same degree of eastward drainage. Yet in these three sites, ranging from about 450 B.C. to the beginning of the Christian era, all organic material from wood to feathers has been preserved in permafrost beneath the active layer. Conversely, there is no preserved organic material other than a few cinders of seal fat in the well-insulated Avinga midden. I concluded from this that while the site typologically must have been occupied sometime after the Killilugak site, it also must have been occupied before the local beginning of permafrost in about 500 B.C.

In earlier excavation I felt that there were indications of vertical drainage through the midden but that if this had been the case there should have been water sorting of such tiny objects as burin spalls, which would have concentrated them at the bottom of the midden. Since this appeared not to be the case (Maxwell 1973a:111), I concluded that the site had initially been a camp on the sandy beach. The 1976 excavation demonstrated that this conclusion was simply the result of the recovery techniques employed. In the earlier years, working through the thawing black mud with trowels and screening the residue under water, our field crew had recovered 40 burin spalls (of 445 total artifacts). In 1976 after the midden had long thawed, drained, and dried, the crew recovered 134 burin spalls (of 370 total artifacts). In other words, the recovery in 1976 was $67/m^3$ versus $5/m^3$ in the earlier excavation. Of these 1976 burin spalls, most modified for use as tools, 68% ($n = 91$) were recovered from within 1 cm of the interface between black midden and sterile yellow sand. The implication is that for a significant period of time water had seeped down through the unfrozen soil above. Additionally, the field crew found in 1976 that there were at least two and perhaps three shallow pit houses on the site. From profiles it was apparent that these had been dug down 15–16 cm below the surface and bordered with rocks. Three hearth areas, presumably in corners of the house pits, were little more than piles of rocks for supporting either oil lamps or chunks of flaming blubber.

Most of the artifacts from the site are indistinguishable from others of the same classes in Early Dorset sites (see Table 5.2). In particular, the nephrite angular-tipped burin-like tools, frequent slate knives with multiple-sawed notches, triangular harpoon end blades, and rectangular soapstone lamps or bowls with square corners are distinctively Early Dorset. But there are also vestigial traits of Pre-Dorset, for instance the frequent use of burin-spall tools, which is absent in Dorset sites. Quartz and quartz crystal has not yet supplanted chert as the major source for many tools as it has in Dorset sites on southeastern Baffin Island, and spalled burins, including two of the distinctive Killilugak type, are more numerous than in most southeast Baffin Dorset sites (Figure 5.22).

To add, then, to our interpretation of the transitional period as discussed in the preceding, there appears to have been a short period, certainly no more than a century and perhaps much less, in which the Dorset adaptive system was well underway. This began before winters became so cold that a wooden-handled knife dropped on the summer ground and covered by winter snow would remain preserved in ice for two and one-half millennia.

6

The Dorset Culture:
Categories of Dorset Activity

INTRODUCTION

The cultural traces Dorset people have left behind have a fascinating, emotional, effect on many of us. Artists and those who appreciate art are intrigued by the skill of their carvers. Tiny ivory animals are so naturalistic and perfectly proportioned that they can appear monumental when photographically enlarged. On a single carving, naturalistic replication may be combined with symbolism and deep magical significance. A complete animal fragment may stand for the whole, as when a lower jaw or split hoof signifies the complete caribou, and some of the human figurines and maskettes seem surely to have been portraits of real people.

To the archaeologist digging in the permafrost, where virtually everything is preserved, there is the frustrating feeling of being almost but not quite capable of understanding the totality of the material culture. Every artifact is made precisely, a point that increases our embarrassment in being unable to determine function. There are numerous small wooden pieces that must have been bound into complex handles or other objects but that may never be identified. Particularly impressive is the ability of these people to live in balance with their environment with such small weapons and without equipment that both earlier and later people found essential for life in the Arctic. Anthropological terms such as "tightly constrained behavior" and "compulsive standardization" have been applied to Dorset people as interpretations of what appear to have been selective food harvesting techniques and widespread standardization of styles.

Modern Inuit fascination is seen in myths and legends, some of which undoubtedly have a thread of oral tradition that stems from ancestral contact. The term "Tunnit" as used today refers to people of the legendary past. In various regions it has been used to apply to the Thule people of 400–500 years ago or even to the Sadlermiut, who died out near the turn of the twentieth century. But many of the stories that are told must relate to the Dorset people. Some of these legends derive authenticity from archaeological evidence. They are said to be dwarfs, or giants, with prodigious strength, and there are a few Dorset tent rings that bear this out. I once excavated such a site on an outwash plain of northern Ellesmere Island. The tent ring, which contained Dorset stone tools, was barely 2 m in diameter, yet the huge boulders that formed the walls ranged from 100 to 200 kg. Each of these rocks had been dragged from several hundred meters away (Maxwell 1960a). According to the stories, the Tunnit, since they had no sled dogs, used this prodigious strength to drag killed walrus home using only a small single-man sled. (The archaeological evidence is that among the Dorset, dogs were very scarce and only small hand-drawn sleds were used.) They loved their wives dearly and dragging such a 500-kg weight at the end of the day seemed child's play, so anxious were they to return to their wives. When they went breathing hole hunting they took their small soapstone lamps (many Dorset lamps are very small), set them burning under their parkas, and then pinned the skirts of the parkas to the snow. When seal appeared, they jumped up in excitement and consequently spilled burning oil over their stomachs. As a result, most of the men's stomachs were scalded and scarred. At night they did not sleep on broad sleeping platforms as the Inuit do, but crawled into little semi-subterranean houses where they slept on narrow benches with their legs extended up the side walls higher than their heads.

One of the more intriguing aspects of Dorset behavior I can only attribute to some ideational constraint: Except for some very late Dorset artifacts, there are no drilled holes in any material through nearly 1000 years of Dorset technology. All holes in hard materials were laboriously scratched in. To the naked eye some of the harpoon head line holes appear round, as they would have to be if made with a drill, but under magnification it is clear that they are not round. This is particularly surprising since the drill is such a useful tool for working bone, antler, and ivory. Both stone drill bits and drilled holes, even in tiny needles, are common in Pre-Dorset although the nature of the drill itself is unclear. In the Thule and Historic periods, the bow drill, with which the drill socket is held between the teeth, was clearly the preeminent fabricating tool. Long foreshafts of ivory, for instance, were cut from a walrus tusk by parallel series of barely touching drilled holes and then broken from the tusk. Of thousands of Dorset artifacts, however, I know of none in which a hole was reamed round by a hand-held sliver of stone twisted for 360°.

Without dogs to drag sleds across the sea ice, without bows and arrows or throwing boards to project harpoon, darts, and lances, without cold-trap tunnel entrances to their winter pit houses, without whale hunting gear or floats for summer kayak sealing, and with only tiny lamps and weapons, the Dorset people, as Meldgaard (1962) originally said, appear to be even less well adapted to Arctic living than their predecessors. Yet there is adequate evidence from Dorset middens that they were remarkably efficient in converting natural resources to human energy. Their dwelling sites attest to a level of adaptive response sufficiently high to allow them even to be selective in their choices of available game.

HUNTING AND FISHING

Obviously, the prime Dorset economic activity was hunting. More than 90% of traditional Inuit food energy came from game animals, clams, and mussels. Among the modern Inuit, wild meat plays the dominant role (Kemp 1971). Consequently, it is logical to assume an equal importance of meat in the Dorset diet. On the other hand, the role of gathered plant foods, rich in some vitamins and minerals scarce or lacking in meat, has probably been underplayed. Today, in season, various species of berries are gathered in buckets and brought back to the tent. The stomach content of caribou, a partially digested salad of lichens rich in carbohydrates, is frequently consumed. But there is also an unmeasured amount of snacking on the leaves of young willow (*Salix* sp.), the flowers and leaves of fireweed (*Epilobium* sp.) and the leaves of sorrel (*Oxyria* sp.), all of which have high concentrations of vitamin C. Various species of edible seaweed are good sources of iron and other minerals. Although we will never have archaeological evidence for Dorset use of these nutritional plant resources, it is a logical presumption that these people did utilize them.

These additions, however, would have been minor compared to the variety of animals killed by Dorset hunters. Middens contain remains of caribou, musk-ox, polar bear, and other inland mammals, birds, varieties of seal, walrus, narwhal, and beluga (see Tables 6.1 and 6.2). To simply list these animals, however, glosses over amazing feats of human skill and endurance. Hunting polar bear with trained dogs and a high-powered rifle, or walrus from a wooden schooner, exposes one to a certain amount of danger. It was more dangerous still in the pre–rifle hunting days when walrus were pursued by a crew of harpooners from a large umiak. But to hunt these dangerous animals without dogs or large boats and within the force range of a man's arm—20 m at best—is incredible.

Land animals, excluding the polar bear, which is more marine than terrestrial, would have been less dangerous. Rogue musk-ox, young males driven from the herd, can be very dangerous. Otherwise, in herds, the musk-ox is genetically programed for defense against wolves, their natural predators. When threatened they form an

Table 6.1

ANIMAL REMAINS FREQUENTLY APPEARING IN DORSET MIDDENS

More Common Mammals	Less Common Mammals
Ringed seal (*Phoca hispida*)	Grey seal (*Halicherus grypus*)
Harbor seal (*Phoca vitulina*)	Beluga (*Delphinapterus leucas*)
Harp seal (*Phoca groenlandica*)	Narwhal (*Monodon monoceros*)
Bearded seal (*Erignathous barbatus*)	Arctic fox (*Alopex lagopus*)
Walrus (*Odobenus rosmarus*)	Arctic hare (*Lepus arcticus*)
Caribou (*Rangifer tarandus*)	Arctic wolf (*Canis lupus*)
Musk-ox (*Ovibus moschatus*)	Common Fish
Polar bear (*Thalarctos maritimus*)	Arctic char (*Salvelinus alpinus*)
	Lake trout (*Salvelinus namaycush*)

Table 6.2

Bird Bone Elements from the Nanook Site[a]

Species	No. of bone elements
Thick-billed murre (*Uria lomvia*)	398
Black guillemot (*Cepphus grylle*)	79
Dovekie (*Plautus alle*)	52
King eider (*Somateria spectabilis*)	43
Unidentified alcids	36
Common eider (*Somateria mollissima*)	28
Glaucous gull (*Larus hyperboreus*)	20
Unidentified duck	8
Iceland gull (*Larus glaucoides*)	2
Common loon (*Gavia immer*)	2
Common puffin (*Fratercula arcticus*)	2
Purple sandpiper (*Erolia maritima*)	1
Rock ptarmigan (*Lagopus mutus*)	1
Willow ptarmigan (*Lagopus lagopus*)	1

[a]Data from Arundale 1976.

arc, or even a square, with horn bosses and curving horn tips facing out. Females and calves stand behind the defense line with one or two dominant bulls at the edges of the line. If a human approaches the herd, a bull will paw the tundra, rub his nose against his foreleg, snort, and finally charge straight ahead. Often one can simply move right or left at the proper moment and the charging bull will pass by to stop and graze. With such moves a human may often approach to within 10 m of the herd. Small wonder that many Arctic explorers have suggested that hunters living on musk-ox would quickly exhaust their source of food.

Polar bears, the only carnivors in North America that will stalk and kill humans for food, could only have been occasional and perhaps unexpected targets for Dorset hunters. Standing 2–3 m tall, these powerful beasts could flick a lance from the strongest man's arms with a twitch of a forepaw. It is hard to believe that Dorset hunters could have killed them unless four or five men, surrounding the rearing giant, dashed in from time to time, sunk their lances deep, and finally exhausted the animal from blood loss. It is certain from their magical art that they did not take the polar bear lightly, but most midden remains indicate that they did kill at least a few with their seemingly insufficient weapons.

Walrus hunting in the open water is equally dangerous. These powerful animals, unlike humans in boats, are capable of moving in horizontal and vertical dimensions. They are fiercely protective of others in the herd. When cows and calves are threatened they do not hesitate to attack even the largest boats. Adults often return to assist and defend a wounded member of their herd. Hunting at a hauling-out place on shore or on a floating ice pan is somewhat safer. But even here there is danger. Hunters approaching a herd on floating ice must be certain that the pan is large enough since the weight of stampeding walrus may be enough to overturn the pan, throwing hunters into the icy water. Small wonder that walrusing is surrounded by a complex of propitiatory behavior on the part of the hunters (Nelson 1969:362).

Our knowledge of Dorset technology and evidence for only kayak-sized boats (Mary-Rousselière 1979a) has led many of us to assume that hunting the 40-ton bowhead baleen whale was beyond Dorset capability. Whalebone sled shoes, which appear in several Early Dorset sites, could be the result of fortunate accident in finding a dead whale beached on shore. All of the whalebone recovered to date from Dorset sites, conceivably could have come from a single skeleton, with fragments traded from place to place. However in some sites such as Nanook near Lake Harbour (Arundale 1976; Maxwell 1973) and those near Pond Inlet (Mary-Rousselière 1976), impressively large sheets of baleen and whalebone detritus raise the question of whether Dorset hunters may not have occasionally attacked these giants. In Mary-Rousselière's judgment (1979a), they would have been easier and safer to hunt than the walrus, which Dorset hunters took in significant numbers. Beluga, which often migrate in large pods to the very ends of narrow bays and along the floe edge were also probably hunted, although their bones are seldom found in Dorset sites. This may have been because this large animal is usually butchered on shore at high tide or on a shelf of fast ice and only the meat is carried back to the settlement.

The only complete list of birds from a Dorset midden comes from the Nanook site occupied for half a millennium before the Christian era (Arundale 1976; see Table 6.2). Notably absent from this list are the Canada goose (*Branta canadensis*), the Snow goose (*Chen hyperborea*), and several species of ducks, other than eider duck, known to breed in the vicinity of the site. This appears to be true as well for other Dorset sites where reported geese and duck bones are rare to absent. In part this may well be reflective of the technology. Without bolas, bird spears, throwing boards, or bows and arrows, Dorset people would be limited in avian hunting. However, during the molt toward the end of July, geese can be chased and captured. Occasionally today, Inuit will capture one or two, tie them to a post inside the tent, and fatten them for later eating. There is no indication that this may have been done in Dorset time. Another bird that one might expect in greater frequency, since it can be captured without weapons is the ptarmigan. (An exception to the preceding statement is the Lagoon site [Arnold 1980], where two species of geese and ptarmigan were common.)

In Arundale's list (Table 6.2), it is significant that bird bone elements appearing with greatest frequency come from birds that nest in great numbers in local rookeries. Of the 692 bone elements Arundale was able to identify from the Nanook and the Early Dorset Morrison site (*n* = 1040), 85% (*n* = 589) come from such rookery birds as murres, guillemots, dovekies, puffins, and gulls. Although eggshells are not preserved in this site, the birds were probably taken while nesting and the eggs were undoubtedly collected. The most profitable manner of snaring the birds would be with nets on the ends of long poles. While there is no direct evidence of such nets in the Nanook site, a number of pieces of musk-ox wool yarn recovered from the midden might well be elements of such nets. The relative frequency of eider duck bones suggests that these also may have been taken with nets while the female was on the nest because they are reluctant to leave the nest while incubating. Eider duck eggs constitute a significant part of the diet of modern Inuit in the vicinity and must have been used by Dorset as well.

In comparison with the preceding, a large sample of bird bones from northern Labrador sites contains a predominance of offshore shear waters, fulmars (Cox and Spiess 1980), and even an extinct great auk (Jordan and Olson 1982).

Although much additional research on the issue is needed, current evidence suggests that Dorset hunters were highly selective in the scheduling of their hunting activities. The faunal residue in a number of sites indicates an emphasis not only on certain species when they are most abundant, but also on specific age sets of certain species when they can be taken in greatest numbers. It appears to have been a carefully timed regime in which the maximum amount of meat could be harvested with the minimum amount of time and energy spent hunting. While this would appear to be the sort of pragmatic response one would logically expect from a hunting group, it does appear to differ significantly from the later Thule exploitation of the same ecosystem. A wider variety of species in greater numbers were taken by the latter. A possible explanation for this is that with the greater hunting range provided by the dogsled and umiak, Thule hunters were able to take advantage of more targets of opportunity. It may also be that the Dorset scheduling system, which required being in specific locales within tight time frames, was a contributing factor to Dorset collapse when upset by intruding Thule hunters.

Sea Mammal Hunting

In Thule and traditional Inuit there was a variety of harpoons and harpoon darts for throwing, thrusting, and projecting with a throwing board. Among these it is possible to distinguish between those used for open-water hunting and those for thrusting through breathing holes in the sea ice. Currently there appears to have been only one type of Dorset harpoon, although there is wide variety in the types of harpoon heads (Maxwell 1974–1975). Its form is such that it could have been used at breathing holes as well as at the floe edge or in the open sea. The Dorset harpoon does not have the toggling flexibility that the Thule one does. In the latter, a bone or ivory foreshaft, bound through drilled holes in the socket, fits loosely and is able to move laterally within the socket (see Figure 8.13). When the harpoon head pierces an animal, the foreshaft bends to one side and the head, fastened to the line, slips off easily. The harpoon line, which has been held tightly to the shaft with a drilled tension piece fitted over a peg on the shaft, now slips off the peg and the weapon disarticulates with only the harpoon head and line attached to the animal. Mechanics of the Dorset harpoon are somewhat different (Figure 6.1). The foreshaft, a long, flat piece cut from caribou leg bone, is tied to the scarfed distal end of the wooden shaft. The foreshaft is bent by steaming so that the harpoon head is brought into the thrusting axis of the shaft. The harpoon line is then pulled tightly against the distal end of the shaft and wedged into a small split in the shaft. When the animal is

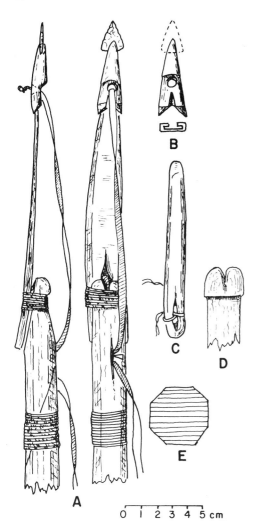

Figure 6.1 Replica of Early Dorset harpoon made with stone burins, burin-like tools, and side and end scrapers (based on artifacts recovered from the Tanfield site, Lake Harbour).
A. assembled harpoon
B. harpoon head with sliced socket
C. caribou tibia foreshaft
D. knobbed end of harpoon shaft
E. octagonal cross section of harpoon shaft

pierced, the foreshaft slides backward along the 25° angle of the scarfed shaft, the head slips off, and the line pulls free from the split in the shaft. Although this weapon could be thrown or thrusted, its mechanics are such that using it in a thrusting manner would be more effective.

A number of wooden harpoon shaft fragments have been recovered from Dorset sites near Lake Harbour. These range in diameter from 1 to 3 cm, with the majority clustering around 2 cm. The shafts were built up of driftwood fragments, joined by simple scarfing, and had knobbed heads at the distal end for binding the foreshaft. They were then adzed and whittled to an octagonal cross section, making them easier to grip with mittened hands. These shafts, particularly those between 2.5 and 3 cm in diameter, would have been equally effective as lances rather than harpoons.

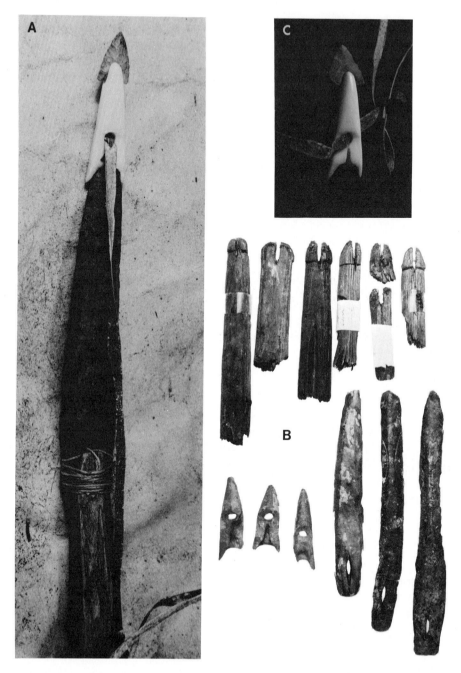

Figure 6.2 Dorset harpoon fragments: A, reconstructed harpoon with wooden shaft, caribou leg bone foreshaft, ivory head, and chert tip; B, three foreshafts of caribou leg bone and antler, six wooden shaft ends, and three harpoon heads of Tyara Sliced type (all from the Early Dorset Tanfield site); C, walrus ivory harpoon head carved with stone burin, burin-like tools, and end and side scrapers (actual size 4.5 cm).

Since the long, caribou leg bone foreshaft is the most common one in Dorset sites and since the distal ends of these foreshafts will fit sockets of both harpoon heads and lance heads, the same shafts, with interchangeable heads, were probably used for both marine and terrestrial hunting (Figure 6.2).

A second type of foreshaft, rare in Early Dorset sites and more common in later Dorset ones, is a small rectangle of ivory (Figure 7.8E). These, scarfed at the proximal ends, would fit on the scarfed ends of the smaller shafts and would be effective only with thrown harpoons. Their increasing frequency in later sites suggests an increase in summer hunting from kayaks on open water.

Harpoon heads were carved from antler, ivory, and occasionally hard driftwood. Fortunately, for typological dating, they differ stylisticly through time, with similar stylistic treatment appearing nearly simultaneously in widely dispersed sites (Figure 6.3). The more noticeable change through time is in the shape of the socket. In early Pre-Dorset, the heads have open sockets in which the foreshafts are held in place by a tight binding passing over the surface of the foreshaft. Foreshafts on such heads could slip easily from the socket and there would be little chance of breakage of the socket walls. By late Pre-Dorset the socket was essentially a closed one with only a small triangular slice on the dorsal surface of the socket. Carving the small socket on the end of a thin harpoon head was obviously more labor intensive than carving an open socket; the small slice has no apparent function, and the increased chance of breakage is obvious from the recovered heads with broken dorsal socket walls. By about 300 B.C. the socket becomes completely closed; then by about A.D. 500 open sockets reappear although the closed socket is retained for certain types.

Paralleling this shift, there are temporal variations in the shape of the dorsal groove proximal to the line hole; in the increasing sharpness of the basal spurs; and in a trend from single line holes, to double line holes that pass from dorsal to ventral surfaces, and finally to asymmetrically placed single line holes close to one lateral edge. Within the trend line of harpoon heads just mentioned, the distal ends may be sharpened and self-bladed or slotted for stone end blades. Since stylistic attributes vary coterminously on both forms, there appears to be little significant difference between self-bladed and stone-bladed forms.

A second harpoon type (Dorset Parallel Sliced in Early Dorset and Dorset Parallel in Middle and Late Dorset) is always slotted for an end blade. It is nearly twice the size of the heads just described and has a transverse line hole parallel to the socket (see Figure 7.1E). A heavy line could be passed through these holes and knotted in front. These heads, presumably for hunting larger seal and walrus, go through some of the same stylistic variations as the contemporaneous ones described previously. Early ones have the small slice in the dorsal wall of the socket and then become closed socketed until the end of Dorset. Through time, they become longer and narrower and the basal spurs become sharper. The chert or quartz-crystal end blades for these and other stone-tipped heads go through similar style shifts, from straight-based triangles with relatively straight lateral margins to forms with deeply incurving bases and delicately serrated edges.

There is little direct or indirect evidence to indicate specific techniques of Dorset sea mammal hunting. The location of many Dorset sites near extensive areas of fast

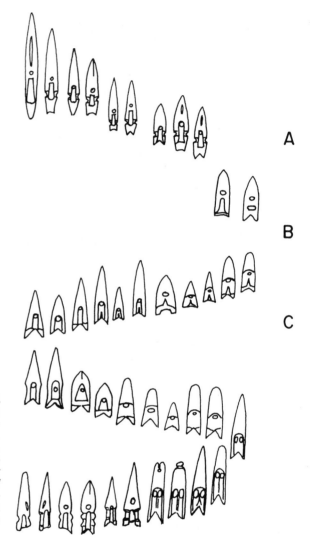

Figure 6.3 Schematic development of seal hunting harpoon heads from (A) Pre-Dorset through (B) a transitional phase to (C) Terminal Dorset. Socket forms change from being open, to widely flanged, to perforated, to narrowly flanged, to closed, and finally return to being open toward the end of Dorset. Line holes are single and centrally placed until Late Dorset when double line holes and asymmetric line holes appear.

ice and polynias suggest the importance of sea ice hunting. This is supported by such artifacts as antler and ivory snow knives for snowhouse building (Figure 6.4), ice creepers for boots, whalebone and ivory sled shoes, model sleds, bear bone ice chisels, and antler ice scoops. The chisels and ice scoops (Mary-Rousselière 1976) suggest breathing-hole hunting for ring seal. The others could be used equally well at the productive *sina* (floe edge).

Open-water hunting may have been more rare. Kemp (1976) has suggested that it was less commonly practiced by traditional Inuit prior to the use of guns and power boats. The Dorset harpoon appears less functional for open-water hunting than for

Figure 6.4 Equipment for hunting on the sea ice: (A) ivory snow knife from the Igloolik region, and (B) antler snow knife from the Late Dorset Talaguak site.

use along the *sina* and at breathing holes. Furthermore no float equipment such as was used in later periods has been recovered from Dorset sites. Nevertheless, young seal, who frequently sleep on the surface of the water, may have been hunted from kayaks. Several wooden artifacts have been identified as toy kayaks. In sites on Navy Board Inlet, Mary-Rousselière (1979a) found what appear to be kayak ribs and a bow piece. Near Lake Harbour in the Nanook and Tanfield/Morrisson sites, our field crew recovered 13 peculiar rectangular wooden planks morticed for 2 rectangular wooden elements (Figure 6.5). Since they appear to be graduated in length we interpreted them as kayak thwarts. This evidence all suggests that Dorset kayaks were close in shape to those of traditional Inuit.

Figure 6.5 One of several wooden pieces graduated in size and interpreted as kayak parts, Early Dorset Tanfield/Morrisson site.

Terrestrial Hunting

There is adequate evidence in Dorset middens of the economic importance of caribou. In fact, some sites such as Nunguvik on Navy Board Inlet and the Ekalluk Lake sites on southern Victoria Island have a predominance of caribou bone. Some Dorset settlements are located along the northward spring migration from the mainland taiga. In at least one instance Dorset hunters pushed 140 km south into the interior at Payne Lake for caribou hunting (Taylor 1958). Other settlements, such as those along the southern coast of Baffin Island, had access only to a resident herd that wintered in highland valleys and moved to the coast and to the eastern part of Nettling Lake from late April to late September. Late summer and early fall are the best times for taking these animals. Earlier, the meat is lean and the skins riddled by warble fly larvae, and later, the hair becomes too thick for winter clothing.

Since the only apparent weapon for caribou hunting was the thrusting lance, it seems likely that hunters could have been effective only by dealing with herds of some numbers rather than by stalking individual animals. By ethnological analogy, they may have used two methods: (1) the *inuksuk* drive, in which converging rows of man-shaped piles of rock, often topped with moss to resemble hair, conceal men, women, and children. While young men run upwind of the herd, drive the caribou toward the rock rows, and panic them by shouting and flapping skins, thus allowing them to be slaughtered by lances; and (2) a method in which a narrow spit of land at a customary crossing place is selected, and the animals are driven into the water and speared by kayakers using either lances or harpoons. The best direct evidence of Dorset use of *inuksuit* comes from Williams Harbour, Labrador (Figure 6.6; Fitzhugh 1981–1982). A number of *inuksuit* near the Ekalluk sites (Taylor 1967) may also have stood since Dorset times.

The caribou lance shaft was a larger version of the one used for harpoons. The head, usually of antler, was long and narrow with sharp edges and either self-bladed or slotted for a stone end blade. Most were slotted for oval side blades near the proximal end (Figure 6.7). The fact that the proximal end was perforated for a line suggests that the lance head was meant to slip from the foreshaft. Presumably a hunter supplied with reserve heads could throw off the line to drag and, slipping a new head on the foreshaft, wound the animal again. There are slight variations in these lance heads, but they do not appear to correlate with time. Essentially the Dorset lance head is unchanged in form from early Pre-Dorset time (Figure 6.8).

Musk-ox hunting appears to have been much less frequent throughout the Dorset sphere, although on Banks Island (Arnold 1980), Karluk Island off the coast of Bathurst Island (Helmer 1980b), and other High Arctic sites their bones are more common in the middens.

It is apparently safe to say that bows and arrows were not used east of Victoria Island. It is difficult to explain the absence of this useful weapon, but in sites on the coasts of Labrador and northern and southern Baffin Island, where quantities of wooden artifacts have been recovered, none can be identified as bow or arrow parts.

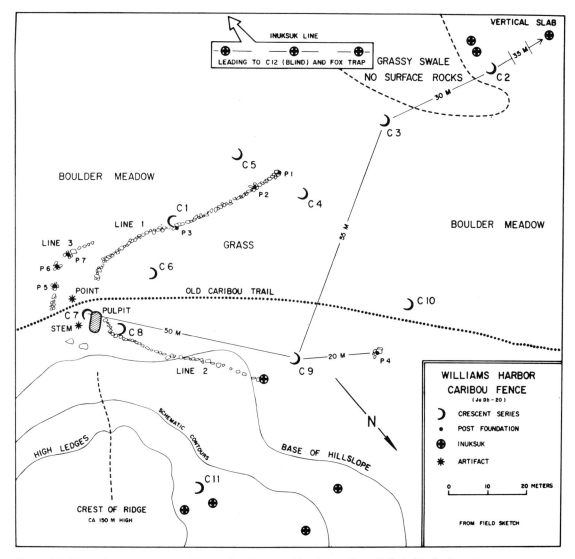

Figure 6.6 Rows of stone *inuksuit* and fences for driving and hunting caribou attributed to the Dorset culture, Williams Harbour, northern Labrador (diagram courtesy of William Fitzhugh 1981–1982).

I found some small, symmetrical, side-notched bifaces that look like arrow tips but were still attached to short, end-notched wooden handles. These were used as knives, as presumably most other side-notched end blades were. On the other hand, McGhee (1969) in the Victoria Island sites of Joss and OdPa-4 found bone shafts slotted for end and side blades (Figure 6.7F) that must have been arrow tips, and Arnold (1980) at the Lagoon site on Banks Island also found arrow tips. Both of

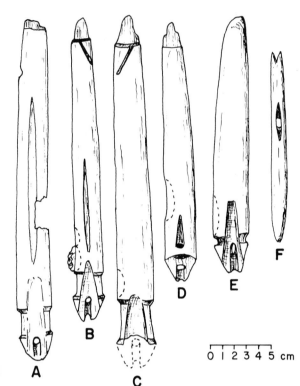

Figure 6.7 Dorset lance- and arrow heads—A–D, Tyara site, Sugluk Island; E, Igloolik; F, Site OdPc-4, Victoria Island (drawings based on selected illustrations from McGhee 1969; Meldgaard 1960a; Taylor 1968).

A.   Pingasut type
B,C,E. Atausik type
D.   Makko type
F.   arrowhead slotted for end and
           side blades

these western sites had traits that seemed to link them in part with developments in western Alaska. These are discussed in greater detail in the section on regional variation.

Under the heading of inland hunting equipment, we should discuss the unusual artifacts recovered from the Nunguvik site by Mary-Rousselière (1979a). He feels

Figure 6.8 Caribou hunting lances of ivory and antler with side blade slots for stone blades, Igloolik region.

these wooden artifacts can only be interpreted as miniature skis on which both ends are upturned in the Lapland manner. Jordan (1980) thinks that several similar specimens at the Avayalik site, where there were many examples of musk-ox wool yarn, may have functioned to spin the yarn.

Fishing

Although there is differential preservation of fish bones in Dorset sites, the location of several of these sites in proximity to fish weirs suggests the importance of fish in the diet. The Arctic char is the favored meat fish in the Eastern Arctic, and since it can be easily filleted it is not surprising that there are few bones in sites at a distance from weirs. Presumably these fish were all taken with small spears. There are no Dorset fishhooks or, except for the most western sites, gorges for line fishing and only a few artifacts that have been interpreted as line weights or lures. The absence of these traits would preclude jigging for tomcod in the open sea or fishing with spear and lure through the ice in frozen lakes. There are a few Late Dorset tridents (see figure 7.24H), but the majority of fish spears were tipped with delicate ivory heads with unilateral or bilateral barbs and were used like harpoons (Figure 6.9). Spearing fish with this implement, probably thrown rather than thrusted,

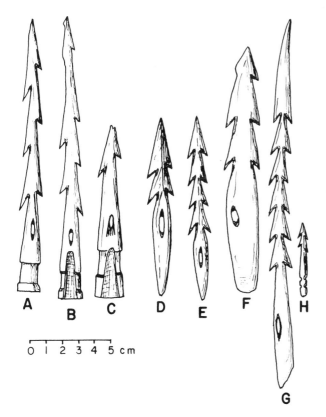

0 1 2 3 4 5 cm

Figure 6.9 Dorset fish spears— A, B, D, Igloolik; C, Tanfield site; E, Basil Norris Bay, Ellesmere Island; F, Mill Island; G, H, Abverdjar site, northern Foxe Basin.

A–C. Early Dorset
D–E. Middle-to-Late Dorset
F–H. Late Dorset

would require extreme accuracy, not only to stab the fish, but also to avoid breaking the fragile tip on rocks. For rapid fishing at a char run it would be much less efficient than the Thule leister with its flexible side prongs that could be quickly spread apart and readied for another thrust.

DOMESTIC TASKS

Butchering

There are currently no published reports on Dorset butchering activities. In the 1960s Murray (1966) initiated such an analysis for the faunal samples from the Lake Harbour region. Subsequently this analysis has been added to and largely verified by Arundale (1976) and Maxwell (1973b). The results of this demonstrate, unsurprisingly, that Dorset women and men performed this task with their customary efficiency and thorough knowledge of game animal anatomy. Murray very rarely found shallow knife marks on bones, indicating that carcasses were disarticulated with sharp knife cuts through the joints. He found knife marks only on the difficult pelvic–femoral joint. At that time he suggested that most, if not all, butchering, at least of small seal, may have been done with microblades. In 1971 I experimentally skinned and butchered a small ringed seal brought me by my Inuit friend Killikti. Initially I used only quartz-crystal microblades in driftwood handle replicas of those recovered from the Tanfield site. Allowing for unfamiliar motor habits the experiment demonstrated the possibility of using only such a small, sharp implement. However, I found the soft, slate end-bladed knife more efficient for separating

Figure 6.10 Reconstructed slate knife and wooden handle used in separating blubber from meat.

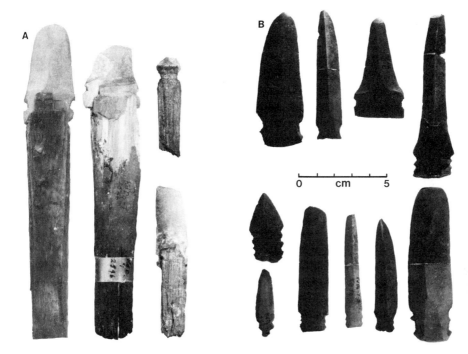

Figure 6.11 Dorset slate knife and knife fragments from the Tanfield site, Lake Harbour; (A) four slate knives with blades still in place and (B) a sample of the several hundred slate knives recovered from this site.

blubber from meat and a chert end-hafted knife for separating femur from pelvis (Figures 6.10 and 6.11).

Both Murray's (1966) and Arundale's (1976) studies demonstrated differential arrivals at the midden site. Small seal carcasses tended to be more complete, with larger animals partially butchered elsewhere. Caribou were characteristically field

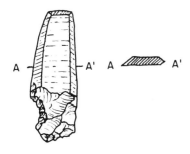

Figure 6.12 Polished Nanook burin-like knife with cross-section.

butchered, with mandibles (presumably with attached tongues), forequarters, and four legs being carried to camp but hindquarter bones usually being left in the field. All caribou bone, including the smallest phalanx had been cracked for marrow.

While many of the end-hafted chert knives may have been used for butchering as well as other functions, there is one type common in core area Dorset sites that appears particularly well suited for meat slicing. This implement, usually of fine-grained chalcedony, is completely polished with one very sharp unibeveled edge (Figure 6.12 and 6.13). Initially I termed this a Nanook burin-like implement based on its resemblance to the Dorset burin-like tool (Maxwell 1973a). However, after examining several hundred under magnification, I can find no signs of wear or heavy use. Alternatively, under 200× magnification, many have meat fibers caught in the polishing striae. This is not surprising since they were initially buried in garbage consisting mainly of meat, yet I would now interpret them as meat slicing knives. Other knives are made of chert, quartzite, and crystalline quartz (Figure 6.14).

Sewing and Hide Preparation

Few of the stone end scrapers from core area sites such as those on northern and southern Baffin Island and Igloolik seem large enough to have been functional in hide dressing. Elsewhere, perhaps because of better available stone, larger lithic artifacts were probably used for skin scraping. On southern Baffin Island most of this work was presumably done with bone scrapers. Cup-shaped fragments of seal

Figure 6.13 Polished chalcedony knives referred to as Nanook burin-like tools.

A. Early Dorset, Tanfield/Morrisson site
B. Middle Dorset, Nanook site
C. Late Dorset, Crystal II site

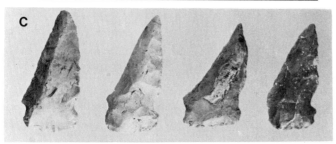

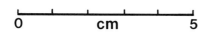

Figure 6.14 Characteristic Early and Late Dorset stone knives.

A. end blades of chert, Early Dorset Tanfield/Morrisson site

B. end blades of quartzite and crystalline quartz, same site

C. transverse-edged chert knives, Late Dorset Crystal II site and polar bear skull, *ulu*-shaped blades cut from caribou scapulae and mounted on wooden handles (see Figure 6.15E), and a variety of bone beamers and fleshers cut from caribou leg bone were all used for this purpose. Caribou leg bones, cut with a burin or burin-like tool, are particularly common in a number of Dorset sites. While most are simply residue from the manufacture of foreshafts and show no edge wear, others, with clear signs of wear, had been used as two-handed beamers or chisel-like fleshers.

Fragments of cut and sinew-stitched skins, numerous ivory and bone needles with oval eyes, and skin patterns cut with microblades all attest to tailored caribou hide and sealskin clothing. Although many Dorset carvings have depicted humans, until recently few of those recovered indicated clothing styles. An ivory carving from northwestern Greenland was a full human figure with what appeared to be a high collar rather than parka hood. However, since the rest of the figure was naked, it seemed doubtful that this could have been part of the costume. More recently Robert McGhee (letter to Maxwell, December 8, 1977) found what is unquestionably a wooden Dorset carving in a Thule house on Bathurst Island. This figure with a characteristically Dorset blowing mouth and tiptoe stance has *kamiks* (sealskin boots), trousers, a double parka without tail or hood but with a three-sided collar (see Figure 6.16). The high-collared rather than hooded parka is substantiated by a peculiar fox–man figure from Mill Island, and a Late Dorset soapstone figurine from northern Labrador (Figure 6.17; Jordan 1979–1980; Clark and Sproull-Thomson

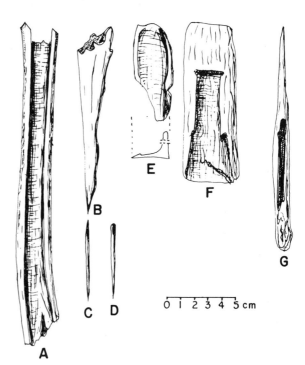

Figure 6.15 Dorset sewing equipment from the Tanfield site, Lake Harbour.

A. two-handed skin scraper cut from caribou leg bone
B. bone awl cut from caribou scapula
C. needle of Early Dorset type with sharpened butt end
D. needle of Late Dorset type (not from the Tanfield site) with rounded butt end
E. *ulu*-shaped scraper cut from caribou scapula
F. wooden scraper handle
G. awl cut from medial spine of caribou scapula

Figure 6.16 Wooden Dorset figure with collared parka from the Brooman Point site, Bathurst Island. The blowing mouth is characteristic of several Dorset carvings of humans and the tiptoe stance is found on several bear carvings (after photograph courtesy of Robert McGhee).

1981). Part of a sealskin cap recovered from the Nanook site would appear to complete the Dorset head gear. We also recovered part of a *kamik* from this site. According to Koojuk, an Inuit woman, who examined it, it was made in the Lake Harbour manner with a bearded sealskin sole, a harp sealskin instep, and a ring sealskin upper.

Dorset sites seem to produce few awls. The occasional sharpened artifacts cut from seal mandible or the medial spine of caribou scapula would appear to be too broad for fine stitching, and yet the tiny bone and ivory needles would seem too fragile for piercing leather. Early Dorset needles are sharpened at both ends and the

Figure 6.17 Tiny steatite figure (2.5 cm tall) of Dorset person with characteristic high-collared parka from the Shuldham 9 site, Saglek Bay, Labrador (courtesy of Richard Jordan).

thicker butt end may have been used as an awl, but later needles are round ended and useless for this purpose (Figure 6.15).

Food Preparation

From the scarcity of other kinds of fire-making equipment we must conclude that the customary technique was simply striking two pieces of flint together. Iron pyrite, which sparks more easily, is common along the southeast coast of Baffin Island but is only rarely found in Dorset sites. Making fire by friction with a wooden drill or plough was not a Dorset practice, although Mary-Rousselière (1979) has reported one charred piece from a Late Dorset house at Nunguvik that might have been the hearth for such an implement. Small curled strips of resinous birch bark, from driftwood, are very common in premafrost middens and would have been convenient tinder.

Hearths as integral parts of axial features in dwellings have been reported from the High Arctic (McGhee 1981b), the Labrador coast (Cox 1978), and the southeastern coast of Hudson Bay (Harp 1976a). Occasionally these are boxes of upright stone slabs but more frequently are flat rocks covered with charred seal fat and bounded by rock pot supports (Figure 6.18). At the Port aux Choix 2 site on New-

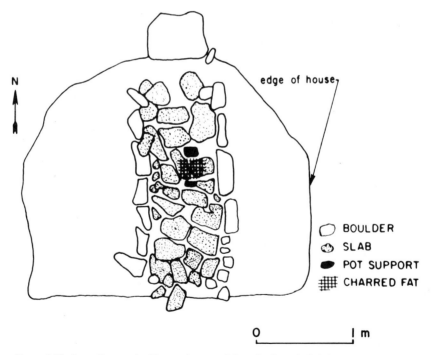

Figure 6.18 Late Dorset dwelling with central hearth, Snowdrift Village, Dundas Island (after McGhee 1981b).

Figure 6.19 Small, rectangular, Early Dorset soapstone lamp from the Tanfield site, Lake Harbour.

foundland (Harp 1976a), some of the linear pits that run through the centers of houses were fire pits.

In sites on northern and southern Baffin Island, well-defined open hearths were very rare. Here soapstone oil lamps were the common source of cooking, heating, and lighting. The stone lamps range in length from tiny (8 cm) to large (50 cm). Soapstone vessels, distinguished from lamps by suspension grooves or holes at both ends, may also be large or small, with some capable of holding hardly more than a small cup of soup. Both lamps and vessels tend to be rectangular and flat bottomed in Early Dorset (Figure 6.19) and more often round to oval in Late Dorset. The fragile vessels often cracked from heat or misuse and were cleverly repaired. Holes were scratched on either side of the crack and the pieces were glued with congealed seal blood and sewed together. Then a rectangular groove cut across the crack was filled with a glued-in strengthening bar of slate or other stone (Figure 6.20). Often red ochre was included in the repair holes. One soapstone repair patch from the Tanfield site would have been a credit to a modern tinsmith: It is designed to fit a hole in the vessel and has an outer flange that is held in place with small steatite rivets (6.20E).

This symbolic association of red ochre, lamps, and pots was particularly prevalent in Late Dorset, when most stone vessels were covered with a red ochre wash.

Toolmaking

Dorset craftsmen appear to have established forms and styles of wood- and ivory-working tools early in the sequence and then to have modified them only slightly over time. For the rough shaping of wood, bone, antler, and ivory, they used adzes of chert or nephrite set in antler sockets and bound to L-shaped driftwood handles. Splitting wedges of bone and antler are common. The average tool kit seemed to have contained a variety of polished burin-like tools with both square- and angular-tipped distal ends. They bound these small gravers to short wooden handles that were longitudinally grooved near the binding notch and down one lateral end for a supporting piece of ivory or bone that kept the graver from rocking backward in the

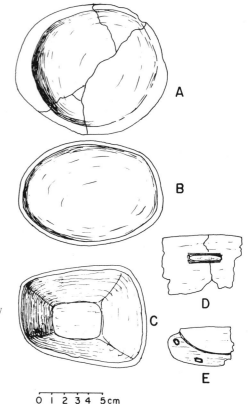

Figure 6.20 Dorset soapstone vessels, probably oil lamps.

A.   Late Dorset, Killikti site, Lake Harbour
B.   Late Dorset, Abverdjar site, Foxe Basin
     (after Rowley 1940)
C.   Early Dorset, Tanfield site, Lake Harbour
D,E. patches for broken vessels, Tanfield site,
     Lake Harbour

0 1 2 3 4 5cm

end-slotted handle (Figure 5.6). These they used for most of the functions performed later by Thule bow drills, cutting even such hard substances as slate and soapstone.

In most Dorset sites the spalled-burin dwindles to only a trace in site inventories or is replaced by ground-and-polished forms. In both northern and southern Baffin Island sites, however, it remains a useful tool, appearing in varying frequencies until Late Dorset. Under magnification most of these spalled burins demonstrate use wear along lateral edges of the burin-spall scar rather than at the corner. They appear to have been used more as fine, very sharp side scrapers rather than as gravers. Their relative frequency in some sites and absence in others may be a function of the seasonality of the site (Maxwell 1980).

Dorset whittlers used a fairly wide variety of medium to small side-notched chert and quartz knives. Many of these are so pointed and symmetrical that they look like arrowheads. Early forms were bifacially flaked and only occasionally asymmetrical, but in Late Dorset assemblages asymmetrical, unifacially flaked knives with one angled edge predominate and take over the function of side scrapers as well. The side-hafted knife also becomes more popular in Late Dorset sites.

End scrapers are present in considerable numbers and in a variety of shapes and sizes down to quartz crystal squares 5 mm on a side. The wear patterns and grooves on hard substances such as ivory and soapstone attest to the use of most of them in carving and shaping materials. There is also a variety of side-notched side scrapers, some of which are such delicate, incurving flakes of quartz crystal that they could only have been used in final scraping of needles and the conical tips of harpoon heads. The regular appearance of discrete variants of these tools in different assemblages implies a high degree of functional specificity for these scrapers, as appears to be true of most Dorset tools.

Published reports include few artifacts that might have been flaking hammers although any segment of antler may have sufficed. Most knappers used pressure flaking for all but the roughest shaping. For this they used ingeneous punches carved from hard walrus penis bone. The field crew recovered both punches and their handles from the Tanfield/Morrisson site. The punch, with rounded distal end, is shaped with an angled, scarfed proximal end (see Figure 6.21B). This was bound

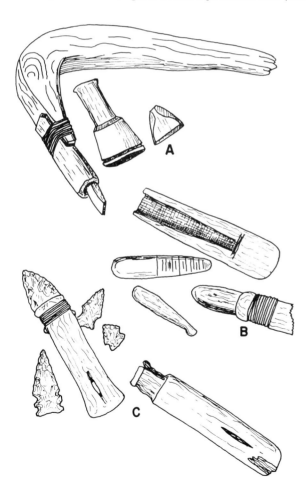

Figure 6.21 Basic items of an Early Dorset tool kit based on artifacts recovered from the Tanfield site, Lake Harbour.

A. adz with driftwood handle, antler adz socket, and nephrite blade

B. flaking punch of wood with tapering grooved handle and scarfed punch of walrus penis bone

C. variety of side-notched knife blades and a wooden handle into a grooved handle on which the groove also slanted from proximal to distal end. When pressure was applied to the flaking end, the two angled surfaces wedged together, tightening the binding. Dorset workmen exerted a high level of control over their materials with these punches, and some of their stonework is beautiful. They had a trick for making some harpoon end blades even sharper than could be done by bifacial retouching. By placing the punch at the distal tip of a stone end blade, they pressed off flutes or spalls from each lateral edge, thus making the tip razor sharp. Punches were also used to press quartz-crystal microblades from chisel-shaped crystals and chert ones from random-shaped cores. These parallel-sided bladelets, less than 10 mm wide, are usually found in profusion in Dorset sites, where presumably they were as multifunctional as the modern pocketknife.

TRANSPORTATION

We have discussed the limited evidence suggesting kayak-like boats for Dorset hunters. The evidence for sleds is much stronger. Shoes for sled runners appear in

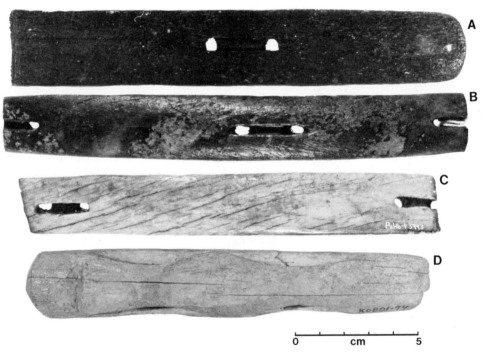

Figure 6.22   Early and Late Dorset sled shoes.

A. shoe of whalebone, Early Dorset Tanfield site
B. shoe of antler, Early Dorset–Middle Dorset Nunguvik site
C. shoe of narwhal ivory, Nunguvik site
D. shoe of walrus ivory with transverse binding slots, Igloolik region, Late Dorset type

earliest Dorset and last until the end of the Dorset period (Figure 6.22). The early ones are broad, flat sections of antler or whalebone perforated from dorsal to ventral surface and bound to the sled runner at the bow end. In shape they are much like Thule ones, for which they may have been the prototype, but with one strange difference. Whereas Thule shoes have two sets of paired holes near lateral margins for lashing to the runners, the Dorset ones have one set of paired holes set in channels at the center of the dorsal surface parallel to the long axis. It is hard to see how these could have been securely bound to the runners. Later Dorset sled shoes are usually of ivory. They are short, jointed segments, each perforated transversely from one lateral margin to the other. There are a number of toy wooden models of these sleds, eight from the Tanfield site alone. If these were proportional to functional ones the latter would have been about 200 cm high and 1.85–2.4 m long with four or five cross slats.

DWELLINGS

Shelters and residences appear in a wide variety of shapes, some being simply clusters of rocks, and are difficult to interpret. The various forms are undoubtedly correlated with seasonal use and perhaps also specific activities (Maxwell 1980). Cox and Speiss (1980) interpret faunal evidence to suggest fall settlements for intercepting harp seal migrating between mainland Labrador and the fringe islands and late winter and spring settlements for hunting at the edge of the fast ice. In some regions the use of winter snowhouses is inferred from snow knives and site locations. On the southeastern coast of Baffin Island, where there is evidence of a large Dorset population, the scarcity of adequate winter structures makes snowhouses probable at least in later Dorset. On the major part of the Early Dorset Tanfield site there are neither boulders nor indications of pits. Stratigraphic evidence indicates that winter houses were above ground structures of sod blocks roofed with skins. Other structures, interpreted by excavators as winter houses, differ from region to region. The axial feature described for Independence I and Pre-Dorset remains an important element of winter houses from the High Arctic to the coast of Labrador, northern Quebec, and both coasts of Hudson Bay. The axial feature may be variously a line of small boulders, a flat pavement, a long trench, or a double line of vertically placed stone slabs. The feature may run through the center of a shallowly scooped-out floor or a pit 50–60 cm deep. Some of the variation can be indicated in the following examples:

1. Feature 3 at the Snowdrift Village site on north Devon Island (McGhee 1981b:50) is presumably a long rectangle, although there is no peripheral boundary or depression of the house floor. The axial feature is 380 cm long, 100 cm wide, paved, and edged with small boulders. Within this feature are two hearths, 2 m apart, flanked by upright stone slab pot supports. A cleared area 90 cm wide on each side of the axial feature provided sleeping space.

2.   Gulf Hazard Site 8 House 1 on the southeastern coast of Hudson Bay (Harp 1976a:132) is roughly circular, 2 m in diameter, with a cleared floor 15 cm deep bordered by a low earthen ridge. The smooth central pavement is made of carefully fitted slabs with hearths and pot supports at each end.

3.   House 2 at Port aux Choix on Newfoundland (Harp 1976a:130) built on the limestone shingle beach is a 4.5- by 4.5-m square. It has been excavated 46 cm deep and the removed limestone shingles stacked against the walls. The axial feature is a combination of stone-lined pits 30 cm deep, some of which are probably hearths. At the rear of the house is a leveled semicircular sleeping platform raised 30 cm above the floor.

4.   A Late Dorset house at Okak 3 on the Labrador coast (Figure 6.23) is roughly rectangular, 7–8 m long and 6 m wide in a pit 50 cm deep. The axial structure is two rows, 5 m long, of narrow upright slabs 1 m apart. This feature is paved and has three hearths with pot supports spaced within it. Pavement is extended along the

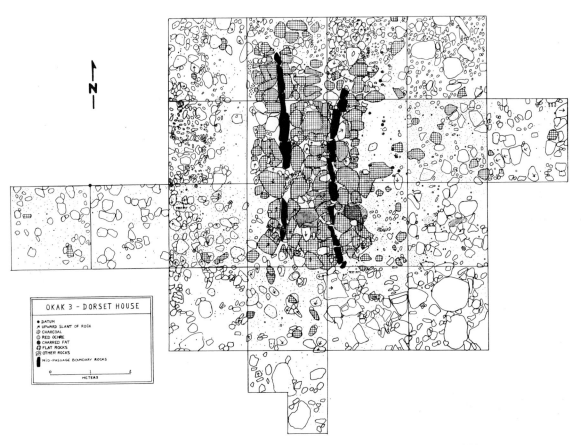

Figure 6.23 Late Dorset house plan from Okak 3 (after Cox 1978).

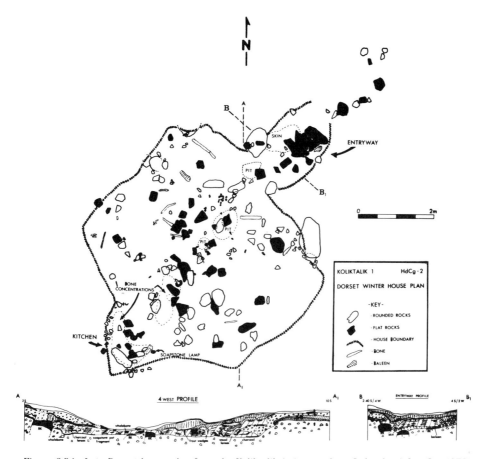

Figure 6.24 Late Dorset house plan from the Koliktalik 1 site, northern Labrador (after Cox 1978).

feature outside of the upright slabs for 50 cm on each side. Lateral to this are two sleeping areas, 1 m wide, of sand and fine gravel.

5. Although the Okak 3 house has no discernible entry, at the Middle Dorset Labrador site of Iglusuaktalialuk 4 West a sod structure with an axial feature has an entrance tunnel, and a Late Dorset house at Koliktalik 1 has a depressed, or cold-trap, entrance tunnel (Figure 6.24).

In the central region of Baffin Island, Foxe Basin, and islands at the mouth of Hudson Bay, the axial feature in winter houses is either rare, absent, or weakly expressed. Meldgaard (1960b) has described the ones at Igloolik as being square to rectangular, approximately 5 m long by 4 m wide, with excavated floors 46–60 cm deep. They have wide, raised sleeping benches along three sides, central fireplace hearths, and house boundaries marked only by low ridges of gravel. At the Morrison site (an integral part of the Tanfield site) on south Baffin Island (Maxwell 1980), an Early Dorset winter house 5 m long and 4.9 m wide had been dug down 46 cm

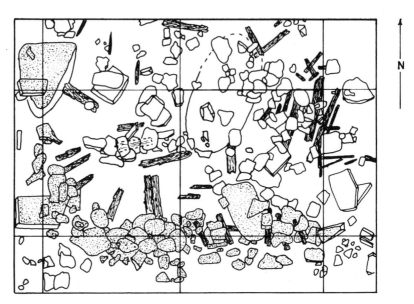

Figure 6.25   Remains of a 40-cm deep Early Dorset pit house at the Morrisson site, Lake Habour. Later site occupants have so disturbed the dwelling boundaries that only the west and south margins are well defined (indicated by stippled rocks). The general house outline is indicated by wooden fragments of the roof framework. The grid is 5-ft squares.

beneath the surface (Figure 6.25). Since it was built originally on a sloping surface, the downslope edge was built up to a 1-m wide, stone sleeping bench the full length of the house, with simply a smoothed-out gravel sleeping area level with the bench on the upslope side. A large glacial erratic boulder filled much of the center of the floor area, and there are no other discernible features within the house. Indications of small cooking areas were scattered in five locations along the floor perimeter; but from the number of vessel fragments recovered from the house, oil lamps were used for most of the cooking and heating. A skin roof was held up with a lattice of short, notched driftwood sticks lashed together, and the roof possibly was covered with snow blocks (Figure 6.25). House 46 at Nunguvik (Mary-Rousselière 1976:42) appears to have been similar. It was 5 m long, 4.5 m wide, and 25–35 cm deep, with small burned areas near the walls.

The Nanook site near Lake Harbour (Arundale 1976; Maxwell 1973a, 1980), although very difficult to interpret, may best be seen as a sort of communal late-winter-to-early-spring dwelling. It is in a small sod pocket, 30 m long, constricted by parallel rock outcrops 16 m apart. Through this runs a single built-up stone wall, 15 m long and 1 m wide, that is parallel to the eastern rock outcrop and 5.5 m to the west of it. West of the wall is the living area, approximately 2.5 m wide, with a floor 60 cm below the top of the wall. Along the west side of the wall, spaced about 1.6 m apart are four kitchen areas marked by quantities of charred fat, partially burned sticks, and refuse. My interpretation of this structure is that it was a line of four skin-covered residences with either a common wall along one end or a long common sleeping bench partitioned into family units.

There is even greater variation in tent platforms used in seasons other than winter. They may be small circular, elliptical, or rectangular areas, 2–3 m in longest dimension, with or without clearly discernible boundaries. They may simply be relatively cleared areas on rocky terraces, marked only by artifact clusters or bounded by large boulders, by a few scattered boulders, or by low gravel ridges. Outside the core area, the axial feature may be indicated in some tent sites by pavements or rows of rocks. Both within and outside the core area, tents used in colder seasons may have either box or built-up hearths.

Late in the Dorset sequence, possibly only after A.D. 500, the people built long-houses, long, rectangular, stone-boulder-outlined enclosures. They have been re-ported from Pamiok Island in Ungava Bay, Diana Bay on the Quebec coast of Hudson Strait, Juet Island near Lake Harbour, Igloolik, Bathurst Island, Victoria Island, and the middle eastern coast of Ellesmere Island. They are usually from 5 to 7 m wide and range in length from 14 m on Juet Island to 32 m on western Victoria Island and 45 m on the Knud Peninsula on Ellesmere Island. Most of these enclosures of large rocks contain little cultural material; only a few caribou bones and a Late Dorset harpoon head was recovered from the 32-m long one on Victoria Island (McGhee 1978). Presumably they were gathering places for ceremonies in snowfree parts of the year when people gather for caribou hunting or fishing. In most there are no indications of roof covering or of daily activities. However, on Knud Peninsula, where Schledermann (1981) found the 45-m long longhouse and three smaller long-house enclosures, there appear to have been foundations for 15–20 tents where as many as 100 people gathered to eat and leave behind bones of geese, duck, fox, hare, seal, walrus, beluga, and narwhal. Outside the enclosures and some distance from them, were rows of built-up hearths, 18 in a 35-m-long row near the longest en-closure. This suggests that each family cooked on its own hearth, taking the food into the enclosure for communal eating. Schledermann suggests that the ice melting early in nearby Flagler Bay drew a vast amount of game and that in the period from May to July Dorset families gathered to hunt and socialize after the long, cold winter. A carbon date on burned willow for the longest enclosure is A.D. 800–900.

Some of the latest Dorset houses, dated after A.D. 1400, are semi-subterranean, with tunnel entrances and whalebone elements in the walls and roofs, and are generally indistinguishable from Thule houses. Yet those reported from Mill Island (O'Bryan 1953), northwestern Hudson Bay (Wenzel 1979), and Igloolik (Meldgaard 1962) contained mainly Dorset artifacts. Particularly confusing is a house at DIA-4 on Diana Bay (Plumet 1979), where construction elements were of both Thule and Dorset type with Thule-like entry, alcove kitchen, and a whale skull and bones in the walls but a typically Paleoeskimo-Dorset midpassage pavement in the northern living room. In the past it has been assumed that the latest Dorset people borrowed construction techniques from the arriving Thule. However, given the evidence from the northern coast of Labrador of pit houses with entry passages dating earlier than the earliest Thule immigration, the borrowing may have gone the other way.

MORTUARY BEHAVIOR

In spite of what is now a large number of known Dorset sites, we know surprisingly little about their treatment of the dead. It may be that the deceased were left in
abandoned snowhouses on the sea ice or left uncovered on the tundra as some
Historic Inuit did. But that does not explain why the few burials we have found, with
their reflections of ideological behavior, were singled out for special treatment.
There is no apparent pattern to suggest that these persons when living had higher
social status than others.

In the middens of both the Early Dorset Tyara site on Sugluk Island and the Later
Dorset Angekok site on Mansell Island there was a single adult mandible, with only
doubtfully associated artifacts. On the Ungava coast at the Imaha site, Taylor
(Laughlin and Taylor 1960) recovered a skeleton associated with a few stone tools,
which while not particularly diagnostic are probably Dorset.

Meldgaard (1960b) has not yet described the Igloolik burials in detail; nor has he
reported the number of them. In general terms, he described them as being of three
types: The first, and most recent, which he considers Thule influenced, is a rectangular box of stone slabs covered by massive boulders. The second, which he says
is the most common, is a round pit, 1 m in diameter and 0.5 m deep, edged with a few
stones. The pits are too small for complete bodies and contain only selected bones
such as mandibles and a few long bones. These are accompanied by artifacts thrown
in without order, which include broken and unfinished tools, miniature nonfunctional harpoon heads, probably carved for the occasion, and some examples of
particularly fine artistic carving. The third type, represented by a single grave, is a
deep (76-cm) pit covered by a gravel mound 50 cm high. A child's mandible and a
single adult long bone were mixed in the pit with scattered items of grave goods.
Charcoal, burned animal bone, and red ochre covered a large square area on the
original ground surface next to the pit. Apparently associated with this area were
split walrus tusks, walrus ribs, and artifacts.

Harp and Hughes (1968) report a similar association of adult and infant remains
from a charcoal-dated house (A.D. 363) at the Port aux Choix 2 site, Newfoundland.
A 20-month-old infant, tightly bound in upright position, had been placed in a pit 50
cm deep and 50 cm in diameter within the central hearth trench or midpassage. The
undertakers had scattered artifacts and an adult human mandible in the pit and then
filled it and capped it with a limestone slab. The grave goods were an interesting
combination of utilitarian and ideational objects, including pieces of unworked
antler and flint, end scrapers and knives, a broken harpoon end blade, a bone
sucking tube, an antler spoon, perforated seal and beaver teeth, and a flat, bone
effigy characteristic of the Newfoundland Dorset style.

Nearby in a cave at Gargamelle Cove, amateurs located a grave or graves containing remains of four infants and four or five adults (Harp and Hughes 1968). Unfortunately there is no indication of whether this had been a mass interment or of
whether they were flesh or secondary burials, but the associated artifacts are
clearly Dorset of the Newfoundland type (Figure 6.26). They included functional

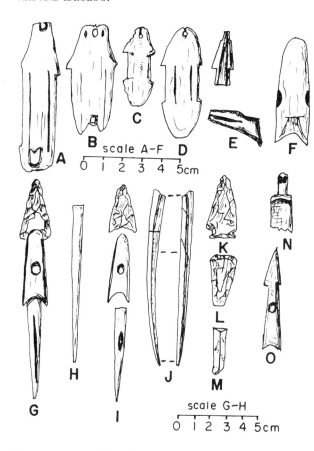

Figure 6.26 Mortuary offerings from Burial 2 at Gargamelle Cove, Newfoundland (drawings based on selected illustrations from Harp and Hughes 1968).

A–D. flat seal and bear amulets of bone and ivory
E. stylized bear heads
F. bone amulet shaped like Dorset walrus hunting harpoon head
G–I. harpoon components (tips, heads, and foreshafts)
J. ivory model of walrus tusks
K. side-notched knife
L. end scraper
M. microblade
N. antler needle case
O. harpoon head amulet (?)

harpoon parts, though some were broken before being placed in the grave, and such ideological items as an amulet box and two thin, bone plates with longitudinal slits. There were buttons or amulets shaped like the transverse-line-hole Dorset Parallel harpoon heads (which do not appear as functional items in Newfoundland Dorset villages) and a number of magico-religious carvings, including miniature walrus tusks and flat, stylized bears. Anderson and Tuck (1974) have reported three additional cave burials, also from Newfoundland, with associated artifacts much like those from Gargamelle Cove.

Physical anthropological analyses of skeletal remains from Newfoundland and elsewhere within the Dorset sphere (Anderson and Tuck 1974; Harp and Hughes 1968; Laughlin and Taylor 1960; Oschinsky 1960, 1964) leave little doubt that these were Mongoloid people with features indistinguishable from modern Eskimo.

ART AND IDEOLOGY

Dorset art has had strong aesthetic appeal to archaeologists and art critics alike (Taylor and Swinton 1967). The skill of carvers in depicting what often seem to be portraits of real persons gives us the rare sensation of seeing Dorset people in a way that looking at stone tools never could (Figure 6.27 and 6.28).

Wood, bone, antler, ivory, and soapstone were all materials for artistic expression. Pieces are usually small but accurately proportioned and often have great anatomical detail. For example, the head of an ivory seal barely 5 cm long recovered from the Tanfield site was cocked as if, while lying on a floating ice pan, it has heard an approaching hunter. Its tiny eyes, its whiskers, and even its small anus are faithfully depicted. Although artistic decoration often embellishes Thule and later Inuit utilitarian objects, this appears seldom to have been the case in Dorset. There are a few harpoon heads with carved human faces but these are probably ideational rather than utilitarian. In fact, as Taylor and Swinton (1967:44) have stated, "most if not all Dorset art [was] concerned with supernatural matters—with shamanism, burial practices, sympathetic magic."

Three-dimensional carvings may be naturalistic, with minute detail, or highly stylized in an impressionistic manner. They may be abstracts in which a single anatomical element, such as a caribou hoof or mandible, stands for the whole animal. This is well illustrated by two delightful small ivory carvings found at Brooman Point, Bathurst Island by McGhee (1981a). They are exactly the same size, approximately 3 cm long. One is a perfect polar bear skull with canine teeth removed; the other is a fleshed-out bear's head (Figure 7.28F).

Line engravings are never curved but rather are exclusively unembellished straight lines that cross, form Xs, are parallel, or are chevroned. Carved animals, particularly bear, are often covered with parallel and chevroned lines that suggest the bones, joints, and skeleton of the animal. On both bears and humans, the face and, if it is part of the carving, the pelvis are covered by an X or two crosses. This skeletal motif has been variously interpreted as an anatomical map for meat divisions and as a flayed, dead animal to ensure magical power over a living one. Many have pointed for explanation to the traditional Inuit belief regarding a shaman's helping spirits. The polar bear is often one of these spirits, and it and the shaman can divest themselves of skin and flesh and fly through the air.

Dorset carvers depicted virtually every animal, bird, and fish in their environment, even the lowly sculpin. More than half of all the recovered pieces, however, illustrate what must have been considered the most dangerous beings, humans and polar bear. Both are often carved with slits in the throat that are filled with red ochre and then closed with a sliver of bone. Humans were represented in a number of ways. Little maskettes, 4–6 cm long, carved from ivory, wood, antler, and steatite have been recovered from both Early and Late Dorset sites. Occasionally these have an incised X across the face, and some have a wedge-shaped piece cut out of the forehead along the X, giving the head a horned appearance. Some of the incised faces may represent tattooing, but others, with part of the face excised, are more mystical. Full-sized masks of driftwood have been recovered from only one small locus in the Button Point site on Bylot Island (Figure 6.29). Two complete ones found there have traces of incised tattooing and had had pegged-in hair and moustaches. There are strange little dolls, usually of wood, with removable arms and legs, and even, in at least one case, a removable erect penis. A complete,

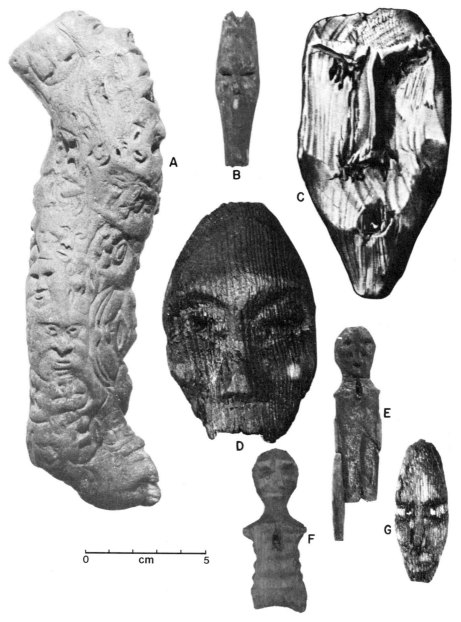

Figure 6.27 Examples of Dorset magico-religious art from several sites. Both E and F have slit throats filled with red ochre.

A.   antler wand covered with human faces, Brooman Point site (courtesy of Robert McGhee)
B.   wooden face with blowing mouth and V cut out in forehead, Saatut site
C.   wooden mask, Avayaluk, Labrador (courtesy of Richard Jordan)
D.G. wooden maskettes, Nanook site
E.   antler female figurine with removable arms and legs, Button Point
F.   wooden figure, Brooman Point

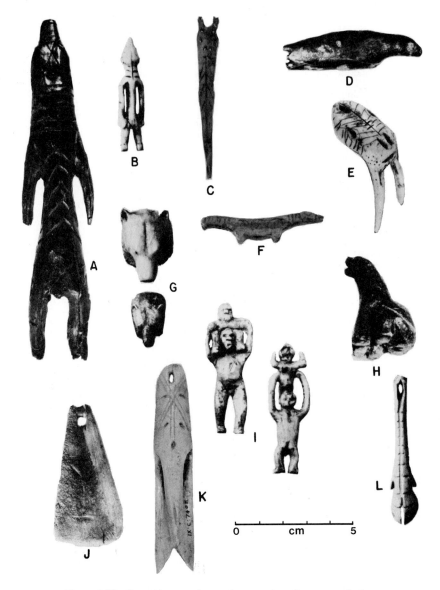

Figure 6.28 Dorset ivory and soapstone carvings from several sites.

A. ivory bear with skeletal engraving, Nanook site, southeastern Baffin Island
B. ivory bear with skeletal engraving, Abverdjar site, northern Foxe Basin
C. ivory composite image (human face/skeletanized bear), Button Point, Bylot Island
D. ivory seal hunting fetish pierced for suspension, Tanfield site, southeastern Baffin Island
E. ivory skeletonized walrus head, Abverdjar site
F. ivory composite image right side, bear/ left side, juvenile walrus, Saatut site, northern Baffin Island

G. two ivory bear heads, Adverdjar site
H. soapstone bear, Shuldham site, northern Labrador
I. two ivory adult figures holding infants, Abverdjar site
J. ivory pendant with lightly engraved human face, Tanfield site
K. ivory harpoon head with two (right side up and upside down) human faces covered by Xs, northern Foxe Basin
L. ivory caribou leg with skeletal engraving, Abverdjar site

0   cm   5

Figure 6.29   Life-size wooden Dorset mask with simulated tattooing from
the Button Point site, Bylot Island. A characteristic double X runs from
forehead to cheeks, vertical lines down forehead and cheeks, and skeletonized backbone down the chin. The mask was apparently originally
equipped with pegged-in hair and moustache.

delicate carving of a human nose raises the question of whether humans might not
have been represented in the abstract as animals often were.

Both Canadian and Greenland Dorset sites have produced segments of caribou
antler covered with clusters of as many as 60 human faces. Most of the faces, carved
in low relief on every possible space of the antler segment, have characteristically
Eskimo faces, but a surprising number of faces are long and narrow with acquiline
features. All of these latter types are from Late Dorset sites, and it may be that these

are portraits of Greenlandic Norse sailors. To date, however, no one has produced direct evidence of contact between Norse and Dorset peoples even though there is now no doubt that they occupied different parts of the Eastern Arctic simultaneously.

Another face, so distinctive that it must represent a person who once lived, appears in carvings as widely dispersed as Bylot Island, Devon Island, northwestern Greenland, Victoria Island, and the head of Foxe Basin and is often an element in the multiface antler carvings. The face is characterized by rectangular or round open

Figure 6.30 Inhaling walrus with flaring nostrils and three ivory Dorset shaman's tubes, with faces characterized by flaring nostrils, tipped by walruses with interlocking tusks from Button Point, Igloolik, and Brooman Point, respectively.

eyes and, particularly, by a markedly pug nose with nostrils facing outward. The face is often indicated on "shaman's tubes," hollow cylinders of ivory tipped by two walrus with interlocking tusks (Figure 6.30). On the specimen from Button Point, the cleft forehead I have mentioned before is indicated by a small notch; and in the one thought to have come from Igloolik this same cleft may be suggested by a small relief carving of a polar bear on the forehead. All of this suggests that the representation may be of a once very famous shaman, well known to the shamanistic fraternity, who suffered from a distinctive deformity. The rather infantile appearance of the face and the cleft condition have been suggested to represent both Down's syndrome and a myelomeningocele condition (see Murdy 1981 for a discussion of a similar deformity among the Olmec of Central America). Alternatively, this human nose resembles the nostrils of an inhaling walrus (Figure 6.30) and thus may be another case of combining humans and animals in the same carving.

Many carvings of game animals, perforated for suspension or for sewing on clothing were probably amulets for magical support in hunting. Other small amulets, such as a bird beak or an animal tooth may have been carried in small, hollow antler boxes, which are fairly common in Dorset sites. But some carvings may have been made just for personal enjoyment. This seems to have been the case with a small ivory figure from the Abverdjar site (see Figure 6.28I). Here a naked man holds a standing infant on his shoulders. The father(?) has tilted his head back to look upwards at his child.

An additional art form, common in a number of sites, is significant for its reflection of magical ritual. These rectangular plaques of ivory carved to represent bear's teeth with overlapping canines (Figure 7.10E) have been called "shaman's teeth." They are not unlike some of the ivory pieces put over mouths of the dead in the Alaskan Ipiutak site, but most of the Dorset ones have tooth-marked ridges on the back and were fitted over the lips of living persons and held in place by clenched teeth. While looking at one it is not difficult to envision a winter's night ceremony in a small pit house lit only by a low flame in the seal-oil lamp. A drum beats hypnotically in monotonous rhythm (drum rims have been recovered from several Dorset sites; see Figure 6.31). Suddenly someone throws oil-soaked marsh cotton on the lamp; it flares, revealing the face of the shaman, his mouth concealed by a gleaming row of ivory bear's teeth.

Beyond the artistic, magical pieces, there are few other indications of ritual and ideology. The occasional incorporation of a caribou or walrus skull in the wall of a dwelling conceivably may relate to some belief system. At the Snowdrift Village site on Dundas Island, McGhee (1981b) found 11 bear skulls and forearm bones, reflective, he things, of some symbolic act. Among traditional Inuit there were strong taboos separating activities related to land animals and sea animals. One of the strongest of these prohibited the sewing of clothing during the late-summer- to-early-fall caribou hunts. After the hunt there was often a move to special camps called sewing places (Damas 1969b). The archaeological record suggests a Dorset parallel to this. While sewing needles are relatively common in a number of sites, there are late-summer- to-early-fall sites in both northern and southern Baffin

Figure 6.31 Wooden drum rim
and handle, Button Point, Bylot
Island.

Island where needles are very scarce. This absence cannot be easily explained by
poor conditions of preservation.

To these suggestions of ideology and religious belief should be added the use of
paint—red ochre and black derived from powdered graphite.

I have mentioned earlier in this chapter the association of red ochre with lamps,
and on several of the carvings there are still traces of red or black washes.

In this chapter there have been strong implications of stylistic homogeneity
throughout the Dorset sphere. To some extent there are strong resemblances
among artifacts of certain types over 1000 km of space. However, by the 1980s it
was becoming apparent that regional differences were greater than earlier recognized. Chapter 7 details some of these regional differences and temporal changes in
technology as they appeared in 1984.

7 Dorset Spatial Distribution and Temporal Change

EARLY DORSET

There is little doubt that the last people to occupy Pre-Dorset sites and to make Pre-Dorset artifacts were the ancestors of Dorset people. Whether or not there may have been an intervening cultural phase—Independence II/Groswater Dorset— there is currently no evidence to suggest the introduction of a significantly different genetic stock. While the fact of a transition is clear, the process is not. Currently the distribution of Pre-Dorset sites and Early Dorset ones is virtually the same, a point that each new season's excavations strengthen. This has led several investigators to interpret the transition as occurring *in situ,* simultaneously, in many parts of the Eastern Arctic. Others, emphasizing the discrete stylistic similarity of Early Dorset artifacts over all of the Eastern Arctic would attribute the process to one of diffusion, although with no clear evidence for a center or direction of dispersal. Still others see the impetus for change developing first in the High Arctic with Independence II and from there diffusing southward. This problem is still moot.

There is more consensus on another part of the process, a change in economic activity, although there is not yet strong empirical evidence to support this. Many authors believe that an important shift toward increased sea ice hunting (or the beginning of this technology) occurred at this time. As discussed in Chapter 5 the time coincides with significant climatic cooling. Settlement locations, the first appearance of such useful items as snow knives, ice creepers, and sleds, and a significant increase in the use of stone lamps all suggest greater use of the fast ice in hunting. On the other hand, at one of the earliest sites, Nunguvik House 46, half of all the faunal remains were of caribou (Mary-Rousselière 1976:44).

Unfortunately, carbon dating is of only limited help in correlating process with time. Earlier we discussed some of the problems with Eastern Arctic dates. The corrections for fractionation and sea reservoir factors suggested by Arundale (1981) appear to provide better fits between some of the dates, but not all of the problems can be resolved by such modifiers. For example, eight carbon samples all of different organic substances from 1 m^2 of the floor of a pit house in the Morrisson site were submitted to Dr. Robert Stuckenrath of the Smithsonian Institution. The expected range of these all were in the range of 500 to 400 B.C. Instead, they ranged in carbon dates from 695 B.C. to A.D. 225.

Currently the best time marker for Early Dorset is still the group of harpoon heads that Taylor (1968) termed Tyara Sliced and Tyara Pointed, to which should be added Dorset Parallel Sliced (Maxwell 1976). The distinguishing feature of this suite is a small triangular slice cut from the dorsal surface of what is essentially a closed, rectangular socket (Figure 7.1). The small slice, which does not appear to have been functional, is an apparent vestige from an earlier form in which the socket is essentially open but flanged on the dorsal surface. At sites where organic material has been perserved, one or more of these three harpoon types occur and they have been interpreted as early in the Dorset sequence. The general time range for this suite is indicated by the corrected carbon dates in Table 7.1. The 8 most reliable of these suggest a period from 550 ± 50 to 300 ± 50 B.C. for Early Dorset. When these dates are supplemented by 3 dates on charcoal from Labrador that Fitzhugh (1976b) and Cox (1978) consider Early Dorset on the basis of lithic artifacts, 535, 505, and 450 B.C., the mean of the 11 dates is 465 B.C. with a standard deviation of 56 years. The sliced harpoon socket was later supplanted by a completely closed socket prior to 270 B.C., as indicated by a reliable date from the Nanook site (see Table 7.3).

Discrete stylistic attributes on other artifacts from these sites also serve as time indicators, although to a lesser extent than harpoon heads. They are discussed in the following brief summaries of Early Dorset sites. (Figures 7.2–7.5 detail the geographic locations of the sites referred to in this discussion of Dorset distribution and change.)

The Tanfield Site

This site in a narrow valley at the southeast corner of North Bay near Lake Harbour, Baffin Island is composed of three coeval components between 6 and 7 m

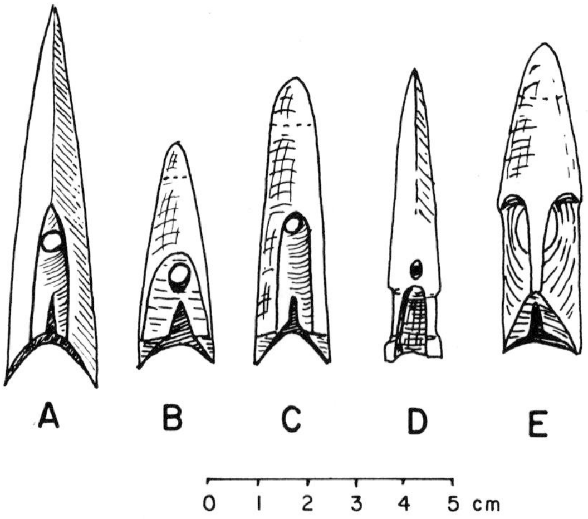

Figure 7.1 Characteristic Early Dorset harpoon heads.

A. Tyara Pointed
B. Tyara Sliced
C. Tanfield Sliced
D. Tunit Open Socket
E. Dorset Parallel Sliced

Table 7.1

RADIOCARBON DATES FOR EARLY DORSET SITES[a]

Site	Lab no.	Material	Uncorrected age (radio-carbon years)	Corrected age[b] (radio-carbon years)	Corrected date (B.C.)
Iluvektalik Is. 1	SI-2510	Charcoal and fat	2845 ± 60	—	895
Alarnerk (22-m terrace)	P-213	Ivory	2910 ± 129	2735 ± 143	785
Karluk Is.	SFU-82	Fox bone	2470 ± 120	2530 ± 120*	580
Alarnerk (22-m terrace)	P-212	Antler	2404 ± 137	2514 ± 141	564
Q-B2, Rose Is.	I-4523	Charcoal	2485 ± 15	—	535
Dog Bight L3	SI-2522	Charcoal	2455 ± 75	—	505
Ballantine	GSC-658	Charcoal	2450 ± 220	—	500
Dog Bight L3	SI-2153	Charcoal	2400 ± 70	—	450
Tyara 3	GSC-701	Seal bone	2670 ± 130	2385 ± 144	435
Tanfield KdDq-7-3	Gak-1280	Sod and twig	2360 ± 144	—	410
Tyara (Layer 2)	GSC-703	Walrus bone	2630 ± 130	2345 ± 144	395
T-1	P-76	Burned seal (?) bone	2632 ± 128	2347 ± 144	397
Karluk Is.	SFU-81	Musk-ox bone	2240 ± 120	2330 ± 120*	380
Karluk Is.	S-1673	Musk-ox bone	2205 ± 130	2295 ± 120*	345
T-1	P-75	Burned seal (?) bone	2508 ± 130	2223 ± 144	273

[a]Data from Arundale 1981, with additions by Maxwell.
[b]Ages have been corrected by incorporating laboratory-derived fractionation and sea reservoir factors. Ages marked with an asterisk have been corrected for fractionation but not reservoir effect.

above the present high-tide line (Maxwell 1973a). The largest component—originally designated the Tanfield site (KdDq-7-1)—covers approximately 1860 m^2 of moss- and grass-covered, flat valley floor of which approximately 7% has been excavated. The density of artifacts and faunal refuse, the depth of cultural midden (60 cm), and the area the component covers all testify to occupation for approximately two centuries by a relatively large band of people. There are no boulders in the midden and only few rocks larger than 3500 cm^3; nor are there any indications of house pits. Faunal analysis and drainage conditions within the valley suggest occupation only in the freezing months when houses were presumably built of sod blocks covered with skins. The second component—originally designated the Morrisson site (KdDq-7-3)—is a westward extension of the Tanfield site, although possibly occupied in somewhat different parts of the year. It contains at least one small, rectangular pit house with side sleeping benches and a roof framework of short lashed pieces of driftwood but no well-defined hearth (see Figure 6.25). This compo-

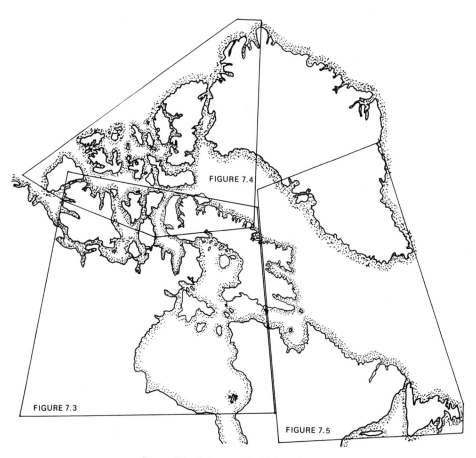

Figure 7.2   Index map for Paleoeskimo sites.

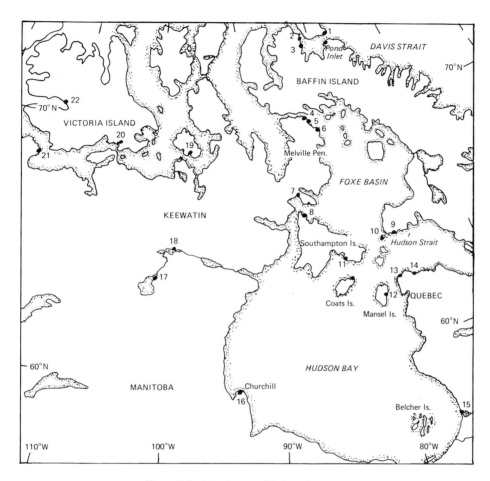

Figure 7.3 Distribution of Paleoeskimo sites.

1. Button Point
2. Nunguvik
3. Saatut
4. Abverdjar
5. Igloolik
6. Hall Beach
7. Naujan
8. Kuk
9. Cape Dorset
10. Mill Island
11. Native Point T-1, T-2, T-3
12. Arnapik, Angekok

13. Ivugivik
14. Tyara
15. Gulf Hazard
16. Seahorse Gully
17. Dubawnt Lake
18. Aberdeen Lake
19. Malerualik
20. Ekalluk River Ferguson Lake, Bell, Ballantine, Buchanan
21. Bernard Harbour
22. Joss

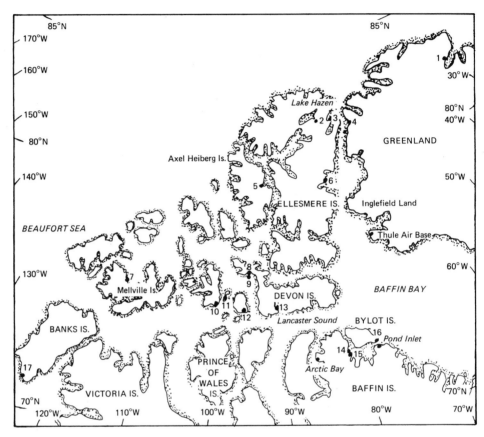

Figure 7.4 Distribution of Paleoeskimo sites.

1. Independence Fjord   10. Brooman Point
2. Ruggles Valley   11. Karluk Island
3. Coneybeare Fjord   12. Resolute
4. Solebakken   13. Maxwell Bay
5. Lake Buchanan   14. Nunguvik
6. Bache Peninsula   15. Saatut
7. McCormick Inlet   16. Button Point
8. Port Refuge   17. Lagoon
9. Dundas Island

nent is covered with rocks and boulders that may be either the residue of other winter houses or of summer tent platforms since the soil is well drained here. The third component—originally designated the Bare Rock site (KdDq-7-2)—is a single rectanguloid tent enclosure of rocks laid on a bare rock outcrop between the first and second components. Typologically its few recovered artifacts are contemporaneous with the other two components.

A fourth component—KdDq-7-1A—lying immediately shoreward from the Tanfield site has only a very thin midden resting on beach sand. Artifact typology

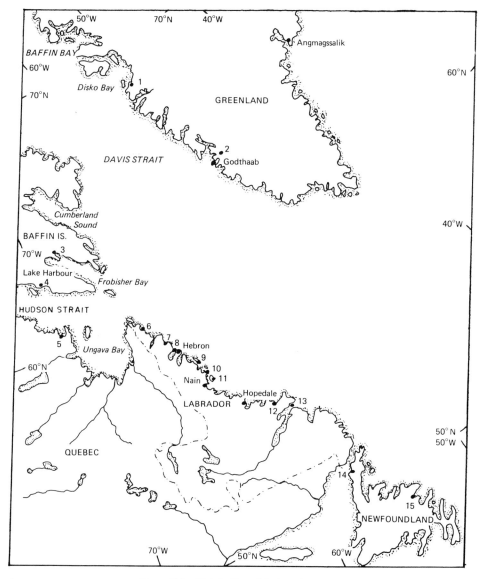

Figure 7.5 Distribution of Paleoeskimo sites.

1. Sermermiut, Sarqaq
2. Itivnera
3. Frobisher Bay, Crystal II, Shaymark
4. Tanfield, Nanook, Kemp, Loon, Closure,
   Killilugak, Avinga, Sandy, Killikti, Talaguaq
5. Diana Bay
6. Avayaluk
7. Ramah Bay
8. Saglek Bay, Rose Island, Shuldham

9. Okak, Illuvektalik Island, Iglusuaktalialuk
10. Thalia Point
11. Koliktalik, Dog Island, St. John's Island,
    Nukasusutok
12. Postville
13. Groswater Bay, Tikoralak, Buxhall
14. Port aux Choix, Gargamelle Cove
15. Shambler's Cove

suggests a later occupation, a point supported by a corrected carbon date of A.D. 65 (GSC 820). A series of excavations indicate that the gently sloping valley was periodically occupied from late Pre-Dorset, based on a corrected date of 1162 B.C. (P-710), to Late Dorset, based on a single tent ring 2 m above present high tide.

The site appears to have had several ecological advantages (Maxwell 1979; Sabo and Jacobs 1980). In midwinter the adjacent North Bay is covered by a perennially stable fast ice expanse of approximately 1000 km² (Figure 7.6). The edge of this floe, a prime source for sea mammals, passes within 2–8 km of the site. The site is on the western edge of the migration route of the southeastern Baffin Island walrus herd and provides easy access to caribou ranges in valleys running inland perpendicular to the coast. Analysis of faunal samples indicate the primacy of seal (84%), primarily ring (*Phoca hispida*) with a few bearded (*Erignathous barbatus*) and a very small number of harbor (*Phoca vitulina*). Caribou constitute 9%, birds (predominantly murres) 6%, and walrus 0.5%, and there are traces of fox, baleen and beluga whales, hare, and polar bear.

The artifacts recovered from the site (7276 stone artifacts and 973 of organic materials) all closely resemble forms and discrete attributes of those from other Early Dorset sites (Figure 7.7). Site elevation, comparable typology and carbon dates all indicate that the site would have been under seawater prior to 600 B.C. and that it was abandoned shortly after 300 B.C. The most diagnostic of the nonlithic artifacts are the harpoon heads of ivory and antler. Of the 58 recovered, 56 are of the suite of sliced heads (Tyara Pointed, 22; Tyara Sliced, 26; and Dorset Parallel

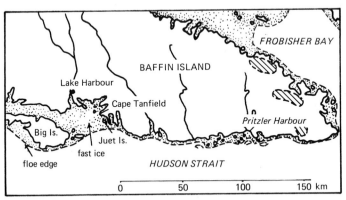

Figure 7.6 Location of the fast ice and floe edge along the southeastern coast of Baffin Island from Big Island to the entrance of Frosbisher Bay. Hatched lines are glaciers (after Earth Resources Technology Satellite [ERTS] photograph for February 16, 1973).

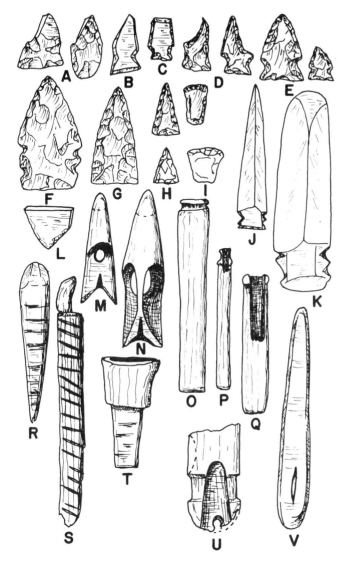

Figure 7.7 Characteristic Early Dorset artifacts from the Tanfield site, Lake Harbour (not to scale).

A. polished and unpolished burins
B,C. angular-tipped and square-tipped burin-like tools
D. side scrapers
E. side-notched knives
F,G. notched and unnotched lance tips
H. harpoon tips
I. end scrapers
J,K. slate knives
L. nephrite adz blade
M,N. Tyara Sliced and Dorset Parallel Sliced harpoon heads
O,P. wooden knife and microblade handles
Q. flaking punch handle
R. walrus-baculum flaking punch
S. crude wooden carving of bear(?)
T. antler adz socket
U. base of lance head slotted for side blade
V. bone foreshaft

Sliced, 4). Four with sliced sockets and slotted for end blades have the line hole in a groove that runs to the proximal end (i.e., Tanfield Sliced). The relative scarcity of the Dorset Parallel Sliced type, with transverse line hole (see Figure 7.7N) and thought to be used primarily in walrus hunting, correlates with the relatively few walrus bones in the midden. Of the remaining two harpoon heads, both of which have closed, unsliced sockets and were recovered from the highest levels of the midden, one is of the Kingait Closed type (Type III in Maxwell 1973a) and the other is of the Nanook Wasp Waist type (Type VII in Maxwell 1973). The Kingait Closed type is also present only in the top level of the Tyara site (discussed in the following section), and this and the Nanook Wasp Waist type are characteristic of the Nanook Middle Dorset site, where the forms appear to have supplanted the sliced heads by 300 ± 50 B.C.

Other characteristic nonlithic artifacts include a quantity of wooden handles for knives, burins, and microblades and a number of pins, harpoon shafts, kayak parts(?), and intricate support pieces. There are many bone foreshafts and the residual split caribou leg bones from which they were cut, cut pieces of whalebone and whalebone sled shoes, antler adz sockets, walrus and seal penis bone flakers, open-socket lance heads with side blades, antler snow knives, ivory fish spears, and wooden toys, including model sleds and one model each of a snow knife, a lance, and a kayak. The site has produced fewer art or ideational artifacts than some other Dorset sites. However, those recovered are similar to ones from other Early Dorset complexes. They include four shaman's teeth of wood and of ivory, wooden removable arms and legs for doll-like figurines, two naturalistic ivory seals, one of which had been deliberately decapitated, a crudely carved wooden bear, a slender wooden pin with bear heads carved at each end, the top of a small antler box or needle case, an ivory shaman's tube, and an antler button.

The more than 7000 lithic artifacts are summarized in Table 7.2. Certain of the more significant facts do not appear in this table. In distinction to late Pre-Dorset and the transitional period there is a marked increase in the use of clear quartz crystal for microblades, outnumbering chert ones 4 to 1, in triangular harpoon end blades, and in certain forms of side and end scrapers. There is also a marked increase in the use of nephrite or a nephrite-like material for angular-tipped burin-like tools and adz blades. The most dramatic increase is in the number of ground-and-polished slate knives in a wide variety of sizes and shapes. Most of these have multiply-sawed side notches. Many of the Early Dorset quartzite side-notched knives (or lance tips) also have multiple notches, although this trait is not restricted to Early Dorset. The true spalled burin, often but not always polished on one or both faces, remains in minor amounts in the assemblage, but burin spalls that appear in major numbers ($n = 174$) in the slightly earlier Avinga site are present only as a trace. While part of this situation may be due to greater difficulty of recovery in the fibrous Tanfield midden, samples that have been fine screened under water have not added to the number. The square-ended, polished Dorset burin-like tool, often of chalcedony, now becomes the dominant grooving tool but is supplemented by the angular-tipped form, which would be useful in carving out the nearly closed harpoon head socket. Another highly polished stone tool, originally termed a Nanook burin-like tool (see Figure 6.12) but now thought to have been a sharp cutting tool, makes its first appearance in this Early Dorset assemblage. Most, if not all, of the side-hafted blades were probably set in the lateral margins of lance heads. They are short, broad, and often semilunate. The side-notched knives of chert and quartzite are symmetrical for the most part—in distinction to Late Dorset ones, which are usually asymmetrical. The triangular chert and quartz-crystal end blades for harpoon heads have straight bases and occasionally are tip fluted. Tip fluting is not as

Table 7.2

LITHIC ARTIFACTS FROM THE TANFIELD SITE[a]

Class	n	Percentage
Microblades	2988	41.1
Slate knives and fragments	1069	14.7
Triangular end blades	699	9.6
Soapstone vessel fragments	451	6.2
End scrapers	432	5.9
End blade tips	368	5.1
Side-notched knives	220	3.0
Dorset burin-like tools	214	2.9
Bifacial unnotched blades	166	2.3
Chert and quartz-crystal microblade cores	138	1.9
Side scrapers	125	1.7
Igloolik angular-tipped burin-like tools	96	1.3
Side blades	80	1.1
Spalled burins	73	1.0
Retouched flakes	54	0.7
Adz blades	46	0.6
Polished burin-like knives	21	0.3
Whetstones	21	0.3
Slate pot menders	5	0.1
Burin spalls	8	0.1
Iron pyrites fragments	2	0.0
	7276	99.9

[a]Components represented here are KdDq-7-1, 7-2, and 7-3.

common a trait on southeastern Baffin Island as it is elsewhere in Dorset assemblages, perhaps as the result of less satisfactory raw material. Many of the concave side scrapers, particularly those of quartz crystal, are incredibly delicate and could only have been used for the final finishing of nonlithic artifacts. End scrapers, both of chert and quartz crystal, range from small (with blades 7 mm wide) to tiny (blades 4 mm wide). Microscopic analysis suggests that these were used in shaping hard organic substances. None of the stone scrapers are large enough to have been effective hide scrapers. The only tools recovered suitable for this purpose are a few made from caribou scapulae and from caribou leg bones. Soapstone and graphite lamp and suspended bowl fragments are uniformly small (from vessels averaging 15 cm long) and are flat-based with rectangular sides. In spite of the excellent preservation in the site only one needle fragment, of ivory, was recovered. This is in contrast to many Early Dorset sites where needles are common. This may be paritally due to recovery problems; but since all excavation was with trowels and samples were fine screened under water, I conclude that their absence coincides with restrictions on sewing during the season of occupation (Figure 7.8).

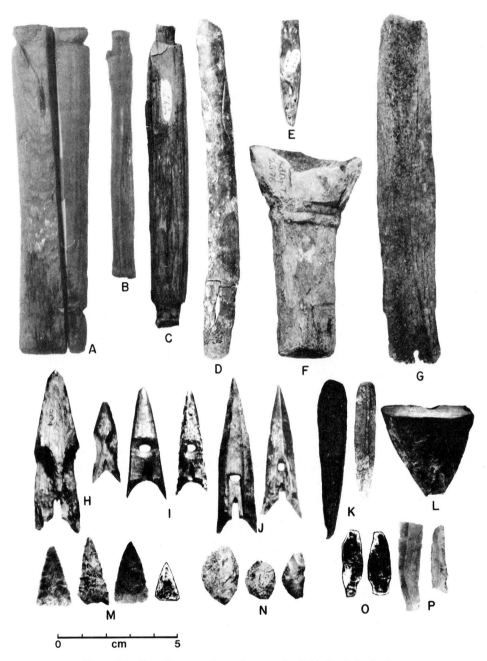

Figure 7.8   Early Dorset artifacts from the Tanfield site, Lake Harbour.

The Tyara Site

Three hundred km due west across Hudson Strait from the Tanfield site is the Tyara site on Sugluk Island off the Ungava coast (Taylor 1968). The midden here, at 16.5 m above present sea level, is much like that at Tanfield, with few rocks and no trace of dwellings, which presumably were of sod blocks. Unlike at Tanfield, walrus constitute nearly 19% of all faunal bones from the site. A similar frequency of walrus bone in the Early Dorset sites around Igloolik suggests that these animals were desirable prey when they were readily available but that Dorset hunters did not travel far from their settlements to hunt them. The midden has three distinct layers, dated (on seal and walrus bone), respectively, 720, 680, and 250 B.C. Applying Arundale's corrective factors to these produces dates of 435 B.C., 395 B.C., and A.D. 35. Consequently there is good correlation between Layers 3 and 2 and the Tanfield site and there is an occupation later than Tanfield in Layer 1. This temporal sequence is well supported by seriation of the 17 harpoon heads Taylor recovered from the site. One, which Taylor termed Tunit Open Socket, was eroded and may be a broken and reworked piece. One from Layer 2 is a self-bladed, sliced socket head of Tyara Pointed type, and 4 (1 from Layer 3 and 3 from Layer 2) are slotted for end blades and have sliced sockets (Tyara Sliced type). Consistent with the proposition that the sliced-socket forms disappear prior to 300 B.C., the harpoon heads from Layer 1 all have completely closed sockets. Three are of Kingait Closed type and 4 of Dorset Parallel type. The latter, thought to be a walrus or large seal hunting head, continues with some minor modifications through the span of Dorset culture. Except for the absence of a slice in the dorsal wall of the socket, it is identical to Dorset Parallel Sliced. Four self-bladed, closed-socket forms with a line hole in a narrow, longitudinal groove Taylor termed "Frobisher Grooved" after the site (Collins 1950) at Frobisher Bay. However, this specific form does not appear in the assemblage from the Late Dorset Crystal II site at Frobisher Bay. It does appear in several middens, such as at T-1, Kemp, Alarnerk, and Nunguvik, slightly later than the sliced, grooved, and stone-bladed form (Tanfield Sliced), and I prefer the term Native Point Grooved after the T-1 site (Maxwell 1976:63).

Nonlithic objects ($n = 91$) that are stylistically similar in both sites are foreshafts cut from caribou leg bones of both a small, rectangular form and a larger, dagger-shaped form, ice creepers, penis bone flaking punches, snow knives or ice scrapers,

---

A. composite wooden knife handle
B. wooden microblade handle
C. wooden burin or burin-like handle with groove for support piece on upper left margin
D. caribou bone foreshaft
E. ivory foreshaft for throwing harpoon
F. antler adz socket
G. antler lance head
H. two harpoon heads of Dorset Parallel Sliced type

I. two harpoon heads of Tyara Sliced type
J. two harpoon heads of Tyara Pointed type
K. two flaking punches of walrus penis bone
L. nephrite adz blade
M. chert and quartz crystal harpoon end blades
N. side blades
O. quartz crystal microblades (photographed on black surface)
P. chert microblades

whalebone sled shoes, awls, wedges, and lance heads (although the variety of lance heads is greater at Tyara). Taylor mentions, but does not illustrate, what he suggests might be a kayak harpoon rest, comparing it to one from the T-1 site (Collins 1957:Plate IV. 23). The one illustrated by Collins is clearly a caribou-scapula skin scraper that was originally fastened to a wooden handle like several at the Tanfield site (see Figure 6.15E). The Tyara site contributes additional traits to the Early Dorset complex. There are perforated ivory weights, which may be for fish lines or bird hunting bolas, a side prong, possibly for a fish spear, perforated fishtail like objects, which may be pendants or needles for stringing fish, and cut and perforated bear canine teeth. Significantly, Taylor recovered 10 needles and 2 needle cases under conditions of no better preservation than at Tanfield.

Art and magic are better represented at the Tyara site. There is a beautiful, widely illustrated, tiny, ivory human maskette from the bottom layer of the site, a carved ivory seal from the second layer, and a walrus head and three bears engraved with a skeletal motif, two of which were found enclosed in an ivory sheath, from the top layer. The provenience of the three bears and sheath in the same square and level with a human mandible and three human ribs led Taylor to suggest they were grave offerings for a shaman.

The T-1 Site

Approximately 390 km northwest of the Tyara site is Native Point on the southeast coast of Southampton Island, the location of the T-1 site (Collins 1956a,b, 1957). The site on a headland 23 m above present sea level covers a flat pasture-like area of more than 75,000 m², although findspots are not continuous over this area. Like Tanfield and Tyara, there are no observable traces of dwellings, no house depressions or surface structures. Below ground there are only a few hearths and small occasional arrangements of flat stones, suggesting floors. The well-drained midden, not frozen when excavated, is 30–50 cm deep. Although no wooden fragments remained in the midden, preservation of bone, antler, and ivory was good. Four carbon dates (all of which contained seal bone in the sample) range from 682 to 110 B.C. (corrected to from 397 B.C. to A.D. 175). Given the extent of this site it is not surprising that the 23-m plateau was sporadically occupied for as much as 575 years. Collins (1956a) considered the eastern part of the site to be culturally distinct from and more recent in time than the western part, a proposition supported by both the carbon-dated samples and typological attributes of the artifacts. Thus material from Test Pit 8 should be the youngest and that from Midden 1 and Trench A the oldest.

Collins and crew excavated about 88 m², recovering more than 25,000 animal bones, 3000 lithic artifacts, and "many" nonlithic materials. A sample of 3873 identified animal bones (Cox and Spiess 1980) indicated the primacy of seal hunting—62.6% were ringed seal and 7.8% bearded seal. Walrus accounted for 11.3%, fox 17.0%, and caribou and polar bear each less than 1%. Collins noted that it is a long distance from this site to the eastern highlands where caribou can be taken even though a number of the recovered artifacts are related to caribou hunting.

Fifty-six km southeast of the site, at Lake Brook, there is a good source of distinctively banded gray-to-black flint occurring in nodules and masses in the limestone bedrock. The ready availability of this lustrous, smooth-textured material contributes to the apparent differences between T-1 stonework and that of other Dorset sites. The same banded flint shows up occasionally in Tanfield Valley middens of various ages, where it stands out from the more inferior local chert. There are some quartz-crystal artifacts from the T-1 site but very few of such metamorphic rocks as quartzite, chalcedony, nephrite, or slate.

Artifact category quantities have not been published, but the lithic tool kit appears similar to Tanfield and Tyara, with some striking differences. There are many microblades but few cores (microblades and other preforms may have been made at the flint source). Microblades are generally longer and straighter than those from southeast Baffin Island sites, which is probably a function of better raw material. At T-1 many end-hafted artifacts had been made from blades (wider than 10 mm) and several, particularly straight-based, triangular end blades, had been only unifacially flaked. Tip fluting on these harpoon head tips is so common that next to microblades the little tip spalls were the most frequent stone artifact recovered. As at Tanfield and Tyara, there are a few true spalled burins, but more polished burin-like tools of both the square- and angular-ended varieties. Retouched burin-spall tools, many pressed from polished burin-like gravers, are more common than at most Early Dorset sites.

At the time of Collin's excavation, the only comparable assemblage was that from the Igloolik sites. Noting some differences between the two assemblages, Collins first referred to the T-1 assemblage as proto- or formative Dorset (1956a). With a larger corpus of data now available for comparison it would appear that the T-1 site fits well with Early Dorset sites elsewhere and that such discrete differences as are present here resemble in degree the slight regional variants in other sites. Unlike the Igloolik and Lake Harbour sites, the T-1 assemblage has "less than a dozen" slate knife fragments, perhaps because of better sources of flint. There are very few soapstone sherds, few side-notched or stemmed end blades, and no concave side scrapers or expanded-edge end scrapers. On the other hand, there are a few rectangular side blades and peculiar triangular side blades with slanting bases and one rounded corner—traits that have not been reported from other Dorset sites.

The styles of recovered harpoon heads relate the site closely to the central Dorset region (Figure 7.9). The suite of early sliced forms—Tyara Pointed, Tyara Sliced, and Dorset Parallel Sliced—dominate the harpoon head complex from the earliest part of the site. In Midden 2, approximately a century more recent, a subtly different sliced form appears in which the line hole is in a deep narrow dorsal groove (Tanfield Sliced). Here also a closed-socket, self-bladed form with a diamond-shaped cross section forward of the line hole (Native Point Grooved) and Dorset Parallel make their first appearance. The sequence parallels that at both Tyara and Tanfield

Figure 7.9 Nonlithic Early Dorset artifacts from the T-1 site, Southampton Island (drawings based on selected illustrations from Collins 1956b).

A. lance head (Atausik type)
B. Dorset Parallel Sliced harpoon head
C. Tyara Sliced harpoon head
D. Tanfield Sliced harpoon head
E. fish spear
F. support piece for burin handle
G. flaking hammer
H,I. foreshafts
J. needle
K. antler needle case(?) or amulet box
L. ivory button
M. ivory bear
N. carving of caribou hoof
O. fish gorge
P. flaking punch
Q. ivory shaman's teeth
R. decorated foreshaft
S. bone blank from which needles have been cut

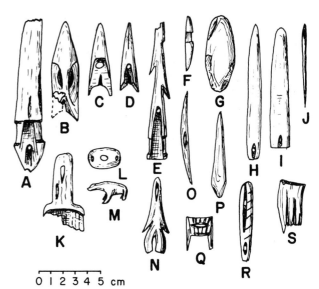

and suggests that occupation of the T-1 site covers the span of at least 500–200 B.C. (for a more detailed description of harpoon head seriation, see Maxwell 1976).

Other nonlithic artifacts compare closely with Tyara and Tanfield. Antler lance heads are virtually the same as are open-socket fish spear heads. There are large and small foreshafts for harpoons and lances, seal and walrus baculum flaking punches, ivory shaman's teeth, small antler needle cases or amulet boxes, burin support pieces, a whalebone sled shoe, and caribou-scapula hide scrapers like those at Tanfield. Like Tyara but unlike Tanfield there are many needles with tiny, scratched-in oval eyes and sharp butt ends and bi-pointed, delicately arcing ivory objects (Figure 7.9O) that may be fish gorges. A number of artistic magical pieces were recovered, including shaman's tubes with carved polar bears, a polar bear, a caribou hoof, a bird beak, and a caribou with skeletal engraving. The only apparent difference between this nonlithic complex and that from other Early Dorset sites is the unusual number of cut bird bone tubes and bone and ivory rings and disks, all of which were mostly from Midden 2.

The Igloolik Sites

The northern Foxe Basin sites on Igloolik and Jens Munk islands are 650 km due north of Native Point (Meldgaard 1960a,b, 1962). These are semipermanent winter settlements of rectangular pit houses 4 by 5 m and 50 cm deep with side benches and floor hearths. At Alarnerk, near Igloolik, Dorset houses are grouped, usually in clusters of five, on raised limestone beach terraces that descend from 22 to 8 m above present sea level, with Early Dorset houses between 22 and 20 m above present sea level. Carbon dates from this elevation, corrected for reservoir factors (see Table 7.1), are consistent with other Early Dorset dates. The size of sites suggest that winter settlements at Alarnerk or Kapuivik on Jens Munk Island might have housed winter aggregates of as many as 100 people and be comparable to the traditional winter aggregation of seal and walrus hunters reported near Igloolik by Damas (1969a). The head of Foxe Basin is one of the ecologically richest in the Eastern Arctic. Melville Peninsula provides access to the large migrating caribou herd from the Keewatin barren grounds, the shallow sea underlain by sediments provides forage for large herds of walrus, Hudson Strait to the south and the Fury and Hecla Strait to the north provide access for beluga and narwhal, respectively, and broad areas of fast ice in winter are available for breathing-hole seal hunting.

Bone, ivory, and antler was particularly well preserved in this limestone country; but unlike northern and southern Baffin Island, wooden artifacts were unfortunately not preserved (Figure 7.10). The harpoon heads at the 22-m level include the familiar triad of Tyara Pointed, Tyara Sliced, and Dorset Parallel Sliced, with, predictably, greater numbers of this latter walrus hunting harpoon head. By the 20-m level, the Tanfield Sliced and Dorset Parallel have appeared, both associated with a few surviving Dorset Parallel Sliced and Tyara Sliced forms.

Other nonlithic traits that have been illustrated or discussed in print have no observable stylistic difference from those of the other Early Dorset sites. The recovered assemblage includes needles with pointed butt ends, walrus-baculum flaking punches, support pieces for burin-like gravers, open-socket lance heads with and without end and side blade slots. adz sockets, large and small foreshafts of bone, antler, ivory, and whalebone, flat sled shoes of whalebone and ivory, open-socket fish spears, and geometrically engraved bone and ivory disks (like those from T-1). Meldgaard (1960a) attributes very few art pieces to this early period at Igloolik.

The frequency of stone tools is apparently much lower in the Igloolik sites than in other Early Dorset sites. This may be due in part to differences in recovery techniques. The lithic artifacts reported are similar to others we have discussed in the preceding. Slate knives and fragments are very common as are triangular end blades with straight bases and fluted tips. There are presumably no true spalled burins, their function having been completely supplanted by the square- and angular-ended burin-like tools. The frequency of microblades and the shapes of concave side scrapers and small expanded-edged end scrapers appear to be virtually the same as at Tanfield and Tyara.

The two published dates from the 22-m level at Alarnerk—one on ivory and the other on antler—can be corrected to 785 ± 143 B.C. (P-213) and 564 ± 141 B.C. (P-212), respectively (see Table 7.1). While the antler date thus corrected is early, it is consistent with the age of the other Early Dorset sites we have discussed. The ivory date, however, would seem to be two centuries too early. There appear to be two alternative interpretations of this. One is simply to consider this date as one among others in the Eastern Arctic to treat with suspicion. The second is to recog-

Figure 7.10 Early Dorset nonlithic artifacts from the Igloolik region, northern Foxe Basin.

A. ivory foreshaft
B. caribou leg bone foreshaft
C. ivory foreshaft for throwing harpoon
D. flaking punch
E. shaman's teeth
F. ivory bear effigy with head and arm amputated
G. antler adz socket
H. bone ice pick
I. antler lance
J. two antler amulet box fragments
K. Dorset Parallel Sliced harpoon head
L. Dorset Parallel Sliced harpoon head
M. two Tyara Sliced harpoon heads
N. Tyara Pointed harpoon head
O. needles with sharpened butt ends
P. miniature lance head
Q. miniature fish spear
R. ivory support pieces for burins or burin-like tools

nize that it is the beginning of Early Dorset and that the earliest manifestation of this culture is in the northern Foxe Basin. Unfortunately there is not yet enough published material to evaluate these alternatives. From published reports, several conversations with Meldgaard, and perusal of the collections in the National Museum of Man, Canada, it appears that the transition from Pre-Dorset to Dorset takes place at Igloolik between the 24- and 22-m terraces. Within this vertical space there is little stylistic change in stone artifacts and very subtle changes in the discrete attributes of harpoon heads from the narrowing of a flanged socket to the forms referred to as "sliced." This suggests that if organic materials had been preserved at such sites as Avinga, discussed in the preceding, and at the earliest carbon-dated Dorset sites in Labrador, discussed in the following, where lithic artifacts so closely resemble those from other Early Dorset sites, their assemblages would have included sliced harpoon heads. The implication of this is that the development of a recognizable Early Dorset may precede such sites as Tanfield, Tyara, and T-1 by as much as a century.

If the Dorset culture has a single locus of development it would be logical to see it taking place in the northern Foxe Basin. Two factors have been suggested for this development: a shift in economy toward more hunting of seal on the sea ice, either at floe edge or through breathing holes, and a rapid population expansion following the transitional period. Both of these might best be satisfied at Igloolik. Damas (1969b) has described the importance of both breathing hole and floe edge seal hunting by traditional Inuit on the vast expanse of fast ice here. He speaks of winter hunting aggregates of more than 100 persons, a winter settlement larger than most in the Eastern Arctic. It is logical to conclude that the coalescence of such a large number of hunters and consequent greater pooling of information could have led to the significant cultural change we term Early Dorset.

The Nunguvik Site

Across the narrow Fury and Hecla Strait and the northwestern corner of Baffin Island, about 400 km from Igloolik, is the site of Nunguvik on the west coast of Navy Board Inlet (Mary-Rousselière 1976). Here 80 house pits along a 1-km stretch of coastline range in age from Early Dorset to late Thule. Half of the number are Dorset, seemingly arranged in clusters of 2–5 houses. In all periods, including Thule, caribou appear to have been the dominant food source. The cultural assemblage from House 46 at 11 m above present sea level is typologically within the range of the Early Dorset sites we have discussed but is also unique in some respects. This typological age is confirmed by a sea mammal bone date that can be corrected to 420 B.C. This winter house is nearly square, 5 by 4.5 m and 35 cm deep. Mary-Rousselière excavated 52 m^2 inside the house and an additional 3 m^2 of midden outside the house. Of the 1873 artifacts recovered, 1748 are of stone and 125 of bone, wood, antler, and ivory (Figure 7.11). Unlike the other Early Dorset sites we have discussed, caribou bone constituted 50% of the faunal residue, with ringed and bearded seal, walrus, and narwhal following in that order of frequency. Quantified information for all tool categories is not available but Mary-Rousselière reports that 9% of the stone tools are true spalled burins and 8% are burin-spalls—an unexpectedly high frequency for an Early Dorset site. Microblades of both chert and quartz crystal constitute 45% of the lithic artifacts and burin-like gravers, both square and angular tipped, 2%. The remaining 36% includes slate and chert knives, some of which have multiple sidenotches, oval, rectangular, and bean-shaped side blades, a slate blade with a wide, rounded end and side notches, concave side

Figure 7.11 Artifacts from the Early Dorset to early Middle Dorset component of the Nunguvik site, Baffin Island.

A. side-hafted microblade in composite handle
B. burin-like tool in handle with support bar to the right
C. wooden knife handle
D. ivory harpoon foreshafts (larger ones of caribou leg bone presumably used for thrusting harpoons)
E. three ivory needles

F. antler amulet box
G. small ivory lance head (larger ones made of caribou antler)
H. walrus penis bone-flaking punch
I. Dorset Parallel Sliced harpoon head
J,K. Tyara Pointed harpoon heads
L. Tyara Sliced harpoon head toy(?) with simulated end blade

scrapers, and expanded-edged end scrapers. Two traits differing from other Early Dorset assemblages are oblique-edged end scrapers more characterisitc of Tanfield Valley Pre-Dorset and end blades with square notches high on the lateral edges. These latter are absent from other Early Dorset sites but are surprisingly like some of the Groswater Dorset forms from Labrador.

The harpoon head complex from this house bears out Mary-Rousselière's contention that the house was reoccupied several times over perhaps a century and a half. The early types, Tyara Pointed, Tyara Sliced, and Tanfield Sliced are present but so also are the somewhat later Dorset Parallel and Native Point Grooved. Additional nonlithic artifacts include a number of longitudinally cut caribou leg bones, needles with pointed butt ends, a whalebone snow knife, several pieces of cut whalebone and baleen, and carved wooden seals and toy harpoons heads. In one of the side walls of the house Mary-Rousselière found a pair of caribou antlers still attached to the frontal bone with the tines symmetrically cut off. Presumably this was used either as hunting camouflage or in some religious ceremony.

The famous and culturally rich Button Point site on Bylot Island a short distance east of Navy Board Inlet has produced artifacts that are unquestionably of this Early Dorset period, as it has of Pre-Dorset and Late Dorset. Unfortunately, according to Mary-Rousselière, the site is so mixed by frost action, it is impossible to separate specific assemblages.

The Greenland Sites

It may be significant that to date no reported sites from Greenland are chronologically or typologically equivalent to the Early Dorset sites in Canada. In fact, the only published Dorset remains in West Greenland, from Sermermiut, postdate the Christian era (Larsen and Meldgaard 1958; Mathiassen 1958). Such apparent absence of Early Dorset is surprising since both Independence II and Sarqaq nearly span in time a transitional period from early Paleoeskimo to developing Dorset. Whether this lack is because there has been little exploratory emphasis on sites of this time period or because such sites do not exist cannot be said at this time. If, in fact, Dorset sites dating prior to the beginning of the Christian era are absent from Greenland, climatic conditions may have been involved. Although there had been cultural contact between Greenland and Arctic Canada during the relatively warm climates of Pre-Dorset–Independence I and the transition–Independence II–late Sarqaq, the abnormally cold climates of 600–500 B.C. may have inhibited such contact. If so, then the development of Early Dorset was restricted to the Canadian Arctic.

M. small antler amulet box
N. Kingait Closed harpoon head
O. Kingait Closed–like harpoon head amulet (without socket and perforated at the distal end)
P. Ivory figure with bear head at one end and young walrus at the other (see Figure 6.27F for a similar figure from the nearby Saatut site)
Q. miniature kayak part(?) (see Figure 6.5)
R. perforated bone plaque with scratched engraving of bird(?) figure

The Karluk Island Sites

Prior to 1977 no Early Dorset site had been reported from the High Arctic north of Lancaster Sound and Barrow Strait. In fact it appeared likely that a retrenchment southward followed Independence II as the climate cooled (McGhee 1976). In that year Schledermann (1978a) located what appeared to be Early Dorset sites on Karluk Island between Little Cornwallis and Bathurst islands at 75°30′ north latitude. In the following two seasons Helmer (1980a, personal communication, 1982) excavated these and additional sites there and at Markham Point a few kilometers to the west and demonstrated the certain presence of Early Dorset this far north.

From a number of locations 8–12 m above present sea level, Helmer recovered several harpoon heads of the familiar Early Dorset suite—Tyara Pointed, Tyara Sliced, Tanfield Sliced, and Dorset Parallel Sliced. These were accompanied by nonlithic artifacts such as lance heads, snow knives, multiply barbed dart heads, foreshafts, flakers, composite handle parts, and needles with elongated eyes and sharpened butt ends. These categories are indistinguishable from those described from other Early Dorset sites. Stone artifacts also are comparable to other Early Dorset assemblages but with some differences in relative frequencies. Many of the triangular end blades are tip fluted but so also are parallel-sided and leaf-shaped bifaces, which are present in greater numbers than in other Early Dorset sites. The relatively large, triangular, microlithic tip spalls from these bifaces are numerous. There are also more parallel-sided blades (equal to, or wider than 11 mm) than in other Early Dorset sites but none of the ground slate knives that are common elsewhere.

A short distance westward at Tu piq Bay near Markham Point on Bathurst Island Helmer located sites with similar assemblages but in these cases some of the tools are of ground slate. The same sliced-socket harpoon heads were here but also two of the Tunit Open Socket type previously reported only from Level 2 at the Tyara site. Other traits that Helmer (personal communication, 1982) considers may place the Tu piq Bay sites early in the Early Dorset period are a side-notched end blade with square notches high on the lateral edges, like those from Labrador's Groswater Dorset, and a burin-like tool that he considers resembles those from Groswater Dorset (this type also resembles those recovered at Killilugak).

Faunal remains differ widely from location to location on both Karluk Island and Tu piq Bay. In some sites small seal predominate, in others musk-ox do, and in still others fox do. Final analysis of these data will tell us much about Dorset adaptive behavior.

Carbon dates from Karluk Island, ranging from 580 to 255 B.C. are consistent with other Early Dorset dates: 2470 ± 120 radiocarbon years (SFU-82) on fox bone, corrected for ^{13}C to 2530 ± 120, 2240 ± 120 radiocarbon years (SFU-81) on musk-ox bone, corrected for ^{13}C to 2330 ± 120, and 2205 ± 120 radiocarbon years (S-1673) on musk-ox bone, corrected for ^{13}C to 2295 ± 120. But these dates and both the similarity of the artifacts to Foxe Basin and Hudson Strait Early Dorset and the fact that there are nearby Independence II houses elsewhere on Karluk Island

(Schledermann 1978b) and at Brooman Point on Bathurst Island leave open the question of whether Dorset is developing here *in situ* from a local transitional phase or is the result of a northward migration.

The Victoria Island and Bernard Harbour Sites

The westward range of Early Dorset extends for approximately 950 km to southern Victoria Island and across Dolphin and Union Strait to Bernard Harbour on the mainland (Taylor 1964, 1967, 1972). Here Pre-Dorset lasts at least until 900 B.C. at the Menez site—2880 ± 105 radiocarbon years (I-2085) on powdered charcoal—and Early Dorset, as defined by the presence of sliced harpoon heads, begins by 500 B.C. at the Ballantine site—2450 ± 220 radiocarbon years (GSC-658) on charcoal. This again raises the processural problem of nascent Dorset. Taylor considers the time gap between the two to be an artifact of sampling and the dearth of archaeological exploration on Victoria Island. McGhee (1976) on the other hand places greater emphasis on the gap and interprets the dates as indicating an abandonment of the region in later Pre-Dorset times and a reentry of Early Dorset people from the east 500 years later. Regardless of the eventual outcome of this discussion, the very close similarity in the discrete attributes of both lithic and nonlithic artifacts between these sites and those of the Foxe Basin–Hudson Strait area points to close and continued information exchange between the two areas.

The Ballantine site on Ekalluk River, which drains Ferguson Lake and empties into Wellington Bay on the southeast shore of Victoria Island, is located in a region of good char fishing, fair sealing, sporadic musk-ox hunting and abundant caribou hunting. This and other sites along the river appear to have been centers for caribou hunting, and some animals possibly were speared in the lake with the same harpoons used for sealing. The lithic complex (Figure 7.12) from the site is typologically comparable to the Early Dorset we have discussed, including a few ground slate knife fragments. The nonlithic assemblage is even more similar to Eastern Arctic sites. Nonlithic artifacts, mainly of antler, include open-socket lance heads with side blade slits, knife or graver support pieces, harpoon foreshafts, a wedge, an adz socket, and a scraper handle. The nine or more harpoon heads are particularly diagnostic, including slight regional variants of Tyara Sliced and Tyara Pointed. A few kilometers eastward at the Ferguson Lake site, Taylor recovered additional traits (Figure 7.13) such as a symmetrically barbed lance head, large, scarf-ended foreshafts, an antler ice pick, and an antler sled shoe. At this site the harpoon heads had narrower slices in their dorsal surfaces and sharper basal spurs and the Native Point Grooved type appeared. These characteristics led Taylor to interpret the site as a somewhat later occupation than that at Ballantine.

The Dorset component of the Buchanan site, which also had a Pre-Dorset component, appears to continue this stylistic trend of mimicking stylistic change in the east. Here most stone and antler artifacts do not differ significantly from earlier ones but sliced harpoon heads become the minority and are replaced in popularity by the closed-socket Native Point Grooved form.

South, on Cambridge Bay, the Newnham site seems coeval with Ballantine, having only Tyara Sliced, Tyara Pointed, and Tanfield Sliced types of harpoon heads. Then, farther south and across Dolphin and Union Strait to the mainland at Bernard Harbour, two sites would appear to be no more than a century later than Buchanan. Here, so distant from the eastern edge of the Dorset sphere, the persistence of Dorset style is remarkable. The site, seven oval and subrectangular tent rings near a

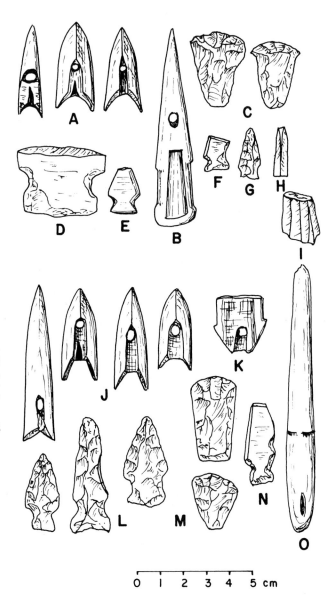

Figure 7.12 Early Dorset artifacts from the Ballantine (A–I) and Buchanan (J–O) sites, southern Victoria Island (drawings based on selected illustrations from Taylor 1967).

A,J. flanged- and closed-socket harpoon heads
B.   lance head
C,M. end scrapers
D.   slate knife base
E.   nephrite burin-like tool base (probably with angular tip)
F,N. Dorset burin-like tools
G.   triangular microlith
H,I. microblade and core
K.   lance base
L.   side-notched end blades
O.   foreshaft

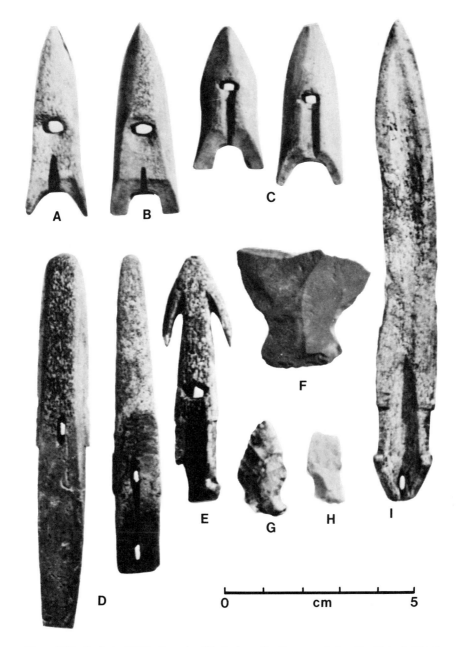

Figure 7.13 Early to Middle Dorset artifacts from the Ferguson Lake site, Victoria Island (after selected National Museums of Canada photographs, courtesy of William E. Taylor, Jr.).

A. Tyara Sliced harpoon head
B. regional variant of Tyara Sliced harpoon head
C. regional variants of Native Point Grooved harpoon heads
D. foreshafts
E. bilaterally barbed lance head
F. slate knife
G. side-notched end blade
H. burin-like tool
I. lance head with side blade slot

good fishing area, contained 247 artifacts. Most of the microblades, biface fragments, and other stone tools are not diagnostic. But there are Early Dorset traits such as tip-fluted, straight-based triangular end blades and the microlithic spalls from the tips, side-notched burin-like tools, and at least one side-notched slate knife fragment. There is a flat whalebone sled shoe of Early Dorset type, a needle fragment, and a single closed-socket harpoon head closely resembling the Native Point Grooved type.

In speaking of harpoon heads, Taylor has pointed out that of some 130 Dorset harpoon heads recovered from west of King William Island none are the Dorset Parallel, transverse line hole type that we have referred to as used in walrus hunting. Since this western region is outside of normal walrus range, the absence of these harpoon heads strengthens the functional inference. Although there is close typological similarity with the east, there are other regional differences at this western edge of Dorset. There is a heavier emphasis on caribou hunting, no multiply side-notched end blades, and triangular end blades, ground-slate knives, and soapstone vessel fragments are all rare (McGhee 1976).

Banks Island: The Lagoon Site

Farther to the west Arnold (1980) has excavated the extremely interesting Lagoon site on the southwest coast of Banks Island. Its carbon dates, all on musk-ox bone, which appears to be a reliable substance for dating, range from 340 to 440 b.c.: 2290 ± 120 radiocarbon years (RL-766), 2320 ± 120 radiocarbon years (RL-765), and 2390 ± 110 radiocarbon years (RL-767). This would place it chronologically contemporaneous with the latter part of Early Dorset in the eastern core area. However confirming this with the typology of the artifacts is more difficult.

The site has certain ecological advantages. Driftwood is much more abundant here than elsewhere in the Central and Eastern Arctic. Seal, musk-ox, and waterfowl are all plentiful, and there are rare appearances of walrus, bowhead whale, and small herds of Peary caribou. Dwelling areas on the site were marked by 9 or 10 shallowly depressed hearth areas of boulders and fire-cracked rock. Surrounding at least one of the hearth depressions, 20 cm deep and 60 cm in diameter, were three vertically placed driftwood posts that would have enclosed a rectangular space 3 m long and 1.6 m wide. Distribution of fire-cracked rock within this space (Arnold 1980:Figure 4) indicate the limits of a kitchen area, with the roof on a larger house supported by the vertical posts. Such a construction is unlike any yet reported for Pre-Dorset or Dorset and is more reminiscent of houses in Alaska where driftwood is more common.

The 334 stone artifacts from the site are of Eastern Arctic type but not sufficiently diagnostic to place them chronologically. Most of the lithic materials are of a gray metamorphosed quartzite and include a number of retouched flakes and blades, end and side scrapers, three burins, a burin spall, and two burin-like tools with square distal ends indistinguishable from Dorset ones. There are large and small side blades, corner-notched, side-notched, and stemmed end blades, one triangular end blade, and basin-shaped lamps roughly made from cobbles. One of the end scrapers has a tranverse edge, a characteristic of Dorset much later than the site could be but a trait that also rarely appears in Pre-Dorset and Early Dorset (as at Nunguvik). The burins and burin spall, while more characteristic of late Pre-Dorset, also appear, though in small quantities, in several Early Dorset sites as discussed in the preceding.

In summary, there is nothing in the lithic technology to preclude including this site in the Early Dorset phase. The opposite is true when the nonlithic artifacts are considered (Figure 7.14).

The 287 artifacts of antler, ivory and bird bone are unlike any in Dorset assemblages. The 9 recovered harpoon heads all have rectangular open sockets and a single lateral proximal spur. Some are unilaterally or bilaterally barbed, others have beds for end blades at the distal end, and most have decorative incised lines running longitudinally down dorsal or ventral faces. An open-socket antler lance head is not unlike those from Pre-Dorset and Dorset sites, but unlike them has an elaborate design of ticked longitudinal and horizontal lines engraved on the ventral surface (opposite to the socket surface). Three barbed points, possibly from fishing leisters,

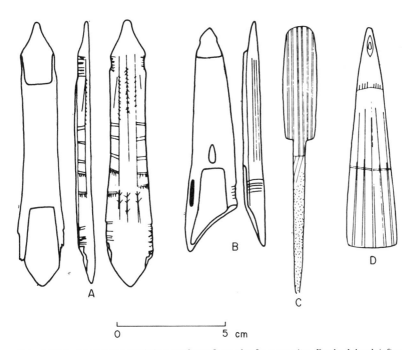

Figure 7.14 Decorated nonlithic artifacts from the Lagoon site, Banks Island (after Arnold 1981).

A. dorsal, side, and ventral view of a lance
B. dorsal and side view of a harpoon head
C. awl
D. pendant

are also decorated as are 2 nail-like engraving(?) tools that had been fitted with hard tips and 9 awls with rectangular handles. Two long narrow points with beds for end blades might be interpreted as arrow points, a trait missing from eastern Dorset. Ninety-three needles and fragments, associated with bird bone needle cases, have round, drilled eyes and round butt ends, characteristics that fit better into Pre-Dorset assemblages than Early Dorset ones but are also present in Alaskan Norton Sites.

In summary, two alternative explanations for this strange complex have been explored by Arnold. The first would relate it to the eastern core area, with some lag in time due to the distance involved. This would require relating such traits as the open-socket harpoon heads to late Pre-Dorset cognates. However it is only the open socket that they have in common, and the asymmetrical proximal spur and engraved designs have more in common with the coeval Norton culture of western Alaska (Dumond 1977; Giddings 1964: particularly Plates 36, 18, and 20, 1967). So, also, do a number of other discrete attributes. This leads to the second interpretation: The site represents contact between Norton and Dorset cultures. Such contact is not unexpected. Several archaeologists have anticipated it, but to date the Lagoon site provides the only empirical evidence. Throughout the long expanse of time, Dorset has the appearance of a closed cultural system, presumably with effective mechanisms of boundary maintenance. Here, at the westernmost border of Dorset culture and the easternmost extension of Norton, such mechanisms may have lost their force. As Arnold (1980:424) states, in referring to such hybridization, "under conditions of low population density—such as would characterize relict populations as well as pioneering groups—the permeability of cultural boundaries would be increased."

The Hudson Bay Sites

Returning eastward, neither the western nor eastern shores of Hudson Bay appear to have been occupied in Early Dorset times. In fact Nash (1976) sees a significant gap in the Paleoeskimo sequence at Churchill between the end of Pre-Dorset in about 900 B.C. and the entry of Dorset people late in the first century B.C. Fitzhugh (1976a) has related this absence to the relatively unsuitable fast ice conditions around the shores of the bay.

Farther out in the bay, around the Belcher Islands, ice conditions may have been more suitable, for Harp (1976b) has located sites here that are Early Dorset by all typological considerations and constitute the most southern penetration of the culture.

Only preliminary reports and photographs are available for these important Belcher Island sites, but a number of significant points can be noted. The islands are low lying, no more than 60 m above present sea level, with the earliest Dorset sites at 55 m above present sea level. This suggests that the islands were beneath seawater until near the end of Pre-Dorset. At least four sites near the northern end of the archipelago—Tuurngasiti 1, 2, 4, and 5—have artifacts that are typologically

A

B   C   D

0   cm   5

Figure 7.15 Lithic artifacts from the Tuurngasiti 2 site, Belcher Islands (photographs courtesy of Elmer Harp, Jr.)

A. side- and corner-notched end blades
B. spalled burins
C. burin-like tool
D. side blades

barely distinguishable from those of the Tanfield site. The highest, and presumably oldest, Tuurngasiti 2, yielded four carbon dates. Two, both older than 1000 B.C., are unacceptable, but two others, 780 and 500 B.C., although early, might be contemporaneous with the Avinga site, which immediately precedes the Early Dorset Tanfield site. Several of the traits from this site resemble stone tools from Avinga (Figure 7.15). There are several spalled burins of a form discretely similar, a number of moderately large side-notched chert knives, and several ground-slate knives with multiply sawed notches. There are several ovate side blades, a few expanded-edge end scrapers, and both square- and angular-tipped burin-like tools. Other Early Dorset traits from these sites include small, rectangular, flat-based soapstone vessels, straight-based triangular end blades, and needles with ovate, scratched-in eyes and sharp butt ends. Most diagnostic are at least three harpoon heads from Tuurngasiti 5—one Tyara Sliced type and two that appear to be most like Kingait Closed. A carbon date from this house, A.D. 610, must be at least 1000 years too recent. The closely related Tuurngasiti 1 site supplied another date, A.D. 370, which is six centuries too young, and a third date, 340 B.C., which Harp considered "far out of line" but which I would consider accurate.

The Early Dorset sites of Tuurngasiti 4 and 5 and the lower terrace at Renouf 2 all had slab-stone box hearths, some with counterweighted pot supports. These features are surprisingly like Independence II hearths, although few other traits are held in common. Their presence is all the more confusing since all of the artifact traits conform to Early Dorset types to the north where stone box hearths have not been reported.

The Coastal Labrador Sites

Soil and climatic conditions here have not preserved organic materials from a time contemporaneous with Early Dorset to the north. However, there is little doubt in the minds of Labrador investigators that an Early Dorset horizon is expressed in lithic artifacts and settlement systems. In summary, Fitzhugh (1980) sees Early Dorset coming into northern Labrador fully formed in the core area and successively expanding southward along the coast. In the process, it displaces the earlier Groswater Dorset, which nevertheless persists coevally as a distinct cultural complex south at Hamilton Inlet until around 250 B.C. Among other traits, the emphasis in economic activities differs, with Early Dorset making a more intensive and efficient use of seacoast resources than Groswater Dorset.

Three charcoal ^{14}C dates (see Table 7.1) span the period from 535 to 450 B.C. A date of 895 B.C. from Iluvektalik Island, more than three centuries too early, is suspect, since the charcoal sample was mixed with fat. North of Nain, artifact traits of Early Dorset in Labrador are essentially those of the core area at T-1, Southampton Island (Fitzhugh 1980) and at Tanfield and Tyara. In the opinions of Fitzhugh, Cox (1978), and Tuck (1975, 1976) these were an intrusion by migration rather than an *in situ* development from the earlier Groswater Dorset. The latter more closely resembles traits of other sites in the transitional period, such as cultural materials from the 24-m terrace at Igloolik, the Killilugak and Avinga sites in Tanfield Valley, and possibly Tuurngasiti 2 on the Belcher Islands. The resemblance is particularly close to Independence II on the basis of the presence in both of midpassage houses.

Early Dorset Labrador houses, on the other hand, are shallow semisubterranean pits without midpassages. In the lithic complex there are triangular, bifacially flaked end blades that are frequently fluted at the tips and have straight or slightly concave bases, end blades with multiple side notching, angular soapstone vessels, nephrite adz blades, notched or stemmed slate knives, and polished burin-like tools, all of which are absent in Groswater Dorset assemblages. In Labrador Early Dorset there was an extensive use of Ramah chert for tools and a high frequency of microblades, circular side blades, and triangular end scrapers.

On the basis of current evidence, Early Dorset people in northern Labrador could not sustain themselves on this rugged unfriendly coast for more than two centuries. Afterwards, five or six centuries may have elapsed before reoccupation. Alternatively, the Middle Dorset site of Avayalik 2, on the basis of both typology and carbon dating, may bridge this gap on the Torngat coast (Jordon 1980).

Summary

In this treatment of Early Dorset we have arbitrarily selected one discrete trait of harpoon heads to mark the end of Early Dorset and the beginning of Middle Dorset. There is no other apparent aspect of cultural change to separate the two, yet the simultaneous and ubiquitous substitution of completely closed-socket harpoon heads for those with small dorsal slices provides a convenient marking point for the beginning of a long period in which more major change took place. Divided thus, the Early Dorset period lasted two centuries from 500 to 300 B.C.

Three hypothetical positions have been advanced for the process by which Dorset developed out of an earlier Pre-Dorset base. These are (1) a regionally specific *in situ* development from local aspects of a widespread Pre-Dorset, (2) a diffused influence from a distinctive High Arctic transitional cultural complex, and (3) an initial development in one cultural center carried outward by both diffusion and migration. Of these, the evidence, in my judgment, best satisfies the latter. The discreteness of trait attributes appearing within less than a century throughout the geographic range of the culture provides a weighty argument in favor of this position. If this was the case, the most logical center of development would appear to have been in the northern Foxe Basin. However, the people there seem to have been in such constant communication with those of northern Hudson Bay, both shores of Hudson Strait, and northern Baffin Island that a shift in economic activity and concomitant artifact style may have been virtually simultaneous throughout this larger region.

In contrast to the smaller sites of late Pre-Dorset, Early Dorset settlements, at least in some seasons, are relatively large, with seasonal aggregates of 50 or more people. In some parts of the range these settlements are more often on exposed outer coasts than in sheltered bays. In the east there is a presumed increase in predation of sea mammals with a concentration on those species that were locally available. Kayak parts and models, sleds, ice creepers, seal oil lamps, and snow knives point to increased hunting activity on both sea ice and open water. In the west, caribou and musk-ox continue to be the dominant prey.

Residence types changed with the seasons. Semi-subterranean houses equipped with side sleeping benches and driftwood roof frames, houses of cut sod, and rectangular tent platforms outlined by boulders all have been reported. The period is marked by an extensive use of slate for knives, quartz crystal for many artifacts, nephrite for adzes and burin-like tools, and, on the northern coast of Labrador, Ramah chert for end blades. There are essentially two forms of harpoon heads: one is small, with a single line hole perpendicular to the socket, the other is larger, with a transverse line hole parallel to the socket. Presumably one was for the smaller species of seal and the other for walrus and bearded seal. There was a marked increase in stone vessels, both lamps and suspended bowls. These are relatively small and rectangular with sloping sides. Triangular end blades have straight bases and are frequently tip fluted, and a fully polished burin-like graver nearly but not entirely supplants the spalled burin. Art forms, carved animals and humans, are present but not as common as they become later. Ideology is expressed on some of these in the form of skeletal engraving. Ideology may also be reflected in the strange absence of drills, which had been present in Pre-Dorset. The labor involved in scratching nearly round line holes in harpoon heads, rather than reaming them out with a stone blade suggests some ideational constraint. There is also tenuous evidence for constraints in the seasonal sewing of skin clothing. One of the strangest absences in at least all but the western islands is the bow and arrow used by earlier

Pre-Dorset people. From the quantity of wooden objects that have now been re-covered from sites such as Tanfield, Nunguvik, and Avayalik we can say with certain-ty that this absence in Dorset sites is not a function of archaeological sampling. Caribou, musk-ox, and polar bear could only have been killed with hand-thrown or -thrusted weapons.

MIDDLE DORSET

I have arbitrarily selected here the time span between the disappearance of sliced-socket harpoon heads and the first appearance of double–line hole ones as the Middle Dorset period (Figure 7.16). On the surface this appears hardly defensi-ble. However, it does conform to some apparent gaps in the ^{14}C sequence (Table 7.3) and to the general impressions of several investigators working in the area. In years, this covers the eight centuries between 300 B.C. AND A.D. 500. At the early end of the sequence there is little stylistic change in attributes, and the tool inventory remains much the same as in Early Dorset. Through time, there are minor shifts in style and more significant changes in settlement patterns. In some regions, particu-larly in Labrador and Newfoundland, these changes in technology and settlement are more pronounced. Coeval with the appearance of double–line hole harpoon heads in the Late Dorset period, there is a more marked change throughout in most of the technical equipment, in art, and in settlement systems. Both the relative stasis of technology and minor cultural changes in Middle Dorset are surprising in light of climatic shifts during this time. Much of the empirical evidence for climatic fluctuation in this period is confusing and even contradictory (see Arundale 1976 and Dekin 1975 for good discussions of this evidence). Generally, in North America it may have been a time of climatic instability, but in the Eastern Arctic the increas-ing cold that began half a millennium before the beginning of Dorset continued to a climax of extreme cold around 150 B.C. Jacobs (1981) has suggested that this led to low terrestrial production and a concomitant reduction of human population at least on Baffin Island. In support of this there appear to be fewer and smaller sites for about four centuries in the latter part of the Middle Dorset period. This is also a period for which no sites have been reported in the High Arctic. Conversely, popula-tion appears to have increased in this period on the Labrador coast (Fitzhugh 1980b). McGhee (1976) has suggested that much of the peripheral Dorset popula-tion was reduced by catastrophism in this cold period.

From the start of the Christian era, a slow warming trend began, a trend that reached its peak between A.D. 250 and 450. It is within the ensuing warm period that populations of Late Dorset expanded, there was a renewed occupation of fringe areas, and Dorset culture reached its apogee of art and technology.

Tanfield Valley: The Kemp and Nanook Sites

The Kemp site is a very small occupation, estimated to cover no more than 84 m^2, approximately 133 m northwest of the Tanfield site and 2 m higher in elevation. The

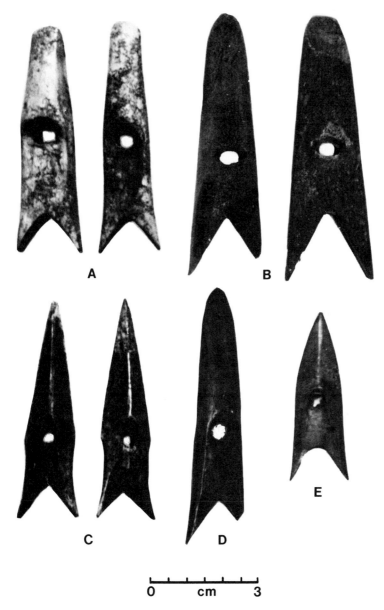

Figure 7.16   Characteristic Middle Dorset harpoon heads.

A. Kingait Closed, Igloolik region
B. Kingait Closed, Saatut site
C. Nanook Wasp Waist, Igloolik region and
    Nanook site
D. Nanook Grooved, Nanook site
E. Native Point Grooved, Tyara site

cultural midden is between two gulleys, at least one of which was coeval with the occupation. The steep western slope of Tanfield Valley rises immediately behind the site, which lies under the lea of a steep, curving, rock outcrop to the south. It is an unlikely location for residences but would be better protected from winter winds than any other part of the valley. This point gives some support to the proposition that winters were continuing to be colder than before.

Barely 12 m² of the site have been tested (Maxwell 1973a), but this has indicated sporadic occupation over two or more centuries. The very few rocks in the midden and the sodden condition of the site suggests settlement only in winter and then in sod- or snowhouses.

Since there was no indication of layering in the homogeneous midden, the 40-cm deep cultural deposit, thick with animal bones, cut wood, and artifacts, was excavated in arbitrary 8-cm levels. Most of the 949 recovered lithic artifacts did not appear to differ significantly in form or frequency from the bottom to the top of the midden. The same category of tools present in the Tanfield site were represented here. Spalled burins, however, were found only in the lowest level, where they constituted 5% of the stone tools in that level. Slate knives continued to exhibit the increasing frequency begun in Early Dorset and then decreased in numbers in the top two levels.

Nonlithic artifacts were relatively scarce (*n* = 57) however they included 15 harpoon heads sufficiently diagnostic to date the site typologically (Figure 7.17). Five of these were too eroded or broken to identify. Six, all from the bottom of the midden, are of the sliced suite (Tyara Pointed, 3; Tanfield Sliced, 2; and Tyara Sliced, 1) and a seventh, from the bottom of Level 4, is of the Tyara Sliced type. A single self-bladed, closed-socket head with its line hole on a raised dorsal platform, from the top of Level 4, was termed Kemp Pointed since it differed from Kingait Closed heads. Two heads from Level 2, closed socketed and slotted for end blades, are of the Kingait Closed type. The situation here parallels that at the Tyara site, where closed-socket harpoon heads displace the sliced-socket ones.

The carbon dates from the site are of only limited usefulness. Driftwood from about the middle of the fourth level dating 90 B.C. (GSC-794) indicates little (see Table 7.3). A corrected charred fat date of A.D. 215 (M-1534) from 20 cm beneath the surface seems a reasonable date for the latest settlement. Based primarily on the recovered harpoon heads, I would suggest that the site was occupied sporadically by two or at the most three families in very cold winters for as many as five centuries, between 300 B.C. and A.D. 200. After this time Cape Tanfield and Tanfield Valley, which are appreciably colder in summer and winter than more inland bays and fjords, was abandoned until much later, in Late Dorset time.

Arundale's (1976) account of the Nanook site is the most complete and detailed treatment of the early part of the middle period. The site is a small pocket 55 m long between two rock outcrops 16 m apart with midden from outcrop to outcrop. Its elevation, at 12 m above present sea level is significantly higher than the earlier Tanfield site 70 m due east but would have been better sheltered in winter than the floor of the valley. In four field seasons 77 m² of the site have been excavated. The

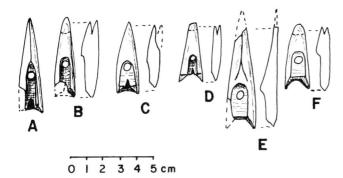

Figure 7.17 Harpoon heads from the Kemp site, Lake Harbour.

A. Tyara Pointed
B. Tanfield Sliced
C. Tyara Sliced
D. Tanfield Sliced
E. Kemp Pointed
F. Kingait Closed

site is a very complex one, with many rocks arranged in barely apparent pattern. Some areas seem intentionally paved, and there appears to be at least one shallow pit house. A long wall 1 m wide built up in three or four courses of rocks and cut sod parallels the eastern rock outcrop and runs the length of the site. Along the western side of this wall were at least four kitchen areas of charred fat, oil-soaked detritus, and sharpened wooden stakes (Maxwell 1980). In my judgment this can best be interpreted as a form of communal living arrangement in which separate family tents were placed along the wall, which then served as an extended sleeping bench.

Arundale has applied rigorous testing to a number of hypotheses about this site, but this work is only briefly summarized here. Eleven carbon dates are available for the site. The earliest, 420 B.C. (on willow twigs), is probably accurate but may well date the natural growth of the site prior to human occupation. In various assessments of the remaining dates, Arundale concludes that settlement began sometime between 420 and 270 B.C. and lasted until A.D. 123. In carefully reasoned arguments she interprets the cultural assemblage as being virtually homogeneous and without change from the bottom of the midden to the top. She concludes that the site was occupied intermittently, but on a relatively regular basis, in the cold seasons of the year and then was abandoned at a time of climatic change. Her interpretation suggests that this coincides with the onset of warmer and wetter weather around the beginning of the Christian era. However, considering the lack of precision in dating the climax of the cold and the beginning of a warming trend, it might also have been abandoned for more sheltered shores when the gradual cooling reached limits of human tolerance on this outer coast.

In the lithic assemblage of 3718 artifacts, there are no discernible changes within various categories from the bottom to the top of the midden. All the categories recovered from the Tanfield site are represented here, and single artifacts from the two sites would be difficult to distinguish. However, when viewed as an assemblage, one has the impression of finer workmanship in the Nanook complex (Figure 7.18 and 7.19).

Whereas some of the triangular end blades at Tanfield were tip fluted, none of the Nanook blades are. In this category there is a tendency toward slightly concave bases. Some of the asymmetrical side blades appear to have been used as side-

Table 7.3

RADIOCARBON DATES FOR MIDDLE DORSET SITES[a]

Site	Lab no.	Material	Uncorrected age (radiocarbon years)	Corrected age[b] (radiocarbon years)	Corrected date
Nanook	Gak-1279	Sod	2220 ± 100	—	270 B.C.
Red Rock Pt.	SI-875	Charcoal	2200 ± 120	—	250 B.C.
Tanfield KdDq-7-1[c]	P-698	Charred fat	2608 ± 50	2143 ± 79	193 B.C.
Saatut	S-671	Seal bone	2405 ± 80	2120 ± 100	170 B.C.
Pamiok	Lv-468	Charcoal	2070 ± 140	—	120 B.C.
Kemp	GSC-794	Driftwood	2040 ± 130	—	90 B.C.
Koliktalik 1-(H2)	SI-2534	Charcoal	1935 ± 95	—	A.D. 15
Tanfield KdDq-7-1[c]	M-1528	Charred fat	2390 ± 150	1925 ± 162	A.D. 25
Nanook	P-704	Sod and grass	1916 ± 61	—	A.D. 34
Tyara (Layer 2)	GSC-702	Walrus and seal bone	2200 ± 130	1915 ± 144	A.D. 35
T-3	P-77	Burned seal (?) bone	2191 ± 120	1906 ± 135	A.D. 44
Tanfield KdDq-7-1A	GSC-820	Charred fat	2350 ± 140	1885 ± 140	A.D. 65
Joss	Gak-1257	Charcoal	1860 ± 100	—	A.D. 90
Iglusuaktalialuk 4W	SI-2508	Charcoal	1860 ± 90	—	A.D. 90
W. Rose Is.	I-5253	Charcoal	1850 ± 100	—	A.D. 100
Koliktalik 1-(H2)	SI-2536	Charcoal	1830 ± 90	—	A.D. 120
Nanook	P-706	Willow twigs	1827 ± 61	—	A.D. 123
DIA-4	QC-628	Burned moss	1810 ± 110	—	A.D. 140

Site	Lab no.	Material	Age[b]	Age[c]	Date
Q. Rose Is.	I-5533	Charcoal	1780 ± 90	—	A.D. 170
T-1	P-62	Charred seal bone	2060 ± 200	1775 ± 55	A.D. 175
Koliktalik 1-(H1)	SI-2533	Charcoal	1775 ± 55	—	A.D. 175
Koliktalik 1-(H2)	SI-2535	Charcoal	1760 ± 90	—	A.D. 190
Port aux Choix 2[d]	P-692	Charcoal	1736 ± 48	—	A.D. 214
Kemp	M-1534	Charred fat	2200 ± 120	1735 ± 135	A.D. 215
Koliktalik 1(H1)	SI-2150	Charcoal	1720 ± 80	—	A.D. 230
Iglusuaktalialuk 4W	SI-2157	Charcoal	1685 ± 70	—	A.D. 265
DIA-4	QC-632	Burned moss	1660 ± 95	—	A.D. 290
St. Johns Is.	SI-2980	Charcoal	1555 ± 90	—	A.D. 395
Avayalik	SI-3997	Willow	1520 ± 60	—	A.D. 430
Avayalik	SI-3009	Willow	1510 ± 60	—	A.D. 440
Napatalik N	SI-1793	Charcoal	1510 ± 100	—	A.D. 440
Koliktalik 1(H1)	SI-2532	Charcoal	1500 ± 95	—	A.D. 450
Avayalik	SI-3886	Charcoal	1495 ± 70	—	A.D. 455
DIA-4	QC-633	Burned moss	1470 ± 100	—	A.D. 480
Koliktalik 1(H1)	SI-2151	Charcoal	1470 ± 100	—	A.D. 480
Moores Is. 1	SI-2155	Charcoal	1450 ± 95	—	A.D. 500
DIA-4	QC-631	Burned moss	1380 ± 100	—	A.D. 570
Koliktalik 1(H1)	SI-2152	Charcoal	1335 ± 90	—	A.D. 615
Port aux Choix 2[d]	P-737	Charcoal	1321 ± 49	—	A.D. 629

[a] Data from Arundale 1981, with additions by Maxwell.

[b] Ages have been corrected by incorporating laboratory-derived fractionation and sea reservoir factors.

[c] Material from two parts of the same sample.

[d] Earliest and latest, respectively, of 11 dates on charcoal.

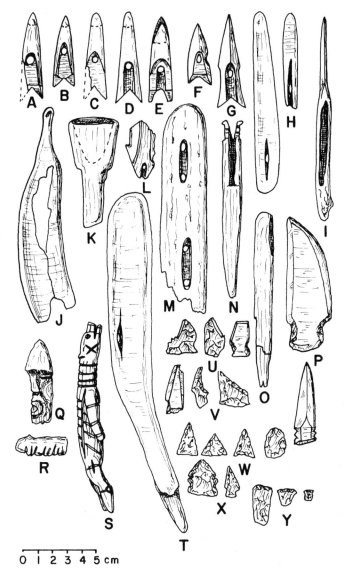

Figure 7.18 Artifacts from the Nanook site, Lake Harbour.

A–C. Kingait Closed harpoon heads
D,E. Nanook Grooved harpoon heads
F. Kemp Pointed harpoon head
G. Nanook Wasp Waist harpoon head
H. harpoon foreshafts
I. awl cut from caribou scapula
J. antler scoop or spoon
K. adz socket
L. base of Atausik-type lance head
M. whalebone sled shoe
N. wooden burin handle
O. wooden side-bladed knife handle
P. slate knife blades
Q. wooden maskette fragment
R. crude ivory shaman's teeth
S. side view of ivory bear
T. antler scoop or snow knife
U. polished and unpolished spalled burins and Dorset burin-like tool
V. Nanook polished knife and side scrapers
W. three harpoon end blades and one side blade
X. side-notched knife blades
Y. end scrapers

0 1 2 3 4 5 cm

hafted knives, and at least one microblade, found in its original wooden handle, was side hafted.

Relative frequencies are similar between the two sites, with a few significant differences. Only 8% of the Nanook lithic tools are slate knives compared to 15% at the Tanfield site, a trend which parallels that at the Kemp site. Spalled burins increase from 1% at Tanfield to 3% at Nanook. For some reason these grooving tools remain, in varying frequencies, in unmixed components throughout the span of

Dorset on the south coast of Baffin Island. Elsewhere in Eastern Arctic Dorset, they appear to have been completely supplanted by the polished burin-like tool. Surprisingly, in view of the fact that this appears to have been a cold weather site in centuries colder than now, there were very few lamp fragments. They represent only 1% of the worked stone objects compared to 6% at Tanfield. Most of the fragments are of flat-based, angular bowls, but at least one is shallow and oval, starting a trend that continues later in Dorset.

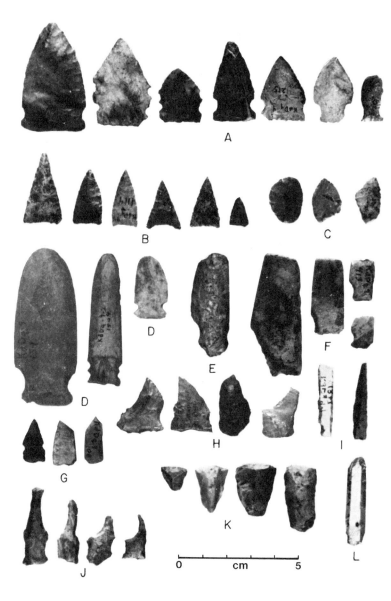

Figure 7.19 Middle Dorset lithic artifacts from the Nanook site, Lake Harbour.

A. side- and corner-notched end blades
B. triangular harpoon end blades
C. side blades
D. slate knives
E. polished knife (Nanook burin-like type)
F. four polished burin-like tools (Dorset type)
G. three angular-tipped burin-like tools of nephrite
H. four spalled burins
I. quartz-crystal and chert microblades
J. side scrapers
K. end scrapers
L. quartz-crystal core for microblades

Of the 50 harpoon heads recovered, 3 are small toys and 6 are too broken and eroded to identify. The remainder are all unsliced with completely closed sockets. Twenty-five are of the Kingait Closed type, slotted for end blades. Four, also slotted, are similar but with the line hole in a narrow groove. The sides of this form are nearly parallel in an elongated bullet shape. I have termed them Nanook Grooved. Nine self-bladed forms are very distinctive, with a line hole in a groove and lateral margins constricted at about the level of the line hole. The type, which I refer to as Nanook Wasp Waist, is probably a more recent variant of the Native Point Grooved type. It appears in Igloolik at the 15-m level (Maxwell 1976). The remaining identified head is one of the Kemp Pointed type. Two fragmentary heads have transverse line holes, but since both are only distal ends, they can only provisionally be considered the Dorset Parallel type.

The 808 artifacts of organic materials include 4 needles, all with pointed butt ends, and 6 whalebone sled runners of an early type. These are flat, with paired lashing holes in the center that are perpendicular to the running surface and connected by a channeled groove. There are also several pieces of yarn, most about 20 mm long, made from twisted musk-ox hair. Their function is unknown, but they must be the result of long-distance exchange since there are no indications that musk-ox ever lived on Baffin Island.

Ten wooden pieces, graduated in size (see Figure 6.5) are carefully made with two rectangular tenoned pieces near a curving edge. The most likely interpretation is that they were framework members of a kayak.

Art, and presumably ideology, is better represented here than at the Tanfield site. There are four small human maskettes made of wood, a fifth of steatite, and a small complete human nose, which—like carved caribou hooves in some Dorset sites— may have been an abstraction for the complete face. There is a two-pronged pendant, which may represent the legs of an animal or human, a crudely carved wooden polar bear with an X across its head, and a beautifully carved ivory polar bear with surface engraving that represents bones and joints (see Figure 7.18S).

At a corrected date of A.D. 65, people making stone tools identical to those of the Nanook complex made a summer camp on what was then a sea beach in the Tanfield Valley (Site KdDq-7-1A) and is now 5.5 m above present sea level. Unfortunately the resulting midden was too thin for preservation of organic materials.

Native Point, Southampton Island: The T-3 Site

Here, at the T-3 site, Collins (1957) excavated a gravel beach ridge 13.5 m above present sea level and 8 m lower than the T-1 site. The midden was thinner than at T-1 and he recovered fewer artifacts, but typologically they are more recent, a point supported by a corrected carbon date of A.D. 44. The site had few mammal bones but a surprising number—11,000—of bird bones. This parallels the situation at the Nanook site, where Arundale (1976) identified a large number of rookery birds.

Collins saw little change in the lithic artifacts from the earlier site (Figure 7.20). As at T-1 there were no concave side scrapers. He recovered no spalled burins but

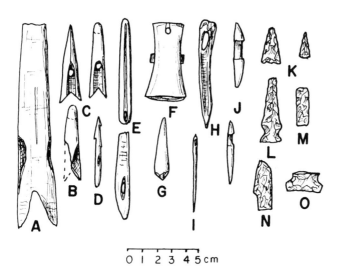

Figure 7.20 Middle Dorset artifacts from the T-3 site, Native Point, Southampton Island (drawings based on selected illustrations from Collins 1956a, 1957).

A. ivory sled shoe laterally perforated
B,C. Dorset Parallel, Native Point Grooved, and Nanook Grooved harpoon heads
D. central barb of fish spear
E. harpoon foreshafts
F. needle case or shaman's tube
G. flaking punch
H. awl cut from medial spine of caribou scapula
I. needle with sharp butt end
J. burin support piece
K. harpoon end blades
L. side-notched end blade
M. side-hafted knife blade
N. unfinished burin-like tool
O. side-notched knife base

0 1 2 3 4 5 cm

did find three spalls from such burins. There was only one unfinished burin-like tool and a spall from a completed tool. Tip fluting on triangular end blades was less frequent although triangular microlithic spalls from this process were present. Conversely, nonlithic traits appear in the T-3 midden that became predominant forms in Late Dorset sites. Unilaterally and bilaterally barbed fish spears have tapering proximal ends that would fit into sockets in contrast to the earlier open-socket ones. The latter forms, unlike the early ones had line holes situated well up from the proximal ends and would have functioned as small harpoons. The only sled shoe fragment is a rectangular bar of ivory perforated from one lateral edge to the other with scratched holes parallel to the running surface. Such sled shoes, nearly square in cross section, were made in sections, with the pointed end of one segment fitting into the V-shaped end of the next. Cutting such a runner from a walrus tusk must have been extremely time-consuming, yet this form continues as the standard sled shoe through Late Dorset.

Needles from T-3, like earlier ones, have points at both ends. They are associated here with a lovely ivory needle case (Figure 7.20F) that Collins considers similar to those of Alaskan design.

Harpoon heads are of expectable types with one exception. This, from the same square and level that produced the carbon sample, is a very small, nonfunctional head of Dorset Parallel Sliced form with only a vestigial line for the slice and chevron incising on the upper part of the dorsal surface. The others are comparable to Dorset Parallel, Kingait Closed, Nanook Grooved, and Native Point Grooved and its later variant Nanook Wasp Waist. Significant additional traits are a cut bear maxilla, a cut polar bear canine, two iron pyrites hammers (or fire starters?), and long, ivory burin support pieces. These latter are the bars that when fastened to a wooden handle keep the grooving tool from rocking backward.

The Northern Foxe Basin Sites

In the sites around Igloolik, Meldgaard has recognized five stages of Dorset culture but has not yet described the diagnostic features in print. Presumably what we are considering here as Middle Dorset would correspond to his Stage 3. The material resembling that from Nanook and T-3 appears to begin at about the 19-m level above present sea level. This level marks the first appearance of a harpoon head comparable to Native Point Grooved. By the 15-m level, this form has transitioned to the Nanook Wasp Waist variant.

At the 19-m level small needles are bipointed and fish spear sockets are still open. Flint has begun to supersede slate for knives and tip fluting of harpoon end blades has declined. By the 18-m level, the Kingait Closed harpoon head, the closed-socket Dorset Parallel, and a few needles rounded at the butt end have all appeared. Art forms seem to increase by the 17-m level, with, among other artifacts, a neatly decapitated ivory polar bear with an engraved skeletal design. At the 15-m terrace, the harpoon complex is the same as that at the Nanook site, including forms of Kemp Pointed, Nanook Grooved, Kingait Closed, Nanook Wasp Waist, and Dorset Parallel. Fish harpoons are of both open-socket and proximal-pointed end types, needles have rounded ends, there is an increase in composite boxes of caribou antler, side-hafted knives appear, and a few of the soapstone lamps are oval shaped. The 14-m level marks the first appearance of the double–line hole harpoon head, which here we are considering diagnostic of Late Dorset.

Navy Board Inlet, North Baffin Island: The Saatut Site

The Saatut site (Mary-Rousselière 1976) is clearly of this Middle Dorset period as indicated by the typology of its artifacts and a corrected carbon date of 170 B.C. The site, 39 km south of the Nunguvik site and 5 m above present sea level, contained 1228 stone artifacts and 838 wood, antler, bone, and ivory.

The lithic assemblage is not particularly distinctive although it does contain some significant items. There were only 2 slate artifacts, 1 resembling an *ulu*. There was 1 spalled burin and only 23 burin-like gravers, indicating little emphasis in this activity. Three of the 78 end scrapers had oblique edges, 41 of the 95 triangular end blades had serrated edges, and there were 3 parallel-stemmed end blades with serrated edges. These 4 attributes, oblique edges on scrapers, serration on the lateral margins of harpoon end blades, and stemmed and serrated lance(?) end blades are all more characteristic of Late Dorset.

Harpoon heads were predominantly of the Kingait Closed type (75%) with Native Point Grooved (21%) and Dorset Parallel (4%) following in importance (Figure 7.21). All of these have deeper and sharper terminal spurs than have Early Dorset

Figure 7.21 Nonlithic artifacts from the Saatut site, Navy Board Inlet, Baffin Island.

A. two harpoon heads of Dorset Parallel type
B. two harpoon heads of Kingait Closed type
C. harpoon head of Saatut Pointed type
D. two harpoon heads of Native Point Grooved type
E. bone dagger(?)
F. four handles for side-hafted microblades or burin-like tools
G. antler adz socket

H. bone awl
I. bodkin
J. needles with square butt ends
K. antler scoop
L. ivory seal effigy
M. ivory bear (top) and young walrus (bottom) effigy (see Figure 6.28F for side view)
N. wooden sled model

toggling harpoon heads. One of the Dorset Parallel heads was slotted for a side blade as well as an end blade. Of the 88 recovered needles only 1 was pointed at the butt end. Carvings and artistic pieces were more common here than in the earlier Nunguvik house. Among the group that included human and bear effigies was a double-ended ivory walrus–bear (Figure 6.28F) and what may have been a tattooing needle decorated with a human face.

Victoria Island: The Joss Site

On the western coast of Victoria Island, along Prince Albert Sound and Minto Inlet, McGhee (1969) located several Dorset sites, including some of the middle period. One, the Joss site, dated A.D. 90 on charcoal and burned caribou(?) bone, is typologically linked both to the earlier sites of Victoria Island and to the core area, although with discrete regional differences. In the stone assemblage there are few triangular harpoon end blades (most Victoria Island harpoon heads are self-bladed), and only a trace of tip fluting remains. Ground-slate artifacts and soapstone vessel fragments are very rare, but the polished burin-like tools do not differ from those found farther east. Of 22 harpoon heads, 21 are closed socketed and only 1 is sliced, all are clearly derived from such earlier forms as those at the Ballantine site. Three barbed heads, either fish spears or dart heads, demonstrate the typological shift noted at T-3, with 2 of the heads being open socketed and 1 having a sharpened proximal end. The needles recovered are all sharp at both ends.

Perhaps the most interesting artifact from this site, duplicated by another from a nearby site (OdPc-4), is what McGhee has interpreted as an arrowhead and compares tentatively to a similar one from the Norton culture of Alaska. The two artifacts are slender shafts of antler that have perforated, scarfed proximal ends and are slotted for end blades and on opposing lateral margins for side blades. These are the only weapons yet identified as parts of a Dorset bow and arrow complex and, like the Lagoon site of Banks Island, may represent one of the few outside contacts in the virtually closed cultural system of Dorset.

Other traits such as antler lance heads, adz sockets, and small antler boxes do not differ typologically from other Dorset ones of this period (Figure 7.22).

The Greenland Sites

The earliest Greenlandic Dorset occupation, as differentiated from Independence II, appears in Disko Bay at the Sermermiut site dated A.D. 123 on plant remains. The cultural materials all point to a Middle Dorset age and therefore may represent a new migration from Arctic Canada rather than an *in situ* development from Sarqaq.

Taylor (1968) has supplied a well-reasoned seriation of various Disko Bay site assemblages that he interprets as closing the gap between these two cultural complexes. His methodology is sound, but I think the results primarily demonstrate developmental trends in Sarqaq that do not bridge the centuries in which Early Dorset was developing to the west. The gap in time between the latest Sarqaq site and Sermermiut Dorset is not less than eight centuries. Furthermore, the Sermer-

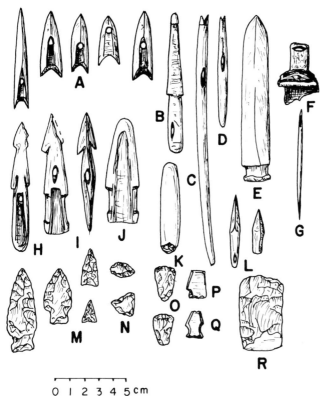

Figure 7.22 Artifacts from the Joss and related sites, Prince Albert Sound, Victoria Island—B, Site OdPc-3; D and R, Site OdPc-4; and the remainder, Joss site (drawings based on selected illustrations from McGhee 1969).

A. harpoon heads
B. foreshaft
C,D. end- and side-bladed arrowheads
E. lance head
F. antler needle case or amulet box
G. needle
H. lance heads
I. dart head or fish spear
J. ice pick
K. flaking punch
L. antler arrowheads
M. knives and harpoon end blades
N. side blades
O. end scrapers
P. burin-like tool
Q. slate knife blade
R. adz blade

miut lithic assemblage (no organic artifacts were preserved) is too close in the discreteness of its traits to stone assemblages of Canadian Middle Dorset to ignore the relation, even though it entails a migration of more than 2000 km across the head of Baffin Bay.

The period between the first and fifth centuries A.D. is the least well known in the Dorset sequence. Through most of the central region of Dorset, there is what appears to have been a population decline or at least a reduction in the number and size of sites. This may, of course, be a function of our limited exploration but that now appears doubtful. Possibly winter and early spring settlements, which produce the most débitage, were now snow house villages on the sea ice, and summer camps were thinly middened and scattered (Maxwell 1980). However, Late Dorset, beginning about A.D. 500, is characterized by distinctive changes in lithic and nonlithic technology. It suddenly appears in marginal areas with no immediate local predecessor even though clearly part of a centrally unbroken continuum. In my 400-km survey of southeastern Baffin Island, I have found only a few traces of small campsites that might have been briefly occupied within these centuries. The same is true for the rest of the Baffin Island coast with the possible exception of the Navy Board Inlet sites of Nunguvik and Saatut. Even in this latter site, the eight-century gap between the two available corrected carbon dates—170 B.C. to A.D. 725—may in part be due to a gap in settlement continuation. My impression of the situation at Igloolik is one of site reduction between the 15-m and 13-m levels, although this may be incorrect. McGhee (1976) suggests a similar gap on Victoria Island between the early part of Middle Dorset and a weakly expressed Late Dorset, which he sees as an immigration from the core area. Late Dorset is widespread and flourishing in the High Arctic, but Middle Dorset has not yet been reported.

Everyone attempting syntheses of Dorset culture has tried to attribute causative factors to climatic change in such episodes of migration, regional expansion, or population change. I am no exception, and, as McGhee (1976) has pointed out, most such attempts have come to grief. These four centuries are particularly confusing from this point of view. Jacobs (1981) in reviewing the evidence, finds that the summer pollen record of southeastern Baffin Island suggests cooler July temperatures. On the other hand, analysis of peat growth indicates a warming trend peaking at about A.D. 450. There is some evidence to support the proposition that the latter part of Middle Dorset was warmer than the early part had been. But as we have discussed earlier, the effect this may have had on fauna and subsequently on humans can be modeled many ways. As noted earlier, warmer, wetter winters mean more snow and icing, which can reduce caribou herds; but, conversely, longer, colder winters, with increased cold stress on calves and more snow compaction, which limits grazing, can also reduce herd size. Warmer winters can reduce the buildup of fast ice and limit seal breeding areas, but long, cold winters that increase the thickness and extent of sea ice reduce breathing space and may also result in decreased population. Obviously, with these variables, we can do little more than state that the period from A.D. 200 to 500 is one of apparent Dorset decline.

The Labrador and Newfoundland Sites

Quite the opposite situation is found on the north and central coasts of Labrador and on Newfoundland. Here the latter part of Middle Dorset between the beginning of the Christian era and about A.D. 500 was a time of maximum Dorset occupation with sites in number and size nearly equaling those of Neoeskimo (Fitzhugh 1980b). Jordan (1980:626) sees this as essentially an *in situ* development from Early Dorset, but with frequent contacts with the core area and borrowing of stylistic attributes developing there. A current gap in carbon dates between the last of Early Dorset (450 B.C.) and the first of Middle Dorset (A.D. 15; Cox 1978) might be interpreted several ways. It might be attributed to the questionable reliability of Arctic carbon dates or simply to the sites that have been sampled. Alternatively, it may reflect a dwindling population followed by a sudden influx of new immigrants. The latter interpretation would fit well with the evidence from farther north of a sudden Dorset population decline.

Most Labrador sites of this period have produced only lithic artifacts. Diagnostic attributes of technology that distinguish it from other periods include unifacially flaked triangular end blades, many of them made by pressing a single flat flake from one face after the biface was formed. Some of these had slightly concave bases. There is a wider range of large and small side-notched bifaces, both symmetrical and asymmetrical. End scrapers tend to be triangular, and distinctive burin-like tools are thin, tabular pieces of polished nephrite with small notches on one or both edges. Soapstone vessels are rectangular, oval ones not appearing until Late Dorset. The Middle Dorset settlements are small nucleated villages of several houses, some with entry tunnels, axial features, and paved sleeping platforms.

Earlier impressions of Newfoundland Dorset, based on materials from the pioneering work of Wintemberg (1939, 1940) and the extensive excavation of Port aux Choix 2 by Harp (1951), were that the island had not been inhabited by Paleoeskimo until it was colonized by Middle Dorset people shortly after the beginning of the Christian era. Since the style of artifacts and art pieces appeared to have had their stimulus in core area Dorset but differed in unique attributes, it was assumed that the distinctive Newfoundland Dorset had developed in virtual isolation after the initial colonization. Later surveys and excavations both in Newfoundland and on the Labrador Coast have questioned both of these impressions. Tuck (1983) has reported small sites with Early Dorset and Groswater Dorset materials, suggesting more of a cultural continuum on the island. The presence of Ramah chert, accessible on the northern Labrador coast, the presence of Newfoundland cherts in Labrador sites near Nain, and distinctive slate knives with interior binding slots rather than side notches in both Newfoundland and Labrador dispel the impression of isolation for Newfoundland Dorset.

The distinctive Middle Dorset sites on Newfoundland have been reported along most of the coast from the northern tip south to the southernmost tip of Cape Ray. Best known of these is the Port aux Choix 2 site near Cape Riche excavated over a number of years by Harp (1951, 1964, 1970, 1976a). Here on two earlier beach lines of limestone shingle 4.6 m and 7.6 m above present sea level, he excavated 20 of 36 house pits. Thirteen of these have been carbon dated, using both charred fat and wood charcoal. The earliest date, a corrected seal(?) fat date, is A.D. 32, and the most recent, on charcoal, is A.D. 629, with a number of charcoal dates clustering around A.D. 400. Within this six century period, Harp sees such homogeneity of cultural traits as to make styles from the earliest houses indistinguishable from those of the latest.

The houses, briefly described in Chapter 6, are square depressions, 4–5 m on a side, scooped from the old beach. The limestone shingle was then carefully stacked along side walls that rise 30–50 cm above the floor level. A series of stone-lined pits, some used as hearths, run from front to back along central floor axes. There are no well-defined entryways, but there are semicircular sleeping platforms of limestone shingle at the rear. The houses, banked with sod cut in summer, were used for a long time. House 2, for example, may have been used for 200 years.

The Port aux Choix settlement was a semipermanent locus from which hunting and fishing forays could be made during many seasons. Its primary use, though, was as a base for hunting the harp seal (*Phoca groenlandica*) that once collected here in great numbers for the pupping season beginning in late February and early March.

In one analyzed house midden sample of 25,000 animal bones, 98% were of this species, with only traces of caribou, fox, beaver, migratory wild fowl, and fish.

In an interesting analysis of the settlement pattern at the site, Harp (1976a) concluded that the bilaterally symmetrical dwellings housed two families or extended families of two or more generations. He considered the minimal viable population for the site to be two households of 6–7 persons each, and in the middle time range, the height of population density, the number of persons living on the site to be 30–50.

Material cultural items from the site unquestionably derive their stylistic impetus from more northern Dorset, but there is such a regional cast to most artifact categories that one would have little difficulty recognizing Newfoundland Dorset in a sample of unknown provenience. The harpoon heads are all closed socketed and slotted for triangular end blades and each is remarkably like all the others. They have a single line hole perpendicular to the socket and occasionally, unlike any others in Dorset, a second line hole forward of the first. The lateral margins are nearly parallel, and both dorsal and ventral faces are flat, giving them a rectangular cross section. While their stylistic progenitor is probably the Kingait Closed type, they differ sufficiently to be considered a separate type—Newfoundland Closed. Dorset Parallel harpoon heads, ubiquitous in core area sites, are present only in nonfunctional form in burial offerings (see Figure 6.26). Harpoon foreshafts (that presumably fit in hollowed, wooden sockets) taper to points at the proximal end unlike the scarf-ended northern ones.

In the lithic assemblage, nephrite burin-like tools are thin and tabular and broad at the base, taper along lateral margins, and have small, single, square side notches. Slate knives, unlike any elsewhere in Dorset, have internal perforations near the base for binding. Side-notched flint end blades, carefully made with occasional multiple notches, include a distinctive type that is beautifully shaped—long, narrow, and thin with square side notches—a form possibly derived from Groswater Dorset. The art of tip fluting appears to reach its apogee here in both numbers and length of tip spalls.

Art forms (see Figure 6.26) utilize the same subjects as in the core area—bear, seal, and walrus—in both naturalized and abstract treatment. Again, the flavor is distinctly regional, with thin, flat, plaque-like pieces and blocky heads of bears and walrus (Harp 1970). Humans, a favorite art subject to the north, are not represented.

Single–line hole, closed-socket harpoon heads and rectangular soapstone vessels, characteristic of more northern Dorset at the beginning of the Christian era, continue throughout the duration of Port aux Choix occupation. Significantly, this regional variant of Dorset does not share in the later stylistic trends that follow elsewhere in Dorset. The Port aux Choix people having once colonized a new niche appear to have continued to live in a balanced equilibrium of ecology and technology cut off from the information network that linked the rest of the Dorset population. This suggests that the stylistic changes taking place elsewhere in Dorset were the result of information exchange over a broad geographic area that encompassed many differing ecological niches. Newfoundland Dorset also demonstrates that the essential "Dorsetness" of technology and ideology could be preserved through six centuries of isolation with remarkable conservatism.

No cogent reasons have yet been advanced for the termination of Newfoundland Dorset; at the end there were only two households on the site. However, the abandonment is within a century of the warm period that marks the beginning of Late Dorset.

Farther to the north, only 25 km south of Labrador's northern tip, the late Middle Dorset Avayalik 1 site has many more of the characteristics of core area Dorset (Jordan 1980). Three willow and wood carbon dates place the site at about A.D. 440, yet many of its artifact traits are very similar to those of three centuries earlier to the north and west. While this may represent something of a local cultural lag, it must be remembered that these three centuries are little known in the north, where this may well have been a period of technological homeostasis.

The Middle Dorset midpassage house at Avayalik was partially destroyed by a Late Dorset house pit but the earlier house appears similar to the later one. If so, it would have been a small (3-m by 3.75-m) semisubsterranean structure with a stone-slab midpassage separating two rock-floored sleeping platforms. Walls were built up with rock and sod, and the roof was framed with driftwood.

The well-preserved nonlithic assemblage of 1050 items (900 of wood) lacked many of the categories normally found in Dorset sites. Two of the harpoon heads were of Kingait Closed type, 3 were of Dorset Parallel type, and 1, a toy like the one from the top level of the Tyara site, was a type Taylor (1968) called Dorset Plain. Wooden artifacts included what Jordan has interpreted as boat frame pieces and boat models. Particularly distinctive are several pieces of musk-ox wool yarn in several different thicknesses.

In the collection of 2500 lithic pieces, there are bifacially and unifacially flaked triangular end blades that have slightly incurving or straight bases and are predominantly tip fluted. Multinotched end blades, also with tip flutes, were probably lance tips. Nephrite burin-like tools vary in shape and include the square- and angular-ended ones of core area Dorset as well as the tabular ones characteristic of Labrador and Newfoundland. There are small, rectangular soapstone lamps and bowls and very few slate knives. The site was rich in art (Jordan 1979–1980), including a wooden maskette 11 cm long, a human face carved on a narrow bar of ivory, and a blocky, ivory bear's head like those from Newfoundland.

In this winter site the predominant source of meat was walrus, presumably taken at the floe edge off the outer coast. Conversely (Cox and Spiess 1980), warmer season's encampments were along protected fjords, where migrating harp seal could be intercepted and there was access to caribou of the interior, a minor but necessary resource.

Summary

For about two centuries after 300 B.C., Middle Dorset culture, its beginning noted only by the substitution of closed-socket harpoon heads for sliced ones, was a continuation of the earlier way of life. Barely perceptible changes in style mark the

material cultures of these centuries. On Victoria Island, both coasts of Hudson
Strait, Southampton and Belcher islands, Foxe Basin, and Navy Board Inlet, people
returned to the same site locations, although the High Arctic and northern Labrador
coast may have been abandoned. In some locales the people seem to have re-
sponded to the gradually increasing cold with communal dwellings and residence
locations better protected from winter winds. An increase in magical carvings,
especially of bears, may also have been a reaction to the increasingly difficult
problem of survival. Slight evidence suggests that in the century before the beginning of the Christian era, winter settlements were moved to snowhouses on the sea
ice or outer islands for floe-edge hunting.

By the second or third centuries A.D. most of the habitual settlement locations,
with some regional exceptions, had been abandoned. For the period from A.D. 200 to
500, I have been unable to locate sites on the southeastern coast of Baffin Island, a
region continually occupied for the preceding 2200 years. The south coast of Hudson Strait, Southampton Island, Victoria Island, and the High Arctic all reflect the
dimunition or disappearance of local inhabitants. In the central core area, the only
sites bridging this time period and demonstrating a continuum of technology and
ideology between the early part of Middle Dorset and Late Dorset are at the head of
Foxe Basin and the north coast of Baffin Island.

Here, in addition to new styles of harpoon heads, other minor trends in material
culture were developed. Slate tools and the tip fluting of triangular end blades
became less popular, with the basal margins of end blades tending to become more
concave. Sewing needles, strangely bipointed in Early Dorset, became rounded at
the eye end. Knives and microblades were occasionally side hafted into bone and
wooden handles, and oval soapstone oil lamps began to take the place of rectangular ones. Fragile, delicately barbed fish spears, once open socketed, were now
pointed at proximal ends for fitting into narrow sockets. Occasional stemmed end
blades with serrated margins began appearing in middens.

In these early centuries A.D., as northern populations appear to have declined
there was a marked increase on Newfoundland and the Labrador coast. While these
Dorset people shared some of the stylistic trends of their northern neighbors, other
styles were retained in their earlier forms. For example, the tip fluting of harpoon
end blades remained as a dominant practice, soapstone vessels continued to be
rectangular, and the stemmed end blades with serrated margins, lance tips(?), did
not appear. These traits, along with such characteristics as slate knives with interior slots rather than side notches, distinctive art forms, end blades with high,
square side notches, and semisubterranean houses with axial features and tunnel
entries, all suggest a certain degree of isolation from cultural stimuli to the north.
These more southerly coastal inhabitants have provided us with the best picture of
Middle Dorset culture from the fourth and fifth centuries A.D.

LATE DORSET

The distinctive artifacts of this late phase are the best known of Dorset materials.
Many now reside in several museums, with only vague references to provenience

where they were deposited by explorers, missionaries, Royal Canadian Mounted Police, and Hudson Bay Company personnel. Why this should be so, why Late Dorset materials should be so much better represented in these collections than earlier Dorset ones is an interesting question. In part it reflects an increase in the number of Late Dorset sites, but the main reason is probably more complex. The majority of Late Dorset sites yet located lie under or adjacent to Thule houses. These are also often the location of nineteenth- and twentieth-century Inuit settlements. The nitrogen-rich sod grows thicker on the old middens, and modern Inuit, cutting sod blocks for their autumn *qarmat* (houses), must have dug up many of the old artifacts. In one collection from Amadjuaq Bay alone, there are more than 200 perfect and complete harpoon heads; the broken and imperfect ones doubtless were thrown away. The sample from unknown sites at Cape Dorset and on Coats Island with which Jenness first defined the Cape Dorset culture was such a collection.

Artifact assemblage and all of the culturally relevant data to be drawn from a Late Dorset site are less well known. Too few Late Dorset sites have been excavated, and of these, few have been published in more than preliminary fashion. Expectably, carbon dating furnishes its characteristic Eastern Arctic confusion. The corrective factors used by Arundale for sea mammal dates would have some Dorset sites occupied after the building of the DEW line. Two charred seal fat dates from Belanger 2 and Gulf Hazard 8, if increased by the factor of 485 years, would place these Dorset sites far in the future, in the twenty-first and twenty-second centuries, respectively. Consequently, I have eliminated from Table 7.4 some of the impossible dates based on sea mammal materials. The remaining dates generally support the estimates that many have made, that Late Dorset begins about A.D. 500 and lasts as a viable culture throughout the Eastern Arctic until about A.D. 1000–1100. Its population, or at least the traits of its culture, diminish under the force of advancing Thule whale hunters. In marginal regions, particularly in a seacoast band from northern Labrador across northern Quebec and down the east shore of Hudson Bay, Dorset survived until as recently as the fifteenth or sixteenth century.

The beginning of the Late Dorset period coincides with, and is probably causally related to, the first warm period in more than a 1000 years. On sites around Igloolik this appears to have taken place at about the 14- or 13-m level of the graduated series of raised beach terraces. To Meldgaard (personal communication, 1977), sites immediately preceding this reflect a transition nearly as pronounced as in the phase before Early Dorset.

A number of distinctive artifact traits provide hallmarks for Late Dorset. These are discussed in the following site syntheses and in the summary, but three stand out as particularly diagnostic. These are harpoon heads with double line holes, triangular end blades with deeply concave basal margins and serrated lateral sides, and side-notched, angular edge knives or scrapers steeply beveled on one face. Less distinctive but equally characteristic of Late Dorset at Igloolik and other sites is a stylistic variant of the walrus hunting harpoon head, Dorset Parallel. Although this basic form had been popular since Early Dorset, the late variants are long and narrow with parallel sides and basal margins that angle steeply toward the midline, giving them very long and sharp proximal spurs (Figure 7.23).

Table 7.4

RADIOCARBON DATES FOR LATE DORSET SITES[a]

Site	Lab no.	Material	Uncorrected age (radio-carbon years)	Corrected age[b] (radio-carbon years)	Date (A.D.)
Nunguvik H-73	S-1206	Botanical material	1550 ± 55	—	400
Nunguvik H-76	S-883	Botanical material	1525 ± 100	—	425
Karluk Is. 25	SFU-87	Musk-ox bone and antler	1420 ± 20	1520 ± 200*	430
Nunguvik H-73	S-1443	Botanical material	1510 ± 65	—	440
Nunguvik H-73	S-846	Botanical material	1490 ± 65	—	460
Sandy	M-1529	Charcoal	1470 ± 110	—	480
Nunguvik H-73	S-1204	Botanical material	1465 ± 85	—	485
Karluk Is. 17	SFU-85	Fox, musk-ox, and bear bone	1380 ± 120	1440 ± 120*	510
Nunguvik H-72	S-478	Burned organic material	1380 ± 95	—	570
Nunguvik H-71	Gak-2339	Burned organic material	1290 ± 120	—	660
Saatut	S-590	Seal (?) bone	1510 ± 135	1225 ± 148	725
Kiliktee	M-1533	Charred fat	1670 ± 150	1205 ± 162	745
Baie Diana	Lv-740	Charred fat	1510 ± 65	1045 ± 89	905
Okak 3	SI-2154	Charcoal	1005 ± 95	—	945
Tuktu	P-177	Caribou bone	709 ± 94	945 ± 100	1005
Okak 3	SI-2506	Charcoal	895 ± 85	—	1055
Baie Diana	Lv-469	Charred fat	1360 ± 90	895 ± 97	1055
Nunguvik H-71	S-766	Botanical material	855 ± 70	—	1095
Gulf Hazard 7	GX-2083	Charcoal	845 ± 120	—	1105
Baie Diana	Lv-471	Charred fat	1300 ± 75	835 ± 108	1115
DIA-4	QC-625	Charcoal	815 ± 110		1135
Gulf Hazard 1	GX-2065	Charcoal	795 ± 160	—	1155
Tuktu	P-176	Antler	649 ± 100	759 ± 106	1191
K'aersut	K-504	Antler	600 ± 150	710 ± 154	1240
Gulf Hazard 8	GX-2068	Wood	550 ± 120	—	1400
DIA-4	UQ-88	Charcoal	490 ± 80	—	1460
DIA-4	UQ-83	Charcoal	475 ± 70	—	1475
DIA-4	GIF-3002	Charcoal	470 ± 90	—	1480
DIA-4	UQ-90	Charcoal	460 ± 105	—	1490
DIA-4	UQ-87	Charcoal	440 ± 90	—	1510
Dog Bight L-1	SI-2523	Charcoal	430 ± 90	—	1520
DIA-4	UQ-93	Charcoal	420 ± 105	—	1530

[a]Data from Arundale 1981, with additions by Maxwell.

[b]Ages have been corrected by incorporating laboratory-derived fractionation and sea reservoir effect. Ages marked with an asterisk have been corrected for fractionation but not reservoir effect.

A site uncontaminated by earlier or later settlements that serves well as a prototype of Late Dorset is also one of the earliest to be reported in print, the Abverdjar site. This single-component site near the head of Foxe Basin is probably near the early end of the Late Dorset period. An educated estimate would date the occupation to about A.D. 600–800. It, like so many sites in the Eastern Arctic, has received only preliminary treatment in the literature (Rowley 1940, 1971–1972), but a pseudo–

site report can be reconstructed with the addition of other sources. In 1960, while the Abverdjar collection was in Denmark, selected artifacts were photographed by the National Museum of Denmark. Elmer Harp, Jr., then a visiting scholar in Copenhagen, took detailed notes while the collection was there. He has very kindly given me access to these and with his permission I am including his trait list in Table 7.5.

Abverdjar Island is one of a group of rocky little granite islands lying between Igloolik Island and the Melville Peninsula mainland. Igloolingmiut, while cutting turf for winter house insulation, first located the site and turned artifacts over to the Reverend Father E. Bazin, O.M.I., who in turn gave them to Graham Rowley. In 1939 Rowley returned to excavate the site, recovering in the process nearly 2000 artifacts, which are now housed in Cambridge University. There is a typological homogeneity to this assemblage that suggests the site was not occupied for more than one or two centuries.

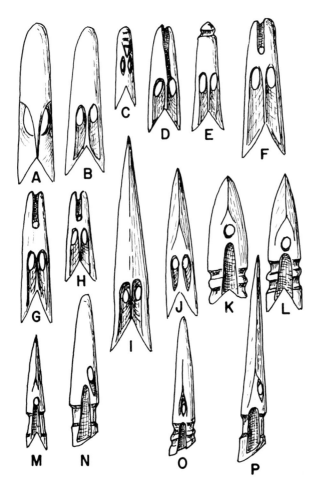

Figure 7.23 Late Dorset harpoon heads from several sites (not to scale): A, C, Kikertardjuk site; B, Abverdjar site; D, F, K, Bell site; G, Joss site; H, Resolute site; I, Dundas Harbour site; J, M, N, P, Crystal II site; L, O, Nudlukta site, Boothia Peninsula.

A.   Type Dorset Parallel
B–H.   Type G
I,J.   Type F
K–M.   Type Ha
N–P.   Type J

Table 7.5

PARTIAL LIST OF ARTIFACTS FROM THE ABVERDJAR SITE[a]

Artifacts[b]	n
Nonlithic	
Harpoon heads	
Dorset Parallel	35
Type G	30
Type F	31
Type Ha$_1$	13
Bone and ivory snow knives*	—
Ivory sled shoes	44
Snow scrapers	8
Ivory spoons or scoops	5
Antler boxes with grooved interior top and bottom for end pieces*	—
Bone and ivory, barbed fish spears with tapered proximal end and lateral line hole	24
Barbed fishing trident	1
Antler and ivory foreshafts with wedge-shaped proximal end	13
Bone and ivory awls	16
Fish spear barbs	12
Ivory ice picks	8
Caribou leg bone scrapers	3
Ivory and penis bone flakers	8
Antler adz sockets	6
Bone knife handles	—
Bone lance head	1
Antler and ivory ice creepers	3
Antler, composite burin handles	57
Bone and ivory needles with rounded proximal ends	52 (116 fragments)
Carvings (mainly of ivory)	
human adult and child, child on adult's shoulders	3
walrus heads and tusks	3
hollowed bear heads	5
hawks	4
geese	4
bar with bear head on each end	1
spatula-shaped stylized bears	37
double ivory rings	3
seal	4
flying bear with chest or belly slit	5
bar with loon head	1
standing caribou	1
caribou hooves	2
human maskettes (1 tattooed)	2
beluga	1
fish	1
antler wands with many carved human faces	2
bone disks with scratched bird(?) designs	3

Table 7.5 *(Continued)*

Artifacts[b]	*n*
Lithic	
Angle-edged, unifacial scrapers or knives	40
End scrapers (15 with flaring edges)	37
Dorset burin-like tools	33
Adz blade	1
Stemmed, slate end blades	2
Stemmed, chert, lance(?) end blades	30
Triangular harpoon end blades (72 chert, 5 quartz)	77
Side-notched end blades (knives)	70
Unifacial, side-notched random flakes (knives)*	—
Microblades (all chert)	29
Small, oval soapstone vessels and fragments*	—
Quartz-crystal microblade cores	6
Quartzite whetstones	13

[a]Data from Harp 1960.

[b]Although no exact number is given for artifacts marked with an asterisk, several of each of these items were recovered from the site.

The settlement is on a sloping turf bank between 7 and 12 m above present sea level, but sea level elevation on this rocky shore may be less relevant than on the limestone beaches of Igloolik. There are four barely discernible hollows, 1 or 2 m in diameter, but Rowley felt that most of the dwellings had been above surface and made of sod blocks. The location is rich in game. Walrus are abundant in autumn, although scarce in other seasons. Seal, both bearded and smaller species, are numerous, as were caribou on the nearby mainland until about the 1920s.

Many of the nonlithic artifacts demonstrate new traits and styles that had not appeared earlier in Dorset culture. Some of these are no doubt functional improvements, but many may simply be innovations in aesthetics. Of the 108 recovered harpoon heads, only the 35 Dorset Parallel ones are continuations of an earlier form. These Late Dorset ones are longer, more narrow, and more sharply spurred than earlier heads (Figure 7.24C). The others are all of new types, which Meldgaard (1977) refers to as Types F, G, H, and J. Type F is self-bladed and closed socketed, with side-by-side line holes set in grooves. At least 5 of this type from Abverdjar have tiny longitude grooves above the line holes. These grooves are too shallow to hold side blades and appear to be only decorative (Figure 7.24B). Type G, with similar double line holes, is slotted for an end blade. Neither these nor Igloolik ones appear to have the small longitudinal groove (Figure 7.24A). There are variants of Type H: Type Ha_1 has an open socket and a single line hole that is medially placed, is self-bladed, and has bilateral basal spurs (Figure 7.24D); 6 of these were recovered at Abverdjar. Type Ha_2 is similar to Ha_1 but has only a unilateral spur (Figure 7.24E); 6 of these were recovered from Abverdjar. Type J resembles Ha_2 but has a laterally placed line hole; 1 of these was recovered from Abverdjar (Figure 7.24F).

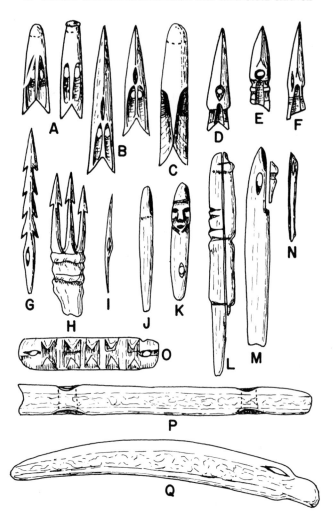

Figure 7.24 Nonlithic artifacts from the Abverdjar site,
northern Foxe Basin (artifacts
not all drawn to same scale).

A.   Type G harpoon heads
B.   Type F harpoon heads
C.   Dorset Parallel harpoon
      head
D.   Type Ha_1 harpoon head
E.   Type Ha_2 harpoon head
F.   Type J harpoon head
G,H. fish spear and trident
I.   fish gorge
J,K.   side-bladed knife
      handles
L–N. composite burin handles
      and support pieces
O.   ice creeper
P.   ivory sled shoe
Q.   ivory snow knife

Meldgaard (personal communication, 1977) suggests that since these Type J
heads are not designed to toggle in the same plane as do other harpoon heads, they
may have been used primarily for fishing. In one collection in the National Museum
of Man from Mansel Island, more than 100 are of this type and it is the most common
in the collection of over 200 heads from Amadjuaq.

Abverdjar harpoon foreshafts differ distinctively from the dagger-shaped caribou
leg bone ones of Early Dorset and, I suspect, reflect a different mechanical princi-
ple. Whereas early ones have a medial perforation at the proximal end for binding to
a scarfed wooden shaft, the later ones have a hole placed well up the piece near one
lateral margin. These are rectangular bars, usually of ivory, square at both ends,
and designed, I suspect, to be bound to the harpoon line and to slip from the shaft as
the head does.

This leads to a tenuous but possible argument that correlates climatic conditions to game procurement. While Thule and traditional Inuit used different harpoon arrangments for floe-edge and open-water hunting as opposed to breathing-hole hunting, Early Dorset people had only the fixed foreshaft system that might have been most effective in floe-edge hunting. A possible reason for population decline in the warmer years of Middle Dorset may have been related to reduced areas of outer coast fast ice and increased instability of the floe edge on which the people depended. To this I would add as a corollary the hypothesis that the population increase in Late Dorset might have been due, in part, to developing skills in breathing-hole hunting. The new technique would then have provided access to the rich sea life under the landfast ice of sheltered bays. Artifacts of this system would have been a different harpoon foreshaft development, ice picks, scoops for removing ice chips from the breathing hole, and an increase in numbers of snow knives, ice creepers, and sled shoes; all of these are reflected at Abverdjar.

No wood was preserved, but bone, antler, and ivory handles indicated that burins and some knives were side hafted in composite handles. Needles of bone and ivory had rounded but scratched, rather than drilled, holes and were blunt and rounded at the eye end. They may have been kept in tubular boxes made of thin plates of antler sewed together and grooved top and bottom on the inside for end pieces. Fishing equipment contained more varied forms than during former periods, including multiply barbed tips with both pointed and wedge-shaped proximal ends and line holes close to one lateral margin, scarf-ended points with or without barbs that might have fit on the side prongs of leisters, a barbed three-pronged trident, and a variety of pierced and unpierced gorges.

Artistic pieces of the site are truly outstanding and several have often appeared in books on Eskimo art (see Figures 6.28 and 7.25). Late Dorset art in general must be considered some of the finest in native North America. The putative magical power of many of these has been stressed, but several appear to have been carved primarily for aesthetic pleasure. The simple list that follows only gives an idea of quantity: 3 ivory figures, each of a naked male with a child on his shoulders; 3 ivory walrus heads with tusks; 5 hollowed-out bear heads; 4 hawks; 4 geese; 9 seal; 6 "flying" bear with slashed bellies or chests; 1 standing caribou; 2 caribou hooves; 1 caribou mandible; 2 human maskettes (including 1 with facial tatooing); 1 beluga; 1 fish; 2 antler bars (1 with 4 carved human faces and the other with 28); 1 ivory bar with a loon head at one end; 1 ivory bar with a bear head at each end; 37 ivory spatulas (some with engraved skeletal design and 1 with a bear head, which are abstract depictions of the flying bear and are diagnostic of Late Dorset); 3 double rings; and 4 oval box bottoms (or plaques) engraved with complicated scratched designs that may represent birds. Many of the animals carved of antler and ivory were embellished with the engraved skeletal designs characteristic of Dorset.

Certain of the lithic traits from Abverdjar are worth mentioning for their importance in serial chronology (Figure 7.26). The triangular harpoon end blades, none of which are tip fluted, all have concave basal margins and a few have finely serrated edges. But the bases are not as deep and the serration is not as frequent as, for example, those at Crystal II, Frobisher Bay. This leads me to judge Abverdjar as having preceded the Frobisher Bay site by a few centuries. The single-side-notched, square-ended, Dorset burin-like tool is present in significant numbers; at this site most were side hafted and had composite handles. The Igloolik angular-tipped form is absent, as it is at Crystal II, but so also is the small-to-tiny corner-notched form with a pointed proximal end I termed "Tiriak burin-like." This latter form is, I think, a later form and is present in the Crystal II assemblage. Soapstone lamps at Abverdjar are small (12–18 cm long), oval, and shallow (3.7–4.5 cm deep). Microblades are relatively scarce, compared to earlier Dorset, and ground-slate knives or lance tips

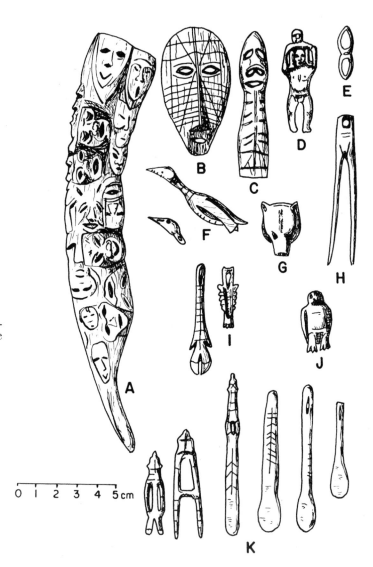

Figure 7.25 Artistic pieces from the Abverdjar site, northern Foxe Basin.

A.   multiple faces on caribou antler
B.   maskette with tattooed face
C,D. human figures
E.   toggle
F.   loon and loon head
G,H. bear and walrus heads
I.   caribou hoof and mandible
J.   falcon
K.   naturalized and stylized polar bears

Figure 7.26 Artifacts from the Abverdjar site, northern Foxe Basin (photographs courtesy of Elmer Harp).

A. harpoon head of Dorset Parallel type
B. three harpoon heads of Type G
C. harpoon head of Type Ha$_2$
D. harpoon head of Type J
E. harpoon head of Type Ha$_1$
F. two harpoon heads of Type F
G. three composite handles for burin-like tools
H. antler adz socket with nephrite adz blade
I. asymmetric chert knife
J. slate knife
K. spalled burin
L. Dorset burin-like tools
M. side blades
N. side-notched end blades
O. transverse-edged knives or scrapers
P. stemmed end blades
Q. triangular harpoon end blades

even more so. There are several parallel-stemmed, flint end blades, some of which are serrated (probably lance tips). Since none of the distinctive antler lance heads have been reported from Late Dorset sites, the lance must simply have been a wooden shaft tipped with a stone blade. There is a wide variety of side-notched and stemmed end blades—both unifaces and bifaces and symmetric and asymmetric—with oblique scraping edges. I would consider at least five of these forms diagnostic

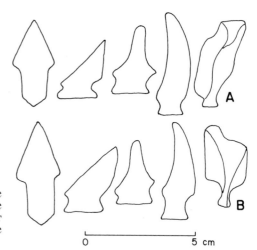

Figure 7.27 Characteristic Late Dorset knife forms: (A) from the Abverdjar site, northern Foxe Basin (after photograph and sketch by Elmer Harp, Jr.), and (B) from the Killikti site, Lake Harbour.

of Late Dorset (Figure 7.27). A few moderately large, oval bifaces and some long, narrow ones are most probably side-hafted knives. The function of concave side scrapers, missing from the site, was apparently taken over by the oblique-edged end blades. End scrapers are slightly less common than in earlier sites. Some are significantly larger, perhaps used for hide treatment, and at least 15 had broadly flaring ends (Tables 7.6 and 7.7).

Table 7.6

ARTIFACT TRAITS FIRST APPEARING IN LATE DORSET

Harpoon heads
   Closed socket, double line hole, and self-bladed (Type F)
   Closed socket, double line hole, and slotted for end blade (Type G)
   Open socket, single medial line hole, and bilateral basal spurs (Type Ha_1)
   Open socket, single medial line hole, and unilateral basal spur (Type Ha_2)
   Open socket, single lateral line hole, and unilateral basal spur (Type J)
Foreshafts with square, chisel-shaped proximal and distal ends and lateral line holes
Side-hafted knives and burin-like tools with composite wood, bone, antler, and ivory handles
Needles with rounded or squared butt ends
Multiply barbed fish spear heads with chisel-shaped proximal ends and lateral line holes
Fishing leister side barbs
Triangular harpoon end blades with concave basal margins and serrated lateral edges (not tip fluted)
Very small, corner-notched burin-like tools with tapered proximal ends (Tiriak type)
Microblades (relatively scarce and irregular in shape)
Parallel-stemmed slate knives or lance heads
Parallel-stemmed chert lance heads with serrated edges
Bifacial chert end blades (knives), often broad, asymmetrical, and rounded at the distal end
Relatively large, unifacial random flakes side notched for hafting
Angle-edged end blades (scrapers or knives; common)
Longhouse rock enclosures, sometimes associated with adjacent rows of hearth platforms

Table 7.7
LATE DORSET ARTIFACT TRAITS CHANGING WITH TIME

Occasional retention of variants of Middle Dorset harpoon head types—Kingait Closed and Native
    Point Grooved
Increase in length and sharpness of basal spurs of Dorset Parallel harpoon head (Meldgaard's [1977]
    Type states E18–E20)
Decrease in Type F harpoon heads and increase in Type G
Increase in Type G harpoon heads with distal rivet hole for metal (?) end blade
Increase in Type H and Type J harpoon heads
Increase in angularity of basal spurs on triangular flint end blades and increase in serration of edges
Increase in size and roundness of side-notched end blades
Marked increase in artistic and magical carvings
Increase in size and in degree of flaring at scraping edge of end scrapers
Increased rarity of side-notched slate knives, bone and antler lance heads, and concave side scrapers
Increase in substitution of chisel-ended fish spear for taper-ended Middle Dorset type
Increase in substitution of corner-notched Tiriak burin-like tool for side-notched Dorset burin-like
    tool, but increase in size of the latter
Marked decrease in use of quartz crystal, slate, nephrite, and chalcedony
Increase in use of metal—copper (native and European) and iron meteoric and European(?)

The Abverdjar inventory is virtually repeated in all its discrete attributes in site after site of the Late Dorset period. In fact the homogeneity of material culture from these sites is such that repetition of the diagnostic traits (see Table 7.6) in the following geographic survey would be needlessly redundant. It was a time of maximum territorial expansion and of cultural participation in a widespread information network. Perhaps this stylistic homogeneity may have been controlled by a vast fraternal order of shamans who shared their secret knowledge. Through more than half a millennium there are only such slight suggestions of stylistic change that we are not yet able to seriate the various categories of artifacts or of sites.

At other sites in the vicinity of Igloolik, this period conforms to beaches between 14 and 11 m above present sea level. This is Meldgaard's (1960) Period IV, and a time when the people were completely adapted to hunting sea mammals, particularly walrus. Longhouses, boulder-outlined enclosures 14 by 17 m, were introduced at the beginning of this period. At Igloolik, as at many Late Dorset sites, there was an extensive use of red ochre. Many of the artistic carvings were colored red, but there was also probably a religious association between red ochre and oil lamps since interiors of these were often painted. A slight indication of temporal change on successively lower beaches is reflected in the increased concavity of harpoon end blade basal margins, the increased sharpness of the proximal spurs of the Dorset Parallel harpoon heads, and the fact that Type H open-socket harpoon heads first appear at Alarnerk on about the 10-m beach level. Here, and south along the peninsula to Hall Beach, as well as far to the north on Ellesmere's Bache Peninsula, some of the Type G harpoon heads are engraved with human faces crossed by X lines.

Northeasterly at the Nungavik site on Navy Board Inlet, Houses 71, 73, and 76 belong to the early part of this late period on the basis of artifact style and carbon dating (Mary-Rousselière 1979a). But harpoon heads remain the Kingait Closed type. This is one of several reasons Mary-Rousselière considers this an isolated region subject to cultural lag where caribou hunting took precedence over sea mammal hunting. Sled models and sled shoes (more than 30 in House 73 alone) increase dramatically. House 73, possibly reused and remodeled, was a cluster of rooms or alcoves surrounding a meter of empty space. Leading into this was a paved entry passage lined with upright stone slabs. The most unique object in this house was a pair of toy wooden skis uptilted at both ends in Lapland fashion. In other late houses he found kayak models, a full-sized kayak rib, and a wooden fire plough, the only fire-making equipment yet reported from a Dorset site. The quantity of baleen in these houses led him to suggest that these people may have hunted the large bowhead whale.

South of here at the Saatut site, most of the traits in the later houses conform to those of Late Dorset elsewhere. Yet here, also, harpoon heads remain of the Dorset Parallel, Kingait Closed, and Native Point Grooved types.

This is not the case at the nearby Button Point site on Bylot Island where Types F, G, and H have been found. This site, hopelessly garbled by frost action and fast eroding into the sea, has been sampled intermittently since 1925 (Mathiassen 1927). Judging by typology alone, it must have been a favored springtime hunting base from Pre-Dorset times to the present, with its largest population concentration in Late Dorset. The site has produced an abundance of mystical carved wooden figures, the most impressive of which are life-sized wooden masks—one complete and three others fragmentary. The fearsome complete mask (Figure 6.29), which once was painted with red ochre and had pegged-in caribou hair and a sealskin moustache, has engraved tatooing like that appearing on other maskettes. An X crosses the face from the forehead to the cheeks and incised vertical lines run down the cheeks. There are small wooden dolls with removable arms and legs, pregnant females and boldly priapic males, bears and humans with slit throats and bellies (the slit filled with red ochre and closed with a carved peg), and a variety of stylized bears (sometimes only suggested by a few engraved lines). Mary-Rousselière believes most of these were originally painted—red for humans and bear and black for seal. With the addition of a number of drum rims and handles recovered from the site, it is not difficult to see Button Point as a ceremonial center. In the springtime as the warm sun was returning, the seals basking on drifting ice waiting to be stalked, and the narwhal returning, it is easy to imagine nighttime ceremonies where rhythmic chants and drumbeats restored the sacred balance of nature. In the dimly lit houses, shamans, frighteningly masked, would manipulate little figures for magical protection from the only predators dangerous to humans—the giant polar bear and humans who were not part of the kinship web.

Late Dorset is well represented in the High Arctic north of Barrow Strait and Lancaster Sound. At present, pending future exploration, there appear to have been three major centers: one bounded by Cornwallis and Bathurst islands and the Grinnel Peninsula of Devon Island, a second in the region around Bache Peninsula on the eastern coast of Ellesmere Island, and the third on Inglefield Land, northwest Greenland.

The first reported of these was the Resolute site on Cornwallis Island (Collins 1952, 1955, 1974–1975). This is primarily a locus of Thule dwellings, both early and late; but on Sites M-1 and M-2 a thin Dorset component lay under sterile sod, which separated it from a Thule component. The recovered harpoon heads are all of classic type, including two with rivet holes at distal ends presumably for metal end blades. In this small collection the number of art forms is impressive. There is a seal, a standing bear, an open-work carving of a falcon with 13 separate perforations, an ivory goose, a stylized engraving of a human face, and 2 grotesque carvings of an ugly woman and a deformed, seated man.

While McGhee (1976) believes this expansion into the High Arctic to be a return after an absence of several centuries through the Middle Dorset period, Schleder-mann (1978b) disagrees and considers the occupation to have been virtually un-broken. In support he cites the results of an extension survey of western Cornwallis, eastern Bathurst, and Karluk islands (1978a). Carbon dates and lithic typology indicate early Paleoeskimo sites dated on (unidentified) bone to 2000 B.C., and there are excavated sites of Early and Late Dorset time. Although he recognizes some inherent difficulties with such a technique, he has plotted the sea level elevation of 263 dwelling localities on 57 sites in this region. The sites range from 23 to 2 m above present sea level, reaching a peak at the late end of the scale with a notable decline between 13 and 11 m. He is tempted to relate this decline to the climatic cooling coincident with Early Dorset, a point supported by Helmer's (1980a,b) ex-cavation of Early Dorset sites between 12 and 10 m above present sea level. Unless otherwise convinced, I am more inclined to put my faith in artifact typology than in site elevation. If, as settlement location indicates, there was an appreciable decline in population, I would see it taking place after the beginning of the Christian era, followed perhaps by complete abandonment and return of people in the Late Dorset period. This would account for the absence throughout the High Arctic of Middle Dorset materials. Late Dorset is certainly well represented on Karluk and adjoining Bathurst islands (Helmer 1980b) by sites containing harpoon heads of Types F and G, and Dorset Parallel, a number of artistic carvings that include antler wands embellished with many human faces, and a longhouse with a row of hearths.

McGhee (1981a) has written briefly about a fascinating Late Dorset site a few kilometers south of Karluk Island on Bathurst Island's eastern coast on Brooman Point. This was a winter settlement of 19 Thule houses 5–10 m above present sea level. In building their rock and sod pit houses, the Thule people had cut through an earlier Dorset site. Encapsulated in the sod, and apparently ignored by the Thule builders, was a lovely collection of wood and ivory Late Dorset carvings (Figure 7.28). My favorite among a group of these carvings of birds, seal, bear, musk-ox, fox, and fish is a tiny (27-mm) ivory bear skull with carefully excised canine teeth. Nearby, and the same length, was a fleshed-out ivory bear's head (Figure 7.28F). There are decorated miniature harpoon heads and an ivory shaman's tube combining walrus and human motifs. Among carvings of human heads and figures there is an

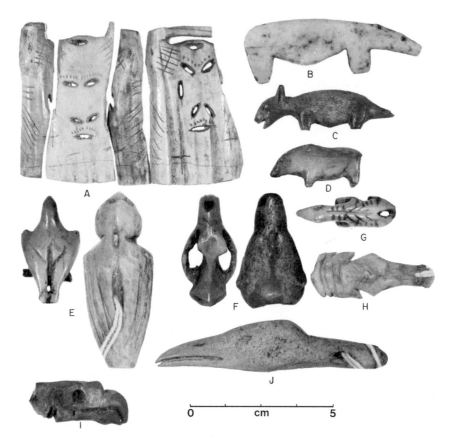

Figure 7.28   Magico-religious artistic carvings from the Brooman Point site, Bathurst Island (courtesy of Robert McGhee).

A. ivory shaman's tube with human faces
   and walruses with interlocking tusks
   (possibly deliberately broken)
B. polar bear
C. fox cub
D. musk-ox calf

E. two falcons
F. polar bear skull and fleshed head
G. polar bear with skeletal engraving
H. sculpin
I. raptorial bird head
J. head of raven or gull

antler tine, well polished by the wear of human hands, with at least 60 carved human faces reflecting both portraiture and mystical fantasy. I must confess that when I held this in my hand I imagined I could feel a slight surge of power.

Apparently all that was left of the original Dorset village were four shallow house depressions, each one containing two lithic artifacts and a carving. A Thule knife handle in the floor of one of these, 80 m from the Thule houses, lends credence to McGhee's belief that the Dorset settlement was close in time to the arrival of early Thule people from the west near the beginning of the second millennium A.D.

Between Bathurst Island and the Grinnell Peninsula of Devon Island, small Dundas Island lies 20 km south of Port Refuge. The Snowdrift site excavated here by

McGhee (1981b) is to date the only completely reported Late Dorset site. This village of five structures, one of four Late Dorset villages on the island, lies between 6 and 12 m above present sea level. Dwelling features are surprisingly like those of Independence II and unlike the Late Dorset houses at Igloolik. They have carefully paved and lined midpassages, 2 m long and 1 m wide and with a large hearthstone in the middle flanked by upright pot supports. On either side were sleeping platforms cleared of cobbles and covered with moss. In the recovered artifact assemblage 7 of the harpoon heads were of Type F, 7 of Dorset Parallel (Type state E18–20 in Meldgaard's (1977) typology) and 1 of Type G. There were both large and small foreshafts. The small ones having lateral perforations may have been used for open-water sealing. The 12 knife handles of ivory and antler are all for side-hafted blades, most with slots so thin they may have held metal blades. This point is supported by the recovery of 3 small pieces of copper and a chunk (38g) of iron that McGhee believes to be of native and meteoric origin, respectively. The 33 needles have rounded or square proximal ends and the soapstone vessels are small, oval-to-round saucers. Art or ideology are represented by 5 drum-rim fragments (of a drum 40 cm in diameter), carvings of miniature harpoon heads, bear, birds, and seal, ivory spatula-shaped stylized bears, toy kayaks, and a crude wooden human figure on which the chest is deeply gouged and the hole pegged with a sliver of wood. Two ivory carvings are of forms occasionally found in Late Dorset sites: One is of joined rings, resembling spectacles, which was also found at Abverdjar (see Figure 7.25E); the other is of joined disks, resembling dumbells.

McGhee sees this as a period in which there was more open-water hunting by kayak. In fact he would question the existence of kayak hunting before this period. He has estimated the site to date from A.D. 1000 plus or minus a couple of centuries (1981:76). On admitedly flimsy evidence, I would suggest it to be fairly early in the Late Dorset period. Although other lithic traits are of Late Dorset type, the few triangular harpoon end blades have straight-to-slightly-concave basal margins and are not serrated. The Igloolik angular-tipped burin-like tool absent from the latest Late Dorset sites is present here, and the tiny, corner-notched Tiriak burin-like tool is not.

Dundas Island, and the Snowdrift Village, are near a well-known polynia, Penny's North Water. Schledermann (1980b) has made an interesting correlation between these game-rich locales and High Arctic prehistoric sites. His recognition of contiguity of polynias and settlement concentrations holds good as well for more southerly sites. Satellite imagery indicates a close relation between southeastern Baffin Island sites and long-recurring polynias.

The northward expansion of Late Dorset people appears only to have been constrained by available land. They penetrated inhospitable Axel Heiberg Island, where Schledermann (1976) and later Sutherland (1977, 1980) found Late Dorset artifacts and harpoon heads of Types F, G, and Dorset Parallel at Buchanan Lake. Dorset people made an apparently brief foray to Lake Hazen, 81°45′ north latitude, on Ellesmere Island and 50 km to the east built a rectangular stone tent enclosure at Basil Norris Bay (Maxwell 1960a). On the Greenland site at Cape Tyson (81°20′) the

Danish explorer Lauge Koch, in 1922 (Mathiassen 1928), found a rectangular tent enclosure with artifacts we would now consider Late Dorset. Farther south, in Inglefield Land and in Comer's Midden at Thule, Holtved (1944) recovered a sufficient number of Late Dorset artifacts under Thule middens to indicate a sizable population divided into a number of communities. Late Dorset can be traced south on Greenland's west coast at least to Upernavik. Around the northern coast and south along the eastern coast, at least as far as Clavering Island, end scrapers of Late Dorset type at Dødemansbugt (Bandi and Meldgaard 1952) suggest penetration of this inhospitable region to 74° north latitude.

Eastward to the middle east coast of Ellesmere Island in the vicinity of Bache Peninsula, Schledermann's (1978c, 1981) continuing work is contributing much to the solution of many problems in Eastern Arctic prehistory. He feels sites there span the time from earliest Paleoeskimo through pioneer Thule and later. He sees this region near an ecologically rich polynia as demonstrating *in situ* development of Eastern Arctic Paleo- and Neoeskimo. At the early end he has reported a buried walrus tusk on the same gravel terrace as, but not associated with, Paleoeskimo remains. Its carbon date—3440 B.C.: 5390 ± 380 radiocarbon years (RI-834)—places it, no matter what corrective factor is applied, well before any other indication of human presence.

We will concentrate here only on the the Late Dorset evidence. The most interesting from the Dorset viewpoint is the Longhouse site on Knud Peninsula partially described in Chapter 6. Four long, rectangular, 1-m high boulder enclosures on the site, the longest being 45 by 5 m, mark a late spring or summer encampment. Close-by the enclosures were rows of 3–18 hearths and platforms encrusted with charcoal and charred fat, the longest row being 32 m. Within the enclosure were food-animal bones but no signs of fire. Typological contemporaneity of artifacts from the hearth row and the enclosure suggest to Schledermann that the cooking was done communally, with the cooks retreating to family enclosures of skin within the stone longhouse for sharing the food. Associated artifacts correlate well with carbon dates from the hearth row of A.D. 800–850 (Schledermann 1981). Harpoon heads are of Types F, G, H (Schledermann 1978c:Plate 3e), and late variants of Dorset Parallel. Foreshafts, composite knife handles for side-hafted blades, and triangular end blades with incurved bases are all of Late Dorset type. The art, which includes a flying loon with skeletal engraving, a bear head, and caribou hooves, feature the only Dorset ivory carving of an Arctic hare I have seen. This timorous crouching creature with ears laid back has the characteristic Late Dorset engraved crosses on shoulders and hips. At least two of the Type G harpoon heads have engraved Xed-out faces like those from Hall Beach and Igloolik.

Whether these long boulder rectangles enclosed individual family tents or open festival halls like the traditional Inuit *qaqqi,* they give us seminal insight into Dorset life. They were certainly built and used at a time of coming together after the long winter during which small hunting bands had scattered. This communal center provided a place and time for reestablishing the warp and weft of kinship and of nonkin dyadic sharing partnerships, a time for selecting mates and introducing

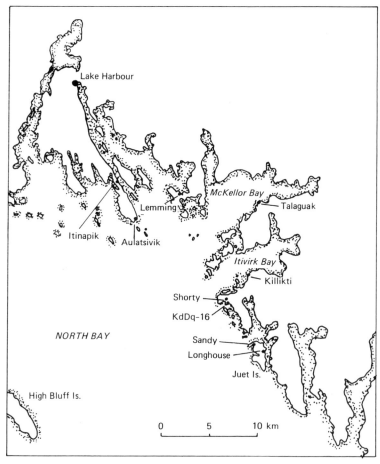

Figure 7.29 Late Dorset components and sites in the vicinity of Lake Harbour, Baffin Island.

babies to the larger society, and most important, a time for reaffirming the complex system of religious and magical beliefs that kept the world of nature in harmony.

The beginning of the Late Dorset period marks a return of Dorset people to the southeast coast of Baffin Island, which they seem to have abandoned for nearly 500 years. At least 10 sites between North Bay and Pritzler Harbour were small encampments of this period. Using our tentative serration of stone artifacts, they would span the full Late Dorset period. Mean winter and summer temperatures and annual precipitation are higher here than in most of the Eastern Arctic. Consequently, few organic artifacts have been preserved in the thin middens, which seldom are deeper than the active zone. However, the many harpoon heads and carvings from farther west along this coast, now in museums, indicate an extensive South Baffin population (see Figure 7.29).

Earliest of these sites is Sandy, dated with willow and driftwood charcoal to A.D. 480 (the site probably dates from little more than 50 years later since driftwood quickly deteriorates on this coast). This site, (Maxwell 1973a) like several of those from the early part of the Late Dorset period, is a small pocket in the rocks barely large enough for a single family, yet sterile bands of sand between three thin midden layers indicate that it was returned to after periods of abandonment. Juet Island, where it is located, is a bleak, inhospitable little island fully exposed to the icy winds and fogs of Hudson Strait. Its only apparent advantage is that it is close to the late winter floe edge. In a complete survey it is clear that the island was briefly occupied fairly early in the Pre-Dorset period, was used by a larger group during the transition between Pre-Dorset and Dorset, and then was not occupied again until Late Dorset, when it was used early and later for two small encampments. At sometime during this period, Dorset people built a 14-m longhouse near the southern end. There is no trace of occupation through the subsequent millennium, but around the beginning of the twentieth century there was a large Inuit village of snowhouses there (Fleming 1956).

On Cape Tanfield, the Late Dorset Shorty site is also a small pocket in the rocks barely 3 by 7.5 m. After the Dorset occupation the center of this space had been dug out for a small Thule house later roofed with 26 whale ribs. This left only a narrow margin around the house pit of partly undisturbed Dorset midden mixed with Dorset materials excavated from the center. From this space we recovered 581 Dorset lithic artifacts. Typological variations in the artifacts lead us to see this as a small encampment periodically utilized for perhaps two centuries. This cannot be demonstrated in the mixed deposit at the side of the Thule house. However in front of the house entry an undisturbed Dorset section had 26 thin bands of midden separated by lenses of sand eroded from the upslope rock wall. Artifacts in this profile were too few for seriation, but it is apparent that the site was returned to many times, perhaps only in one season of the year. Surprisingly, although faunal bones were well preserved, we did not find a single worked piece of bone, antler, or ivory. Of the 449 recovered animal bones, 380 were of ringed seal (minimum number of individuals [MNI] = 30), 3 of bearded seal (MNI = 2), 16 of walrus (MNI = 2), 32 of caribou (MNI = 3), 3 of fox (MNI = 2), and 15 of eider duck (MNI = 2). Age sets of these animals suggests a specialized type of hunting. Twenty-five of the ringed seal were neonates or yearlings and one was a young juvenile, as was one of the walrus. This evidence plus the duck bones best satisfies the following reconstruction: From late May to early June, when young sea mammals were basking on the ice shelf and after the ducks had returned, small groups of three to five male hunters would return to the area, throw skins over the rock outcrop, and hunt along the south coast of Itivirk Bay.

This same pattern of small Late Dorset seasonal encampments either in small bedrock pockets or on open tundra is repeated at the Lemming site on Okiavilialuk, at Tiriak on Juet Island, at Itinapik on the peninsula southwest of Lake Harbour, and at a number of small transient camps between Lake Harbour and Pritzler Harbour. Aulatsivik (Cape Wight), was, and is still today, a favored late spring camping ground. From here, canoes can be hauled to the floe edge and basking seal can be taken east and west of the peninsula. This cape is now too disturbed for archaeological excavation, but in small spots at various elevations we have found Pre-Dorset and Early and Late Dorset artifacts.

The Killiktee site, deeper in Itivirk Bay, and the Talaguak site, on an arm of land between Itivirk and McKellar bays, are both larger and later in Late Dorset than the sites just mentioned, yet the evidence suggests that they too were seasonal. Stone tools recovered in a few hours excavation at the Killiktee site (corrected carbon date A.D. 745) have the same discrete attributes as those from the Abverdjar site. The excavations at the Talaguak site have concentrated on the Thule houses. However, all of these later houses had been cut through earlier Dorset middens, and in some the compacted Dorset surface provided the base for Thule sleeping platforms (Sabo 1980). In all probability most of the grassy, 213-m wide headland is sporadically underlaid by Dorset midden.

The Dorset stone tools encapsulated in the sod blocks of Thule houses, and one ivory sled shoe of Late Dorset type, are typologically contemporaneous with the Killiktee site and Abverdjar. Because so many of these late sites are transient and seemingly only inhabited in warm months, I have suggested (Maxwell 1980) that at least on this coast winter villages were made up of snowhouses on the fast ice.

One hundred and thirty km to the north, the Crystal II site on the banks of the Sylvia Grinnell River at the outskirts of the town of Frobisher Bay is clearly a Late Dorset fishing encampment. The site, no more than 2.5 m above the high tide that reverses the river's current, was first excavated by Collins (1950). He found that five Thule pit houses had cut through an earlier Dorset midden separated from the later Thule occupation by a layer of sterile sod. Where part of the Dorset deposit was protected from cycles of freezing and thawing, nonlithic artifacts were well preserved and fit into a Late Dorset time frame (Figure 7.30). Harpoon heads are of Types F, H, J, and a late variant of Kingait Closed. The assemblage included bone and antler composite handles for holding side-hafted knives and one ivory spatula with a bear head and skeletal engraving (Figure 7.30E). In subsequent years (Maxwell 1972) my field teams excavated the part undisturbed by Thule houses and recovered 980 stone artifacts. All of these are of late type. Most diagnostic are the number of oblique-edged end blades, expanded-edged, flaring end scrapers, stemmed and side-notched end blades, and skillfully flaked harpoon tips with deeply incurved basal margins and finely serrated edges. Burin-like tools include the square-ended Dorset burin-like, but also the corner-notched Tiriak type, and only one tip fragment of an Igloolik angular-tipped form. Unlike Dorset sites elsewhere in the Eastern Arctic, but like those of all periods I have excavated on the southeastern coast of Baffin Island, Crystal II contained spalled burins (7.3% of the stone tool assemblage). Since this, like other late sites, is so close to the present tide line and since the site contained no other tools of a Pre-Dorset type, the spalled burin on southeastern Baffin Island must be seen as a regional variant and not the result of the site contamination.

Over most of the site, the midden was too thin to protect organic materials from

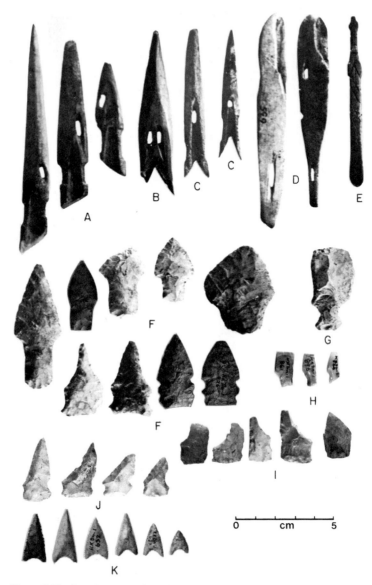

Figure 7.30 Late Dorset artifacts from the Crystal II site, Frobisher Bay (after selected Smithsonian Institution photographs, courtesy of Henry B. Collins).

A. harpoon heads of Type J
B. harpoon head of Type F
C. harpoon head of Type Ha$_1$
D. two composite handles for burin-like tools
E. spatula-shaped effigy of bear with skeletal engraving
F. stemmed, corner-notched, and side-notched end blades

G. side-notched flake knife
H. side-hafted burin-like tools
I. spalled burins
J. transverse edged knives or scrapers
K. harpoon end blades (all with fine marginal serration)

disintegration. It was an unpatterned jumble of rocks reshuffled by successive families as they robbed older tent rings for their own dwellings. But one of these tent enclosures at the northeast corner was undisturbed. It was a barely outlined rectangle of rocks with a cleared sleeping space along one side and a deposit of charred fat but no hearth at an opposite corner. There was no trace of an axial structure that could be considered a midpassage.

Sporadic Dorset sites have been reported from farther north along the eastern coast of Baffin Island, but so far none are earlier than Late Dorset. Because much of this coast is submerging rather than rising, earlier sites may be underwater.

South, across the Hudson Strait, there are sites with artifacts diagnostic of the Late Dorset period from the northeastern tip of Labrador (Leechman 1943) westward to Payne, Diana (Plumet 1979), and Wakeham (Barré 1970) bays. The Nuvuk Island site near the northeastern corner of Hudson Bay (Leechman 1943) is clearly late, with its harpoon heads of F, G, and J types, Late Dorset lithics, and carved figures of a man with a removable penis, a bear, and a swan.

Late Dorset people returned to the Belcher Islands, apparently after an absence of several centuries and settled at the Kingaaluk 1 site (Harp 1976b). They crossed and settled on the stepping-stone islands of Mansel and Coats across the north end of Hudson Bay. In the collection that Burwash sent to Jenness (1925) from this latter island, there were literally hundreds of harpoon heads with lateral line holes (Type J) as well as many of Types F, and G, and late forms of Dorset Parallel. Presumably these were associated with carved shaman's teeth, bear head spatulas, and peculiar engraved and carved bone disks.

Collins' (1956b, 1957) T-2 site on Southampton Island, closer to present sea level than T-1 and T-3, is of this Late Dorset period. From here Late Dorset can be traced through harpoon heads and other diagnostic traits to the north shore of the Boothia Peninsula (VanStone 1962), to Cresswell Bay on Somerset Island (Taylor 1967), to the south shore of King William Island (Mathiassen 1927), and to Victoria Island. In fact, given the necessary exploration time, energy, and money, I suspect that one would find Late Dorset sites on all the shores of the Canadian Arctic Islands and adjacent mainland with the exception, perhaps, of Prince Patrick, Mackenzie King, and Borden islands.

On southeastern Victoria Island, the Late Dorset materials of the Bell site (Taylor 1964, 1967, 1972) differ enough from those of earlier sites on the island that both McGhee (1976) and I see them as artifacts of people returning from the east after an absence of some centuries. The site had stratified, but not always separable, Late Dorset and Thule components, with rectangular house depressions, some probably dug by Dorset people. Harpoon heads are of Late Dorset types. Most are slotted for end blades (Type G), two have strange longitudinal grooves running from the distal end to double line holes, and one has a rivet hole in a channeled groove for a perforated end blade in the Thule fashion. These two attributes, the longitudinal grooves and rivet hole most resemble harpoon heads from the very Late Dorset site at Resolute, Cornwallis Island. One open-socket harpoon head is of Ha_2 type, with median line hole and single lateral spur. The site also produced a number of wooden pieces—human maskettes and bears incised with skeletal motifs.

Farther west on Victoria Island at Prince Albert Sound (McGhee 1969) a large, rectangular stone enclosure 31 m long, 7.6 m wide, and 0.5 m high contained little cultural midden but at least one Late Dorset harpoon head of Type G.

Prior to the late 1970s, northern Labrador was largely terra incognita to archaeologists, with no evidence of Late Dorset occupation. Beginning in 1977, the Torngat Archaeological Project, the first large-scale multidisciplinary attack on the Arctic since the Fifth Thule Expedition, discovered and sampled 350 prehistoric sites between Okak and the northern tip (Fitzhugh 1980a). Among these, several sites have the diagnostic lithic traits detailed in the preceding for Late Dorset. Much of the data is not yet analyzed or published. But available evidence indicates a time gap between Middle and Late Dorset and few transitional tool forms. Consequently it may be a new and late movement of Dorset people onto this coast from the north. The most completely described site is at the southern boundary of Late Dorset, Okak 3 on Okak Island (Cox 1977, 1978). A large semisubterranean house at this site (described in Chapter 6 in the sectioned title "Dwellings") has a paved axial feature (midpassage) with hearths and pot supports but no discernible entryway. This differs distinctively from the Middle Dorset houses on Labrador, which are deeper and do have tunnel-like entrys. Surprisingly, although the stone tool traits seem to come from the Foxe Basin–Baffin Island region, this house form does not. It does, however, appear in northern Labrador, on the northern Quebec coast, and in southeastern Hudson Bay. The virtual identity of this house form to those reported from the High Arctic and its absence from the intervening sites is one of the mysteries of Dorset culture.

Because middens are so thin in these Labrador Late Dorset houses, they may only have been used in fall and early winter and then deserted for snowhouses on the fast ice or outer islands in the colder months (Fitzhugh 1980a). Such evidence supports my contention that late winter villages on southeastern Baffin Island were on the sea ice. In this latter region of extreme tidal fluctuation, rising and falling seas of winter build up such bands of broken shore ice that movement from land to flat sea ice is exasperating and time-consuming. Such time could better be spent hunting at the floe edge or breathing holes from close-by houses already on the smooth ice.

Point Revenge Indians dominated the Labrador coast south of Nain, preventing a southward expansion of Late Dorset people. But to the north, from Okak to the Button Islands, there are late settlements in virtually all habitable bays and fjords. Stone artifacts recovered from them are replicas of Late Dorset forms ubiquitous in the Eastern Arctic.

One of the most interesting of the Late Dorset Labrador sites is the large village of Shuldham 9 on Shuldham Island in Saglek Bay (Clark and Sproull-Thomson 1981; Thomson 1981, 1982). Recovered materials indicate that the island was occupied in virtually all the phases of Paleo- and Neoeskimo, but most intriguing are the soapstone art objects from Late Dorset houses carbon dated around A.D. 1340. The houses have the familiar axial features, and the utilitarian lithics are characteristic of Late Dorset elsewhere. The many soapstone figures, however, while having a Dorset flavor are delightfully unique (Figure 7.31). One carving of a bear cub has the

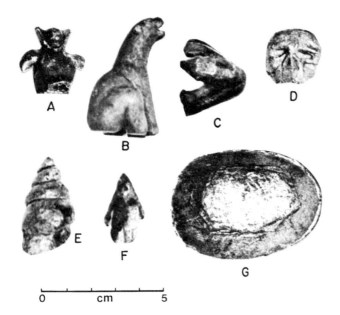

Figure 7.31 Magico-religious artistic steatite carvings from the Shuldham site, Shuldham Island, Saglek Bay, Labrador (after photographs courtesy of Callum Thomson).

A. human figure with upstanding collar
B. polar bear
C. polar bear cub
D. human skull
E. periwinkle shell
F. human figure with hooded parka (possibly representing Thule or Norse stranger)
G. miniature lamp or bowl

animal sprawling with legs outstretched and forepaws resting on them; another has a cub raising its head in a plaintive howl. One figurine depicts a 3-cm high human with an upstanding Dorset-type parka collar sitting impassively; another carving is of a human couple vigorously coupling. One crudely carved human figure has both a high Dorset collar and a Neoeskimo-type parka hood. The assemblage also includes a soapstone seashell, human skull, and bird head. Though the carvings in their relative crudeness do not reflect the finished techniques of Dorset ivory carvers; with their emphasis on bear and human figures, they nevertheless conform to basic Dorset themes. Had organic materials been preserved at this site, they surely would have reflected a rich range of ivory, antler, and wooden carved art.

The persistence of Late Dorset on the Labrador coast based on carbon dates establishes its contemporaneity with both Thule and Norse settlements farther to the north.

TERMINAL DORSET

By A.D. 1000 Dorset demography and culture had clearly reached a climax and was in a balanced state of equilibrium within its ecosystem. A century later it had ceased to exist as a viable culture over most of its previous range. In 1960 the explanation for this sudden event was relatively simple. At about A.D. 1000 Thule whale hunters from northern Alaska had intruded on Dorset territory. With their more efficient technology permitting productive open-water hunting, particularly of the huge bowhead whale, they had simply substituted new ways of life for the old. With no apparent evidence for wholesale slaughter of Dorset people, it was assumed that some of them had assimilated the new technology. Other less flexible individuals, driven from favored hunting spots to less productive sites, had ultimately starved, while still others had taken refuge in marginal regions of the Eastern Arctic. Ultimately, it was thought, we would find strong archaeological evidence of contact between the Dorset and Thule cultures.

In 1984, the presumed scenario is much the same but with added complexity. Carbon dates, even treated with deserved scepticism, only rarely indicate overlap of the two cultures in the same locale; hypotheses about borrowed traits remain mainly inferential; and in spite of the subsequent excavation of many Late Dorset and Early Thule sites, there is not yet empirical evidence of contact. Both cultures are often present on the same sites, but thin, sterile layers between the two and Dorset artifacts encapsulated in the sod blocks of Thule houses indicate sequential rather than synchronous occupation. Jordan (1979) and Bielawski (1979) are among many authors who have inferred the borrowing of traits between the two cultures. The traits most commonly cited are ivory sled shoes, snow knives (presumably for snowhouses), and extensive use of iron for end blades and soapstone for lamps and pots, all of which Thule people may have borrowed from Dorset. Contemporaneous Dorset people are thought to have borrowed the cold-trap tunnel entryway and raised sleeping platform from Thule architects. However, the early appearance of tunnel entries in Labrador Middle Dorset raises doubts about the direction this trait may have taken.

A common explanation for the reduction of Dorset people in the central part of the Eastern Arctic, if indeed they were not all quickly assimilated into Thule villages, hinges on the nature of the two economies. Faunal evidence from many sites suggests that Dorset people primarily hunted species abundant within a day's travel of the home settlement. They did not, for example, hunt walrus if the local migration terminated 100 km away. They intercepted migrating harp seal in narrow channels (Cox and Spiess 1980), concentrated on rookery birds rather than on the more elusive migratory fowl, and specialized in the selective hunting of age-sets of animals when these were most abundant and least wary. This strategy required detailed knowledge of local animal behavior and precise timing of hunting activity through the year. The Thule economic pattern, facilitated by their long-distance umiak and dogsled travel, seems to be more one of hunting targets of opportunity and exploiting a greater variety of food resources. They were better organized for cooperative activity by virtue of their training as whaling crews. Had Thule people moved in, for example, to a critical fishing river at the right time, Dorset people would simply have avoided the newcomers and deprived themselves of this resource. By itself such an event would not have led to starvation, but repetition of similar episodes over a period of time would inevitably lead to decreased reproductive and survival rates. In this regard, epidemic may also have played a role. The immigrant population, with earlier sporadic contacts with more southerly and Siberian people may have introduced diseases for which Dorset people, long isolated, had no natural immunity.

Not all Dorset settlements were submerged by Thule culture. Current evidence indicates that for three or four centuries after Thule people had dominated most of the northern Eastern Arctic, a coastal band of Dorset villages extended from northern Labrador, across the Ungava coast, and down Hudson Bay's east coast to Gulf Hazard. This coastal control may have blocked a southern penetration of the early Thule diaspora.

Terminal Dorset concluded at Igloolik with settlements on the 8-m strand line at Alarnerk and K'aersut. A corrected carbon date on antler at the latter site is A.D. 1240, presumably at least a century after Thule people entered the area. Houses at this level containing Late Dorset artifacts have tunnel cold-trap entrances, side storage and cooking alcoves, and elevated rear sleeping platforms—all in the Thule fashion. Graves in Terminal Dorset at Igloolik, the only location at which they have been reported, are large Thule-like rock cairns. A very late, Terminal Dorset house at Nunguvik, carbon dated 5 years after an adjacent Thule house, had a paved tunnel entryway, a partially paved floor, and a storage alcove near the entry. Most of this house's artifacts were of Late Dorset type, but the one recovered harpoon head, not yet described, is of a type new to the Dorset inventory (Mary-Rousselière 1979a).

Much of our difficulty in recognizing the process of cultural interaction between Terminal Dorset and early Thule comes from the nature of the sites. Over most of the Eastern Arctic, Thule migrants settled on the same spots previously occupied by Dorset people. On rugged, rocky coasts such as those on southeastern Baffin Island, these were the only flat spaces suitable for houses. More important, the nitrogen-rich Dorset middens had produced thick layers of sod so useful for the walls of Thule houses. Consequently there are often more Dorset objects encapsulated in this sod in the interior fill of Thule houses than artifacts of the latter culture. The Shorty site, where the first hour's digging excited the excavators with the possibility of demonstrating contact and assimilation, is such an example. The house here was of unquestionable Thule design, with 26 bowhead whale ribs left lashed together when the house was abandoned. As I have stated earlier, there were 581 Dorset lithic artifacts in and around the house and only 2 Thule ones—a whalebone fish lure and a whalebone mattock. Sadly, the second hour's digging clearly demonstrated that the Thule house had been dug through an earlier Dorset midden.

A better example is House 9 at the Talaguak site, also near Lake Harbour (Maxwell 1981; Sabo 1981). Inside this early Thule house there were 86 Dorset artifacts (and 128 Thule ones). When our crew cut through the stone and sod back wall we could see clearly the boundary where Thule architects had cut through a Late Dorset midden in excavating the pit for their house. Careful plotting of artifacts demonstrated that (1) all Dorset artifacts in the interior of the house lay closer to the surface than did Thule ones, (2) all Thule artifacts lay in association with interior features—fireplaces, floors, and storage compartments—whereas no Dorset ones did, and (3) most Dorset artifacts were within a 50-cm horizontal distance from the outer walls. The conclusion was inescapable: Dorset artifacts in the house had come from sod blocks used in building up walls of the Thule house that had later collapsed inward.

A situation similar to this may or may not account for the structure on Mill Island

(O'Bryan 1953) that has long been seen as a possible fusion of traits from Dorset and Thule. Architecture of the house does not differ from other Thule residences. The thin layer of debris on the floor indicates only a short occupation, but the mixture of Dorset and Thule materials in it can be interpreted three different ways: It could have been (1) built by Thule people and later reoccupied by Dorset families, (2) constructed by Thule people on an earlier Dorset site, or (3) constructed by strongly Thule-influenced Dorset builders. O'Bryan opted for the last interpretation and there is some evidence to support him. Of the 400 artifacts recovered from inside and adjacent to the house, only 11 were clearly of Thule type (Figure 7.32). Two miniature harpoon heads, possibly toys, had drilled sockets and, although not of diagnostic types, were probably Thule. The remaining harpoon heads were of Late Dorset type as were art carvings and most lithic and nonlithic artifacts. The Thule artifacts, such as 2 wooden throwing boards, a drilled harpoon socket, and a drilled knife handle, show no influence from Dorset styles. Perhaps the most significant item was a cache of 5 Dorset needles inside a stone compartment on the sleeping platform.

The faunal refuse in the house was characteristic of neither Dorset nor Thule hunting practices. O'Bryan estimated a minimum number of 29 individual caribou, 2 narwhal, 9 individual polar bear, a "surprisingly large" number of fox, and the remains of a very few hare, duck, geese, and ptarmigan. If it were not for the cache of Dorset needles carefully stored by the residents, I would consider it likely that this was another example of sequential site use.

Better examples of the blending of cultural traits, if not of direct contact, come from the Tuvaaluk Project on the northern Ungava coast (Plumet 1979). Whereas over most of the Eastern Arctic there is an overlapping of Thule and Dorset houses; on the coast west of Ungava Bay, sites of the two cultures are not on the same spot. According to Plumet, even when Dorset and Thule sites are nearby, the settlements are separated due, he feels, to microecological differences.

One of the richest sites along this coast, DIA-4 on Diana Bay, was occupied for at least 1000 years (Badgley 1980; Plumet and Badgley 1980) according to both carbon dates and lithic artifacts (nonlithic ones were not preserved). The very well-preserved House A on this site, carbon dated A.D. 1480 on charcoal from the kitchen area, is particularly illuminative of the Terminal Dorset period (Plumet 1979). Prior to excavation it was assumed to be a Thule house, with its large rocks, many ribs and scapulae of bowhead whale, and tunnel entry blocked by a whale skull. But stream erosion of part of the west wall exposed a Dorset soapstone lamp covered with red ochre and stone tools diagnostic of Late Dorset. Excavation of the house demonstrated a strange miscegenation of architectural traits. The northern part of the interior living space was typically Dorset, with paved midpassage, stone boxed lamp support, and lateral sleeping spaces. The southern half was equally typical of Thule houses, with broad paved floor, cold-trap 30 cm below the level of floor paving, and tunnel entry 3 m long. Part of the west wall had been constructed by cantilevering overlapping large stone slabs held in place by whale ribs, a trait characteristic of Greenlandic late Thule. There was little doubt that the house had

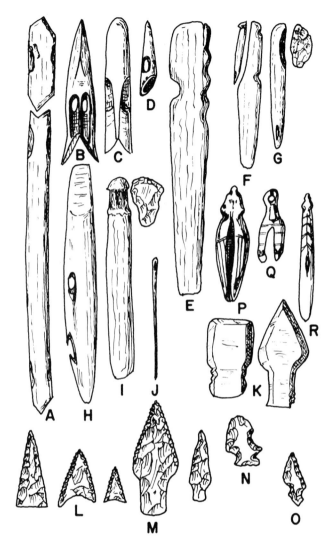

Figure 7.32 Artifacts from the Mill Island site (drawings based on selected illustrations from O'Bryan 1953).

A. two segments of laterally perforated ivory sled shoe
B. Type G harpoon head
C. Dorset Parallel type harpoon head
D. toy harpoon head of Thule type
E. Thule type wooden throwing board
F. composite burin handle
G. side-bladed knife handle and blade
H. ivory harpoon foreshaft
I. end scraper and wooden handle
J. needle with rounded butt
K. slate knife blades
L. harpoon end blades
M. stemmed lance blades
N,O. side scrapers
P. ivory bear-headed falcon
Q. human or bear effigy
R. bear-headed ivory spatula (all artifacts are not drawn to same scale)

been built on a single occasion and by people whose artifact inventory consisted solely of Dorset tools.

House A and other data from the site demonstrate unequivocally coexistence of Thule and Dorset people for two or three centuries in the Eastern Arctic. But it still does not answer questions regarding the nature of contact between the two. Did Thule people avoid the coasts of Ungava and northern Labrador? Did the two ethnic groups live side by side in uneasy truce, the one borrowing better residence forms and perhaps even whale hunting, the other borrowing the technique of snowhouse building and stone lamps? The probable exposure of Dorset people to the more efficient gear for open-water hunting of Thule culture, with its floats, toggles, and disarticulating harpoon, but their failure to adopt it provides further evidence of Dorset conservatism. The impression of a closed Dorset cultural system is reinforced by this and by the fact that at various times and in various places Paleoeskimo people were exposed to forest edges and the ecotones between forest and tundra yet did not appear to have utilized forest mammals in their economy or to have borrowed from neighboring people such energy-efficient tools as bow drills or bows and arrows. It is not surprising that at least some of the Dorset remnant retained this technological conservatism in the face of what appear to have been more efficient Thule tools and weapons.

Cultural conservatism is well demonstrated by the unmixed Late Dorset site Harp (1976a) excavated at Gulf Hazard. This outlet to Richmond Gulf is far south on the eastern coast of Hudson Bay and probably outside the range of the earliest Thule migrants. The houses here, ranging in charcoal dates from A.D. 1105 to 1400, are of unquestioned Dorset type. House 1 at Gulf Hazard 8 is particularly striking. The shallow pit around 5 m in diameter is barely outlined by a ridge of gravel. Through the center was a very carefully paved axial feature of fitted stone slabs. Two vertically boxed hearths in the axial feature, filled with charcoal and burned blubber, were bordered by cantilevered pot supports. The house is virtually identical to those described from the Late Dorset Snowdrift site more than 2000 km to the northwest. The persistence of this house form for at least 3400 years from early Independence I to Late Dorset and its geographical spread adequately documents Paleoeskimo conservatism.

Equally intriguing is the fact that in House 1 of Gulf Hazard 1, carbon dated to A.D. 1155, Harp (1974–1975) recovered a harpoon head-shaped amulet of copper. Extensive analyses of this artifact indicate that it was of European origin. It could only have come from Norse settlers either by long-distance trade in an exchange network or through direct contact.

Did Dorset people survive into the twentieth century? On Greenland's southeastern coast, the drift ice of the East Greenland current kept the Inuit of Angmagssalik in near isolation for several centuries. Differences in several of their cultural traits suggested to Meldgaard (1960a) that they might represent the assimilation of Thule and Dorset traits. Their concern with magical flying-bear spirit helpers, an elaborate development of shamanism, and secret shaman language, and grotesque artistic carvings all point to possible Dorset origins.

The mysterious Sadlermiut of Southampton Island have been particularly noteworthy as possible remnants of Thule-influenced Dorset people. They were not discovered by Europeans until the nineteenth century. Then by the winter of 1902–1903, they were virtually exterminated by an epidemic probably introduced by a sick sailor from the SS *Active* who died in the late summer of 1902 and was buried at Lake Harbour.

Mathiassen (1927) learned from the Aivilik that the Sadlermiut had been a self-isolating people, refusing to marry into other tribal groups, speaking a strange dialect, and seeking avoidance rather than relation with others. Inuit from Lake Harbour and Cape Dorset, taken to Southampton by the *Active* for whale hunting, spoke of them as being extremely strong and smelling excessively of rancid blubber (Pitseolak 1975). According to these accounts they were unwilling to enter into the postcontact trade networks by which copper, iron, and soapstone were circulating. They were, however, noted for skill in flint knapping, a technique that had virtually disappeared elsewhere.

Collins (1956a) and Taylor (1960) researched the possibility that the Sadlermiut may have represented a blend of Thule and Dorset cultures by excavating houses at Native Point and on Coats Island. The results were inconclusive, largely because the houses had been occupied too late in the nineteenth century. However, the frequent use of vertical rock slabs in the pit houses and particularly the very Dorset-like stemmed and broadly side-notched flint end blades recovered there leave the questions open. The excavation of earlier Sadlermiut houses may some day add to the solution. The houses excavated by Mathiassen (1927) at Kuk on the northern shore of the island were earlier. However, except for the flaked stone artifacts, the recovered cultural material can best be attributed to Thule origins. Dorset artifacts were found, both in the excavations and in collections made by local Inuit, but those illustrated are characteristic of much earlier Dorset and were probably encapsulated in sod for the houses. There is one possible exception: On the sleeping platform of one prehistoric Sadlermiut house there were two shaman's tubes with carved bear heads and skeletal engraving that are unquestionably Dorset carvings (Mathiassen 1927:Plate 67; 3,4). Whether these were coeval with the house construction or collected by Sadlermiut from an ancient midden must remain moot.

8   Thule Whale Hunters

INTRODUCTION

Some time near the beginning of the second millennium A.D., western Alaskan Inuit, presumably speaking an archaic Inupiat, began an eastward migration that by the thirteenth century had dominated the coasts of Arctic Canada and Greenland.

The archaeological taxon for the migration, culture, and people—Thule (pronounced Danish-fashion, Tuleh)—derives from one of the earliest and seminally productive interdisciplinary researches in anthropology: Between 1921 and 1924 one of the most impressive teams of archaeologists, anthropologists, and natural scientists ever assembled compiled the data for 34 volumes of what is still the most complete description of the Canadian Arctic. Sailing from Copenhagen in a small ship, they iced in for the winter in Repulse Bay at Danish Island near a Hudson Bay post. From here, exploring by dogsled, Kaj Birket-Smith, Therkel Mathiassen, Helge Bangsted, Knud Rasmussen, Peter Freuchen, and Jacob Olsen collected the data that became foundational to every schoolchild's knowledge of Eskimo life.

Mathiassen, occasionally helped by Birket-Smith, Rasmussen, and Olsen, had responsibility for the archaeology. He began his excavations close to the winter harbor on the north coast of Repulse Bay at the Naujan site of 18 semi-subterranean pit houses and several graves, meat caches, and boat supports. The assemblage from the 12 houses he excavated in a single short summer differed, in his mind, significantly enough from cultural traits of the living Central Eskimo—Aivilingmiut, Netsilingmiut, and Iglulingmiut—to warrant a new archaeological term. In 1910 the irrepressible humanists Knud Rasmussen and Peter Freuchen had started a small trading post near what is now the large air base on northwestern Greenland. They named it after the ancient term for the farthest north—Ultima Thule. The trading post became the jumping-off place for several Danish expeditions, notably Lauge Koch's impressive sledge journey on the coast of northern Greenland. Mathiassen chose Thule as the appropriate name for this archaeological culture discovered on the Fifth Thule Expedition.

It is worth the space here to recount, in Mathiassen's words, some of his excavation difficulties, since they are so similar to those that some of us, precluded from helicopter use, still experience.

As matters turned out, however, I was unable to devote myself exclusively to archaeology in the brief summer; some ethnographic, carthographic [sic] and natural-historic work had necessarily to be done in this season too; but in periods when conditions made it possible I concentrated principally upon the excavations.

The system of excavation which I employed, and which was also used by the other members of the expedition when at all possible, naturally had to be adapted to the conditions: the short time available, the frozen ground, the lack of proper equipment and implements, packing materials etc. which one must have on an expedition as compared with the equipment available when excavations of settlements are undertaken at home; in addition I was quite alone on the work as a rule. (Mathiassen 1927:1–3)

In spite of these problems, he recorded discoveries in 10-cm levels and treated organic specimens in "glycerine-carbol," techniques that were not always followed in Arctic excavations until the later 1960s.

In his definition of the Thule tradition, Mathiassen may have done his work too well. With exemplary speed he published his work on the archaeology of the Central Eskimo (1927) 2 years after Jenness (1925) had defined a different cultural complex in the Arctic—the Cape Dorset culture. Thule was well defined and understandable by ethnographic extrapolation; Dorset was enigmatic, probably older, and intriguing. For nearly half a century Arctic expeditions focused first on Dorset and then on its earlier progenitor. Thule was virtually ignored until new concerns in archaeology with process, behavior, and ecological strategy led to revived interest in its prehistory. The description of Thule culture that follows in brief description is essentially that engendered by Mathiassen. For several decades it was accepted as dogma. Since 1975 many facets of this description, and of the origin of Thule culture, have been raised to careful scrutiny, which is treated later *ad passim*. The Mathiassen model remains an ideal background against which archaeologists, born two generations later and equipped with better training, can test their trowels.

To Mathiassen the hunting of large baleen whale was the preeminent facet of Thule economy. Since this activity, the large boats that made it possible, and an abundance of wood for boats and houses were basic to the Thule lifeway (Mathiassen 1927:184), the culture could not have originated in the Central Arctic. Therefore Eastern Thule must have been a northern Alaskan or Siberian culture modified to fit the virtually woodless coasts of Arctic Canada. He concluded that this Alaskan culture had moved eastward initially not by diffusion but by a migration of people.

Traits that defined Thule (Mathiassen listed more than 100) were not greatly different from those of traditional Inuit. Dogsleds, kayaks, and umiaks not only made possible greater hunting ranges, but also the accumulation of larger and heavier household supplies and the capacity for transporting them to new settlements. Houses were relatively large, deep pits lined with huge boulders, sod, and whalebone, roofed with whale rib and jaw frameworks covered with skin and sod, and entered by long tunnels opening onto a paved floor. To further retain heat these houses had rear sleeping platforms raised above floor level. Weaponry—harpoons, lances, spears, darts, throwing boards, bows, and arrows—was diversified to accommodate hunting activities both on sea ice and in open water and such varied game as birds, seal, and whale. Most cutting tools were of slate rather than flint. Household utensils for both men's and women's work, extensive use of drills, differently bladed tools for cutting snowhouse blocks, beating frost from clothing, and scraping rime ice from the skin of kayaks, and literally hundreds of different toggles, handles, and plugs all attest to extreme functional specificity and concern with gadgetry.

Just looking at the Thule inventory gives one the impression of adaptive equipment adequate to meet any regional situation. It is logical that Meldgaard's (1960a) first exposure to Canadian Dorset culture led him to conclude that these people, in contrast to the Thule, were inadequately prepared, recent migrants from the south.

Such thoughts may have influenced Mathiassen's interpretation of the Dorset artifacts he recovered. Two years before publishing his monograph, Jenness (1925) had identified Dorset as a separate and distinct culture and concluded that it was older than Thule. In spite of recovering Dorset artifacts in nearly all the houses and middens he excavated and correctly identifying them, Mathiassen (1927) continued to maintain that Dorset harpoons and other tools were merely stylistic and possibly regional variants of Thule culture. In the matter of Thule origins he was in direct opposition to his ethnographer colleague Birket-Smith. The latter (1929) rejected Mathiassen's theory of an Alaskan homeland. Working on an evolutionary model of development from primitive to advanced, he saw Thule origins among the inland Caribou Eskimo, whose rudimentary equipment was the most primitive in the Eskimo realm. The two were in closer agreement on the final disposition of Thule. Both saw marked trait differences between Thule and the traditional Central Eskimo of the nineteenth and twentieth centuries. To Birket-Smith this signaled a later migration of Eschato Eskimo to the coast. Mathiassen saw direct ancestral linkage between Thule people and the living Polar Eskimo but was less sanguine on the ancestry of the Central Eskimo. It was not until the 1960s and 1970s that this issue was laid to rest with empirical evidence that modern Inuit of the Eastern Arctic are, indeed, the descendants of Thule people.

Following his work in the Central Arctic, Mathiassen returned to carry on archaeological excavations in Greenland. Here he recognized a Viking influence on the later Thule culture and identified a separate complex for this hybrid, which he termed Inugsuk. In the course of his work he had nearly retraced the full extent of the Thule diaspora.

Although we have discussed earlier the logical course of contact between Dorset and Thule cultures it bears another look from the viewpoint of the Thule cultural system. Dorset culture was clearly an adaptive Arctic system. Its people survived, thrived, and multiplied over a 1500-year period (twice as long if we add Pre-Dorset). Yet there is no comparison between the adaptive power of Dorset equipment and that of Thule. Beyond the equipment level there are other factors of Thule adaptive strength. Whale hunting may or may not have been a frequent activity, but the successful hunt of a single 40-ton bowhead whale in a year would provide each individual in a typical Thule community of five families with between 2 and 4 kg of meat a day (and quantities of flammable blubber) for the full year. More important in the contact between cultures, the organization of labor, specialization of duties, and nature of command structure inherently crucial to hunting huge whales would carry over into social structure, enabling Thule people to take concerted action in a way not possible for the loosely knit Dorset bands. Large boats and dogsleds permitted access to sea hunting farther from land and on more distant parts of the floe edge as well as making the move of whole communities to better hunting locations relatively easy. Cleverly designed harpoons that disarticulated on striking a seal and were equipped with inflatable bladders to keep the animal afloat, side-pronged bird spears with striking radii of 10 cm, throwing boards, and bows and arrows all can only be seen as more efficient weapons for harvesting the game potential. Small wonder that Thule hunters had little difficulty in dominating the more favored coasts of the Eastern Arctic.

THE INITIAL INVASION

Many hypotheses have been advanced for the location and time of impetus for the original Thule invasion. Mathiassen, although seeing it as emanating from Alaska, considered Birnirk of the Point Barrow region, known from collections made 35 years before the Fifth Thule Expedition, to be too recent to be the origin point. He saw the Old Bering Sea culture later identified by Collins (1935) as a more likely progenitor. Subsequently, Collins (1940) in an sequential seriation of styles in art and harpoon heads, suggested an age of A.D. 500–900 for Birnirk, making this culture a logical birthplace for Eastern Thule. However, Ford (1959), basing his conclusions on the excavation of deeply stratified settlement mounds in the vicinity of Point Barrow, questioned this opinion. He saw the stylistic sequence, particularly of harpoon heads, as indicating that Eastern Thule began after Birnirk and early in the following Nunagiak phase—a time he estimated as being closer to A.D. 1250. This estimate of time coincided more closely with that of Holtved (1954) who had considered the Nûgdlît site of northwestern Greenland, certainly one of the oldest Thule sites in Greenland, to date toward the end of the thirteenth century (1954:99). The advent of Arctic carbon dates shifted the end of Birnirk backward, closer to Collin's original estimate of A.D. 900 and close to the shift in the Bering Strait region from Old Bering Sea to Punuk culture.

At this point Taylor (1963a), using newer evidence based primarily on harpoon head typology, hypothesized that Birnirk had existed as far east as the Amudsen Gulf by A.D. 900, that the Birnirk to Nunagiak development occurred generally along the coast between Point Barrow and Victoria Island, and that a proto-Thule development intervened between Birnirk and Nunagiak spreading to Greenland by A.D. 1100. In 1963 Taylor (1972) excavated the Jackson and Vaughn sites on Cape Parry hoping to find proof of these hypotheses. Unfortunately, Taylor considered the wooden-floored and -roofed semi-subterranean houses to be typologically closer to Nunagiak and therefore too recent for the beginning of Thule. His estimate of A.D. 1200 for the Jackson site was not confirmed by carbon dates of A.D. 744: 1206 ± 100 radiocarbon years (M-1509) and A.D. 744: 1176 ± 100 radiocarbon years (M-1508). However, these were derived from samples of sealskin and charred seal fat, respectively. If the factor of 465 years is added, as Arundale (1981) recommends, their age is closer to Taylor's estimate.

The introduction of Thule carbon dates, which appeared to cluster around A.D. 1000, led McGhee (1970b) to conclude that Thule had developed from a Birnirk base shortly before the latter's end, and then moved rapidly eastward within one or two centuries. He saw neither specific traces of population pressure in the west nor developments of new and more efficient technology in the Birnirk homeland at this time. But, on the other hand, he pointed out that the date of A.D. 900 for terminal Birnirk coincided with the end of the Scandic climatic episode (Bryson and Wendland 1967), a transition between the cool Sub-Atlantic episode of 550 B.C.–A.D. 400, and the warmer-than-present Neo-Atlantic of A.D. 900–1200. This warm period throughout the Northern Hemisphere, known as the Medieval Warm Period, was marked by extensive European migration toward northern shores, for example, the Norse expansion into Iceland, Greenland, and ultimately south to Newfoundland. There was less drift ice in the Atlantic and a more northerly boundary of the Arctic pack ice around Spitsbergen.

Such an increase in temperature may have limited the southerly extent of pack ice in the Beaufort Sea off the northern coast of Alaska. Reduced sea ice in the Parry Channel from M'Clure Strait in the west to Lancaster Sound in the East may have allowed pods of the bowhead whale of Alaska and the Greenland whale of the east (both *Balaena mysticetus*) to mingle in one continuous distribution. This led McGhee to a model for Thule development based on the changed environmental conditions and modern Inuit whaling practices on the Arctic coast of Alaska.

Along the Alaskan coast the whales migrate easterly in the spring. If conditions of temperature, ice, and wind are right, a narrow shore lead opens up. This restricts whales close to shore in a relatively narrow strip of water where a large community of hunters may take as many as 15 whales in a single week. On the other hand, since whales tend to stay close to the ice edge, if the southern limit of the Beaufort pack ice lies too far from shore this type of hunting becomes impossibly dangerous.

The western gulfs and straits of the Canadian Arctic Islands are the normal summering grounds of the bowhead. Therefore less sea ice and the opening of these waters to the interisland basins and channels of the east would increase the hunting period to a full summer rather than just the fall and spring migration. This open-water hunting would require some modification in technique, involving sighting and chasing whales with umiaks and kayaks. While this method might have been less productive than whaling from shore leads during annual migrations it could be done over a longer period of the year and from more island locations. This change to an open-water whale hunting technique, characteristic of Eastern Thule, may also account for the small size of settlements compared to those of Alaska. In the restricted waters between the Canadian Arctic Islands neither large fleets of umiaks for pursuing whale far at sea nor aggregates of many hunters on shore leads would be effective. While the whaling crew of adult males from a community of five or six families might retrieve a whale in only occasional years, this supply of meat and blubber added to the take of dependable seal and caribou would be more than adequate for the small settlement.

Changing climate of the Neo-Atlantic would not only have opened up rich eastern feeding grounds for baleen whales, it would have altered other factors in the eco-system critical for maritime hunters. Less pack ice and thinner accumulations of winter ice might lead to local increases in walrus and bearded seal but would reduce the availability of suitable denning sites for the ringed seal (McLaren 1958), on which most Arctic communities ultimately depended. Since Dorset people appear to have been particularly dependent on this species, a reduction in this prime source of food may have contributed to the ease with which Thule people dominated the east.

McGhee's model is a persuasive one but its major premise, that whale hunting was the driving force, has been questioned by Stanford (1976). At the Walakpa site, 35 km west of Point Barrow, Alaska, he excavated 17 sequential occupation layers that clearly demonstrated a continuum from the beginning of the Birnirk culture to a late Western Thule of A.D. 1400.

Birnirk, which began about A.D. 500 reached a late stage at A.D. 980: 970 ± 90 radiocarbon years (Gak 2298). At the Walakpa site the earliest Thule date was A.D. 1110: 840 ± 90 radiocarbon years (Gak 2297). However Stanford considers Thule to have begun around two centuries earlier in the vicinity of Point Barrow. In the successive layers of the Walakpa site he found little faunal or technological evidence of whaling activity. In fact he questions whether this was a regular factor in late Birnirk economy. Conversely he found ring seal to have been the basic food species, as they were in most Eastern Thule sites. Progressive reduction in the individual size of these animals toward the upper layers of the Birnirk midden suggested both overhunting and decrease in newborn and subadult pups due to restriction in fast ice denning sites. Stanford concluded that the impetus for an eastward migration around A.D. 1000 was due primarily to a search for better sealing waters.

A more recent explanation returns to an earlier suggestion by Collins (1952). To him the artifacts he recovered from one of the earliest Eastern Thule sites at Resolute, Cornwallis Island, showed strong Punuk influences. This Bering Sea culture had developed a significant emphasis on whale and walrus hunting by about A.D. 800 and, to Collins, might have been a force in the Thule migration. In the late 1970s and early 1980s Schledermann's excavations at Bache Peninsula, Ellesmere Island, (Schledermann and McCullogh 1980) supported this suggestion with artifacts that demonstrated even stronger Punuk traits. As is usual in the Arctic, harpoon head styles provide the best clues to both cultural influences and time. The earliest in Eastern Thule, clearly derived from the west, are the Sicco and Natchuk types (described in the following discussion). In a convincing attribute analysis Yamaura (1979) contends that the former of these was derived from Punuk origins and the latter from Birnirk ones.

To summarize the resultant hypothesis, Punuk people were moving eastward during the latter part of the tenth century, pushed in part by population pressure in the west. It was a time of warring factions in northeastern Siberia and population expansion in the islands of the Bering Sea. The appearance of armored vests of bone slats (Bandi 1974–1975) and fearsome spears more effective for terrifying and killing humans than animals testify to local Punuk conflict. In their eastward move they brought with them a whale hunting economy. Seen thus, Eastern Thule in its initial development was a composite of Punuk and Birnirk traits. The pressure for movement from the Alaskan coast was an amalgam of factors that included warmer climates, reduced seal population, population pressure from the west, and increased emphasis on hunting the bowhead whale, which were already moving eastward.

Establishing the precise time for the initial eastward expansion has proved difficult. The location of sites and evidence of regional ecology suggest that it took place during the warmer climates of the Neo-Atlantic episode (Andrews and Miller 1979). But as yet there is no empirical evidence to suggest whether this was at the beginning around A.D. 900 or toward the end around A.D. 1200. Carbon dating appears to be of little help in this matter. Savelle (1980) has listed all the available Thule carbon dates to 1980. These 97 dates, on a wide variety of organic substances and from 12 different laboratories, fail for the most part to confirm the hypotheses of individual investigators. Twenty-one of the carbon dates in Savelle's list, which have central tendencies prior to A.D. 1000, average to A.D. 930, a date for Canadian Thule that most would consider a century too early. Four willow dates, often considered the more accurate, average A.D. 888, seven wood and charcoal dates average A.D. 920. On the more recent end of the list are many dates that are equally unacceptable. The situation has led to the tempting but dangerous acceptance of "good" dates, those that fit an investigator's estimates, and rejection of "bad" dates, those that do not, and the application of a variety of modifiers to bring carbon dates into harmony with hypothesis. Recent evidence of the variety of "fossil" carbon in the arctic tundra and maritime landscape and of differential uptake by various life forms (Schell 1983) suggests that we may be many years away from the ability to use Arctic carbon dating with any precision.

In light of the preceding statement, to say that the initial migration took place between A.D. 1000 and 1100 is questionable; yet this is the period that appears most popular among workers in the field. This estimate is compounded of a number of factors. In spite of the difficulties with carbon dating there is a greater clustering of central tendencies in this period, particularly when allowance for sea reservoir effect is taken into consideration. Sea level elevation of settlements, although treated with caution contributes to the estimate as do apparently sequential variations in house types. Ultimately, most researchers have placed the greatest reliance on changes in artifacts, particularly when they correlate with similar changes in the Alaskan sequence. However, attempts to seriate artifact styles have not yet been very successful. Stanford (1976) states that in the sequential Birnirk and Thule layers of Walakpa only harpoon heads and the tangs (proximal ends) of antler and bone arrowheads are useful time markers. While the angularity of shoulders and knobs on the tangs of the latter change through time in Alaskan sites, they appear to be less reliable guide fossils in the Eastern Arctic. For example, tangs with sloping

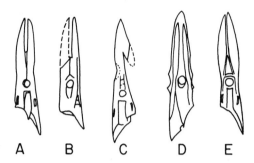

Figure 8.1 Western Arctic Thule harpoon heads.

A. Tasik
B. Nuwuk
C. Natchuk
D. Alilu
E. Sicco

shoulders appear early in Thule at Walakpa and those with sharp shoulders appear late. However, at the Ruggles Outlet site on northern Ellesmere Island (Maxwell 1960a), which is certainly late in the Thule sequence, the shoulders on three arrowhead tangs are sloping rather than sharply squared.

Changing harpoon styles have been somewhat more useful for dating Eastern Thule sites. In particular, five types recovered from late Birnirk and early Thule sites

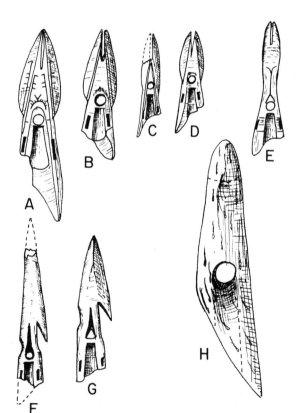

Figure 8.2 Early Eastern Arctic Thule harpoon heads. A from Nûgdlît, northwestern Greenland; B, G from southern Devon Island; C, F, H from Resolute, Cornwallis Island; D, E, from Thule, northwestern Greenland (drawings based on selected illustrations from: Collins 1952; Holtved 1944, 1954; Taylor 1963b).

A–D. Sicco type
E.   Tasik(?) type
F,G. Natchuk type
H.   whaling harpoon head

in the Point Barrow vicinity are restricted to only a few sites in the Canadian Arctic (Taylor 1963b). Consequently, these types—Tasik, Nuwuk, Natchuk, Alilu, and Sicco—are considered to date the earliest sites in the east (Figures 8.1–8.3).

Tasik (Figure 8.1A) has an open socket, a single asymmetrical lateral spur, nonfunctional side blade slots, two lashing slots, and a blade slot in the same plane as the line hole. In the east it has been reported only from the Vaughn site near Cape Parry (Taylor 1972) but may also be in the northwest Greenland assemblage.

Nuwuk (Figure 8.1B) is closed socketed with a single lateral spur and an end blade slot in the same plane as the line hole and is often decorated with incised lines, including an inverted Y over the line hole. The type has been reported from the Vaughn and Jackson sites near Cape Parry, Lady Franklin Point on Victoria Island, and the Umanaq and Nûgdlît sites on northwestern Greenland.

The Natchuk type has an open socket, a single lateral barb, an opposing nonfunctional or vestigial side blade slot, and lashing slots. To date it has only been reported from a site on southern Devon Island and House N at Site M-1 at Resolute (Figures 8.1C and 8.2F and G).

The Alilu type (Figure 8.1D) has a closed socket, a lateral asymmetric spur, and a blade slot at right angles to the line hole. Some of this type have vestigial side blade slots and raised ridges for decoration. One from the Jackson site may be of this type and it is present in the Semmler Collection from the vicinity of Lady Franklin Point.

The Sicco type (Figures 8.1E and 8.2A–D) is the most widespread in the Eastern Arctic and actually more common there than in the Point Barrow vicinity. It has an open socket with a thin blade slot parallel to the line hole. Its most distinguishing feature is a pronounced wasp waist and decorative lines that are often raised. Taylor (1963a) traced the eastward distribution of this type from the Booth Islands off Cape Parry to Lady Franklin Point on the southwestern shore of Victoria Island, north to House N at the M-1 site on Cornwallis Island (Collins 1952), to the south coast of Devon Island (possibly Maxwell Bay), to the eastern coast of Ellesmere Island at Buchanan Bay (Lethbridge 1939), and across Kane Basin to Nûgdlît (Holtved 1954) and Thule (Holtved 1944). Subsequently the type has been reported from Minto Inlet on the west coast of Victoria Island (McGhee 1970b), Brooman Point on Bathurst Island (McGhee 1981a), and Skraeling Island off the eastern coast of Ellesmere Island (Schledermann and McCullogh 1980).

If these five types, particularly the Sicco, do indeed identify sites on the earliest Thule immigrants, then the course of migration is apparently clear: Possibly following bowhead whales, they would have coasted along the mainland into Amundsen Gulf through the straits and gulfs south of Victoria Island into Victoria Strait, then north through Peel Sound or M'Clintock Channel and east through Barrow Strait and Lancaster Sound, and finally north along the east coast of Ellesmere Island and across Kane Basin into northwestern Greenland (Figure 8.4).

If we consider eastern sites, the traits of which most closely resemble those of the Western Arctic, to be the earliest, then the sites of Nûgdlît and Ruin Island in northwestern Greenland and Skraeling Island and other sites around Buchanan Bay on eastern Ellesmere Island must represent initial Eastern Thule. Grouped into a

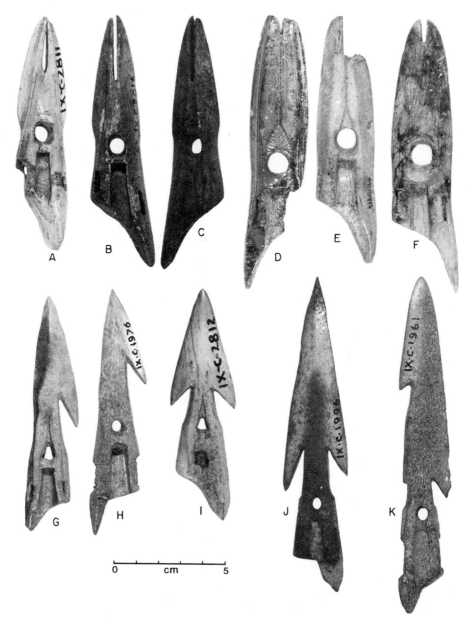

Figure 8.3 Variations of Early Eastern Thule harpoon heads—A and G from Maxwell Bay, Devon Island and others of uncertain Eastern Arctic provenience but from the general Foxe Basin–northern Hudson Bay region.

A.   Sicco type
B,C. modified Sicco type with raised decorations but diminished "wings"
D–F. Mathiassen's (1927) Type 3 with variants of inverted Y design
G.   similar to Natchuk type with single lateral barb, incipient side blade opposite barb, grooved binding slots, and inverted Y above the line hole
H.   Mathiassen's (1927) Type 2 with single barb and binding notches
I–K. Variants of Mathiassen's Type 2

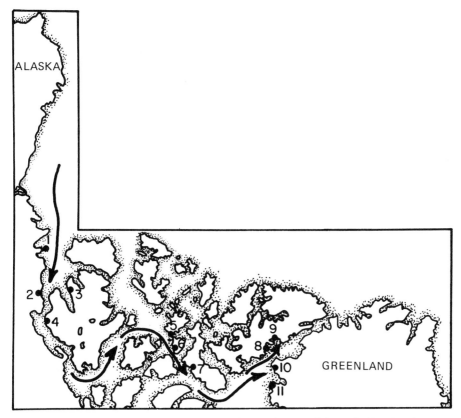

Figure 8.4 Early Thule sites in the Eastern and Central Arctic and the probable migration route.

1. Cape Parry
2. Inman River
3. Minto Inlet
4. Lady Franklin Point
5. Brooman Point
6. Resolute
7. Maxwell Bay
8. Skraeling Island
9. Buchanan Bay
10. Nûgdlît
11. Thule

Nûgdlît–Ruin Island phase first by Holtved (1954) and augmented by a series of Ellesmere Island excavations carried out by Schledermann and McCullogh (Schledermann 1978c, 1980a; Schledermann and McCullogh 1980), the phase is distinguished by a distinctive house style, western-related artifact traits, and associated Norse materials. The Skraeling Island sites, as yet published only in preliminary form, have small, square-to-roundish semisubterranean houses with short entry passages and kitchen antechambers entered from the living area but paralleling the entry and lack raised sleeping platforms. The form, Schledermann thinks, is similar to Alaskan houses. Associated with these dwellings are *qaqqi* (festival structures), large square foundations up to 7 m long made of sod, whalebone, and huge boulders and roofed with large sections of baleen overlaid by skins.

Houses on the site have contained decorated harpoon heads of Sicco type (Figure 8.5A) as well as closed-socket whaling heads, two needle cases of western design (Figure 8.5B and C), examples of Barrow Curvilinear Stamped pottery, and an ivory brow band with western decorative engraving (Schledermann and McCullogh 1980). In most of the houses excavated there were a number of Norse articles of wood, iron, copper, and cloth.

Many Eastern Arctic archaeologists would be happy if carbon dates for the Nûgdlît–Ruin Island phase ranged within the eleventh century. A few do and some are too early in the ninth century for the Norse materials associated with them, but the more reliable dates cluster around the end of the twelfth to end of the thirteenth century. This leads to three competing hypotheses: (1) The radiocarbon assessments do not reliably date the sites, (2) the initial Thule expansion into the east did not begin much before A.D. 1200, and (3) while the more southern parts of the Eastern Arctic may have been occupied as early as the eleventh century, it was not until the beginning of the thirteenth century, toward the end of the Neo-Atlantic episode, that people either from the Punuk Islands or from Point Barrow but strongly influenced by Punuk culture took a northward course to the Eastern High Arctic.

There are a few data in the more southern Arctic to support Hypothesis 3. Since 1980, the impression of most who work in Eastern Arctic prehistory is that the High Arctic migration was followed in the thirteenth century by a move south from Ellesmere Island and Greenland to colonize such "classic" Thule sites as Naujan on Repulse Bay. However, again using the Sicco harpoon head as a clue, there may be reason to suggest that an early, and perhaps the earliest, immigration followed a southern rather than northern route. Schledermann (1979:135, quoting a personal communication from Arnold) states that five harpoon heads from the Naujan site are of the Sicco type. Several Sicco heads, now housed in the National Museum of

Figure 8.5 Punuk-type (A–C) and Eastern Thule-type (D) artifacts from Ellesmere Island (drawings based on selected illustrations from Maxwell 1960a; Schledermann 1978c, 1981).

A. Punuk-like Sicco harpoon head from Bache Peninsula
B,C. Punuk-like needle cases from Skraeling Island
D. Eastern Thule type needle case from the Ruggles Outlet site

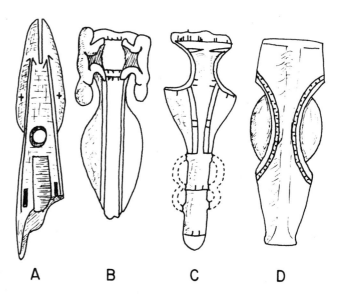

A   B   C   D

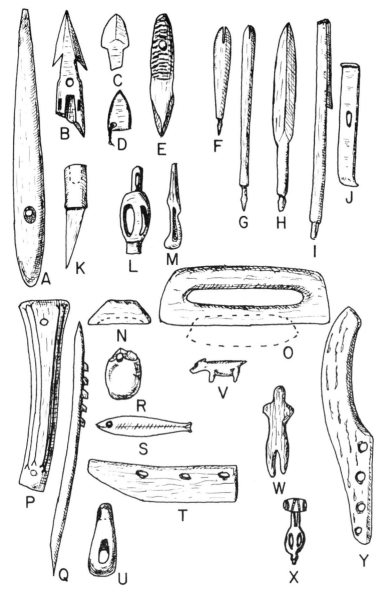

Figure 8.6 Early Thule artifacts (not to same scale) from House B at site M-1 from Resolute, Cornwallis Island (A–I, K, M, N, P–U, W, X) and houses at the Nûgdlît site, northwestern Greenland (J, L, O, V, Y) (drawings based on illustrations from Collins 1952, 1955; Holtved 1954).

A.	foreshaft	Q.	bird spear side barb
B.	Thule Type 2 harpoon head	R.	bola weight
C,D.	harpoon end blades	S.	fish lure
E.	ice pick	T.	toy dogsled
F–I.	arrowheads	U.	dog trace toggle
J.	sinew twister	V.	carved animal
K.	harpoon socket	W.	wooden female figurine
L.	seal float toggle	X.	carved female pendant (to be
M.	toy throwing board		worn with the female figure
N.	toy *ulu* handle		upside down
O.	*ulu* handle	Y.	snow knife handle
P.	knife handle		

Canada, are from an unspecified site in the Calthorpe Islands, a group at the northern end of Foxe Basin, and from unidentified sites in the general Foxe Basin region. Furthermore, House 9 at the Talaguak site near Lake Harbour (Maxwell 1981; Sabo 1981) has a number of western features that may have diffused southward from the Nûgdlît–Ruin Island phase or may have come directly from Alaska.

Although no one has yet established a detailed seriation of classes of Eastern Thule artifacts, it is apparent that from the beginning these migrants had a material culture inventory adequate for efficient adaptation to the ecosystem. We discuss in more detail some of the apparent stylistic variations developing over time in the following section. For now, limiting statements to only such early findspots as contained Sicco harpoon heads, such as Nûgdlît Houses 13A and B, 24A and B, and 29 and Resolute House N and Area M-1 House B, we find a surprisingly complete

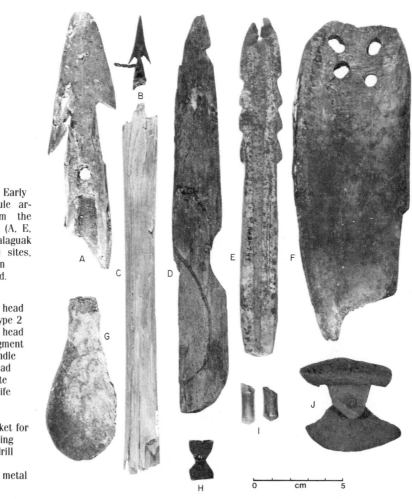

Figure 8.7 Early Classic Thule artifacts from the Okiavilialuk (A, E, J) and Talaguak (B–D, F–I) sites, southeastern Baffin Island.

A. Type 2 harpoon head
B. model Type 2 harpoon head
C. bow fragment
D. sling handle
E. lance head
F. composite snow knife blade
G. scoop
H. drill socket for fine drilling
I. jadeite drill bits
J. *ulu* with metal blade

inventory of equipment with its genesis in Alaska (Figure 8.6). Open-water hunting is represented by kayaks and umiaks displayed as toys and incised carvings, whale hunting harpoon heads up to 21 cm long, seal and walrus hunting harpoon heads, harpoons with heavy sockets and movable foreshafts, line stoppers, throwing boards for projecting lighter harpoon darts, float mouthpieces, toggles, plugs, and swivels to tire sea animals once harpooned, and gut skin waterproof parkas. There were ice picks, wooden stool legs, snow knives, shovels, dog trace buckles, and sled parts, all associated with both sea ice, floe edge, and breathing hole hunting. For land hunting and fishing there were bows, arrows, quiver handles, lances, bird spear side prongs, fish lures, and leisters. Domestic tools included both men's and women's knives, bow drills, whalebone mattocks for digging house pits, soapstone lamps and bowls, and occasionally poorly fired pottery and lamps made of clay and sandstone. At both Resolute and Nûgdlît sites there are fragments of iron knife blades. Two that have been analyzed are of meteoric origin, presumably from the huge meteorite near Thule carried back by Peary to the American Museum of Natural History, but others may have been of Norse origin. Since meteoric iron side-bladed knives were recovered from the Late Dorset sites of Abverdjar and Inuarfigssuak, knowledge of the large meteorite, as well as the use of soapstone lamps, may have passed from Late Dorset to Thule people.

Houses at the Talaguak and Okialivialuk sites near Lake Harbour, Baffin Island (Sabo 1981) may be nearly as early as the Resolute and Nûgdlît sites. Artifacts from these houses (see Figure 8.7) are probably characteristic of an early part of the Eastern Thule period.

EXPANSION AND THE CLASSIC THULE PHASE

Presumably between the twelfth and fourteenth centuries there was a marked expansion of Eastern Thule in both population and geographic extent. High Arctic settlements increased, but more impressive was the proliferation of permanent settlements to the south. By the end of these two centuries Thule people had spread along both coasts of Hudson Strait into Hudson Bay, up the coast of Foxe Basin, and along the coasts of islands to the north. To the west there were settlements from Banks and Victoria islands and along the mainland from the Mackenzie Delta to the Melville Peninsula. Villages spread from the western coast of Greenland across the northern coast, then ice free, and well down the eastern side. Apparently only Labrador, Quebec, and the most northwestern islands of the Arctic Archipelago were avoided (Figure 8.8).

This is referred to as the "classic" period of Thule development, being characterized by Mathiassen's rich finds at Naujan and marked by permanent winter settlements of large semi-subterranean houses of stone, sod, and whalebone. The archaeological record indicates this vast area as one of remarkably homogeneous culture and one within which information flow appears to have been virtually constant. This also suggests that while population expansion may have been due partly

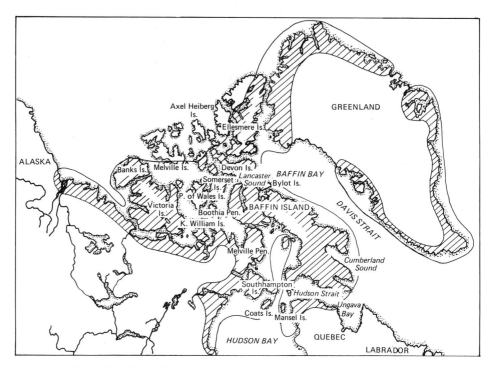

Figure 8.8   Distribution of Classic Thule (shaded areas) in the Eastern Arctic.

to optimal ecological conditions and partly to an absorbed Late Dorset contingent, there undoubtedly was a continuing eastward drift of Alaskan natives as they learned of favorable hunting conditions in the Arctic Archipelago. The Thule activities discussed in the following section refer primarily to this classic period of expansion.

CATEGORIES OF THULE ACTIVITY

Attempting an inventory of Thule material culture becomes a seemingly endless task of trait listing. These were perhaps the most gadget-oriented people of prehistory, nearly as much so as we are today, and monographic reports on Thule excavations can consequently make for hard sledging. Furthermore, with the blessings of permafrost we know virtually as much about their possessions as we do about those of modern Inuit. For example, I once found in a northern Ellesmere Island dwelling for a single family, occupied for only one or two winters, three distinctively different toggles. From ethnographic analogy these three, of quite different shapes, were used to tow dead seal behind kayaks, one being inserted through the septum of the nostrils, a second through the skin of the neck, and the third through skin at the navel. No one, archaeologist or Inuit, has yet been able to tell me why one would need such different towing devices or under what conditions they would have been used. This is particularly baffling since Lake Harbour Inuit, who have hunted successfully with me in my kayak, simply puncture the skin of the seal's tough upper lip and pass a line through the hole, and the seal streams smoothly behind.

Since an emphasis on whale hunting is one of the distinguishing features of Eastern Thule, at least in its first few centuries, we can begin with a short discussion of these largest of mammals (Figure 8.9). Prior to the heavy commercial whale hunting pressures of the eighteenth through twentieth centuries, both toothed and baleen whales must have been relatively common in the Eastern Arctic given proper ice conditions for these air breathers. Of the toothed whales probably only the relatively small beluga (*Delphinapterus leucas*) and narwhal (*Monodon monoceros*) were hunted extensively. A third toothed Arctic species, the 10-m long carniverous killer whale (*Grampus orca*) was probably considered too dangerous for small-boat hunting, as it is today. A baleen cutout from the Bache Peninsula region of Elles-mere Island (Schledermann 1981:598) has the characteristic profile of a sperm whale (*Physeter catodon*). However the huge baleen whales appear to have been the prime Thule targets. These whales have cavernous mouths filled with springy 3- to

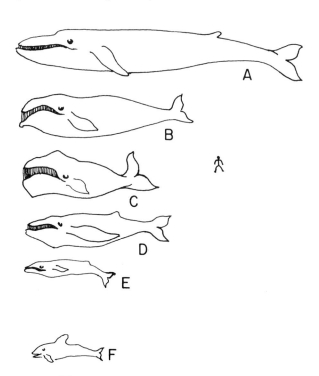

Figure 8.9 Whales of the Eastern Arctic (human figure to same scale).

A. blue whale
B. right whale
C. bowhead whale
D. humpback whale
E. minke whale
F. killer whale
G. narwhal
H. beluga whale

5-m-long sheets of baleen, the commercial whalebone once used for corset stays and buggy whips. They feed on tons of miniscule plankton by sounding, a process of taking in quantities of organism-rich water and, by pressing their huge tongues against the baleen filter, expeling the seawater but retaining the plankton.

The most common of the large Eastern Arctic baleen whales was the Greenlandic or bowhead (*Balaena mysticetus*). Adults of this species range in length from 4.5 m to 18 m, averaging about 13 m, and weigh 3 tons per linear meter. Their most notable physical feature, their highly arched heads, are nearly one-third the animal's total length with heavy outward-splayed lower jaws that are loosely joined at the center and range in length from 2 to 5 m. The bowhead eastern migration route is relatively short, with winters spent close to the southern edge of pack ice around 60° north latitude. These whales would have been reasonably easy to hunt. They tend to feed near the surface and often sleep there. Their heavy blanket of blubber keeps them afloat when dead even during the springtime when the salinity of the seawater is greatly reduced. They are not prone to use their immense tail flukes in defense and, like the north Atlantic black (*Eubalaena glacialis*), swim at speeds of only 2–4 knots, well within the capacity of umiak paddlers.

The northern range of the North Atlantic black (or right) whale, equally as large as the bowhead, tends to coincide with the southern limits of the latter. Its head is smaller and less arched and consequently its baleen plates are only about 3 m long. The species was hunted in the southeasterly part of the Thule range as was the much smaller (10-m) minke whale (*Balaenoptera acutorostrata*), which feeds closer to shore.

It is doubtful whether the other two available baleen species inhibiting these waters were hunted by prehistoric whalers. The 15-m long humpback (*Megaptera nodosa*), with flippers nearly one-third its total length, is an acrobat, often standing on its head, thrashing the water with its giant tail flukes, and lifting its tremendous bulk clear of the water—clearly too active for paddling hunters. The blue whale (*Sibbaldus musculus*) might simply have been too large to hunt. This is the largest of all living animals, with a recorded length of 31 m and weight of more than 130 tons. It is a fast swimmer, prefers the open ocean far from shore, and migrates annually from the Arctic to the Tropics.

The huge bowhead whale had great economic value for Thule people. The average adult animal would provide 15,000 kg of good meat and *muktuk,* the outer skin, which tastes like oily mushrooms and is considered a delicacy in the Arctic. Nine thousand kg of blubber would have been available for cooking, heating, and illuminating oil lamps. The tough, springy baleen and hard, heavy bone, which is solid unlike the hollow bones of other mammals, had multiple uses. On most sites where skulls have been found, the base of the skull has been broken out, indicating that the brains were also eaten. The two lower jaws, 2–5 m long, made good roof rafters for the subterranean houses, as did the shorter maxilla. In one Thule house on Somerset Island, McCartney (1980:532) found 8 whale skulls lining the inner wall. Presumably the formerly attached maxilla, and separate mandibles had been used for roof supports, providing 32 heavy rafters.

Useful though the killing and recovery of a bowhead whale would have been to a relatively small Thule community, it was probably only an occasional occurrence. The staple game that made time available for whale hunting were the various species of seals, caribou, and walrus. Pragmatic and omniverous Thule hunters utilized a wider range of resources than Dorset people had in the same localities. Hare, wolves, fox, birds, and in certain regions musk-ox all appear in numbers in the middens as do egg- and clamshells. In general the faunal composition of sites seems to reflect the taking of more targets of opportunity. This is logically due to better means of transportation but also to more efficient weapons such as bows and arrows, throwing boards, slings, bolas, and bird spears. In the eastern part of the range, particularly after whaling declined, walrus, beluga, and narwhal appear to have been more important food sources than they had been in many Dorset localities. There is more Thule evidence for stone wolf and fox traps than for Dorset ones, and while stone fish weirs might have been initially laid by Dorset fishers, they were undoubtedly expanded by Thule ones.

Although they made efficient use of virtually all available food resources, in the last analysis it was the consistent reliability of seal harvesting and the predictable caribou migrations that remained a major factor in the location of the semipermanent winter settlements. The most common seal species hunted was the ubiquitous ringed seal (*Phoca hispida*), followed, respectively, by the much larger bearded or square flipper seal (*Erignathous barbatus*), the harbor seal (*Phoca vitulina*), the migrating harp seal (*Phoca groenlandicus*), and, on Greenland, the migrating hooded seal (*Cystophora cristata*).

Sea Mammal Hunting

If the plethora of whalebone and baleen in houses and middens were not sufficient evidence for whale hunting, Thule artifacts would be. The whaling complex requires adequate weaponry, cooperative human effort, and a large boat. For at least early and classic Thule there is archaeological evidence for all these. If one combines data from sites throughout the east (Figures 8.10 and 8.11) the following picture emerges. The whaling harpoon had a large, thin, triangular end blade of slate. This was often drilled near one corner but was not riveted to the harpoon head, indicating that it was tied to either the head or the harpoon line and designed to release and remain embedded in the animal. The toggling harpoon head of whalebone or ivory was large, 12–24 cm long, with a closed socket, a single unilateral basal barb, and an end blade slot at right angles to the line hole. A few heads had two parallel raised lines bordering the line hole. The harpoon head type does not appear to have changed through time, with the possible exception that those from the earliest sites appear to taper to sharper distal tips whereas those from later sites tend to have blunt ends. The foreshaft was large, usually made of whalebone, with a single central perforation and a conical, rounded butt end. This fitted into a round, drilled socket fastened to the wooden harpoon shaft with a single scarfed and pinned joint. It is apparent that the foreshaft, tightly bound to the wooden shaft rather than to the

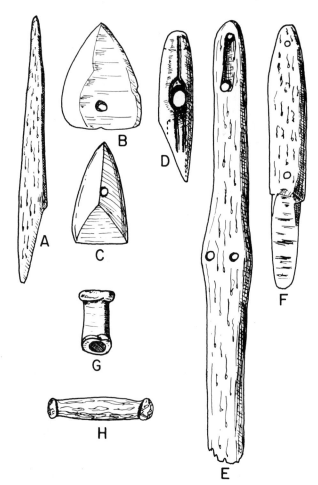

Figure 8.10 Whale hunting gear from the Naujan site, north Repulse Bay (artifacts not drawn to same scale; based on selected illustrations from Mathiessen 1927).

A. fixed foreshaft
B,C. slate harpoon end blades
D. decorated harpoon head
E,F. lance heads
G. bladder mouthpiece
H. wooden bar for lashing the bladder float to the harpoon line

socket, was meant to move slightly to either side when thrust into the animal, thereby releasing the head from the foreshaft. Plug mouthpieces, carved plugs, and line swivels indicate that seal and walrus bladders, and probably whole sealskins were inflated, plugged shut, and tied to the harpoon line. These floats were thrown overboard to tire the whale and force it to the surface after harpooning.

The whale hunting boat (umiak) with built-up driftwood frame and bearded sealskin covering is depicted by wooden toys and wooden boat parts and in at least four Thule engravings (Figure 8.12). One of the engravings (Figure 8.12B) suggests that whale hunting combined both individual kayakers and umiak crews. The umiak form appears virtually identical to those still used in Alaska. In the engravings, crews range from four to seven persons. Based on modern whaling accounts (Nelson 1969:217), the Thule umiak, with harpooner in the bow, helmsman in the stern, and three or four paddlers, would approach the whale from the rear as it rose to breathe.

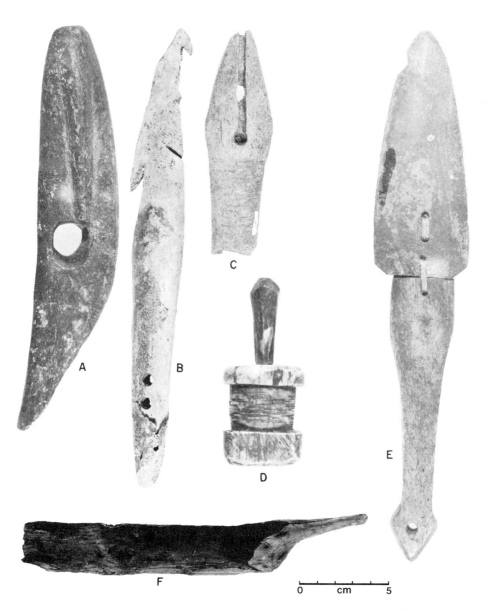

Figure 8.11 Whale hunting gear from (A, D) unknown sites in the Eastern Arctic; (B) Talaguak site, southeastern Baffin Island; (C, F) Peale Point site, Frobisher Bay, Baffin Island; (E) north side of Stratchcona Sound.

A.   harpoon head
B,C. lances
D.   inflation nozzle for sealskin float

E.   flensing knife
F.   fragment of wooden umiak model

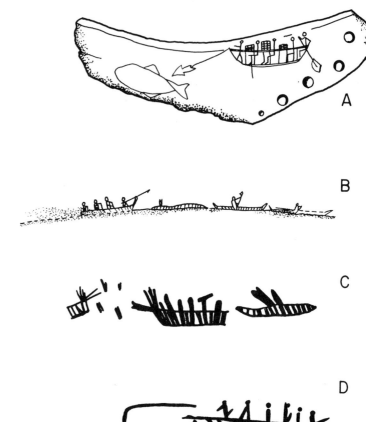

Figure 8.12 Thule engravings of whale hunting scenes.

A. on whalebone snow knife from Resolute, Cornwallis Island
B. on ivory drill bow from Arctic Bay
C. on ivory pendant from Cape Dorset
D. on ivory drill bow from Cumberland Sound

In the few seconds during which it surfaced, the harpooner would try to strike a vital spot and the man directly behind him would throw out the floats. Tiring the animal might take several harpoons and floats, but final killing would be accomplished with special heavy, slate-tipped lances also found in Thule sites. The Cape Dorset engraving (Figure 8.12C) shows the whale being towed tail first to a coastal settlement. Where the tidal range was negligible, the butchering would have to be done in shallow water. On the south coast of Baffin Island, with 6–12-m tides, whales could be floated ashore at high tide and butchered when the tide went out. Where tidal range was less extreme the whale would have to be flensed while floating.

There is a greater variety of kits for killing smaller sea mammals. The presence of quite different harpoon head forms in close association with each other suggests the use of separate types for specific animals and for open-water versus ice hunting. However, it is only speculation to try to relate forms to specie or season of use. Unlike the Dorset heads, some of the Thule specimens, particularly certain forms of the barbed Type 2 (described in the following discussion), have line holes so close to the proximal ends that they would not have toggled; others would have rotated within the body of a struck animal perpendicular to the pull of the line.

The mechanical principles of the disarticulating Thule harpoon differ significantly from the Dorset ones I have described. On the Thule harpoon, a small tension piece with multiple holes was fastened to the harpoon line (Figure 8.13). Three-quarters down the length of the harpoon shaft, an ivory peg was inserted in the shaft and the tension piece fitted over this peg. This held the line between harpoon head and tension piece tightly against the axis of the harpoon shaft. The movable ivory or antler foreshaft had a rounded proximal end that rested in a fixed and drilled socket piece. In earlier forms the foreshaft was bound to the shaft rather than the socket; in later forms it was bound to the socket. As long as tension was maintained along the

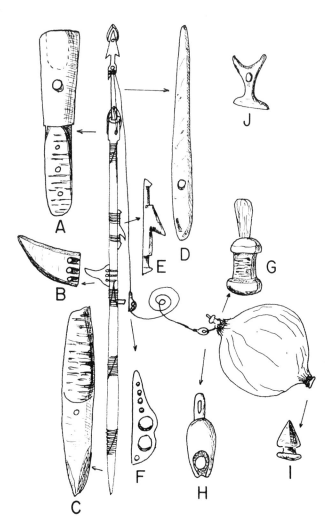

Figure 8.13 Reconstruction of a Thule sealing harpoon from artifacts recovered from sites in the Thule district.

A. socket
B. hand rest
C. ice pick
D. movable foreshaft
E. harpoon line stop
F. tension piece
G. float mouthpiece and stopper
H. toggle for fastening float to harpoon line
I. plug for repairing float
J. harpoon rest, lashed to the deck of the kayak

harpoon axis all of the parts would stay in a straight line. But the shock of striking an animal would tip the foreshaft to one side, shortening the distance between head and pegged tension piece. The tension piece would slip free, loosening the head and line from the harpoon. A kayaking hunter would then throw overboard the coiled line and the inflated float fastened to the line with toggles and swivels.

As in the Dorset period, harpoon heads and their stylistic variation provide the most reliable device for the typological dating of assemblages. A detail of the breadth of discrete attribute variation that has been used for this purpose is beyond the scope of this book (see Ford 1959; Holtved 1944; Jordan 1979; Mathiassen 1927; Stanford 1976 for more complete classifications). Essentially these discrete modifications revolve around five major forms, which Mathiassen (1927) originally designated Thule Types 1–5 (Figure 8.14).

Type 1 (Figure 8.14A and B) is open socketed, with drilled lashing holes (or lashing notches), a single lateral spur, and neither barbs nor end blade. It does not appear in the early Resolute and Nûgdlît sites and is relatively rare in classic Thule deposits. The fact that it has drilled lashing holes rather than slots cut for this purpose and that it has been recovered from Naujan on Repulse Bay and Comer's Midden at Thule but not from the earlier sites on Greenland's Inglefield Land suggests that the form appeared during the later expansion phase. Jordan's (1979) seriation of Greenlandic harpoon heads places it in the middle fourteenth to late fifteenth centuries. Ford (1959:80–82) related the type to the Birnirk–Nunagiak type—Tipiruk Open Socket—and considered the eastern form to have first developed in Alaska from an earlier prototype. From its form, however, it might equally well be a bladeless form of Type 3 and have developed in the east.

Type 2 with its many variants is the most ubiquitous and best known of the Thule types (Figure 8.14C–G). In its ultimate development and distribution it spread from the Bering Strait westward along the Siberian coast to the mouth of the Kolyma River and eastward to Greenland. It is open socketed and laterally barbed. Its ancestry was clearly in the early Birnirk Open Socket type, with opposing flint side blades, unilateral but multiple basal spurs, and no end blade. The Birnirk Open Socket type does not appear in Thule sites, but the type that succeeds it in the west, Natchuk Open Socket, is associated with the earliest assemblages in the east and may have been the prototype for Type 2. The Natchuk type has a single carved, unilateral barb and lacks a side blade opposite the barb but has only a vestigial side blade platform or small slit. The unilateral basal spur often has an additional small knob as a vestige of a second spur.

By classic time, the derived Thule Type 2 form is most often symmetrically barbed (Figure 8.14C) with a single spur. Through time the following discrete changes take place: The barbs, usually placed in a bilaterally symmetrical pair may in later sites become a multiple set of barbs. Ventral and dorsal faces of early forms are often decorated with incised Ys or filled triangles, but this decoration disappears after classic time. Line holes tend to shift from triangular to round. Although the baleen binding that held the head to the foreshaft passed through notches, cut slots, or drilled holes without significant difference in relative age at the Walakpa site, this

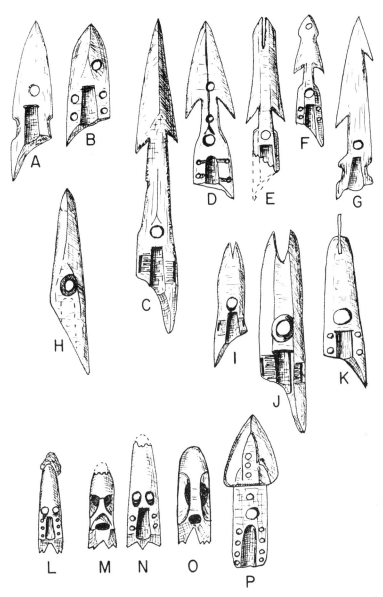

Figure 8.14 Characteristic Thule harpoon heads from several Eastern Arctic sites—A, B, D, K from Naujan, north Repulse Bay; C, I, J from Crystal II; Frobisher Bay; E, F, H, L, N, O from the Thule district; G from Memorana, Victoria Island; M from Lonesome Creek, Ellesmere Island; P from Quililukan, Pond Inlet.

A,B. Type 1   H. Type 4
C–G. Type 2   L–P. Type 5
I–K. Type 3

attribute is considered to be a reasonably reliable time marker in the east. Here cut notches and slots seem to precede drilled holes for lashings. Such is the sequence in Jordan's seriation of Greenlandic harpoon heads (1979).

In general the basal spurs become shorter and less angular, and additional knobs on the basal spur disappear early. A few of the earliest forms have small vestigial barbs or lateral ridges at the level of the line hole. In latest Thule, particularly in the western part of the range, the socket may become closed or a riveted end blade of slate or metal may be added in a slot that may be either parallel or perpendicular to the line hole.

Type 3 is open socketed with a slot for the end blade parallel to the line hole and a single lateral basal spur. In some early forms the line hole is on a raised platform and the lateral edges are beveled. The earliest eastern manifestation of this type and a prototype is the one we have discussed as Sicco. Through time the raised ornamentation and lateral constriction diagnostic of the Sicco type become less pronounced until by classic time the Type 3 head lacked decoration and had nearly parallel straight sides. The binding that early was through cut notches or slots later was made through drilled holes (Figure 8.14I–K). Although Ford (1959:82, 83) considered Thule Type 3 to have developed in Alaska from the earlier Tasik Open-Socket type, the sequence above can be traced within the Eastern Arctic. In this light it is interesting to note that one harpoon head from an early house at Inuarfigssuaq on northwestern Greenland, which Holtved considered a broken and reworked Type 2 (1944:Plate 3 No. 9), has the symmetry, end blade slot, and incised decoration that more closely resembles the Tasik type (Figure 8.2E).

Type 4, with closed socket, end blade at right angles to line hole, and single basal spur, is a smaller version of the whaling harpoon head (Figure 8.14H). It is less common than either Type 2 or 3 and changes little through time from the beginning of Thule to the end. According to Mathiassen (1927) this type was still being used by Iglulingmiut for walrus hunting in the twentieth century.

Type 5 is a flat harpoon head slotted for a slate or iron end blade with either two line holes perpendicular to the blade slot or one line hole passing laterally from one edge to the other. It may be either closed or open socketed, with multiple drilled lashing holes and bilateral basal barbs that are often bifurcated (Figure 8.14L–P). This type was not present in the classic Naujan site but is in the assemblage at the later site of Quililukan near Pond Inlet. On northern Ellesmere Island and on the western coast of Greenland, it is associated with frequent tools of European metal and other aspects of Norse influence. This type is common in the Inugsuk culture (Mathiassen 1930) and probably does not predate A.D. 1400.

There is less sequential variation in the rest of the artifact complex for hunting smaller sea mammals. But it is clear from the appearance of various components in the earliest sites that the whole kayak hunting complex with its attendant gadgetry was well established before the eastward migration. The harpoon parts, including floats and hardware, were much as I have described for whaling, although smaller. In addition to thrusted and thrown harpoons there were smaller darts with fixed, tanged heads and attached bladder floats for projecting with wooden throwing boards. There was also a variety of pins and plugs for closing the wounds of killed seal so that the blood, used in cooking, would not be lost.

The hunting kayak, based on toy models and recovered parts, was much like more modern ones, with a small cockpit, carved rests on deck for harpoons and lances, and a circular stand for the coiled harpoon line aft of the cockpit. Complete gut skin parkas stitched with waterproof seams have been recovered from the Nûgdlît site. These would have covered all the upper body except for the face, and the long skirt would have been tied around the cockpit coaming so that no water could get in if the kayak tipped over.

There is equal evidence for ice hunting from floe edge and through breathing holes. The same harpoons may have been used at breathing holes as for open-water hunting but, like those used today, had with a fixed rather than movable foreshaft. The ice hunting complex (Figure 8.15) included ivory or bear bone ice picks on the butt ends of harpoons, scoops for removing floating ice chips from the breathing hole, claw-shaped scratchers for attracting seal, antler probes for determining the configuration of the cone-shaped breathing hole, and tubes for drinking fresh melt water on the ice surface. There were three-legged stools of wood or whale scapula for waiting at the breathing hole and snow goggles for eye protection, not only for bright sunny days, but also for those with thin overcast when the sky and snow are the same eye-straining shade of white. Knives of ivory or whalebone for building snow block igloos on the sea ice appear to have gone through a sequential development from composite forms with blades lashed to the handle to a one-piece knife with a single shoulder and later to a bilaterally shouldered form. In the dogsled complex there is also a change from trace buckles with two sets of holes at right angles to each other to buckles with two holes in the same plane.

Terrestrial Hunting

Killing lances, probably used to dispatch both sea animals and large land game either had broad self-blades or were slotted or stepped for end blades of slate or metal. The lance proper had no foreshaft but was lashed directly to the shaft with a scarfed joint. However, free, open-socket, reserve lance heads, similar to harpoon heads but without line holes, were carried and could be slipped on a harpoon foreshaft. Lances would have been useful in killing walrus where they hauled out on rocky islets and in hunting caribou from kayaks in lakes (Figure 8.16E and F). This latter technique, used by traditional Inuit, is demonstrated by engravings on a Thule drill bow (Figure 8.21). Runners would drive frightened animals into lakes where kayakers could spear them. The hollow hair of the caribou would keep dead animals afloat until they could be recovered. A similar technique on land used the *inuksuit* (converging lines of piles of stone built to resemble men). Behind these, hunters would hide as runners drove the animals between the rows of stone. Although ringed seal was the dominant food species throughout the Eastern Arctic, at a number of sites, such as those on Victoria Island and the Nunguvik site on northern Baffin Island, caribou far outnumbered seal in the food remains.

The primary Thule weapon for caribou, and probably polar bear, hunting was the bow and arrow. The small Thule bow was sharply recurved and built up with jointed fragments of driftwood stiffened by plates of musk-ox horn or antler and backed with sinew. There was a special ivory gadget, a sinew twister, for tightening the cables of plaited sinew that gave the bow what little power it had (Figure 8.6J). Its effective range was probably not much more than 10 m. In stalking caribou, Thule hunters

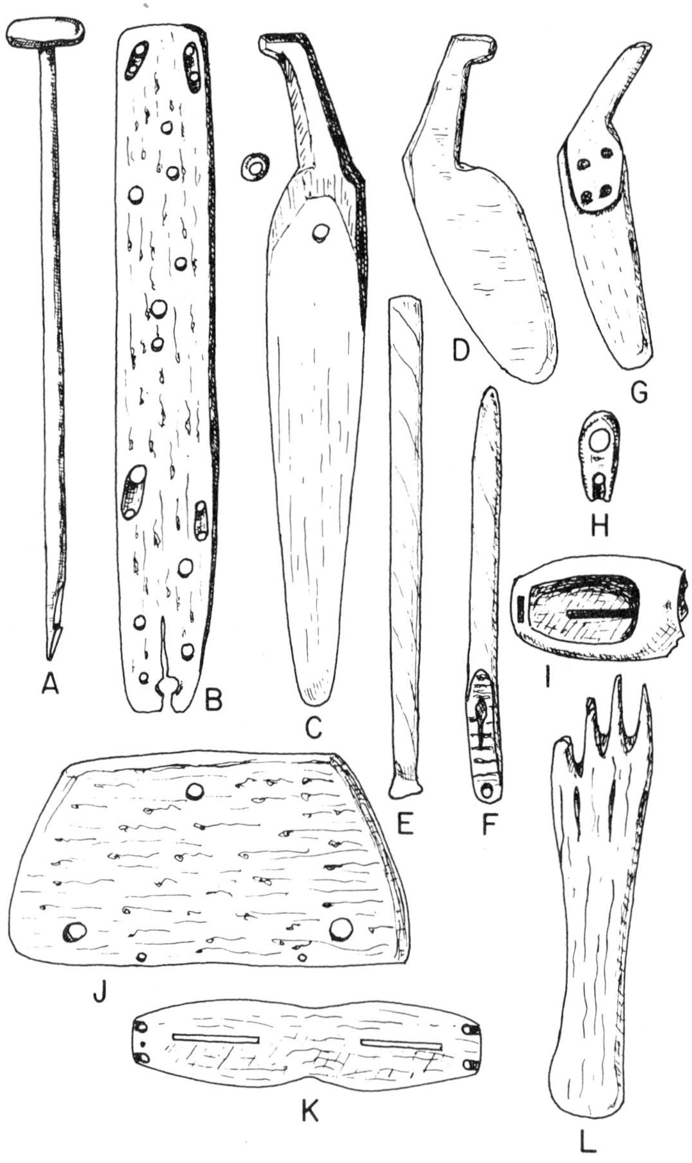

Figure 8.15 Thule equipment for hunting on the sea ice—A–C, E, H from the Ruggles Outlet site, Ellesmere Island; D, F, G, I, J from the Thule district; K from the Memorana site, Victoria Island; L from the Quililukan site, Pond Inlet.

A. probe for testing consistency of snow for igloo building
B. whalebone sled shoe
C. whalebone snow knife and ivory lanyard button
D,G. snow knives
E. narwal ivory tube for drinking melt water on the surface of the ice
F. narwhal ivory fixed foreshaft for breathing hole hunting
H. ivory dog trace toggle
I,K. snow goggles
J. wooden sealing stool seat
L. scratcher for attracting seals

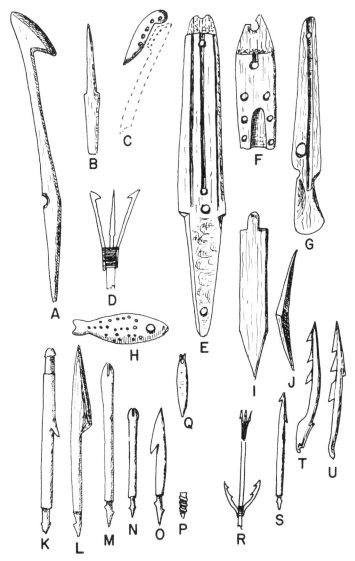

Figure 8.16 Thule fishing and land-hunting equipment—A, C, M, Q from the Ruggles Outlet site, Ellesmere Island; B, G, K, N–P, R–U from the Thule district; E, F, H–J from the Naujan site, Repulse Bay; L from the Crystal II site, Frobisher Bay.

A–C. leister parts
D. artist's reconstruction of a leister
E. fixed lance head
F. removable lance head for use with harpoon
G. wooden throwing board
H. fish lure
I. notched end of composite bow
J. antler bow brace
K–P. arrow heads
Q. needle for stringing fish
R. artist's reconstruction of a bird spear
S–U. bird spear parts

may have covered themselves with caribou hides. Such appears to be the camoflage on three of the men depicted on the Arctic Bay drill bow (Figure 8.20A; Maxwell 1983).

Arrowheads, of bone, antler, or ivory, either self-bladed or slotted for end blades, had long, conical tangs that were forced into wooden shafts (Figure 8.16K–P). At Walakpa these proximal tangs were useful late Birnirk and early Thule time indicators. The earliest had sloping shoulders, ending in a simple, conical tang. Later arrowheads had sharp shoulders, some with bilaterally symmetrical, small knobs on the tang and some with the offset lateral knobs. The sharpness of the shoulder and location of the tang knobs appear not to be as useful as time markers in the east. Some of the early eastern ones had egg-shaped slotted ends with a medial ridge around the circumference of the tang. Through time this ridge became two knobs, first bilaterally symmetrical and then offset. The latest development, presumably the result of European contact, was a threaded tang that was screwed into the arrow shaft. Arrows were kept in a skin quiver with a long, ivory or antler handle. This artifact and the drill bow were the objects most often decorated with engraved designs.

There were specialized weapons for hunting birds. The most ingenious was the multibarbed spear probably projected with a throwing board from a kayak (Figure 8.16G and R–U; although an engraving from Martin Frobisher's voyage of 1576 shows one being thrown by hand). The bird spear had several sharp points at the tip and two or three curving, barbed side prongs fastened three-quarters down the length of the shaft. This weapon effectively acted like a shotgun, with a lethal shot pattern of 15–18 cm. Flying birds were also caught with bolas of heavy whalebone tied with sinew or snagged with hooks at the ends of sticks from baited hiding places. Sharp-tipped gorges and "gull hooks," sticks with inset, angled prongs wrapped in baleen, were tied to lines and embedded in lumps of blubber for shore birds. Sealskin slings with pebbles for ammunition served for birds and small game as did baleen snares. For fox and wolf there were ingenious stone box traps with

Figure 8.17   Exterior (A) and interior (B) of a stone fox trap at the Lonesome Creek site, northeastern Ellesmere Island.

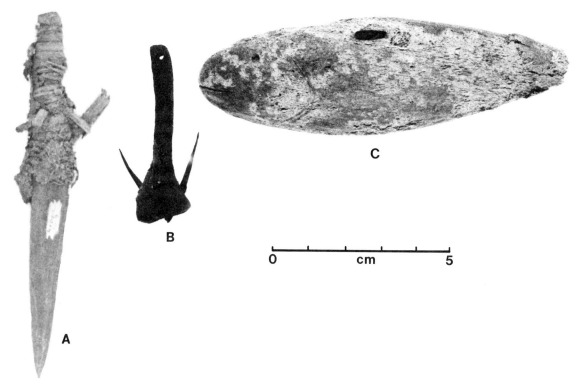

Figure 8.18 Thule lake-ice fishing equipment—A, B from the Talaguak site; C from the Shorty site, southeastern Baffin Island.

     A. gull hook of wood and baleen
     B. fish hook of pierced seal metacarpal and three small bird beaks
     C. whalebone fish lure

cantilevered and balanced entryway rocks or heavy deadfalls (Figure 8.17A and B). A fox dislodging the bait on the balanced bait stone at the back of the box upset a balanced pile of boulders and closed the box.

    The favored implement for fishing was the *kakivak*, a three-pronged leister with a fixed central point and springy side barbs (Figure 8.16A–D). The side prongs were of two types: a single bar of antler with a hook-shaped barb at the end (Figure 8.16A) and a composite hook drilled and fastened to a neck of wood or antler (Figure 8.16C). These leisters were used at the stone weirs in streams where the ana-dromous Arctic char migrated annually to the sea. Since a number of Thule sites have produced fish lures of bone or ivory, the leister may also have been used for fishing through the frozen surface of lakes. In this technique, used by Inuit today, a hole is cut in the lake ice, the lure suspended on a line, and the kakivak used to spear a fish attracted by the lure. A small Thule artifact, which may have been a hook for jigging for tomcod, was made of a seal metacarpal drilled with three holes through which were inserted the small sharp beaks of birds (Figure 8.18).

Food Preparation

By ethnographic analogy, there is a distinction between Thule men's knives and women's knives, the latter being used for butchering and a multiplicity of household tasks. The woman's knife, *ulu,* is most distinctive and with its broad, curved blade resembles an old-fashioned lettuce chopper. Today, and among traditional Inuit, there is a close identity between a woman and her *ulu* and *kudlit* (seal oil lamp). I once visited an old campsite on Big Island off the south coast of Baffin Island and found among the debris an *ulu* made from a saw blade. I showed it to an Inuit friend who said without hesitation, not knowing where it had come from, "Oh yes, that was my grandmother's." I returned it to his family, but to me it looked like a hundred others.

Early *ulu* blades were made of slate, but by A.D. 1400 most were made of European iron. The earliest version of the handle, derived from Birnirk, is a simple, wide crescent of bone or wood (Figure 8.19C). This form continued into historic time, but around the "classic" time of the Naujan site some handles had large central holes (Figure 8.19D). With the increasing use of iron the blade was riveted to a metal tang fitted into a wood or bone handle in a T shape.

Men's knives, used for butchering and other cutting tasks, had a wide variety of forms. There are none that have been specifically identified as whale flensing knives but some of the lances with larger blades could have been used for this purpose. Some knives with long handles for two-handed use were undoubtedly used for flensing walrus and large seal (Figure 8.20L and R). Some of the earlier small, end-bladed knives were decorated with geometric engraving, but this practice decreased in later Thule. There were both short and long side-bladed knives as well as combination tools with both end and side blades. Some knives with composite handles resembled those common in Late Dorset. As with the ulu, the blades changed from slate or flaked chert (rare) to very small end blades of both meteoric and European iron early in the development of Eastern Thule.

Fire-making equipment included both the wooden spindle and hearth used with the bow drill and kits of pyrites and flint (Figure 8.20Q, S, and T). In the Nûgdlît–Ruin Island phase, which appears to have been the earliest Thule period in the High Arctic, cooking was done over open fires of willow, driftwood, and seal fat in antechambers separated from the main living room by a low lintel. At House 9 on the Talaguak site near Lake Harbour (Maxwell 1981; Sabo 1981), a dwelling that should date to shortly before A.D. 1200, there were two open-hearth fireplaces at the two front corners of the living room. These were later capped and became platforms for blubber lamps. Large triangular oil lamps of soapstone, with solid bar or knobbed wick ledges and wicks of marsh cotton, displaced the smoky open hearth early in the development of Eastern Thule. Above them hung large deep rectangular soapstone bowls suspended from the rafters by lines that passed through drilled holes in the corners. The use of soapstone for this purpose was probably acquired from Dorset people. In Alaska, lamps had been made of pottery fired in the heat of plentiful driftwood. In a few early Thule sites there are traces of both a crude, poorly fired

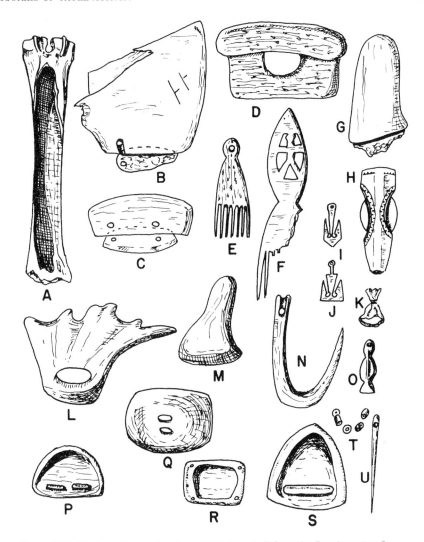

Figure 8.19 Thule equipment for domestic tasks—A, K from the Resolute site, Corn-wallis Island; B, E, H, I, N, T from the Ruggles Outlet site, Ellesmere Island; C, D, F, G, J, L, M, O–S, U from the Thule district (artifacts are not drawn to same scale, based on selected illustrations from Collins 1952, 1955; Maxwell 1960a; Holtved 1944).

A.	two-handed hide scraper	O.	needle case–shaped pendant
B–D.	*ulus*	P.	toy oil lamp
E,F.	combs	Q.	bear skull skin scraper
G.	scraper with metal blade	R.	toy soup bowl
H–J.	needle case and thimble holders	S.	toy oil lamp
K.	dog skin thimble	T.	amber beads
L,M.	antler and bone hide scrapers	U.	needle with drilled eye
N.	meat hook		

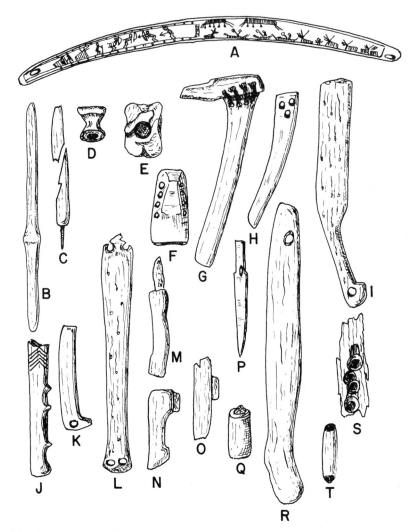

Figure 8.20 Thule equipment for domestic tasks—A from a grave near Arctic Bay, Baffin Island; B from the Crystal II site, Frobisher Bay; C–E, I, K, M, T from the Ruggles Outlet site, northeastern Ellesmere Island; F, G, H, J, L, N–S from the Thule district (drawings based on selected illustrations from Collins 1950; Holtved 1944; Maxwell 1960a).

A.	bow drill with engraved scene of bow and arrow warfare, old men and children, tents, and hunting caribou by kayak and whale by umiak
B,C.	bow drills (C with iron tip)
D,E.	ivory and caribou astragalus socket pieces
F–H.	adz parts
I.	frost scraper or snow beater
J,K,M.	end-bladed knife handles (M with iron blade)
L,R.	two-handed flensing knives for whale and walrus
N,O.	side-bladed knives with metal blades
P.	marlin spike
Q.	iron pyrite strike-a-light in a bone handle
S,T.	fire drill and wooden hearth

pottery and composite lamps of sandstone and clay, but the trait does not last long in the wood-scarce east. The characteristic Barrow Curvilinear Stamped pottery of Alaska has been reported only from west of Victoria Island and the Buchanan Bay region of Ellesmere Island (Schledermann 1981).

There was a wide variety of utensils in the cooking and food storage complex. There were ladles and skewers for taking meat from boiling pots, blubber and meat hooks for hanging supplies to house rafters, and in the Norse-influenced Ingusuk period in Greenland even bone, horn, and wooden copies of European spoons. There were meat trays of wood and whale scapula, storage vessels with wooden bottoms and sides of curved baleen stitched with strips of baleen, pails with bone or antler handles, and wooden bowls and buckets. In fact, counting heavy soapstone lamps and bowls, the household equipment of an average Thule family may have weighed close to 500 kg compared to less than 50 kg for a Dorset family. Surplus meat that could not be kept in stone lockers inside the house or in storage chambers off the tunnel entry were cached in hollows covered by stone boulders or in pits dug into the permafrost. In the more southern Thule range, meat could not be kept fresh through the full year this way, but slightly rotten meat was probably considered edible as it is today. My Inuit friend Killikti once showed me how all of the edible meat of a single walrus could be stored in one poke, tightly packed, made of the walrus' hide. There is a danger, however, in keeping meat thus packed in anaerobic condition, and probably there were occasionally fatal cases of botulism among Thule people who kept meat this way too long.

Hide Preparation

Hide working and stitchery is, and probably always has been, a source of Inuit pride. Preparing the skins for clothing is arduous work. All connective tissue and fat must be scraped from the interior, the grain of the skin must be broken to render it flexible, and for some purpose all the hair must be removed. From ethnographic analogy caribou hides—for inner and outer winter parkas, trousers, socks, and boot tops—were softened by repeatedly scraping the inner surface. There is no report of the Inuit having used the brains of the caribou in tanning as the American Indian used that of deer, nor was smoke tanning feasible. Skins for the summer *kamiks* (boots of sealskin) had to be waterproof. To prepare them, the inner skin was scraped clean and rolled hair side in until it had rotted to a black color; then it was dehaired and soaked in a bucket of family urine, which stood near the entryway. The skins were then sewed with a waterproof stitch that angled through layers of over-lapped skin without penetrating either layer. Since such boots stiffen like iron when dried after being wet, they were first stretched with a wooden or bone stretcher then chewed to render them soft and pliable. For dress boots and decorative inserts, sealskins were left out to bleach white in temperatures below −30° C.

Skins of the bearded seal were used for boot soles, strong lines, and the skins of umiaks. Preparing line was a man's task. The hide was cut in a series of circles about 5 cm wide that were then slipped over the seal's head. With sharp knives or shavers, these circles were cut into tough lines 5 mm wide and 12–14 m long that were waterproof and equally useful on land and in the water. Both bearded sealskins and, occasionally, walrus skins were used for the skins of umiaks. Many were too thick for this purpose and had to be laboriously split by women with their ulus.

Thule women used a variety of scrapers for these purposes, all probably functionally specific. There were split caribou metatarsal two-handed beamers, cup-shaped fat scrapers of ivory and seal or polar bear skull, L-shaped wooden handles with stone blades characteristic of Alaska (disappearing early in the east), and curved sections of blades set in bone or ivory handles (Figure 8.19L, M, and Q). The most common hide scraper was a cut caribou scapula with the medial spine removed. This was done by first drilling a series of fine holes on both sides of the spine and then snapping it off. These medial spines were often sharpened for use as awls as were other split animal and bird bones. Stitching was done with ivory or bird bone needles with tiny drilled eyes (Figure 8.19U). When not in use these needles were stitched into a soft piece of leather with a carved ivory stopper at one end which was threaded through an ornamental ivory needle case. The other end of the leather strip was tied to an anchor-shaped ivory holder for the simple loop of dog skin that served as a thimble (Figure 8.19H–J and K). These needle cases were elaborately carved and decorated with incised geometric ticked lines and must often have been heirlooms. In a house on northern Ellesmere Island I once found a beautiful one that must have been used for teething since it was marked with perhaps generations of baby teeth.

As Mathiassen (1927) demonstrated, these needle cases went through a stylistic development from a western, tubular form engraved with a human representation to one in which the arms became wings (see Figure 8.5C). In time the cutout arms were left filled in, and the typical Eastern Thule case has broad semicircular wings on each side (see Figure 8.5D).

Manufacturing

There is such a plethora of artifacts in many Thule houses, particularly of such hard materials as stone, bone, antler, and ivory, that artifact making must have required nearly as much time as hunting. The most distinctive and often-used Thule implement was the bow drill. The sense of identity between a man and his bow drill (and arrow quiver handle) was such that these implements were often elaborately engraved and included with the dead as grave goods. A particularly beautiful ivory bow from a grave near Arctic Bay is rich with depictions of settlements, caribou and whale hunting expeditions, and interband warfare (Figure 8.20A, 8.21, and Maxwell 1983).

The Thule and traditional Inuit bow drill is indeed an ingenious device. The mechanism itself is virtually world wide. The bow, a curved object of any material, has a loose cord that is wrapped around a spindle. One end of the spindle rests in a smooth socket; the other, with a tip of stone or metal, does the drilling as one saws back and forth with the bow. The difficulty with most drills is that one needs one hand to saw the bow, a second to hold the spindle socket, and a third to hold the

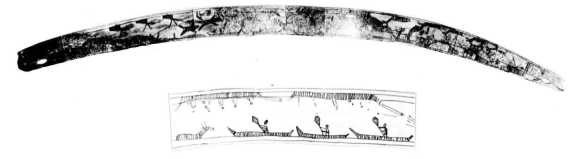

Figure 8.21 Obverse side (badly eroded) and opposite-side detail of ivory drill bow, 42.3 cm long, from Arctic Bay, Baffin Island, showing scenes of whale, bear, and caribou hunting and of men fighting with bows and arrows.

object being drilled. Thule craftsmen overcame this difficulty by holding the socket, often the naturally shaped ankle bone of a caribou, in their teeth, thus leaving one hand free to hold the piece being drilled. Since the thin cord would often work up the spindle and tangle in the socket, they carved a median ridge on the spindle. This tool was to Thule men what the burin and burin-like tool was to Dorset artisans. Rather than grooving a walrus tusk to split off a narrow bar of ivory, they would drill a series of impinging holes in parallel lines and then split out the section between the lines.

A close functional second was the adz (Figure 8.20F–H). This was a simple tool with an inverted L-shaped driftwood handle and a heavy whalebone socket lashed through drilled holes to the short arm of the L and fitted with a stone or metal blade. With these two tools and a wide variety of whittling knives Thule craftsmen did such intricate work in ivory as carving interlocking chains and swivels (Figure 8.25).

The intricacy of carving, the thinness of slots for end blades, the rusty stains on such slots, and the absence of such a useful tool as the burin has suggested to Blaylock (1980) and others (McCartney and Mack 1973) that the use of iron by Thule workers was much more prevalent than we have previously thought. These authors consider that the availability of meteoric and European iron in the east may have been one of the factors leading to the Thule migration. Iron tools are present, though rare, in even the earliest sites, but they preserve badly, even in permafrost. It has even been suggested as more appropriate to consider the Thule as Iron Age rather than Stone Age hunters. For example, there were no slate artifacts in the Nûgdlît site and few in Greenlandic Thule sites in general.

Dwellings

We have already discussed the salient features of the distinctive Thule winter house, with its semi-subterranean floor, tunnel entryway, whalebone, skin, and sod roof, and rear sleeping platform of flat stones with baleen mats under caribou skins for insulation (Figure 8.22). But there are other details worth mentioning. The entry

Figure 8.22 (A) Whale rib roof framework, *in situ,* of a small Thule house at the Shorty site, south-eastern Baffin Island, and (B) the same house, barely 2 m in diameter and 1.5 m high, with reconstructed roof framework.

end closest to the living area usually ended in a deep pit that acted as a sink and a trap for cold air. Consequently one often entered the house through a hole in the living room floor. These entry tunnels were often 5 m or more long and barely 50–60 cm high and wide. In summer when one looks at an entry that has been excavated it is almost impossible to imagine wriggling through it in a bulky skin parka, pausing halfway along to beat the frost from one's clothing with a knife-shaped beater, and entering the house without knocking the whole structure down.

Many house interiors were elaborate, with paved meat and blubber lockers, vertically placed rocks for roof supports, and sleeping platforms raised on pillars to provide storage space underneath. There are still questions about the sequential development of eastern houses. The prototype is undoubtedly the square-to-rectangular, semi-subterranean, wooden-floored and -roofed houses of Alaska. But as Mathiassen (1927) pointed out, it is as difficult to build a square house with whale ribs and jaws as it is to build a round house with wood. The Jackson and Vaughn site houses of Amundsen Gulf, which are presumably early in classic time (Taylor 1972), are square with wooden floors and roofs, but since they have many traits more closely tied to the west it is questionable whether they should be considered of Eastern Thule type. Sites we have considered as belonging to the initial migration, Nûgdlît, Ruin Island, and Buchanan Bay, have semi-subterranean houses that are square to rectangular with open-hearth kitchens in antechambers off the living area and occasionally storage antechambers. They lack raised sleeping platforms or roof rafters of whalebone.

House 9 at the Talaguak site near Lake Harbour (Maxwell 1981; Sabo 1981) contained artifacts characteristic of the classic period of about A.D. 1100 (Figure 8.23). However, the house, which had been renovated and modified at least three times, displayed traits that might illuminate the sequence in house types. The initial house was rectangular with two open-hearth kitchens at both corners in the front of the living space. Two storage antechambers opened into the long tunnel entry with an inside, paved meat locker in one back corner of the house. As first constructed, it had a roof framework of whale ribs covered by a thick walrus skin. The floor was paved but there was no raised sleeping platform. Scraps of bearskin in the back corner opposite the meat locker indicated that the family slept here on the paved floor insulated from the cold by the heavy skin. In a later development, a raised, square sleeping platform was built in this corner and covered with flat flagstones. In the latest phase the open hearths, where fires of willow and seal fat had burned, were capped and made into platforms for oil lamps.

This sequence suggests that the typical Eastern Thule house, which was round and had a semicircular sleeping platform occupying the back half of the house, may have been a later development.

With the increasing cold of the fourteenth century there was an apparent increase in Arctic sea ice with a concomitant decrease in whales and whale hunting. Several authors have suggested that after around A.D. 1300 in Hudson Bay and Foxe Basin there was an abandonment of the deep winter pit houses in favor of villages of snow

Figure 8.23 Deep Thule winter house at Pritzler Harbour (A) and view to the north (B) and to the south (C) of excavated Thule House 9 at the Talaguak site, southeastern Baffin Island. String grid lines are 2 m apart.

block houses on the fast ice. This is thought to result in larger winter village aggregations since breathing-hole hunting can best be accomplished by several people watching a number of holes to which the seal may come. On southern Baffin Island the winter settlements were in snowhouses at least by the beginning of the twentieth century, but there is no empirical evidence to indicate when this change in winter houses took place. Whalebone pit houses with skin roofs were still being used in 1576 when Martin Frobisher entered the bay that bears his name (Mathiassen 1927:Vol. 2, p. 136). Mathiassen distinguished between the Thule winter houses and the *qarmat,* autumn shelters made in the same house pits but covered with lighter skins, used by traditional Inuit after the Thule period (Figure 8.24). But there is little archaeological evidence with which a distinction can be made between these autumn *qarmat* and a winter house. Sabo (1981) has demonstrated that Thule-type pit houses were used well into the historic period. In northwestern Greenland among the Polar Eskimo, whose culture changed the least from the preceding Thule, the house type remained much the same but with cantilevered slabs of rock substituting for whalebone. Sod houses continued in use in Greenland well into the twentieth century and in Labrador until the late nineteenth and early twentieth centuries.

The small number of houses on many Thule sites has raised the question of whether they reflect the presence of enough adult males to constitute a whaling crew (Freeman 1979). In contrast there are sites with a greater number of houses, such as Nûgdlît with 62 houses and Nunguvik with 50. Unfortunately, the changes in style of most Thule artifacts is not sufficiently rapid to allow us to determine contemporaneous occupations on single sites. For example, Stenton (1983) has excavated 5 of 11 Thule houses at the Peale Point site near the village of Frobisher Bay. These 5 were occupied in at least three distinctly different time periods. The implication of this is that few houses could have been contemporaneous.

In a survey of Thule sites in the Eastern Arctic (McCartney 1979), 4–6 houses is a

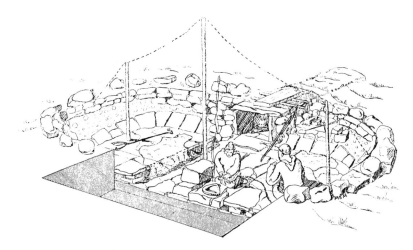

Figure 8.24 Reconstruction of a *qarmak*—originally built for two families, later occupied by a single family—at the Ruggles Outlet site, northeastern Ellesmere Island, and photograph of the sleeping platform showing a mixture of female human bones and dog bones and a woman's comb under the fallen roof pole.

number that frequently appears. A survey of modern Inuit winter settlements on the southeast coast of Baffin Island from 1930 to 1970 (Maxwell 1979) indicates that this has been the average size of winter villages and may be the result of a dis- covered adaptive efficiency in hunting, village size thus depending on the available land and sea game.

Where historic records are available, this permanent settlement size remains fairly consistent. Holtved (1944:9–14) in a demographic analysis of Polar Eskimo in the Thule district through an 11-year period beginning in 1923, found an average annual population of 259.6 individuals. These were grouped in an average of 12.6 settlements, with 4.3 families per settlement and 4.67 individuals per family. This is paralleled by McGhee's work (1976:114) in which he finds an average of 4.5 houses for 26 settlements on the Victoria Island coast. In this article he cites Dunning's 1966 study of 48 Central Eskimo units with an average of 4.6 dwellings per unit.

This picture of winter hunting bands of 20–25 persons is not consistent with the one I presented earlier of the traditional Netsilingmiut and Igloolingmiut winter aggregates of more than 100 persons in snow block villages on the sea ice during *aglu* (breathing hole hunting). This suggests, if McGhee and McCartney are correct in their interpretation, that when the permanent winter villages were abandoned between A.D. 1300 and 1500 in favor of snowhouse villages, there may have been a major change in the social system. While the hunting band of 4–6 families may have remained a cohesive unit of about the same size with internal integration throughout the year, the large snowhouse aggregates would have led to significant social change. The sphere of social interaction, including more non-kin dyadic meat-shar- ing contracts and an increased mating universe, would certainly have widened. In many settlements the role of *umialuk* (whaling boat captain) would have changed to that of *isumatak* (the "thinker" who in winter controlled the division of meat taken on the sea ice).

Thule summers were spent in tents, and rock tent rings and meat caches are the most ubiquitous cultural features on the surface of the Eastern Arctic. Thule tents were circular, 2.5–3.5 m in diameter, with skirts of skin tents held down by a ring of boulders. According to a few engraved designs on ivory, the supporting tent poles must have all sloped toward the back from an H- or A-shaped frame at the doorway. In these designs the tent poles are much longer than one would expect to locate in the shore drift. Although it would be impossible to prove empirically, wood must have been a major trade item among Thule bands.

A characteristic Thule settlement complex can be illustrated by the situation at Talaguak near Lake Harbour (Sabo 1981). There are 12 pit houses, although these were not occupied contemporaneously. Parts of the small peninsula are marshy and other parts are underlain by Dorset midden; both have produced thick sod for building. In the rocky hill behind the site there are several fox traps and at least one grave, both types of stone structures presumably dating from Thule time. There is a good running-water stream within 0.25 km of the houses. Approximately 0.5 km north along the coast is a complex of stone tent rings in a better location for summer camping (and away from the rotting carcasses as they thawed from the winter snows). This is at the top of a huge, smooth, sloping exposure of bedrock that extends from lowest to highest tide line. It would have been ideal for floating whales ashore at high tide to be butchered at low tide and for beaching kayaks and heavy umiaks. Many bleached whalebones and both umiak and kayak stands of piled-up boulders indicate this site's use for both purposes. At both summer and winter location there are a number of piled-rock meat caches. Extending north along the shore of McKellar Bay there are similar meat caches on most prominent landmarks where they would be available for unsuccessful hunters. At the tops of the highest hills are *inuksuit*. While these are still made by children everywhere they camp, they are nevertheless valuable navigation aids when traveling along this sharply dissected coast with its fringing islands. It would be logical to suppose that some had been made for this purpose by Thule travelers.

Mortuary Behavior

In the Alaskan homeland, Birnirk–Nunagiak people placed their dead, with accompanying grave goods, in wooden houses or house-like wooden cribs. Without driftwood supplies this was impossible in the east. By classic Thule time this practice had been modified to substitute heavy boulder cists for the log tombs. These large beehives of heavy rocks, larger than meat caches, covered box-like structures of flat rock within which the dead lay extended. We do not know what the earlier pattern of burial may have been. In spite of an extensive early occupation of Inglefield Land with many settlements, Holtved (1944) found no graves associated with these sites. The inclusion of grave goods in classic Thule burials does not appear to have followed any regular pattern. Some, of men, women, and children, are relatively richly accompanied, while others have very few or no artifacts.

Certainly the frequency of stone cist graves in the vicinity of Thule settlements indicates that treatment of the dead was quite different from that practiced by Dorset people or by the historic Netsilik, who left the dead uncovered on land or sea ice. McCartney (1977) uses the frequency of graves at Silumiut in comparison to the apparently short-term use of the whalebone houses to suggest that after snowhouses on the fast ice became the standard winter dwelling, the people still returned to land to enclose the dead in the stone vaults. However, Merbs (1971), who studied the orientation of more than 200 graves at this site and others at Naujan, concluded that they were oriented to the rising or setting sun. Comparing these orientations to the solstices, he concluded that most interments would have been made in summer. This leads to the hypothesis that seasonal differences in treatment of the dead may have emerged and that winter dead were exposed on sea ice or frozen land without permanent covering. In time this may have culminated in such practices as reported for the traditional Netsilik, who left the dead exposed in the open regardless of season.

Art and Ideology

Just as Birnirk in the west reflects a decline in art when compared with the earlier Old Bering Sea culture, so does Thule in the east when compared with Dorset. Occasional three-dimensional carvings in wood and antler demonstrate that the craftsmanship was there, but there simply appears to have been little concern with either freestanding art or the esthetics of decoration. Unlike Dorset artists, Thule carvers were more apt to decorate utilitarian objects, although even these are rare (Figure 8.25 and 8.26). They tend to be more common early than late and appear most often on certain selected classes of objects. Harpoon heads, although not sockets or lance heads, were occasionally engraved with an inverted Y proceeding distally from the line hole toward the tip or with triangles filled with horizontal or vertical lines above the line holes. Men's knives, although not the snow knives,

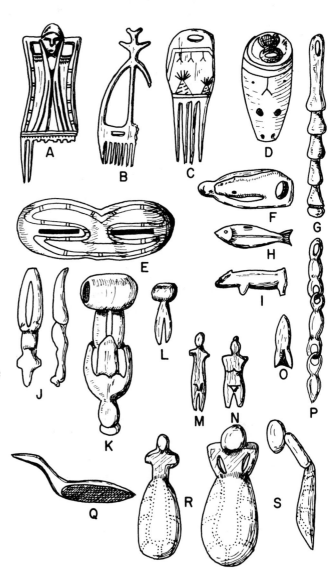

Figure 8.25 Thule   artistic carvings from several sites.

A–C. women's combs
D.   harpoon socket
E.   snow goggles
F.   float toggle
G.   ornament
H.   fish lure
I.   bear effigy
J,K.   female effigies
L.   whale's tail effigy
M,N.   human dolls
O.   whale effigy
P.   linked chain
Q–S.   tingmait (bird and
       human figures)

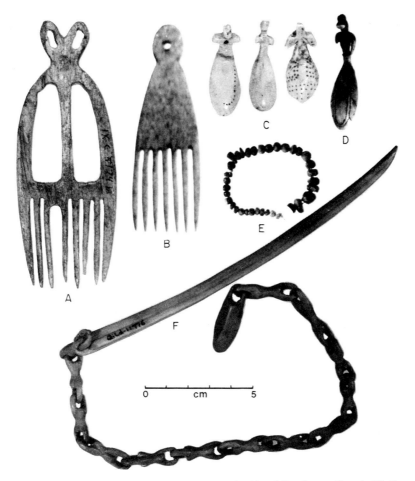

Figure 8.26 Thule carvings from (A) the north side of Strathcona Sound, (B) the Ruggles Outlet site, northeastern Ellesmere Island, (C, D) unknown sites in the Eastern Arctic, (E) the Lonesome Creek site, northeastern Ellesmere Island, (F) the Brooman Point site, Bathurst Island.

A,B. whalebone combs
C,D. ivory tingmaits (D with topknot hairdo; photograph by Jane Sproull-Thomson)
E. amber beads
F. ivory meat fork and linked chain

sometimes had engraved Ys or parallel lines, and women's combs and needle cases, but not ulus, had engraved designs of straight, often spurred, lines. Later, perhaps after metal began to be used extensively for drill points, rows of drilled dots became common design elements.

Combs were among the artifacts most often decorated (Figure 8.26A and B). The outlines of their handles varied and some were beautifully carved with cutout shapes or relief elements that often represented human figures. Fish lures, carved three-dimensionally of ivory, antler, and whalebone, were representational, often to a degree exceeding their function, with eyes, gill slits, and mouths all depicted. Drag handles and toggles were occasionally carved in the shape of animals or animal heads, often bears or bear heads, as were the ends of quiver handles. But pail handles and bows for drills were more often ornamented with engraved designs than with animal carvings. Some of these engraved designs included scenes from life, with stick figures representing humans and animals in hunting scenes.

The most common of the three-dimensional figurines, both in wood and ivory, is a human figure without arms or with arms represented only by stumps. For a few the sex is indeterminate, but most are clearly women. They are often depicted with a loin cloth and boots, topknots, and amulet straps crossed over the chest. The prevalence of the topknot harido in Greenlandic sites was once thought to have been due to Inugsuk or Norse influence. But its common appearance in sites earlier than Inugsuk and farther to the west than Inugsuk influence could have spread indicates that it was probably the fashionable Thule hair style. A few of the figurines depict Norsemen. The most dramatic of these (see Figure 9.4, p. 304), from an early Thule house at Okiavilialuk near Lake Harbour (Sabo and Sabo 1978), has a carved robe, collar, and cross incised on the chest.

Second to the human figurines, both in numbers and distribution, are tiny ivory floating birds, usually loons. These may be completely representational or have a loon body and a human (usually female) torso in place of the loon head and neck. Several were decorated on the back with rows of lines or dots that, as Sproull-Thomson (1979) has noted, depict a women's parka. Boas (1888) described a modern Inuit game played with pieces like these called *tingmiujaq,* and this name (or *tingmait*) is usually given to the little floating birds. The distribution and numbers of both these and the human figures suggest a greater ideological importance for them for Thule people than simply as games and toys. Sproull-Thomson (1979) has pointed-ed to the frequency of female figurines and the association of women and diving birds on the *tingmait.* This, she suggests, may represent a Thule origin for traditional Inuit ideology in which the most important supernatural figure is Sedna (or Nuliajuq), the sea goddess. Sedna lives at the bottom of the sea and from there controls the actions of the sea animals. The loon, a diving bird, provides the metaphysical link between the surface and sea and between women and Sedna.

There is a wide range of forms, predominantly pendants, that may simply have been decorations, or may have a deeper meaning as amulets for ensuring success in various activities. These include teardrops and rows of teardrop shapes, linked chains and swivels, perforated animal teeth, and stylized whales. One frequent object is a perforated barrel-shaped bead with an inverted female figurine hanging from it (Figure 8.25K). Carpenter (1973) has made the ingenious suggestion that these were fetishes for pregnant women to aid in head-first deliveries. If this were the case, an ivory pendant from the Bache Peninsula of Ellesmere Island (Schledermann 1981:598) with three inverted female figures must either represent triple the insurance or indicate a desire for multiple births.

In the early Thule House B, at site M-1 at Resolute, Collins (1952:50) recovered a

Figure 8.27 Nangissat, a line of rocks for a jumping game, from the Lonesome Creek site, northeastern Ellesmere Island.

sealskin necklace with a gull head and small, attached skin pouches. This can easily be recognized as a good luck amulet, but of the many amulets a Thule person may have worn and carried, most, by ethnographic analogy, may have been of bird and animal parts and not recognizable as fetishes to the archaeologist.

Other than these there is less reflection of Thule ideology than that of the earlier Dorset or later traditional Inuit. There are, for example, no reported masks or maskettes. Drum rims and handles for the large, flat, skin-covered drum are present in all Thule phases. But whether they were used in religious ceremonies as well as in secular song contests we may never know.

Toys and Games

If Thule carvers were sparing in their artistic work, they certainly were not in the making of toys. Most are sufficiently well made to be recognizable as the work of adults for children. To cover the range of these bone, ivory, antler, wood, and baleen objects would be simply to repeat the descriptions I have already given for the utilitarian material culture. There are model umiaks, kayaks, and dogsleds, soapstone lamps, ulus and men's knives, harpoons, lances, fish spears, and bows and arrows. In fact virtually everything used by adults was copied in miniature form, often in simple, silhouette baleen cutouts. There are also balls made of lashed strips of baleen, and baleen "whizzers"—toothed disks and propeller shapes that when whirled through the air produce a roaring noise. The *ajaqaq*, a variant of the cup-and-pin game, was played with a variety of perforated bones, often a seal humerus. There are also *nangissat*, long rows of flat rocks for playing a jumping game (Figure 8.27), where only Thule people are likely to have made them. Many of the Thule summer settlements have within the complex much smaller tent rings and little fans of pebbles that probably represent dogs and dogsleds. As is true today among the Inuit, much of children's play was geared to preparation for adult activities.

From Classic Thule to Historic Contact

There is little agreement between experts on various time phases of Thule culture. Few material culture traits other than discrete alterations in harpoon head styles fall into sets of widespread and sequential patterns. Furthermore, some of the larger sites, such as Naujan at the head of Roes Welcome Sound and Nûgdlît in northwestern Greenland, were unquestionably occupied over several centuries. Treating site assemblages from such localities as cohesive wholes has often led to confusion between early and later traits. The lack of agreement over separating the Thule period into temporal phases is reflected in the plethora of terms that appear in the literature. "Early," "earlier," and "earliest Thule" are often used. Nûgdlît–Ruin Island phase, Pioneer phase, Expansion, Later Expansion, Classic period, Baleen period, Developed Thule, Modified Thule, and Inugsuk are among the more formal designators employed to signify cultural change within the general period. There is further difficulty in distinguishing a terminal point for Thule culture. In so far as most would now agree that modern Canadian Inuit are direct descendants of the Thule invasion, the period could be seen as continuing into the present. On the other hand, contact with Western cultures has so modified Thule culture that considering modern settlements as basically Thule is like treating modern London as simply an extension of English culture in 1066. This is further complicated by the fact that Euro-American contact occurred at markedly different times in different regions. This ranges from Martin Frobisher's journey to Baffin Island in 1576 to John Ross' discovery in 1818 of Polar Eskimo who are said to have thought themselves the only humans in the world. Such recognition of a period of contact and beginning Western acculturation ignores the effect of Norse impact that now appears to have been as early as both Thule Eskimo and Vikings were present in the Eastern Arctic.

In this volume I follow the somewhat timid course of recognizing four general phases: an initial entry, a classic expansion, a postclassic modification, and historic contact

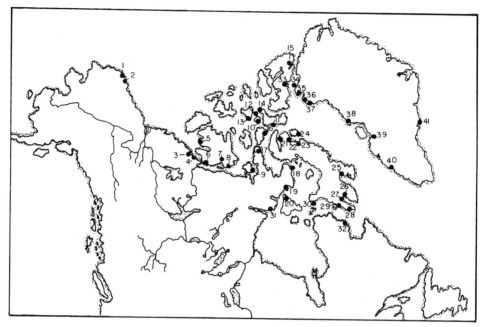

Figure 9.1 Thule sites.

1. Walakpa	15. Ruggles Outlet	29. Talaguak and Shorty
2. Point Barrow	16. Learmouth	30. Mill Island
3. Vaughn	17. Levesque Harbour	31. Silumiut
4. Jackson	18. Igloolik	32. Diana Bay
5. Memorana	19. Naujan	33. Skraeling Island
6. Lady Franklin Point	20. Kuk	34. Ruin Island
7. Bell	21. Arctic Bay	35. Nûgdlît
8. Pembrook	22. Nunguvik	36. Thule
9. Malerualik	23. Mittimatalik/Quililukan	37. Umanaq
10. Resolute	24. Button Point	38. Inugsuk
11. Maxwell Bay	25. Cumberland Sound	39. Sermermiut
12. Karluk Island	26. Crystal II	40. Kangamiut
13. Brooman Point	27. Peale Point	41. Angmagssalik
14. Snowdrift Village	28. Pritzler Harbour	

THE INITIAL ENTRY

Hypotheses about the origin of Eastern Thule and its expansion into the Eastern Arctic have been discussed in the preceding chapter, but certain points can stand additional analysis here. It is reasonably clear that the majority of early Eastern Thule sites were occupied by communities whose ancestors lived in the house mounds of late Birnirk along the northern Alaskan coast near Point Barrow. However, by the beginning of Thule, Birnirk culture had already been strongly influenced by new hunting techniques and material artifacts introduced from islands in the Bering Sea. The resulting configuration cannot easily be separated into component parts (i.e., Birnirk traits and Punuk ones). Prior to this, however, earlier in late Birnirk, a pure Punuk influence in the form of whale hunting, whaling harpoon heads, and the characteristic Sicco harpoon head appear in the Birnirk middens as an alien intrusion (Stanford 1976:113). It is these Punuk traits, associated with Western house styles, that characterize the earliest Eastern High Arctic sites. The restricted distribution of these traits and their short duration in the east suggest a different cultural configuration from the later classic Eastern Thule. It may have been that a relatively small number of seaborne Punuk communities, forced by increasing population on the home islands and following whale as they coasted along the summer limit of pack ice, were the first to have moved eastward. Some of these communities may have settled on the Alaskan coast. Others, by-passing the Western Canadian Arctic and much of the Central Arctic, may have penetrated to the eastern corner of the High Arctic. Perhaps within the same century, many more communities departing the Alaskan coast with a cultural inventory that now included both Punuk and Birnirk traits began infiltrating the more southern shores of the Canadian Arctic. For these latter hunters, the characteristic hunting weapon would have been the double-barbed Thule Type 2 harpoon head developed from earlier Birnirk prototypes and ideally suited for breathing hole hunting. The implication of this is that, while the hypothetically pure Punuk invasion of the Eastern Arctic may have been the first of these migrations, it was limited in scope and short in duration. It is then the subsequent amalgam of Birnirk and Punuk culture in a migration involving many more people and covering greater expanses of shore that we now consider typical Eastern Thule.

One of the surprising points about what we are calling here the Punuk invasion is the evidence emerging since the 1970s of strong Norse contact. Since the Norse sagas refer only to voyages no farther north than Upernivik (73° north latitude) and then only in the fourteenth century, it had long been assumed that Thule sites with metal objects must have been late in the sequence. It is now clear that the Vikings were penetrating northward at least as far as 79° north latitude less than 50 years after the initial Norse settlement of Brattalid on southern Greenland. Schledermann's (1981) discovery of chainmail armor, woolen cloth, iron boat rivets, and other iron objects demonstrates not only that the natives on eastern Ellesmere were securing iron and other materials from the Norse, but also that they had a surplus of iron, unused locally and untraded to other communities. From this time on iron, both from the large meteorites on Cape York used previously by Late Dorset people and from European smelters, became a critical part of Thule assemblages. In fact, knowledge of this iron may have been one of the many factors that lured these migrants to the east (McGhee 1983).

THE CLASSIC EXPANSION

During this phase there was a marked increase in Eastern Arctic population and proliferation of settlements along all but the Labrador, Quebec, and eastern Hudson Bay shores. The prototype of classic sites has long been the first one systematically excavated—the Naujan site. The tendency in the literature has been to characterize other sites as earlier or later than Naujan—sometimes on the basis of discrete attributes but often on admittedly impressionistic bases. Much of what we have discussed in the preceding chapter in the section titled "Categories of Thule Activity" refers to materials recovered from Naujan-age sites. It was a period in which there was a marked homogeneity of traits, reflecting an active and persistent information network throughout the Eastern Arctic. While midden remains attest to omnivorous diets and efficient harvesting of all meat sources in the environment, overwhelming evidence (McCartney 1980) indicates that bowhead whale hunting was a frequent and important activity during this phase. Valuable as the meat, blubber, bone, and baleen would have been to a community, it may have been that sociopolitical factors and religious belief systems involved in hunting these huge mammals were equally significant in strengthening the social web and world view of the people. Schledermann (1979) has referred to this as the "Baleen period" and house sites of this time are often so filled with the tough, fibrous material that they are difficult to excavate.

Houses of the classic phase were large, deep pits lined with huge boulders, cut sod, and whale skulls and vertebrae and were entered through long, narrow tunnels. Roof frameworks were of whale jaws and ribs and driftwood timbers. Over these stretched walrus or bearded seal skins covered with cut sod and, in winter, blocks of snow. It is often frustrating to be excavating remains of such a house in the freezing rain while standing in pools of melting permafrost and to think how cozy such a house would have been when heated with three or four large, soapstone lamps of flaming seal oil.

Few artifacts can be ascribed exclusively to this classic phase; those that presumably are characteristic of it have already been discussed. Snow knives are more often composites, with lashed-on handles and short blades, but single-piece forms are present, as are composite knives in later sites. Classic arrowheads tend to have sharp shoulders on the tang, a trait found earlier in the east than in the west, but this attribute is not a particularly reliable time indicator. The only reasonably reliable time-linked trait is in the treatment of Types 2 and 3 harpoon heads. In these open-socket forms the binding that held the foreshaft in the socket passed either through notches or cut slots in early examples and through drilled holes in later ones.

Perhaps one of the best examples of classic Eastern Thule, and possibly earlier than Naujan, is House 42 at the Nunguvik site on Navy Board Inlet (Mary-Rousselière 1979b). This two-family dwelling, entered through a hole in the floor from a deep cold-trap in the tunnel entry, has been carbon dated on *Cassiope tetragona* (heather), at A.D. 1090 (S-477), with a date of A.D. 1235 (S-516) on similar material from a platform later laid on top of the earlier one. Artifacts recovered from this early house are of general Thule character and of only limited use in seriating discrete traits. For example, the long snow knife of whalebone is of a single piece with one shoulder on the concave margin. The tangs of four antler arrowheads span the possibilities of form: One is sharp shouldered with two small knobs on the tang, one, egg shaped at the distal end and slotted for an end blade, has sloping shoulders and knobs, one has a four-sided tang with sloping shoulders, and one has a square tang with slightly beveled base. Of two *ulu* handles, one is a single bar while the other has a large cutout finger hole in the handle. An ornamented boot creaser and a fragment of a decorated needle case have a slightly Western aspect, but on a dog trace toggle both holes are in a single plane. Several wooden female dolls are represented both with and without hair topknots. Only the harpoon heads conform to statements made earlier about time-linked traits. Types 2, 3, and 4 are represented. Those of Types 2 and 3 have cut binding slots, and one, of Type 3, has slightly constricted lateral margins reminiscent of Sicco heads and a vestigial side blade slit on one edge. This site assemblage demonstrates well the difficulty of discussing cultural change in the Thule Period on the basis of artifact attributes alone.

The small site of Crystal II on the outskirts of the town of Frobisher Bay (Collins 1950) is of this classic phase and although not carbon dated is commonly considered to precede the Naujan site by a few years. Discrete attributes on the artifacts recovered from the two of four subterranean houses that had not been earlier disturbed suggest that this is one of the earliest Thule sites in the more southerly Eastern Arctic.

The location has several ecological advantages. It is on the bank and near the mouth of the swiftly flowing Sylvia Grinnell River, an excellent fishing spot for the anadromous Arctic char. With a local tidal differential of as much as 12 m, the river runs upstream at high tide, producing a still water pool, ideal for launching boats, adjacent to the site. At high tide, seal follow fish into the river, and in the autumn large pods of beluga are common at the head of Frobisher Bay. When Charles Francis Hall visited the area in the mid-nineteenth century (Hall 1874) there were many caribou herds inland from the head of the bay. The major disadvantage to the site is its location approximately 150 km northwest of the winter floe edge. This restricted winter sea mammal hunting to ringed seal at the breathing holes.

The excavated Houses 3 and 4 are characteristic of Eastern Thule and demonstrate no particular Western traits. The harpoon heads, however, have discret attributes that are generally considered early in the sequence (Figure 9.2). Types 1, 2, 3, and 4 are all represented. Of the first 3 open-socket forms, only 3 of Type 2 have drilled lashing holes; the remaining 10 of this type and the 4 of Type 3 have cut slots or notches. Several of the Type 2 heads have incised inverted Ys above the line hole; all have long, sharp, basal spurs, and at least 1 has marginal ridges from opposite the line hole to the base. One of the Type 3 heads, although not decorated in the Sicco manner, has a marked constriction of the lateral margins at the level of the line hole. Several of both Types 2 and 3 have a small slot at right angles to the distal end of the open socket where a small sliver of ivory could be inserted for protection to the socket—generally an early trait in Eastern Thule.

The tangs of antler arrowheads have both sharp and sloping shoulders (Figure

Figure 9.2 Classic Thule hunting equipment from the Crystal II site, Frobisher Bay, Baffin Island (after Smithsonian Institution photographs, courtesy of Henry Collins).

A. Type 2 harpoon head with gouged binding slots
B. Type 2 harpoon head with binding notches
C. Type 3 harpoon head with gouged binding slots
D. Type 3 harpoon head with binding notches
E. Type 3 harpoon head with curving lateral margins similar to the Sicco type
F. Type 4 harpoon head

G. harpoon socket
H. arrowhead slotted for end blade
I. four self-bladed arrowheads
J. bird spear side barb
K. ivory ice pick
L. harpoon foreshaft
M. bone bola weight

9.2H and I), the single complete whalebone snow knife is of a single piece, with one shoulder on the concave edge, and the dog trace toggles have both holes in the same plane.

Except for one flaked chert scraper, which is probably Thule (Collins 1950:Plate X, No. 4), all of the flint and slate tools that Collins recovered can now be identified as belonging to a Late Dorset component abandoned well before the Thule settlement. This would suggest the use of iron, since disintegrated, for blades. While this may have been true for the thin slots on knife handles, the end slots on harpoon heads are probably too wide to have held anything but a stone blade. This situation suggests that iron may have been too scarce at this early date to be used for anything less carefully curated than a knife.

The presence of classic Thule winter houses this far away from the floe edge is surprising since traditional Inuit winter hunting usually depended on both the breathing hole harpooning of ringed seal and the taking of bearded seal, walrus, and beluga at the floe edge. However, Stenton (1983) excavating the Peale Point site 13 km to the west of Crystal II found adequate evidence of sufficient meat to support winter inhabitants of 11 pit houses ranging in time from classic Thule to historic contact. Quantities of whalebone and baleen in the earliest of these suggest a major locational advantage for hunting the bowhead whale. This site lies at the northern end of a long, submarine channel that extends down to Hudson Strait and provides a natural passageway for the huge mammals. The oldest pit house yet excavated on the site, House 2, was probably initially occupied at nearly the same time as the Crystal II houses. After 10 cm of midden, including quantities of baleen, had built up on the paved floor the house was repaved, and approximately 7–10 cm of midden, including whale ribs and sheets of baleen, accumulated on this second floor. This stratified house with an isolated lower layer provides good empirical proof of harpoon head changes from the classic phase to a postclassic one (Figure 9.3). Harpoon heads of Types 2, 3, and 4 on the earlier floor have notched or cut slots for binding, and one bilaterally barbed Type 2 head with long, sharp, basal spur is close in form to the Natchuk type but without a vestigial slit for a side blade.

The more recent occupational phase, from the quantities of baleen on the upper floor, is well within the period of intensive whale hunting, but the open-socket harpoon heads have drilled holes for lashing to the foreshaft. This upper floor midden also contained a closed-socket head of Type 5, which is generally considered to be more characteristic of the latter part of the developed, or postclassic, Thule.

The earliest excavated house at the Talaguak site near Lake Harbour, House 2, was also stratified, with two paved floors and a midden between (Sabo 1981). The earlier of the two floors is as old as Naujan or possibly slightly older. Its midden contained the early, and rare, Type 1 harpoon head with slight lateral constriction below the line hole, a prominent spur, and a raised area around the line hole that tapered toward the distal end. Although the lashing passed through drilled holes, this attribute is also present on the Naujan Type 1 heads. A medial fragment of a Type 2 had had cut binding slots, significant "lateral ridges," and an inverted Y filled with cross-hatching above the line hole. A Type 3 head, also with cut slots, had a

Figure 9.3   Late Postclassic artifacts from House 2 at the Peale Point site, Baffin Island.

A.   side-bladed knife handle with slots at bottom left, upper left, and top left (slot in the upper two-
     thirds has been filled with a wooden plug and top and bottom slots had traces of iron blades
B,C. late forms of Type 2 harpoon heads
D.   bow fragment
E.   arrowhead
F.   fixed lance head

slight lateral constriction, a sharp basal spur, and a reinforcing bar above the open socket. Other artifacts in this earlier midden were four dog trace toggles (three with holes in the same plane and one with holes perpendicular to each other), an antler arrowhead with sharp shoulders, a small *ulu* with an iron blade and an ivory handle, and a segment of carved ivory chain. The upper midden contained, among other artifacts, a Type 2 harpoon head with multiple side barbs, drilled lashing holes, a Type 5 harpoon head.

House 9 at this same site also had traits that suggest it was as old as Naujan if not older. As has been discussed earlier, the rectangular house had two interior open-fire kitchens and initially lacked a raised sleeping platform—all early and more Western traits. The two harpoon heads from the floor are of Type 2, with cut lashing slots, marginal grooved ridges, and reinforcing bars in the distal ends of the open sockets. One may have been single barbed but is badly eroded. A snow knife from this house was of the composite type. Particularly significant are the number of nephrite or jadeite artifacts from this house since this material is very rare in classic sites and absent in later ones. The artifacts of grass-green stone include harpoon end blades, drill bits, an adz fragment, an ax, and a small, polished disk. It is tempting to suggest that this material was carried from Alaska. However, the local Dorset people made extensive use of a nephrite that may occur naturally on the south coast of Baffin Island (for artifacts from this site see Figure 8.7).

One of the most interesting early Thule houses in the Lake Harbour region is House 8 at Okiavilialuk, also stratified, with an earlier component typologically coeval with Naujan (Sabo 1981). A small compartment in the bottom floor contained a small wooden figurine (Figure 9.4) that is carved in the Thule manner but unquestionably represents a Norse figure clothed in European style with its hooded cloak and incised cross on the chest (Sabo and Sabo 1978). This, like the chainmail and boat rivets from the High Arctic suggest that Thule Eskimo had personal contact with Norse Vikings from the time they arrived in the Eastern Arctic.

The Silumiut site excavated by McCartney (1977) on the west coast of Roes Welcome Sound, about 190 km south of the Naujan site, appears to date from the latter part of the classic phase. Four carbon dates on wood indicate a span from A.D. 1130: 820 ± 100 radiocarbon years (Gak-2748) to A.D. 1260 690 ± 100 radiocarbon years (Gak-2759). The earlier part of the site was probably coeval with Naujan, and the later part seems to have postdated Naujan. This assessment is partially supported by trait attributes: Types 2 and 3 harpoon heads have both cut slots and drilled holes for binding, although Type 5, the later type, is absent from the site. Arrowhead tangs have both sloping shoulders and sharp shoulders, with small offset knobs on the conical tangs. Most of the *ulus* have cutout finger holes, and the snow knives are composite forms with lashed-on blades.

G.	miniature *ulu* with slate blade	L.	leister side barb
H.	two slate harpoon end blades	M.	wooden float bar
I.	bladder dart inflating nozzle	N.	bird spear side barb
J,K.	dart heads	O.	wooden snow goggle fragment

Figure 9.4   Wooden early classic Thule figurine from the bottom of a house on the Okiavilialuk site, Lake Harbour. The costuming, including a robe and cross on the chest, is that of a Norseman of the twelfth century (life-size).

There was no sharp cultural break marking the end of the classic phase, but from the middle of the thirteenth century to the middle of the fourteenth, changes were occuring in the basic character of Thule culture. There were major expansions from the High Arctic southward of Lancaster Sound into Cumberland Sound, Foxe Basin, and the Gulf of Boothia. In part this expanding population entered waters good for whaling, but they also moved into regions such as Banks and Victoria islands where whales were rare and human ecology relied more heavily on other species. Mc-Cartney (1977) has suggested that with the end of the classic period at such sites as Silumiut, where whaling had previously been important, seal hunting on the sea ice took precedence over whaling and the deep winter pit houses on land were abandoned for snowhouses on the fast ice.

THE POSTCLASSIC MODIFICATION

With expansion into somewhat different ecological niches, the notable homogeneity of material culture that had characterized the classic phase became attenuated. Nevertheless, the similarity of artifact traits throughout the Eastern Arctic indicates that regardless of whether hunting strategy focused more on walrus, caribou, narwhal, or musk-ox, a strong network of information exchange persisted.

In part the redistribution of people that characterized the postclassic phase may have resulted from growing population pressure, but more probably climatic change was the primary factor. Between A.D. 1400 and 1600, summers of the waning Pacific climatic episode were growing colder and the Little Ice Age of the Neo-Boreal episode, with its advancing glaciers on Greenland and Baffin Island, was beginning. In some localities the drifting pack ice of summer may have increased to the point where, although individual pans floated freely, total ice cover may have been so complete as to make boat hunting dangerous to impossible. In more southerly latitudes a longer persistence of fast ice along the shore may have constrained the launching of umiaks and shortened the period of deep-water hunting. Most critical to whale hunting in many places would have been the increased size of drifting ice fields, too vast for whales, which normally must breathe every 4–5 minutes.

As Schledermann (1979) has demonstrated, there is adequate site evidence from the decreasing amounts of baleen for a steady decline in bowhead whale hunting after A.D. 1400. Cessation of whaling and complete dependence on other game animals was regionally variable. In the High Arctic the latter part of the sixteenth century seems to mark the end of open-water hunting, by umiak or kayak. Prior to this date the sea mammal–rich waters of Davis Strait, Baffin Bay, Kane Basin, and Robeson Channel had been an open ecotone between Atlantic and Arctic Basin waters. Whaling and other forms of kayak and umiak open-water hunting in summer had extended at least to 80° north latitude on the Canadian side and perhaps farther on the northwestern Greenland coast. Even as the weather was cooling, a few restless explorers were trying to extend their hunting ranges beyond reasonable northern limits. On the Arctic Basin coast of Greenland, unnavigable ice-bound waters today, Knuth (1952) found the complete frame of an umiak, since carbon dated to A.D. 1490 (K-566), where presumably a small hunting band beset by ice had had to abandon their transportation. Presumably dating from about the same time is a peculiar find at 80° north latitude on the northwestern Greenland coast (Mathiassen 1928) of an assemblage of gear from the warm-water kayak complex developed in southwestern Greenland, which would have been useless along the ice-choked shore where it was found.

The Lonesome Creek and Ruggles Outlet sites of northeastern Ellesmere Island have been estimated to date to this modified phase at the end of the fifteenth century. In this High Arctic region, boat hunting in any season is impossible today and presumably would have been then. Although stalking basking seal in late spring and summer would have been feasible, faunal remains indicate that fishing and the hunting of fox and musk-ox was much more important. The Ruggles Outlet site on Lake Hazen, 40 km from the coast (Maxwell 1960a), is particularly informative of the postclassic modified phase as a result of its tragic abandonment. Evidence here can best be interpreted as the remains of a single family occupying a shallow *qarmak* roofed with skins (see Figure 8.24). They stayed here only long enough to accumulate the remains of a few foxes and a single musk-ox before the man apparently died and was laid to rest under a pile of rocks outside the house. From the evidence on the sleeping platform, the widow, left alone, ate their three sled dogs and died, two whalebone combs still in her hair. The significance of these remains is that they constitute the complete inventory of a single family during a short period of time.

Unfortunately, only one harpoon head, an unfinished one of Type 4, was recovered from inside the house, but the approximately coeval Lonesome Creek site on the coast produced two of Type 5. In the Ruggles Outlet house were many types of spears for fishing; arrowheads, both self-bladed and slotted for end blades, with sloping shoulders and offset knobs on conical tangs; a complete whalebone snow knife with shoulders on both lateral edges; three dog trace toggles of walrus and narwhal ivory; end-hafted knife handles; an ulu with crude handle and iron blade; a drill and two drill sockets; wooden fire drills; a narwhal ivory drinking tube; a winged needle case; and sled shoes with both simple holes for pegs and channeled holes for binding.

Significantly, a small, end-hafted knife blade is of smelted (Norse) iron, whereas the iron-bladed *ulu,* an iron drill bit, and a second drill bit from the Lonesome Creek site are of meteoric iron (P. Sutherland, letter to M. S. Maxwell, April 11, 1983). Further evidence of the diffusion of European materials to this site comes from the remains of the dogsled. One runner was collected by the ill-fated Greeley expedition of 1881 and since lost. The other, excavated in 1958, formed the roof of the entry tunnel and was a single, thick, sawed board.

Today, cold air draining off the mountains into the basin of Lake Hazen may keep temperatures below −45°C for a full month. It may be that after A.D. 1600 temperatures even lower than those today constituted a constraint to normal human life in spite of the availability of a large resident musk-ox herd. Hunters away from the artificial heat of houses may have suffered deep body heat loss that could not be successfully regained when they returned to shelter and food. Under such severely cold conditions the food gained through hunting could not make up for energy lost while hunting; therefore their energy input−output ratio reached a critical deficit. Whatever the reason, much of the High Arctic appears to have been abandoned by the 1600s.

Farther to the south, whaling, although decreasing in importance, continued for various lengths of time depending on the location. At Igloolik (Mary-Rousselière 1979b), on the northern coast of Hudson Strait (Pitseolak 1975; Sabo 1981), and on the Labrador coast (Schledermann 1979) a limited amount of whaling continued until historic time. Elsewhere, where ice conditions precluded whaling because of reduced breathing space for whales or conditions dangerous for skin boats or where whaling had never been of major importance, economic activities altered toward greater dependence on local game species. On Banks, Victoria, and King William islands throughout the classic and postclassic phases Thule people had been much more reliant on a complex of ringed seal, caribou, and fish; whaling seems never to have been of great importance. Pritzler Harbour on the southeastern tip of Baffin Island, a site of 16 Thule pit houses not yet excavated, may be an important settlement of the postclassic phase. Here few whalebones are exposed on the surface, but there are quantities of walrus bones and skulls around the house pits. If summer floating ice conditions in Hudson Strait were then as they are now, hunting for whale in a skin boat far from land would have been very dangerous.

In the stratified houses of Okialivialuk and Talaguak the upper cultural layers have little baleen and are distinguished by modified harpoon heads such as multiple-barbed variants of Type 2 and the flat heads of Type 5. Still later single-component houses at these two sites are shallower and have less midden accumulations, suggesting shorter seasonal use and moves to snowhouses in the coldest winter months.

Quililukan near Pond Inlet at the northern end of Baffin Island (Mathiassen 1927) has long been seen as a site that bridged both the latter years of the classic phase and most of the modified postclassic. Virtually all variations are represented in the 60 harpoon heads recovered. Types 1–3 predominate, but according to Mathiassen there is greater variation in these than expressed at Naujan. There are Type 2 heads of classic type but also variants with drilled lashing holes, multiple side barbs, and slotted ends for stone or iron end blades. Most significant, there is a marked increase in Type 5 heads, which in time became the dominant harpoon form in the east.

Beyond these attributes there are few traits that can be considered diagnostic of postclassic time. Snow knives are both single pieces and composites with lashed-on blades, single-piece snow knives have both single and double shoulders, arrowheads have conical tangs with both sloping and squared shoulders, with and without small offset knobs on the tangs, and ulus have both single bar handles and handles with cutout finger holes. For the most part all of these traits continue well into the historic period.

Although changes in artifacts may have been less than diagnostic, there were important changes in other aspects of culture according to Mathiassen. Quililukan, he states (1927:145), was less rich in baleen than Naujan had been, suggesting reduced whaling, and the later houses were shallow, skin-covered pits (*qarmat*) occupied in autumn before the winter snow was of sufficient texture for snow block igloos.

By the end of this postclassic phase there were fewer activities common to the complete Thule sphere. The ensuing greater emphasis on regional ecologies led, according to McGhee (1974), to such separate "tribes" as the Copper Eskimo, Netsilingmiut, Aivilingmiut, Sadlermiut, Igloolingmiut, Nugumiut, and others first contacted by European, Canadian, and American explorers.

CONTACT AND THE HISTORIC PERIOD

The first European contact of Thule Eskimo was clearly with Norse settlers from the Greenlandic eastern and western settlements, which at their climax had more than 4000 inhabitants (McGovern 1979, 1980). The nature of this contact, its influence on Thule culture, and the distribution of Norse materials in Thule sites is still little known. Norse sagas written two and three centuries after the fact say little of intercourse with native people, yet from the emerging archaeological record it is clear that the diffusion of Norse metal—iron and smelted copper—was widespread early in Eastern Thule development (McGhee 1981c). Earlier, Mathiassen (1930), basing his interpretation on Sermermiut sites around Disko Bay, had identified a separate cultural complex, Inugsuk, dating, he estimated, to the late fourteenth and early fifteenth centuries. This Inugsuk culture was distinguished by the frequency of such Norse goods as chessmen, barrel staves, sawed timbers, long-handled spoons and iron implements. Since then, it has become apparent that similar European materials had been acquired by Thule Eskimo through diffusion or direct barter virtually as early as they had arrived in the east (McGhee 1983). An exchange of goods between the two peoples would have been logical. The Norse settlers were under heavy church pressure for the tithing of income. The most acceptable items for fulfilling church requirements to Norway and ultimately to Rome were gyr-falcons, in high demand for hunting, walrus ivory, and polar bear skins. The Vikings had neither sufficient technology nor opportunity for taking this prey from the environment and so were dependent on native hunters. In one account (cited in McGhee 1983) 400 ivory walrus tusks were shipped from Greenland to Norway. On the other hand, iron tools received in trade were far more functional to the Eskimo than their native brittle slate ones.

The passage of iron as far west as the Silumiut site was probably along native exchange routes, but there is some archaeological evidence to suggest more direct encounters between the two people. Schledermann's finds of chainmail armor, boat timbers and rivets, woolen cloth, iron knife blades, and the base of a wooden barrel on Ellesmere Island's Buchanan Bay suggest to him the remains of a boat load that had either wrecked on shore or been attacked and the sailors slaughtered by the natives. The arm of a trader's small bronze balance scales recovered from a Thule house on the western shore of Ellesmere Island (Sutherland 1977) might more likely be attributed to the presence of a trader rather than the result of long-distance trade. Perhaps the most convincing argument for at least occasional face-to-face contact comes from the small wooden figurine from House 8 at Okiavilialuk (Sabo and Sabo 1978). Those who have viewed the figurine agree that it could only have been carved by a Thule Eskimo who had actually seen a Norseman in European dress.

The collapse of the Norse settlements by the beginning of the fifteenth century curtailed the addition of new European iron into the exchange system. Yet it is clear that the iron earlier acquired continued to circulate in trade.

Following the demise of the Norse settlements, further contacts between Thule descendants and Europeans varied from one to four centuries, depending on local isolation. The earliest contacts were logically on eastern coasts, as explorers searched for a northwest passage to the rich markets of the Orient. Martin Fro-bisher made three adventuresome voyages between 1576 and 1578, discovering the bay that bears his name. On the first voyage he found what he thought was a rich gold deposit on Kodlurn Island, but this was later found to be worthless iron pyrites. His contacts with local natives, then living in pit houses, were unfriendly, and he ultimately lost five of his crew. In successive trips to mine the "gold," he lured a native close to his ship with a shiny trinket; then with a strong heave of his arm he lifted Eskimo and kayak aboard ship and kidnapped him to England. As a last memento he received a Thule arrow in the rump, but history does not record whether the tang of the arrowhead had a sharp or sloping shoulder.

In 1585, 1586, and 1587 John Davis explored the east coast of Baffin Island, entering Cumberland Sound. He lost two men to unfriendly Eskimo on the north coast of Labrador. George Davis sailed up the east coast of Baffin Island in 1602 and penetrated some distance westward through Hudson Strait. Hendrick Hudson in 1610, enroute to discovering Hudson Bay, encountered friendly Eskimo near Cape

Wolstenholm. A year later, after the mutiny that set Hudson adrift in a small boat, the remaining crew stopped there again, and, after initial friendly trading, the Inuit attacked the sailors and killed several of them. It was not until two centuries later, from the early nineteenth century on, that many Inuit met people from the Western world.

For nearly three centuries the sailing route through Hudson Strait into Foxe Basin and Hudson Bay was the one first used by Davis and Hudson. Since drift ice was less thick along the south coast of Baffin Island, vessels would strike north from Cape Chidley, Labrador and make for Saddleback Island in the Middle Savages, the only major landmark along this coast (Figure 9.5). From there they would sail north-westerly along the shore to Big Island and then cross the strait to Charles Island off the Quebec coast. From the late seventeenth to early nineteenth centuries there were frequent voyages along this route during the summer. Large groups of Baffin Island Inuit would gather at Saddleback and Big Island in anticipation of ship arrivals, gathering eiderduck eggs as they waited. Most of the early exchanges between sailors and Inuit were friendly, but occasionally an apparently peaceful trading session would erupt in violence. In part such attacks may have been related to a growing scarcity of iron on which the natives had now grown dependent.

Figure 9.5 View of Saddleback Island from the southeastern coast of Baffin Island. This distinctive island served as a landmark for early sailors crossing Hudson Strait.

The occasional early contacts appear to have had little effect on native culture other than the introduction of a few items of European manufacture. The first significant impact came with Franklin's 1845–1848 expedition and the ultimate loss of his ships and full crew of 129 men. In the following 12 years more than 100 ships searched unsuccessfully for survivors. During this period there were 33 ship winterings (Baird 1949), with ship captains letting their ships freeze in safe harbors and continuing the search with the summer breakup. It was these winterings, a technique followed later by whalers anxious to stretch the commercially valuable whaling season, that produced the major impact of European and Canadian culture on the Inuit descendants of the Thule people.

From the middle of the nineteenth century on, commercial activities of the Western world played an increasing role in altering Inuit culture. Inuit crews were hired as harpooners and oarsmen for whale boats to be sent out from mother ships, and many men, and some of their wives, would spend the summer on such ships. The S.S. *Active* operated a mica mine at Lake Harbour in conjunction with its whaling activities, employing many of the local men as miners. Commercial trapping of white fox for trade with the Hudson Bay Company kept men on the traplines for months and away from the winter seacoast hunting. In turn this left families more dependent on goods from the store purchased with the skins. Wooden boats and guns quickly replaced skin boats and harpoons. With the coming of missionaries and police, major components of the nonmaterial culture were permanently altered.

Although outside the scope of this study of prehistoric development, the period of contact and subsequent changes in Inuit culture is increasingly becoming the focus of Arctic archaeologists. A succession of Basque, French, German, and English left their impact on Labradoran Inuit culture from the seventeenth through the nineteenth centuries (Kaplan 1980). Hans Egede's 1721 missionary endeavors in Greenland marked the beginning of continuous involvement between Danes and Inuit, and the acceleration of commercial whaling and exploring through Davis and Hudson straits left its archaeological traces on southern Baffin Island (Sabo 1981; Schledermann 1975). The quantity of historical archaeology now in process in the Eastern Arctic will shortly be sufficient for a book of its own.

In 1954 the Distant Early Warning Line was begun with stations every 80 km along the 70th Parallel from Cape Dyer, Baffin Island, to Cape Lisburne, Alaska. This was the first major opening up of the Eastern Arctic, and the increase in airborne logistics converted most of the Inuit population to wage economies and motorized boats and snowmobiles. By 1965 the traditional system of adaptation had virtually ceased. In essence this decade brought the first dramatic cultural change in the 4000-year history of such settlements as Pond Inlet, Igloolik, and Lake Harbour.

References

Anderson, D. D.
  1970 *Akmak: an early archaeological assemblage from Onion Portage* (Fasc. 16). Acta Arctica, Copenhagen.
Anderson, J. E., and J. A. Tuck
  1974 Osteology of the Dorset people. *Man in the Northwest* 8:89–97.
Andrews, J. T., and H. H. Miller
  1979 Climatic change over the last 1000 years, Baffin Island, N.W.T. In Thule Eskimo culture: an anthropological retrospective, edited by A. P. McCartney. *National Museum of Man Mercury Series, Archaeological Survey of Canada Paper* 88:541–554. National Museums of Canada, Ottawa.
Arnold, C. D.
  1980 A Paleoeskimo occupation on southern Banks Island. *Arctic* 33:400–426.
  1981 The Lagoon site (OjR1–3): implications for Paleoeskimo interactions. *National Museum of Man Mercury Series, Archaeological Survey of Canada Paper* 107. National Museums of Canada, Ottawa.
Arundale, W. H.
  1976 *The archaeology of the Nanook site: an explanatory approach.* Unpublished Ph.D. dissertation, Department of Anthropology, Michigan State University.
  1981 Radiocarbon dating in Eastern Arctic archaeology: a flexible approach. *American Antiquity* 46:244–271.
Badgley, I.
  1980 Stratigraphy and habitation features at DIA.4 (JfEl–4): a Dorset site in Arctic Quebec. *Arctic* 33:569–584.
Baird, P. D.
  1949 Expeditions to the Canadian Arctic. *The Beaver* March, June, and September.
Bandi, H-G.
  1974 Metallene lamellespamzer der Eskimos auf St. Lorenz Insel, Alaska. *Folk* 16:83–94.
Bandi, H-G., and J. Meldgaard
  1952 Archaeological investigations on Clavering Ø, northeast Greenland. *Meddelelser om Grønland* 126:4.
Barré, G.
  1970 *Reconnaissance archéologique dans la région de la baie de Wakeham (Nouveau Québec).* La Société d'Archéologie préhistorique du Québec, Montreal.
Barry, R. G., W. H. Arundale, J. T. Andrews, R. S. Bradley, and H. Nichols.
  1977 Environmental change and cultural change in the eastern Canadian Arctic during the last 5000 years. *Arctic and Alpine Research* 9:193–210.

Bielawski, E.

    1979 Contactual transformations: the Dorset–Thule succession. In Thule Eskimo culture: an anthropological retrospective, edited by A. P. McCartney. *National Museum of Man Mercury Series, Archaeological Survey of Canada Paper* 88:100–109. National Museums of Canada, Ottawa.

Birket-Smith, Kaj

    1929 *The Caribou Eskimos.* Report of the Fifth Thule Expedition 1921–1924:5 Copenhagen.

Blaylock, S. K.

    1980 *Thule bone technology from Somerset Island, central Canadian Arctic, N.W.T.* Paper presented at the Society for American Archaeology Annual Meeting, Philadelphia.

Boas, F.

    1907 The Eskimo of Baffin Land and Hudson Bay. *American Museum of Natural History Bulletin* 15.

Bryson, R. A., and W. M. Wendland

    1967 Tentative climatic patterns for some late Glacial episodes in central North America. In *Life, Land and Water,* edited by W. J. Mayer-Oakes. University of Manitoba Press, Winnipeg.

Carpenter, E.

    1973 *Eskimo realities.* Holt, Rinehart and Winston, New York.

Clark, B., and J. Sproull-Thomson

    1981 *Spirits of earth and water.* Newfoundland Museum, St. Johns, Newfoundland.

Collins, H. B.

    1935 Archaeology of the Bering Sea Region. *Smithsonian Annual Report for 1933,* pp. 453–468. Smithsonian Institution, Washington, D.C.

    1940 Notes and news, Arctic. *American Antiquity* 5:233–234.

    1950 Excavations at Frobisher Bay, Baffin Island, N.W.T. In Annual Report of the National Museum of Canada for 1948–49. *National Museum of Canada Bulletin* 123:49–63.

    1952 Archaeological excavations at Resolute, Cornwallis Island, N.W.T. Annual Report of the National Museum of Canada for 1950–51, *National Museum of Canada Bulletin* 126:48–63.

    1955 Excavations of Thule and Dorset culture sites at Resolute, Cornwallis Island, N.W.T. *National Museum of Canada Bulletin* 136:22–35.

  1956a Archaeological investigations on Southampton and Coats islands, N.W.T. Annual Report of the National Museum of Canada for 1954–55. *National Museum of Canada Bulletin* 142:82–113.

  1956b The T-1 site at Native Point, Southampton Island, N.W.T. *Anthropological Papers of the University of Alaska* 4:63–89.

    1957 Archaeological investigations on Southampton and Walrus islands, N.W.T. Annual Report of the National Museum of Canada for 1956. *National Museum of Canada Bulletin* 147:22–61.

    1958 Present status of the Dorset problem. *Proceedings of the 32nd International Congress of Americanists, Copenhagen,* 1956, pp. 557–560.

    1974 Additional examples of early Eskimo art. *Folk* 16–17:55–62.

Cox, S. L.

    1977 *Prehistoric settlement and culture change at Okak, Labrador.* Unpublished Ph.D. dissertation, Department of Anthropology, Harvard University.

    1978 Paleo-Eskimo occupations of the north Labrador Coast. *Arctic Anthropology* 15:96–118.

Cox, S. L., and A. Spiess

    1980 Dorset settlement and subsistence in northern Labrador. *Arctic* 33:659–669.

Damas, D.

  1969a Characteristics of Central Eskimo band structure. In Band societies, edited by D. Damas. *National Museum of Canada Bulletin 228:* 116–138.

  1969b Environment, history and Central Eskimo society. In Ecological essays, edited by D. Damas. *National Museum of Canada Bulletin 230:46–64.*

Dekin, A. A., Jr.

    1975 *Models of Pre-Dorset culture: towards an explicit methodology.* Unpublished Ph.D. dissertation, Department of Anthropology, Michigan State University.

1976 Elliptical analysis: an heuristic technique for the analysis of artifact clusters. In Eastern Arctic prehistory: Paleoeskimo problems, edited by M. S. Maxwell. *Memoirs of the Society for American Archaeology* No. 31:79–88.

Dumond, D. E.

1972 Prehistoric population growth and subsistence change in Eskimo Alaska. In *Population growth: anthropological implications,* edited by B. Spooner. MIT Press, Cambridge.

1977 *The Eskimos and Aleuts.* Thames and Hudson, London

Fitzhugh, W. W.

1972 Environmental archaeology and cultural systems in Hamilton Inlet, Labrador: a survey of the central Labrador Coast from 3000 B.C. to the present. *Smithsonian Contributions to Anthropology* No. 16. Smithsonian Institution, Washington, D.C.

1976a Environmental factors in the evolution of Dorset culture: a marginal proposal for Hudson Bay. In Eastern Arctic prehistory: Paleoeskimo problems, edited by M. S. Maxwell. *Memoirs of the Society for American Archaeology* No. 31:139–149.

1976b Paleoeskimo occupations of the Labrador Coast. In Eastern Arctic prehistory: Paleoeskimo problems, edited by M. S. Maxwell. *Memoirs of the Society for American Archaeology* 31:103–118.

1980 Preliminary report on the Torngat Archaeological Project. *Arctic* 33:585–606.

1981 A prehistoric caribou fence from Williams Harbor, northern Laborador. Proceedings from the 11th Annual Chacmool Conference, October 1978. University of Calgary, Alberta.

Fleming, A. L.

1956 *Archibald the Arctic.* Appleton-Century-Crofts, New York.

Ford, J. A.

1959 Eskimo prehistory in the vicinity of Point Barrow, Alaska. *Anthropological Papers of the American Museum of Natural History* 47.

Fredskild, Bent

1973 Studies in the vegetational history of Greenland. *Meddelelser om Grønland* 198:4.

Freeman, M. M. R.

1979 A critical view of Thule culture and ecological adaptation. In Thule Eskimo culture: an anthropological restrospective, edited by A. P. McCartney. *National Museum of Man Mercury Series. Archaeological Survey of Canada Paper* 88; pp. 278–285. National Museums of Canada, Ottawa.

Giddings, J. L., Jr.

1956 A flint site in northernmost Manitoba. *American Antiquity* 21:255–268.

1964 *The archaeology of Cape Denbigh.* Brown University Press, Providence.

1967 *Ancient men of the Arctic.* Alfred Knopf, New York.

Gordon, B. H. C.

1975 Of men and herds in Barrenland prehistory. *National Museum of Man Mercury Series. Archaeological Survey of Canada* No. 28. National Museums of Canada, Ottawa.

1976 Migod-8000 years of Barrenland prehistory. *National Museum of Man Mercury Series. Archaeological Survey of Canada Paper* 56, p. 310. National Museums of Canada, Ottawa.

Hall, C. F.

1864 *Life with the Eskimaux.* Sampson Low, Son, and Marston, London.

Harp, E., Jr.

1951 An archaeological reconnaissance in the Straits of Belle Isle area. *American Antiquity* 16:203–221.

1958 Prehistory in the Dismal Lake area. *Arctic* 11:218–249.

1960 Abverdjar collection. Data available from author, Department of Anthropology, Dartmouth College, Hanover, N.H.

1964 The cultural affinities of the Newfoundland Dorset Eskimos. *National Museum of Canada Bulletin* 200. Queens Printer, Ottawa.

1970 Late Dorset art from Newfoundland. *Folk* 11–12:109–124.

1974   A Late Dorset copper amulet from southeastern Hudson Bay. *Folk* 16–17:33–44.

1976a Dorset settlement patterns in Newfoundland and southeastern Hudson Bay. In Eastern Arctic prehistory: Paleoeskimo problems, edited by M. S. Maxwell. *Memoirs of the Society for American Archaeology* No. 31:119–138.

1976b Report on archaeological investigations in the Belcher Islands during the summer of 1975. Manuscript on file, Archaeological Survey of Canada, National Museum of Man, Ottawa.

Harp, E., Jr., and D. R. Hughes

1968   Five prehistoric burials from Port aux Choix, Newfoundland. *Polar Notes* 8:1–47.

Hayden, B.

1972   Population control and hunter/gatherers. *World Archaeology* 4:205–221.

Haynes, C. V., Jr.

1966   Elephant hunting in North America. *Scientific American* 214:104–112.

Helmer, J. W.

1980a Early Dorset in the High Arctic: a report from Karluk Island, N.W.T. *Arctic* 33:427–442.

1980b Preliminary report of the 1979 Crozier Strait Archaeological Project. Manuscript on file, Department of Archaeology, University of Calgary.

Holtved, E.

1944   Archaeological investigations in the Thule District. *Medelelser om Grønland* 141. C. A. Reitzels Forlag, Copenhagen.

1954   Archaeological investigations in the Thule District (Pt. 3): Nûgdlît and Comer's Midden. *Medelelser om Grønland* 146. C. A. Reitzels Forlag, Copenhagen.

Irving, W. N.

1957   An archaeological survey of the Susitna Valley. *Anthropological Papers of the University of Alaska* 6:37–52.

Jacobs, J. D.

1981   Environment and prehistory, Baffin Island. Manuscript on file, Department of Geography, University of Windsor, Canada.

Jenness, D.

1925   A new Eskimo culture in Hudson Bay. *Geographical Review* 15:428–437.

Jordan, R. H.

1978   Introduction. In Symposium on central Labrador archaeology. *Arctic Anthropology* 15:1–8.

1979   Inugsuk revisited: an alternative view of Neo-Eskimo chronology and culture change in Greenland. In Thule Eskimo culture: an anthropological retrospective, edited by A. P. McCartney. *National Museum of Man Mercury Series. Archaeological Survey of Canada Paper* 88, pp. 149–170. National Museums of Canada, Ottawa.

1979   Dorset art forms from Labrador. *Folk* 21–22:397–417.

1980   Preliminary results from archaeological investigations on Avayalik Island, extreme northern Labrador. *Arctic* 33:607–627.

Jordan, R. H., and S. L. Olson

1982   First record of the great auk (*Pinquinas impennis*) from Labrador. *The Auk: A Quarterly Journal of Ornithology* 99:167–168.

Kaplan, S. A.

1980   Neo-Eskimo occupations of the northern Labrador Coast. *Arctic* 33:646–658.

Kemp, W. B.

1971   The flow of energy in a hunting society. *Scientific American* 225:104–115.

1976   Inuit land use in south and east Baffin Island. In *Inuit Land Use and Occupancy Project report* (Vol. 1), edited by M. M. R. Freeman. Dept. of Indian and Northern Affairs, Ottawa.

Knuth, E.

1952   An outline of the archaeology of Pearyland. *Arctic* 5:17–33.

1954   The Paleo-Eskimo culture of northeast Greenland elucidated by three new sites. *American Antiquity* 19:367–381.

1967a Archaeology of the Musk Ox Way. *Contributions du Centre d'Etudes Arctiques et Finno-Scandinaves* No. 5, Paris.

1967b The ruins of the Musk Ox Way. *Folk* 8–9:191–219.

1968 The Independence II bone artifacts and the Dorset evidence in north Greenland. *Folk* 10:61–80.

1981 Greenland news from between 81° and 83° North. *Folk* 23:91–111.

Larsen, H.

1962 The Trail Creek caves on Seward Peninsula, Alaska. *Proceedings of the 34th International Congress of Americanists 1960,* pp. 284–291. Vienna.

1968 Trail Creek, final report on the excavation of two caves on Seward Peninsula, Alaska. *Acta Arctica* 15:7–79.

Larsen, H., and J. Meldgaard

1958 Paleo-Eskimo cultures in Disko Bugt, West Greenland. *Medelelser om Grønland* 161:1–75.

Laughlin, W. S., and W. E. Taylor, Jr.

1960 A Cape Dorset culture site on the west coast of Ungava Bay. In Contributions to anthropology in 1958. *National Museum of Canada Bulletin* 168:1–28.

Leechman, J. D.

1943 Two new Cape Dorset sites. *American Antiquity* . . 4:363–375.

Lethbridge, T. C.

1939 Archaeological data from the Canadian Arctic. *Journal of the Royal Anthropological Institute* 69:187–233.

Lowther, G. R.

1962 An account of an archaeological site on Cape Sparbo, Devon Island. Contributions to anthropology in 1960. *National Museum of Canada Bulletin* 180:1–19.

McCartney, A. P.

1977 Thule Eskimo prehistory along northeastern Hudson Bay. *National Museum of Man Mercury Series. Archaeological Survey of Canada Paper* 70. National Museums of Canada, Ottawa.

1979 Archaeological whale bone: a northern resource. *University of Arkansas Anthropological Papers* 1. University of Arkansas Press, Fayetteville.

1980 The nature of Thule Eskimo whale use. *Arctic* 33:517–541.

McCartney, A. P., and D. J. Mack

1973 Iron utilization by Thule Eskimos of central Canada. *American Antiquity* 38:328–339.

McGhee, R. J.

1969 An archaeological survey of western Victoria Island, N.W.T., Canada. *National Museum of Canada Bulletin in Anthropology* 232:158–191.

1970a Excavations at Bloody Falls, N.W.T., Canada. *Arctic Anthropology* 6:53–73.

1970b Speculations on climatic change and Thule culture development. *Folk* 11–12:172–184.

1974 Beluga hunters: an archaeological reconstruction of the history and culture of the Mackenzie Delta Kittegaryumiut. *Newfoundland Social and Economic Studies* 13. Institute of Social and Economic Research, Memorial University of Newfoundland, St. Johns.

1976 Paleoeskimo occupations of Central and High Arctic Canada. In Eastern Arctic prehistory: Paleoeskimo problems, edited by M. S. Maxwell. *Memoirs of the Society for American Archaeology* 31:15–39.

1978 Canadian Arctic prehistory. *National Museum of Man. Archaeological Survey of Canada.* National Museums of Canada, Ottawa.

1979 The Paleoeskimo occupations at Port Refuge, High Arctic Canada. *National Museum of Man Mercury Series, Archaeological Survey of Canada Paper* 92. National Museums of Canada, Ottawa.

1980 Individual stylistic variability in Independence I stone tool assemblages from Port Refuge, N.W.T. *Arctic* 33:443–453.

1981a A tale of two cultures: a prehistoric village in the Canadian Arctic. *Archaeology,* July and August.

1981b The Dorset occupations in the vicinity of Port Refuge, High Arctic Canada. *National Museum of Man Mercury Series, Archaeological Survey of Canada Paper* 105. National Museums of Canada, Ottawa.

1981c The Norse in North America. In *The Vikings and their predecessors,* edited by K. Gordon. National Museum of Man, National Museums of Canada, Ottawa.

1983   *The Eastern Arctic: forty centuries of prehistory, half a century of archaeology.* Paper delivered at the 16th Annual Meeting of the Canadian Archaeological Association, Halifax.

McGhee, R. J., and J. Tuck

1976   Un-dating the Canadian Arctic. In Eastern Arctic prehistory: Paleoeskimo problems, edited by M. S. Maxwell. *Memoirs of the Society for American Archaeology* 31:6–14.

McGovern, T. H.

1979   Thule–Norse interaction in southwestern Greenland: a speculative model. In Thule Eskimo culture: an anthropological retrospective, edited by A. P. McCartney. *National Museum of Man Mercury Series, Archaeological Survey of Canada Paper* 88:171–188. National Museums of Canada, Ottawa.

1980   Cows, harp seals and churchbells: adaptation and extinction in Norse Greenland. *Human Ecology* 8:245–275.

McLaren, I. A.

1958   The economics of seals in the Eastern Canadian Arctic. Arctic Unit Circular I, Mimeograph on file, Fisheries Research Board, Canada.

MacNeish, R.

1956   The Engigstciak site on the Yukon Arctic coast. *Anthropological Papers of the University of Alaska* 4:91–111.

Mary-Rousselière, G.

1964   The Paleo-Eskimo remains in the Pelly Bay region, N.W.T. National Museum of Canada Contributions to Anthropology 1961–1962. *National Museum of Canada Bulletin* 193:62–183.

1974   Preliminary report of archaeological investigations at Nunguvik and Saatut. Manuscript on file, Archaeological Survey of Canada, National Museums of Canada, Ottawa.

1976   The Paleoeskimo in northern Baffinland. In Eastern Arctic prehistory: Paleoeskimo problems, edited by M. S. Maxwell. *Memoirs of the Society for American Archaeology* 31:40–57.

1979a A few problems elucidated and new questions raised by recent Dorset finds in the North Baffin Island region. *Arctic* 32:22–32.

1979b The Thule culture on north Baffin Island: early Thule characteristics and the survival of the Thule tradition. In Thule Eskimo culture: an anthropological retrospective, edited by A. P. McCartney. *National Museum of Man Mercury Series, Archaeological Survey of Canada Paper* 88:54–75. National Museums of Canada, Ottawa.

Mathiassen, T.

1927   Archaeology of the Central Eskimos, the Thule culture and its position within the Eskimo culture. *Report of the Fifth-Thule Expedition,* 1921–1924:4. Glydendalski Boghandel, Nordisk Forlag, Copenhagen.

1928   Eskimo relics from Washington Land and Hall Land. *Meddelelser om Grønland* 71:3.

1930   Inugsuk, a Mediaeval Eskimo settlement in Upernivik District. *Meddelelser om Grønland* 77:4.

1958   The Sermermiut excavations. *Meddelelser om Grønland 161:3.*

Maxwell, M. S.

1960a *An archaeological analysis of eastern Grant Land, Ellesmere Island, N.W.T. In Contributions to Anthropology in 1960. National Museum of Canada Bulletin* 180:20–55, Ottawa.

1972   Preliminary report of excavations at the Crystal II site. Manuscript on file, Archaeological Survey of Canada, National Museum of Man, National Museums of Canada, Ottawa.

1973a Archaeology of the Lake Harbour district, Baffin Island. *National Museum of Man Mercury Series, Archaeological Survey of Canada Paper* 6. National Museums of Canada, Ottawa.

1973b Faunal analysis of the Tanfield site. Manuscript on file, Department of Anthropology, Michigan State University.

1974 An early Dorset harpoon complex. *Folk* 16–17:125–132.

1976   Pre-Dorset and Dorset artifacts: the view from Lake Harbour. In Eastern Arctic prehistory: Paleoeskimo problems, edited by M. S. Maxwell. *Memoirs of the Society for American Archaeology* 31:58–78.

1979   The Lake Harbour region: ecological equilibrium in sea coast adaptation. In Thule Eskimo culture: an anthropological retrospective, edited by A. P. McCartney. *National Museum of Man Mercury Series, Archaeological Survey of Canada Paper* 88:76–87. National Museums of Canada, Ottawa.

1980   Dorset site variation on the southeastern coast of Baffin Island. *Arctic* 33:505–516.

1981   A southeastern Baffin Thule house with Ruin Island characteristics. *Arctic* 34:133–140.

1983   A contemporary ethnography from the Thule period. *Arctic Anthropology* 20(1):79–187.

Meldgaard, J.

1960a   Origin and evolution of Eskimo culture in the Eastern Arctic. *Canadian Geographical Journal* 60:64–75.

1960b   Prehistoric sequences in the Eastern Arctic as elucidated by stratified sites at Igloolik. *Selected papers of the 5th International Congress of Anthropological and Ethnological Sciences, 1956.* University of Pennsylvania Press, Philadelphia.

1961   Sarqaq-folket ved Itivnera: Nationalmuseets undersogelser i sommeren 1960. *Tidskritet Grønland* January:15–23.

1962   On the formative period of the Dorset culture. In Prehistoric relations between the Arctic and Temperate Zones of North America, edited by J. M. Campbell. *Arctic Institute of North America Technical Paper* 11, Montreal.

Merbs, C. F.

1971   Sir Thomas Rowe's Welcome. *The Beaver* 301:16–24.

Møhl, U.

1972   Animal bones from Itivnera, West Greenland. *Meddelelser om Grønland* 191:6.

Murdy, C. N.

1981   Congenital deformities and the Olmec Were-Jaguar motif. *American Antiquity* 46:861–871.

Murray, P.

1966   Faunal analysis of the Nanook site. Manuscript on file, Department of Anthropology, Michigan State University.

Nash, R. J.

1969   The Arctic Small Tool tradition in Manitoba. Occasional papers of the Department of Anthropology, No. 2. University of Manitoba, Winnepeg.

1972   Dorset culture in northeastern Manitoba, Canada. *Arctic Anthropology* 9:10–16.

1976   Culture systems and culture change in the Central Arctic. In Eastern Arctic prehistory: Paleoeskimo problems, edited by M. S. Maxwell. *Memoirs of The Society for American Archaeology* 31:150–155.

Nelson, R. K.

1969   *Hunters of the northern ice.* University of Chicago Press, Chicago.

Nichols,

1967   Pollen diagram from Sub-Arctic central Canada. *Science* 155(3770):10–16.

Noble, W. C.

1971   Archaeological surveys and sequences in central District of Mackenzie, N.W.T. *Arctic Anthropology* 8:102–135.

O'Bryan, D.

1953   Excavation of a Cape Dorset culture site, Mill Island, west Hudson Strait. *Annual Report of the National Museum of Canada, 1951–52.* National Museum of Canada, Ottawa.

Olsson,

1972   The pretreatment of samples and the interpretation of C-14 determinants. In climatic changes in the Arctic area during the last ten thousand years, edited by Y. Vasari, H. Hyvarinin and S. Hicks, *Acta Universitatas Ovlvensis, series A*(3):8–37. Oulu, Finland.

Oschinsky, L.

1960   Two recently discovered human mandibles from Cape Dorset sites on Sugluk and Mansel islands. *Anthropologica* (n.s.) 2:212–227.

1964   *The most ancient Eskimos.* Canadian Research Centre for Anthropology, The University of Ottawa, Ottawa.

Pitseolak, P.

1975   *People from our side.* Hurtig Publications, Edmonton.

Plumet, P.

1979   Thuleens et Dorsétiens dans L'Ungava (Nouveau-Québec). In Thule Eskimo culture: an anthropological retrospective, edited by A. P. McCartney National Museum of Man Mercury Series, Archaeological Survey of Canada Paper 88:110–121. National Museums of Canada, Ottawa.

Plumet, P., and I. Badgley

1980   Implications methodologiques de fouilles de Tuvaaluk sur l'étude des établissments dorsétiens. *Arctic* 33:542–552.

Rasmussen, K.

1931   The Netsilik Eskimos: social life and spiritual culture. *Report of the Fifth Thule Expedition* 1921–1924:8. Glydendalske Boghandel, Nordisk Forlag, Copenhagen.

Rosing, J.

1962   Palaeoeskimoerne. In *Bogen om Grønland*, pp. 29–37. Politikens Forlag, København.

Rowley, G.

1940   The Dorset culture of the Eastern Arctic. *American Anthropologist* 42:490–499.

1971   Notes on the Cambridge University collection: some unique pieces. *Artscanada* 162 and 163:116–120.

Sabo, D., and G. Sabo, III

1978   A possible Thule carving of a Viking from Baffin Island, N.W.T. *Canadian Journal of Archaeology* 2:33–42.

Sabo, G., III

1981   *Thule culture adaptations on the south coast of Baffin Island, N.W.T.* Unpublished Ph.D. dissertation, Department of Anthropology, Michigan State University.

Sabo, G., III, and J. D. Jacobs

1980   Aspects of Thule culture adaptations in southern Baffin Island. *Arctic* 33:487–504.

Savelle, J. M.

1980   *An appraisal of Thule archaeology.* Unpublished M.A. thesis, Department of Anthropology, University of Arkansas.

Schell, D. M.

1983   Carbon-13 and Carbon-14 abundances in Alaskan aquatic organisms: delayed production from peat in Arctic food webs. *Science* 219:1068–1071.

Schledermann, P.

1975   Thule Eskimo prehistory of Cumberland Sound, Baffin Island, Canada. *National Museum of Man Mercury Series, Archaeological Survey of Canada Paper* 38. National Museums of Canada, Ottawa.

1976   A Late Dorset site on Axel Heiberg Island. *Arctic* 29:300

1978a Distribution of archaeological sites in the vicinity of the proposed Polar Gas pipeline and staging area, N.W.T. Mimeograph available from Polar Gas Project, Calgary.

1978b Prehistoric demographic trends in the Canadian High Arctic. *Canadian Journal of Archaeology* 2:43–58.

1978c Preliminary results of archaeological investigations in the Bache Peninsula region, Ellesmere Island, N.W.T. *Arctic* 31:459–474.

1979   The "Baleen Period" of the Arctic whale hunting tradition. In Thule Eskimo culture: an anthropological retrospective, edited by A. P. McCartney. *National Museum of Man Mercury*

Series, *Archaeological Survey of Canada Paper* 88:134–148. National Museums of Canada, Ottawa.

1980a Notes on Norse finds from the east coast of Ellesmere Island, N.W.T. *Arctic* 33:454–463.

1980b Polynias and prehistoric settlement patterns. *Arctic* 33:292–302.

1981 Eskimo and Viking finds in the High Arctic. *National Geographic* 159:575–601.

Schledermann, P., and K. McCullogh

1980 Western elements in the early Thule culture of the eastern High Arctic. *Arctic* 33:833–842.

Solberg, O. M.

1907 Beitrage zur Vorgeshlichte der Ost-Eskimo. *Steinerne Schneidergerate und Waffenschärfen aus Grönland* 2, Hist.-Fil. Klasse 2, Kristiana.

Spaulding, A. C.

1958 The significance of difference between radiocarbon dates. *American Antiquity* 23:309–311.

Sproull-Thomson, J.

1979 Recent studies in Thule art: metaphysical and practical aspect. In Thule Eskimo prehistory: an anthropological retrospective, edited by A. P. McCartney. *National Museum of Man Mercury Series, Archaeological Survey of Canada Paper* 88:485–494. National Museums of Canada, Ottawa.

Stanford, D.

1976 The Walakpa site, Alaska. *Smithsonian Contributions to Anthropology* 20. Smithsonian Institution, Washington, D.C.

Steensby, H. P.

1917 An anthropogeographical study of the origin of Eskimo culture. *Meddelelser om Grønland* 53:39–288.

Stefansson, V.

1921 *The friendly Arctic: the story of five years in polar regions.* Macmillan Company, New York.

Stenton, D.

1983 *An analysis of faunal remains from the Peale Point site (KkDo-1) Baffin Island, N.W.T.* Unpublished M.A. thesis, Department of Anthropology, Trent University.

Sutherland, P.

1980 Archaeological survey on northern Ellesmere Island and eastern Axel Heiberg Island (summer 1980). Manuscript on file, Archaeological Survey of Canada, Ottawa.

1981 Archaeological excavation and survey on northern Ellesmere Island and eastern Axel Heiberg Island (summer 1981). Manuscript on file, Archaeological Survey of Canada, Ottawa.

Taylor, W. E., Jr.

1958 Archaeological work in Ungava, 1957. *Arctic Circular* 10:25–27.

1960 A description of Sadlermiut houses excavated at Native Point, Southampton Island, N.W.T. *National Museum of Canada Contributions to Anthropology, 1957.* National Museum of Canada Bulletin 62:53–99.

1962 Pre-Dorset occupations at Ivugivik in northwestern Ungava. In Prehistoric cultural relations between the Arctic and Temperate Zones of North America, edited by J. M. Campbell. *Arctic Institute of North America Technical Paper* 11, Montreal.

1963a Hypotheses on the origin of Canadian Thule culture. *American Antiquity* 28:456–464.

1963b Implications of a Pre-Dorset lance head from the East Canadian Arctic. *Arctic* 16:129–133.

1964 Interim account of an archaeological survey in the Central Arctic, 1963. *Anthropological Papers of the University of Alaska* 12:46–55.

1967 Summary of archaeological field work on Banks and Victoria islands, Arctic Canada, 1965. *Arctic Anthropology* 4:221–243.

1968 The Arnapik and Tyara sites: an archaeological study of Dorset culture origins. *Memoirs of the Society for American Archaeology* 22.

1972 An archaeological survey between Cape Parry and Cambridge Bay, N.W.T., Canada. *National Museum of Man Mercury Series, Archaeological Survey of Canada Paper* 1. National Museums of Canada, Ottawa.

Taylor, W. E., Jr., and R. McGhee

    1979   Archaeological material from Cresswell Bay, N.W.T., Canada. *National Museum of Man Mercury Series, Archaeological Survey of Canada Paper* 85. National Museums of Canada, Ottawa.

Taylor, W. E., Jr., and G. Swinton

    1967   Prehistoric Dorset art. *The Beaver* 298:32–47.

Thomson, C.

    1981   Preliminary archaeological findings from Shuldham Island, Labrador, 1980. In Archaeology in Newfoundland and Labrador, 1980, edited by J. Sproull-Thomson and B. Ransom. *Historic Resources Division, Government of Newfoundland and Labrador,* Annual Report 1.

    1982   Archaeological findings from Saglek Bay, 1981. In Archaeology in Newfoundland and Labrador, 1981, edited by J. Sproull-Thomson and C. Thomson. *Historic Resources Division, Government of Newfoundland and Labrador, Annual Report* 2.

Tuck, J. A.

    1975   Prehistory of Saglek Bay, Labrador: Archaic and Palaeo-Eskimo occupations. *National Museum of Man Mercury Series, Archaeological Survey of Canada Paper* 32. National Museums of Canada, Ottawa.

    1976   Paleoeskimo cultures of northern Labrador. In Eastern Arctic prehistory: Paleoeskimo problems, edited by M. S. Maxwell. *Memoirs of the Society for American Archaeology* 31:89–102.

    1983   Contract archaeology at Memorial University. In Archaeology in Newfoundland and Labrador, 1982, edited by J. Sproull-Thomson and C. Thomson. *Historic Resources Division, Government of Newfoundland and Labrador, Annual Report* 3.

VanStone, J. W.

    1962   An archaeological collection from Somerset Island and Boothia Peninsula, N.W.T. *Art and Archaeology Division of the Royal Ontario Museum Occasional Paper* 4, University of Toronto.

Wenzel, G.

    1979   Analysis of a Dorset–Thule structure from northwestern Hudson Bay. In Thule Eskimo prehistory: an anthropological retrospective, edited by A. P. McCartney. *National Museum of Man Mercury Series, Archaeological Survey of Canada Paper* 88:122–133. National Museums of Canada, Ottawa.

Wilkinson, P. F.

    1972   Oomingmak: a model for man–animal relationship in prehistory. *Current Anthropology* 13:23–44.

Wintemberg, W. J.

    1939   Eskimo sites of the Dorset culture in Newfoundland (Pt. 1). *American Antiquity* 5:83–102.

    1940   Eskimo sites of the Dorset culture in Newfoundland (Pt. 2). *American Antiquity* 5:309–333.

Wissler, C.

    1918   Archaeology of the polar Eskimo. *Anthropological papers of the American Museum of Natural History* 22. American Museum of Natural History, New York.

Wright, J. V.

    1972   The Aberdeen site, Keewatin District, N.W.T. *National Museum of Man Mercury Series, Archaeological Survey of Canada Paper* 2. National Museums of Canada, Ottawa.

Yamaura, K.

    1979   On the origin of Thule culture as seen from the typological studies of toggle harpoon heads. In Thule Eskimo prehistory: an anthropological retrospective, edited by A. P. McCartney. *National Museum of Man Mercury Series, Archaeological Survey of Canada Paper* 88:474–484. National Museums of Canada, Ottawa.

Yellen, J. E., and H. Harpending

    1972   Hunter gatherer populations and archaeological inference. *World Archaeology* 4:244–253.

Index

47,767

DATE		
NOV 2 5 1988	APR 3 1996	
DEC 1 3 1988	APR 2 9 1996	
FEB 1 4 1990	APR 2 7 1996	
MAR 0 2 1990	MAR 2 0 1999	
MAR 1 9 1990	APR 0 1 1990	
APR 0 3 1990		
Vaug	APR 1 9 2003	
	APR 0 8 2005	
Dec 18 716	MAR 5 2005	
OCT 1 0 1993	MAR 1 6 2007	
NOV - 1 1993		